MANAGER'S
LIFETIME GUIDE TO THE
LANGUAGE OF
POWER

JAMES HOLTJE

MANAGER'S
LIFETIME GUIDE TO THE
LANGUAGE OF
POWER

JAMES HOLTJE

PRENTICE HALL
Paramus, New Jersey 07652

Library of Congress Cataloging-in-Publication Data

Manager's lifetime guide to the language of power / edited by James
  Holtje
    p.   cm.
  ISBN 0-13-894882-8 (cloth)
  1. Business communication   I. Holtje, James.
  HF5718.M367 1997
  658.4'5—dc21   97-11600
                                                          CIP

Printed in the United States of America

10 9 8 7 6 5 4 3 2 1

ISBN 0-13-894882-8

Attention: Coporations and Schools

Prentice Hall books are available at quantity discounts with bulk purchase for educational, business, or sales promotional use. For information, please write to: Prentice Hall Career & Personal Development Special Sales, 240 Frisch Court, Paramus, NJ 07652. Please supply title of book, ISBN number, quantity, how the book will be used, date needed.

PRENTICE HALL
Career & Personal Development
Paramus, NJ 07652
A Simon & Schuster Company

On the World Wide Web at http://www.phdirect.com

Prentice-Hall International (UK) Limited, *London*
Prentice-Hall of Australia Pty. Limited, *Sydney*
Prentice-Hall Canada Inc., *Toronto*
Prentice-Hall Hispanoamerica. S.A., *Mexico*
Prentice-Hall of India Private Limited, *New Delhi*
Prentice-Hall of Japan, Inc. *Tokyo*
Simon & Schuster Asia Pte. Ltd., *Singapore*
Prentice-Hall do Brasil. Ltda., *Rio de Janerio*

CONTENTS

Section Four—LETTERS

Section Five—SELLING

Section Six—NEGOTIATIONS

INTRODUCTION

As a businessperson, you have much to worry about. From the start of a typical business day until finish, you will likely perform myriad tasks ranging from reassuring clients, maintaining office peace, developing new business, finishing up old work, pleasing the boss, disciplining subordinates, not to mention putting out any number of fires before they burn out of control. Sound familiar? If this sounds like you on a good day, read on.

When you barely have enough time for lunch, what time do you have to worry about communications? The answer is, you better have some time to spare.

Why is communications important in today's business world? The answer lies in a cliché you've probably heard about a million times: "We live in an Information Age." Think about that phrase. "Information Age." Much like the "Industrial Age," which spans the lifetimes of virtually all readers today, the new Information Age will touch everyone in ways both profound and subtle and will literally change the way we do business. It will change the way *you* do business. Almost nothing will be the same.

Information is rapidly becoming perhaps the most important commodity in business today. Whether you work in pharmaceuticals, manufacturing, insurance, publishing, or whatever the field, information is rapidly changing the business landscape, and smart businesspeople are learning not to buck the trend, but to ride it, and use it to their benefit.

And it's much more than e-mail, web pages, and teleconferencing. These are only the latest developments in the information revolution. The sheer volume and use of information would stagger the managers and businesspeople of only a generation ago. Managing information and presenting it in ways that convey your meaning precisely and with flair is the challenge we all face as information becomes the lifeblood of tomorrow's economy.

Manager's Lifetime Guide to the Language of Power will be a tremendous asset to you as you begin to navigate this new business landscape. For example, as you probably know, there are fewer layers of management in many companies today. As a result, there is a lot more direct communications up and down the chain of command. This means more communications responsibilities for remaining managers. Can they possibly have all the necessary communications skills down pat?

Or how about on the other end of the scale? More and more smaller companies are blossoming with niche specialties. While they may have skills in some areas, do they have all the communications skills they need for the business? No one can be virtually perfect in every single facet of business, after all.

This book will help the overworked businessperson who may not make communications his or her first priority, but unquestionably must communicate effectively to various "audiences" both inside and outside the company. Best of all, this book is geared toward businesspeople who don't have much time to waste and aren't looking for theory, but need practical—real-world—solutions to real communications problems.

Can't think of how to begin that memo? This volume provides tips, hints, and even examples of how to started. Panicked about that speech you have to give at the next sales meeting? Relax. This book will teach you how to get started, what to say, and how to say it. It even offers tips on how to get over stage fright.

Can't find the right words for that sales letter? Not to worry, we include sample texts and valuable tips to make writing easy. Don't know how to handle a constant critic on your staff? This volume will provide all the verbal ammunition you need. No matter what the communications challenge you face on the job, this extensive volume will point you in the right direction and offer tips on how to say it or write it in style.

Best of all, this volume is not only invaluable in terms of nuts-and-bolts help on the job, it also offers you the very best of Prentice Hall's best-selling business titles for the price of one volume. It features chapters from some of Prentice Hall's most competitive business books as well as introductory remarks, sidebar pieces and summary points to help you retain the information you've learned. Each section of this book covers a particular communications topic and features individual chapters from previously published Prentice Hall books from such authors as Jack Griffin, James van Fleet, and Harold Meyer, and more.

You get only the best of business communications right at your fingertips. You'll see. It will be a well-thumbed reference for a busy executive like yourself for many years to come!

You don't have to be Shakespeare to get ahead in business today, but you do have to know how to speak and write well enough so you can advance in today's demanding work world. *Manager's Lifetime Guide to the Language of Power* will help you get there and give you the edge you really need.

Good luck.

A personal note of thanks to Tom Power, executive editor at Prentice Hall, for his work in realizing this important volume.

James Holtje

MANAGER'S
LIFETIME GUIDE TO THE
LANGUAGE OF
POWER

JAMES HOLTJE

SECTION ONE

MEMOS

INTRODUCTION—MEMO WRITING: PUTTING IT IN WORDS

It's no exaggeration that memo writing is the lifeblood of written business communications. For the vast majority of companies—large and small—virtually no aspect of business hasn't been summed up in crisp, concise, and well-phrased memos that communicate, inform, direct, and keep the wheels of business humming smoothly.

If you're like most businesspeople, you will likely write hundreds, if not thousands, of memos during your entire working life. Whether it's a memo announcing promotions, requesting a proposal, or detailing plans for a company social event, this will be the most-used form of written communication you'll use. While new technologies are promising high-tech ways of communicating using voice, images, and data, the standard written "To: From: Subject:" format which we know so well will likely be with us for a long time to come.

Yet, as you know, not every memo that crosses your desk is worthy of publication. Far from it. Some are poorly organized, badly expressed, or meander aimlessly. Like any other form of communications, poor memo writing reflects poorly on the writer. And in our Information Age, poor communications skills are a definite liability.

This chapter will help you understand the fundamentals of proper memo writing, how to structure them, what to say, and what *not* to say. It will also provide real-world models that you can use directly use as prototypes for memos that best fit your individual business needs. It will give you the edge you need to expressing yourself clearly and concisely to get the results you want. It will show you how to use time-tested methods that can work in virtually any business environment.

Further, model memos are provided as "memo templates" for your own writing needs. These templates are excellent references for the busy businessperson who doesn't have the time to sit down and draft a tome. Each offers suggested phrasings, structure, and language. Additionally, practical tips at the end of each memo keep you on course: reminding you of what needs to be conveyed in specific situations.

Whether it's a memo on getting equipment inventoried, inspiring employees to fulfill a rush order, or squashing a nasty rumor, this chapter will give you real world examples of what to say—and how to say it.

CHAPTER 1

THE NUTS AND BOLTS OF MEMO WRITING

To: The Reader

From: The Author

Subject: Memo Writing—The Basics

Whether you're a business pro who's just fired off your thousandth memo, or this is your first day on the job and the boss wants a memo on his desk by 10 A.M., knowing and internalizing the basics of memo writing will significantly improve your business communications skills.

No one likes to read poorly-written or poorly-structured memos. It takes up too much time. When was the last time you were handed a long-winded, meandering, and virtually indecipherable memo? Be honest, we've all gotten them. Like everyone, you probably thought: What in the world is this person trying to tell me? Perhaps you've politely asked the person later what he or she had in mind. Remember, the best writing is always expressed in clear, simple sentences. Memos are no exception. Organized writing reflects organized thought.

That's why it is so important to make sure this most basic form of business communications is virtually "internalized," so the next time you sit down to write, your thoughts are clearly, cogently, and confidently conveyed.

In the following chapter, Cosmo Ferrara, author of Prentice Hall's *Writing on the Job* details what he describes as the six principles of good memo writing. They are the six most important items you'll need to keep in mind for day-to-day business communications.

HOW CAN I DEMYSTIFY MY MEMOS?

You're straight out of school, where the only writing you did was for tests and term papers. Your boss has just asked you to write a memo. You've heard of memos, but what exactly is a business memo? What's the best way to write one?

Or you've been writing and reading memos for a number of years now. Some seem to generate positive response, while others generate indifference or confusion. You've decided it's time to find out what makes memos work so yours can be more effective. This chapter shows you how to clear up muddled memos and make them effective vehicles of communication.

THE WHAT AND WHY OF MEMOS

A business memo is a short, written document that conveys requests, directives, advice, or information from one member of an organization to another. Despite the widespread use of telephone mail and electronic mail, the memo still prevails as the cornerstone of official interoffice communication because it offers a tangible, durable record of a message being sent.

With the rapid movement of personnel from job to job and from company to company, hard-copy records enable those left behind to carry on without major disruptions to the organization. Memos often provide such records.

Memos are written on a range of subjects, from the office picnic to a company restructuring. Memos should be clear and brief. And because it is an interoffice communication, the memo is generally informal in style.

HOW *NOT* TO WRITE A MEMO

If you were a manager and received the following memo, would you read it? Why? How would you respond to it? Would you know exactly what it is asking you to do?

To: All Managers

From: Mr. Bigg

Date: 9/9/9_

Subject: Professional Appearance

I had a client visit me at the office yesterday, and as we were walking out, we passed a number of staff, both professional and support. While everyone was polite, the client made some remarks about the way some people were dressed. As I walked back to my office alone, I was thinking about the client's remarks and the potential effect of them on our business relationship. I then took a closer look at the same people we had passed. Feeling now that this was becoming an issue, I proceeded to walk around the entire floor (some of you may have noticed me) to make an overall assessment of our appearance. On a scale of 1 to 10, I'd have to rate us about a 6, which is not acceptable.

So I went back to my office to think about the problem. Last night before going home I stopped off at the library and picked up a copy of *Dress for Success,* by John T. Molloy. It includes some good material on business dress. I'd like to share some of it with you.

One suggestion he makes, which I will ask all manager to apply, is to hold a staff meeting and discuss appropriate attire. Molloy goes on to say that a poor first impression loses more sales than anything else. He also says that you have a better chance of making the sale if you are dressed conservatively. Conservative need not be corny, however. So be informed about fashion issues so you're not considered way out of touch with today's world.

You can get your people to improve their appearance by setting a good example and dressing professionally yourself. Be clear about how you want employees to dress for work. Compliment employees who look great; express dismay when they don't. When you have to criticize a person's appearance, don't mix that in with other work issues.

I realize that telling people how to dress is no easy task, but no one said managing people is easy.

WHAT GETS A MEMO READ?

Managers in Mr. Bigg's office might read his memo, but only because his authority commands their doing so. On its own, the memo has little going for it.

For one thing, the memo is long and rambling, taxing the reader's patience to find out where it is going. The excess verbiage not only bores the reader but also buries the memo's key points and purpose. Some managers may feel the purpose is merely to convey information, because of Mr. Bigg's statement: "I'd like to share some of it with you." Actually, the purpose is to get managers to do something. But the directive is not emphasized. It is given almost as an aside: "One suggestion he makes, *which I will ask all managers to apply,* is to hold a staff meeting . . ." Only the most alert managers would see the statement as a directive.

Similarly, Mr. Bigg is vague about the dress standards he wants set. What does he mean by "conservative"? Or by "corny"? Or by being "informed about fashion issues"?

In addition, what Mr. Bigg wants from his managers is no easy task. Yet he gives no real help as to how they can accomplish it.

Furthermore, does Mr. Bigg expect any reporting from his managers? Does he want to know of their progress? By a certain date? Mr. Bigg gives no indication of when he wants this task accomplished or how he wants managers to report to him. Such open-ended directives can easily be ignored.

Mr. Bigg no doubt spent much time writing this memo. And his managers spent time reading it and trying to interpret it. Chances are, though, their time was wasted, because the memo as constructed probably will not achieve what the writer wants. He has not made that clear.

SIX PRINCIPLES OF GOOD MEMO WRITING

1. Specify the Subject

Most companies use a preprinted form to standardize and simplify memo writing. Use the "subject" line on these forms to bring the reader close to the subject quickly. Instead of a generic subject head like "Professional Appearance," as in Mr. Bigg's memo, use a more specific title like "Improving the Professional Appearance of the Staff." This kind of heading tells more about the subject—that something is going to be done about *improving* personal appearance. Readers react more strongly when they infer from the subject heading that something is being asked of them.

Another reason for using a specific subject head has to do with *future use of the memo*. A typical project in most offices may produce as many as twenty or thirty memos. A generic head on those memos does not help someone researching the project some time later. For example, if all thirty memos carry a generic subject head like "Loss Protection Plan," the researcher will have to read the contents of each memo to find the one he wants. To eliminate all that reading and simplify the search, use a more specific subject head like "Implementing the Loss Protection Plan." Or use the generic head with various subheads, such as

Loss Protection Plan—Equipment Needs

Loss Protection Plan—Cost-Benefit Analysis

Loss Protection Plan—Implementation: Phase I

A specific subject head indicates more precisely what the memo covers. Such specificity helps the reader get into the memo. It also helps in filing the memo and searching the file later.

IS MEMO WRITING DEAD IN THE ELECTRONIC AGE?

One of the advantages of using e-mail to transmit your memos—especially if you work in a large company or are separated from your clients—is that the information is instantly sent, and almost instantly received. No more interoffice envelopes with names crossed-off, or standing on line waiting for a curled-up rolls at the fax machine. Also, because messages are stored electronically, information can be archived both on disk and/or in print, a great advantage over print only. Some U.S. companies report saving thousands of dollars a year by using e-mail on either the Internet or various company "intranets"—which after all cost only the amount of a local phone call to a nearby service provider versus expensive overnight services, or long-distance phone bills for faxes.

When writing memos using e-mail bear in mind that just because this is a "new" medium it does not mean the protocols of memo-writing should be ignored. Information should still be concise, to the point, and convey your thoughts clearly. Further, do not abuse the privilege. Just as no one likes to see their inbox filled with memos on trivial matters that can be solved with a brief conversation, no one likes to see their e-mail account flooded either. Check with your company about their policy on using e-mail to transmit memos and other business related messages. If they don't have a policy—as many don't—here's your chance to write a memo that could lead to real cost savings. See you in cyberspace!

---

2. State Your Purpose Clearly

Most memos are written for one of three reasons:

To give readers information

To get readers to make a decision

To move readers to act

When you know beforehand the purpose you are working toward, you will cut out extraneous matter and highlight the critical—ideally, in the first sentence or paragraph. In the example, Mr. Bigg's purpose is to get managers to act, to take steps to improve appearance. But he does not state his purpose until the third paragraph. Some readers may not get that far with some memos. And by stating the purpose almost parenthetically as he does (*which I will ask all of our managers to apply*) he does not call attention to it.

Stating the purpose up front is like running a meeting from an agenda—you have an outside discipline focusing you on the essentials. You are less likely to ramble. Any by stating the purpose up front, you make it obvious to your readers what you are about.

If you find yourself having trouble stating the purpose of your memo, use this basic trigger: "The purpose of this memo is to. . . ." That statement can get you started in the right direction, and it cannot be ignored or misunderstood by your readers.

One exception to this principle of stating the purpose up front occurs when persuasion is involved. In such instances, you may want to coax the reader into the memo before stating your purpose.

3. Limit the Content

Restrict the content of the memo to:

❑ What the reader *needs* to know

❑ What the reader *wants* to know

In the example, the only background needed is that Mr. Bigg is displeased with staff dress. The managers do not need to know all the details of his sojourn around the office and of his trip to the library. What they *do* need to know, however, and what they *want* to know, is what they should do about the problem. The worst thing a memo can do is imply that something is expected of the reader but not be clear on what that something is.

By being conscious about limiting the content, you're more likely to include the important information. Having done that, you'll see no need to add extraneous matter. Therefore, learn to review your memos and cut out all that is not helpful to the reader.

4. Save the Details for the Attachments

When readers need more than a few details to follow a directive, put those details in attachments. You saw in the example what happened with Mr. Bigg did not do that. He tried to summarize the book he read, doing little justice to the book and giving little real help to his readers. But by putting the specific guidelines and suggestions in attachments, you can give the level of assistance readers need to do what's asked and still keep the memo itself short and focused.

5. Put the Most Important Information First

If you put unimportant information up front, hoping to "build up" as you go, you may lose your readers. They may never get to the important stuff. Mr. Bigg, for example, may be justified in thinking his managers need an explanation for his call for this action, but that explanation is less important than the directive. That explanation may be included, but more succinctly, and later in the memo.

6. Highlight with Visual Cues

Effective memos make it easy for readers to grasp key thoughts. Highlight important information by using:

- ❒ A specific subject title
- ❒ Meaningful headings and subheads
- ❒ Underlining and boldfacing
- ❒ Bulleting
- ❒ Numbering and lettering

Mr. Bigg's memo is one solid block of print. Readers are forced to read every sentence of every line to grasp the message. That may be asking too much of busy people. By using visual cues, you can draw attention to key elements. Such highlighting may be enough to pique the reader's interest, and it will certainly emphasize key points.

SOME POINTERS ABOUT FORM

Use first and last names on the "To" and "From" lines in the logistics portion of the memo. Memos often become part of a project's permanent file and remain with it long after individuals connected with it have moved on. Full names make tracing either party more realistic.

The memo does not need a greeting, as a letter does. Some people, however, like to use a greeting when writing to someone they know. They feel a simple "Jack" or "Hi, Joan," softens the formality of the printed communication. A clos-

THE INVERTED PYRAMID

If you've ever written an Op-Ed piece for a newspaper, you'll know exactly what this term means. Writers use this term to describe starting with the most important material first, then working your way to the least important. An inverted pyramid helps visualize the process—from bigger to smaller. It's also a useful metaphor to keep in mind for memo writing. Always start with your most important information at the top, then work your way down.

Just like a newspaper editor who must decide what's "newsworthy," managers must decide which priorities they wish to communicate. Studies show that many readers do not always read much beyond the headlines. Fewer still read beyond the first couple of paragraphs. Just as journalists must capture the readers' attention to get them to read on, you too must make sure they're hooked, and ready to read to the end. Approach memo writing the same way. Ask these questions: what's the most important information I'm trying to communicate, the second, the third, and so on? Soon the outline will take shape. Stuck? Can't figure out what's the best way to start? One technique works particularly well. Describe exactly what you want to say to a colleague or friend. You'll find it's often easier to say it in plain English first, *then* to commit yourself to writing. More often then not, you'll begin with the most important information. Call it a "verbal first draft," but it works!

ing is not required either, but *the writer's signature or initials are*. They verify that the person whose name appears on the "From" line did indeed write the memo.

Include your telephone extension number next to your name in the logistics portion of the memo. You may get a quicker response if you make it easier for readers to contact you. Don't give the reader a reason not to respond, and do all you can to encourage a quick response.

Try to limit memos to one page. A one-page, double-spaced memo is visually inviting, and is more likely to be read than a longer, cramped memo. If you must use single spacing to keep the memo to one page, do so. Whenever your memo is single-spaced, be sure to skip a line between paragraphs.

Whether you indent the first line of each paragraph or use the block form is a personal or company choice. If you use the block form (no indenting), however, skip a line between paragraphs.

MODEL MEMO

To: All Managers
From: Mr. Bigg
Date: 9/9/9_
Ext.:   1234

specific subject head   Subject: Improving the Professional Appearance of the Staff

The professional appearance of some of our staff   **purpose**
is not what it should be. I'd like you to hold a
group meeting with the people reporting to you
to raise the level of appearance to a professional
standard.

subhead   *The Standard to Maintain*

One of the attachments to this memo gives *seven*   **highlight**
guidelines for professional dress I'd like you to
convey to your people. These guidelines were
drawn from *Dress for Success,* a book by John T.
Molloy, which many individual and companies
are using as their standard.

details in attachment   I have also attached some *detailed suggestions*   **space between paragraphs**
that can help you explain the issues and make this
a positive experience for all. I suggest you red
these before calling your meeting.

subhead   *What Prompted This?*

A client walking through our office made a dis-   **less important**
paraging remark about staff appearance. I'm tak-
ing that as a signal to address the situation before
it becomes a problem.

due date   Please let me know by 10/9/9_ how you have   **highlight**
handled the matter and what the results were.

initials of writer   ajb

—Memo Checklist—

DECIDE ON YOUR PURPOSE:

- ❏ *To inform*
- ❏ *To call for a decision*
- ❏ *To move to action*

SPECIFY YOUR SUBJECT ON THE SUBJECT LINE.

STATE YOUR PURPOSE IN THE FIRST SENTENCE OR PARAGRAPH.

SELECT YOUR CONTENT TO ACHIEVE YOUR PURPOSE.

LIMIT THE CONTENT TO WHAT THE READER NEEDS AND WANTS TO KNOW.

PUT THE MOST IMPORTANT INFORMATION FIRST.

HIGHLIGHT THE MOST IMPORTANT INFORMATION WITH VISUAL CUES.

USE ATTACHMENTS FOR LENGTHY DETAILS.

FOLLOW THE CONVENTIONS OF YOUR COMPANY'S MEMO FORM.

Summary Points

- Memos are among the most common form of everyday business communications.
- Try limiting memos to one page where possible.
- Remember the six principles.

   Specify your subject upfront.

   State your purpose clearly—answer *what* it is you want done.

   Limit the information to what the readers needs (or wants) to know.

   Don't clutter—keep details for the attachment section.

   Like a newspaper article, start with the most important information in the lead paragraph.

   Get your point across! Use visual cues like headings and subheads, **bold,** bullets, underlining, *italics,* and so on.

CHAPTER 2

BASIC MODEL MEMOS: REAL-WORLD EXAMPLES

Now that we've mastered the basics of memo writing, it's time to move on to some real-world prototypes you can use—right now, or anytime—to help you compose winning memos that get action. How many times have you been given the assignment to "write-up a memo" and distribute it to employees, only to sit in front of your PC staring at an empty screen? Believe me, you're not alone. The model memos that follow from Cynthia Barnes' *Model Memos for Every Business Occasion* can be applied with obvious modifications to almost any situation your own firm faces. Once you find the heading that most clearly resembles your own circumstances read the memos carefully, and pay extra attention to the tips— they're specifically designed to keep you focused and on track.

If you're really at a loss for words, try this little trick: Write down the whole memo as written in the section. For example, write out the memo on making a hiring recommendation to personnel. Once you've written out the text, you've already got a starting point. Because you'll likely be working on a computer, you have the luxury of changing the name, changing a few details here and there, and *voilà*! Your new memo is complete. You can even save specific memos on your computer's hard drive or a disk under a specific name, especially if you'll be needing the text fairly frequently. Don't worry if the two texts seem similar, most memo writing is fairly formulaic anyhow. If it gets the point across in as few words as possible, you've achieved what you set out to do—that should make the boss happy!

MODEL MEMOS FOR DAY-TO-DAY OPERATIONS

Operating effectively from day to day, sometimes moment to moment. This is what makes—or breaks—your business, whatever your business. The short-term, day-to-day actions you take will determine your organization's long-term

But you know, all too well, that you'll have to take a new short-term action, just as soon as you've handled the last problem or challenge. And you'll have to communicate your ideas to your boss, your co-workers, or your subordinates. Whether you're announcing a job opening, canceling an appointment, delegating a work assignment, getting equipment or supplies, collecting time cards, or hiring a new worker, writing memoranda to describe your short-term actions steals valuable time from your day: each day, every day.

Now, writing those routine memoranda doesn't have to rob you of valuable time. The memoranda in this chapter will communicate your ideas about routine matters. Turn to the page you need, have the memo typed, and send it out: another day-to-day matter gets resolved. Use one of the phrasing alternatives or add a few words, if needed, to say what you mean and mean what you say.

Day-to-day memoranda writing has been done for you. So you can spend time with the more important business of working or managing the work of others. You can now spend your time where it counts: Improving your organization's bottom line.

ANNOUNCING A JOB VACANCY

TO:
FROM:
DATE:
SUBJECT: JOB VACANCY

Qualified employees are encouraged to apply for the Management Analyst II position (Job Announcement #20371) currently open in the Finance Department. October 1, 19—, marks the closing date for applications.

This position is vacant because of Ms. Susan Capra's recent promotion to Analyst III. Consistent with our company's policy of promoting from within whenever possible, interested employees need to submit the following information to the Personnel Department, no later than 5:00 P.M., October 1, 19—:

1. an updated application form

2. a letter of application, outlining your qualifications for the position

3. a current resume

Before you apply, stop by the personnel office to review the job announcement. The new Analyst II should be notified by October 21, 19—. Best of luck to all applicants.

Memo Writer Tips

1. Name the job and department in the very first sentence. Those who are interested can read on; those who are not may stop here.
2. Be sure you include deadline information in the first paragraph.
3. It's a good idea to explain why this vacancy has occurred. This will short-circuit rumors and may provide potential applicants with additional motivation to apply.
4. Make sure you provide details about what information must be submitted by when, and encourage readers to review the job announcement before they apply. This way, employees won't waste valuable time applying for a position if they are not fully qualified.

Phrasing Alternatives

PARAGRAPH 1

If you meet the qualifications for Sheet Metal Worker II, please submit your application for this job by Friday, August 2.

A vacancy in the Credit Collections Division is scheduled to occur on November 14, 19—. All interested and qualified employees are encouraged to apply by November 26.

Qualified workers interested in applying for Radiology Technician should submit application materials to the personnel office no later than July 17, 19—.

PARAGRAPH 2

Max Larson has accepted a position in the Charlotte office, creating this vacancy. If you are interested in this position, send an updated application form and letter of application to Sue Knowles, Room 206, by 4:30 P.M., August 2.

Budget allocations have enabled us to hire an additional Collections Representative. Those who meet the qualifications should send the following to the personnel office by November 14:

1. Form 3405
2. A current resume
3. A letter of recommendation from your immediate supervisor

PARAGRAPH 3

A job description is available on the Job Vacancy Announcement Board, Suite 706. Review this carefully before submitting your application package.

Contact the personnel department for a copy of Job Announcement #34566. Make sure you meet the qualifications before you apply. Good luck!

ANNOUNCING A LAY-OFF

TO:
FROM:
DATE:
SUBJECT: LAY-OFF

Sales of door fasteners have steadily declined for the past two years. This decline makes it impossible for the company to continue to manufacture these items without, ultimately, affecting sales in other areas.

For this reason, all workers on the fastener production line will be laid off, effective Friday, April 4, 19—, at 4:00 P.M. Your final paycheck, including two weeks' severance pay, will be ready by that date. Pick your check up in the payroll office on April 4.

I am very sorry this lay-off could not be avoided. I want to thank you all for the hard work you've given to this company. As openings become available in other areas, you may be called back to work, according to applicable personnel policies.

Memo Writer Tips

1. Explain why the lay-off has become necessary.
2. Tell workers who will be laid off, when.
3. Discuss any procedures for recalling workers, applicable union policies, unemployment insurance benefits, etc.

Phrasing Alternatives

Paragraph 1

Company profits have dwindled by 35 percent this year. These dwindling profits have prompted me to study areas where we might cut back on personnel, in order to preserve some jobs.

House Bill 1136 passed on March 5 mandated a reduction in force of Health and Human Services counselors.

The holiday season has ended. This means Abbott Department Store must return to pre-holiday personnel levels.

Paragraph 2

Much to my regret, you will be laid-off at the end of your shift on Friday, March 3, 19—. Your last check, including one month's severance pay, will be mailed to you no later than March 10.

Counselors hired within the last year will either be offered other positions within the agency or laid off, based on job performance and seniority factors. These status changes will begin on Monday, October 9, 19—. Human Resources will schedule an appointment with each counselor affected by this action within the next 30 days.

Seasonal employees hired within the past 90 days will be laid off after Friday, January 15, 19—. You may pick up your final paycheck before you leave work on that date.

Paragraph 3

Thank you for all your hard work. I wish we could have avoided this lay-off, but declining profits simply make that impossible at this time.

I appreciate your service and dedication. Union guidelines specify that employees may be called back to work, if additional work becomes available, according to seniority rights. The personnel office will provide you with information about filing your employment insurance claims.

Your loyalty and outstanding performance are greatly appreciated. Perhaps you'll have the opportunity to work for us again next season.

ANNOUNCING A PROMOTIONAL EXAMINATION

TO:
FROM:
DATE:
SUBJECT: PROMOTIONAL EXAMINATION, CLERK-TYPIST

The promotional examination for Clerk-Typist will be given on Monday, February 3, 19—, from 8:00 A.M. to 12:00 noon in Room 1238. Employees who plan to take the examination must register with the personnel office by 4:00 P.M., Friday, January 1.

No materials, including briefcases, handbags, etc., can be taken into the examination room. No one will be admitted to the examination room after 8:00 A.M. SHARP.

Study booklets are available in the personnel office.

Memo Writer Tips

1. The first sentence should include what, when, and where specifics about the promotional examination.

2. Discuss any restrictions or special conditions in the second paragraph so employees come properly prepared on exam day.

3. Provide information about available study materials, etc.

Phrasing Alternatives

PARAGRAPH 1

The examination for Occupational Health Nurse has been scheduled for Saturday, April 11, 19—. The exam will begin promptly at 9:00 A.M. and last until 1:00 P.M. To register, contact Marge Miller at ext. 410 no later than Wednesday, April 8.

Now is the time to register for the upcoming promotional exam for Supervisor I, Production. The test will be given on Monday, May 4, from 7:30 A.M.–10:30 A.M. You must sign up in the human resources office by April 22 if you plan to test.

PARAGRAPH 2

You will be permitted to use pocket calculators and dictionaries during the exam, but no other articles, even handbags or briefcases, will be allowed in the testing room. Arrive by 7:30 A.M. or you will not be allowed to take the examination.

Plan to bring #2 pencils with you, but no other supplies can be brought into the examination rooms. Doors to the testing room will be locked at 8:55 A.M. If you do not arrive before then, you will not be permitted to test.

ANNOUNCING A SALES CONTEST

TO:
FROM:
DATE:
SUBJECT: SALES CONTEST

Land five new accounts this month and win an all-expenses-paid vacation for two to Hawaii. The Hawaiian Feast Sales Contest begins today. The winner will be announced on Friday, May 13th.

Here are the contest rules:

- Accounts must be ones Landmark Enterprises has never handled before. Prospects you are currently working are okay.
- Each new account must place at least a $500.00 order by May 11.
- A completed "New Account Data Sheet" must be submitted to your Account Manager for each new account.

The lucky winner and his/her companion will fly to Hawaii for a three-day stay at the Honolulu Hilton on Maui. In addition, the winning go-getter will take along $500.00 spending money.

Go get those new accounts and get yourself a well-deserved vacation—on us. A real Hawaiian Feast is just five new accounts away.

Memo Writer Tips

1. Describe what sales personnel have to do and what they can win in the first sentence. Use a sales pitch to get their attention right away.
2. Be sure to include a deadline so people know how long they have to achieve the goal.
3. Outline contest rules and/or restrictions.
4. Close the memo by offering additional details about the prize and a few motivational words.

Phrasing Alternatives

PARAGRAPH 1

Sell $2,000 or more in products this month and win yourself a two-day stay at the Copper Junction Lodge. Our quarterly sales contest begins May 3 and runs through May 31.

The Peak Achiever Sales Contest starts next Monday and ends on November 30. All you have to do is generate 25 new leads and get at least one new account. Your price . . . $150.00 in cash!

PARAGRAPH 2

Contest rules are outlined below:

The easy-to-follow contest regulations are outlined below:

PARAGRAPH 3

Getting new leads can now earn you a substantial cash award. Start making those phone calls now!

A few new sales will entitle you and your guest to an all-expenses-paid vacation valued at more than $500. Sell big! Win big!

CANCELING AN APPOINTMENT

TO:
FROM:
DATE:
SUBJECT: APPOINTMENT CANCELLATION

Unfortunately, I won't be able to keep our Friday, November 18 appointment for 3:00 P.M. The General Manager will be flying in from the coast, and we'll be touring each job site Friday afternoon.

    I'll call you Monday and reschedule.

Memo Writer Tips

1. Put all pertinent facts in the first sentence: day, date, time.
2. Briefly explain why you're canceling.
3. Say how, when, and whether you plan to reschedule.

Phrasing Alternatives

PARAGRAPH 1

    I'm sorry I'll have to cancel our 8 A.M. appointment on August 3. I'm really backlogged on the Hammerfield Project, so I'll have to reschedule.

    Can we reschedule our April 14 appointment? When I made it, I didn't realize I had another appointment scheduled for the same day and time.

PARAGRAPH 2

I'll have my secretary call and reschedule.

Let's plan it for later that same week. I'll call to set up another time.

COMMUNICATING SECTION GOALS*

TO:
FROM:
DATE:
SUBJECT: PERFORMANCE GOALS FOR 1989

Provided below are suggested goals for the 1989 Performance Plan.

1. Develop and implement an accountability structure that clearly defines each senior manager's authority and responsibility in carrying out District goals and programs.

2. Implement employee selection and performance management programs that maximize the productivity of all employees in accomplishing district goals and programs.

3. Develop a district-wide healthcare benefits cost containment program.

4. Develop an operational plan with timelines for implementing the Affirmative Action Plan.

Memo Writer Tips

1. List the goals for your unit or section, beginning with the most ambitious goals.
2. Detail each in one to two sentences.

Phrasing Alternatives

PARAGRAPH 1

Below are listed this year's goals for our department

The 19— goals for the Utilities Department is as follows:

The goals and objectives below describe the plans and undertakings I would like to see us achieve over the coming year.

---

*This memorandum was written by the Director of Administration of a metropolitan transportation district.

DELEGATING ASSIGNMENTS

TO:
FROM:
DATE:
SUBJECT: NEW ASSIGNMENT: GREAT FALLS PROJECT

You've been selected to monitor work on the Great Falls Project. When a job needs to get done—and get done well—your name is one of the first to come to mind. Your skills will most assuredly make this project a successful one.

Plan to update me bi-weekly on the project's progress. If you have any questions about the file I've attached, let's meet next Wednesday to discuss specifics.

Memo Writer Tips

1. "You've been selected" or "You have been chosen" lets your reader know he/she brings special talent to the new assignment. In the same sentence, name the project or new assignment.

2. Address what role you plan to play and how you plan to support their efforts.

Phrasing Alternatives

PARAGRAPH 1

I'm turning over to you the follow-up on the job we did for Knowlton and Company. I know you'll make sure they're satisfied with our services.

Because you've had previous training experience, you have been chosen to provide orientation for the three new employees in our section.

PARAGRAPH 2

Let me know when the job is complete. If you need anything from my office, just let me know.

Laura Brigham can provide you with technical support. I'll check back with you in a few weeks to see what progress you've made.

DISTRIBUTING THE ORGANIZATIONAL CHART TO NEW PERSONNEL

TO:
FROM:
DATE:
SUBJECT: ORGANIZATIONAL CHART

Your job is an important one and fits into our company as outlined on the attached organizational chart. Discuss problems, questions, suggestions, etc. with your immediate supervisor, Mr. Rand. When necessary, he'll communicate your concerns to upper management.

    Welcome aboard!

Memo Writer Tips

1. The organizational chart establishes "chain of command." Let your new employees know this, while welcoming them to the organization.
2. Spell out how problems should be addressed, and close on a positive note.

Phrasing Alternatives

PARAGRAPH 1

    Attached is a copy of the organization chart for our agency. Your immediate supervisor is your link to management, as you are the link to subordinates under your direction. Use the chain of command outlined when you have problems or questions.

    Here is the organizational chart for our operation. It will acquaint you with our structure and where you fit in the overall management hierarchy.

ENCOURAGING WORKERS TO MAKE CHARITABLE CONTRIBUTIONS*

TO:
FROM:
DATE:
SUBJECT: UNITED WAY CAMPAIGN

The United Way is once again asking for our support. Let's give generously again this year. Our agency goal is $5,000, one thousand dollars more than last year's total contributions.

Return the attached card to the Personnel Department if you decide to contribute through payroll deduction. Give until it helps! Thank you for your continued support.

Memo Writer Tips

1. Include a company or departmental goal as an incentive. Employees like feedback on where their money has gone.
2. Keep this memo short, as it is one employees are accustomed to receiving.

Phrasing Alternatives

PARAGRAPH 1

Once again, it is time to give to those less fortunate than ourselves, through your tax-deductible donations to the United Way Campaign. The $23,000 you donated last year went to fund a variety of helpful projects in your community.

Please give—and give generously—to this year's Charitable Fund Campaign. We raised $1,700 last year and should be bale to raise at least $2,000 this year.

PARAGRAPH 2

Completed payroll deduction cards should be returned to Employee Relations by March 31. Give whatever you can afford. Every little bit helps.

---

*This memorandum was written by the Personnel Director of a community-based, job training program.

Payroll deduction forms will be included in next week's pay envelopes. Fill out your form and return it to Rhonda by April 1. Thank you for your donations to this worthy organization.

EXPLAINING AN ORDER DELAY TO SUBORDINATES

TO:
FROM:
DATE:
SUBJECT: ORDER DELAY

The piping ordered for the Valve Assembly Unit has not yet arrived. I checked with purchasing, and according to the supplier, the pipe should arrive by this Thursday. The supplier has been instructed to ship the supplies overnight delivery, since I know you can't begin reconstruction of the unit until this material arrives.

Memo Writer Tips

1. Outline what order has been delayed and why.
2. Let the reader know when the shipment can be expected.

Phrasing Alternatives

PARAGRAPH 1

The chip we need to complete the interface of our new telephone system will arrive by 5:30 P.M. tomorrow. In the interim, we are limited to receiving incoming calls on the main switchboard number (333-3333). Advise all your clients to use this number until further notice.

The drill bit you need is not in stock at Abrams Company. I am checking with other vendors to find the part and will deliver it to you as soon as it comes in.

The test kits you ordered on 2/6 are on back-order. In order to have enough kits for this week, I am issuing a purchase requisition today so we can get kits from a local supplier. This supplier has promised delivery by Monday.

FILLING TIME CARDS/SHEETS OUT CORRECTLY

TO:

FROM:

DATE:

SUBJECT: TIME CARDS

Please fill out your time cards as follows:

1. Write in your employee number.

2. Record the number of hours you work each day.

3. Total our hours for the week at the bottom of the card.

4. Sign and date the card at the bottom.

5. Place completed time cards in the box marked "payroll" next to the time clock.

A sample time card is attached.

Completing time cards properly saves us time and reduces the chances for errors in calculating your paychecks.

Memo Writer Tips

1. List the steps involved in completing the time card or sheet.

2. Attach a sample so employees can see how to fill the cards out correctly.

Phrasing Alternatives

PARAGRAPH 1

Time sheets should be filled out according to the following procedure:

If you fill out your time cards as outlined on the attached sample, we can eliminate many of the payroll errors we have had recently.

GETTING A JUMP ON THE OFFICE RUMOR MILL

TO:
FROM:
DATE:
SUBJECT: RUMOR CONTROL

The rumor mill has been at it again. There is no truth—I REPEAT, NO TRUTH—
to the rumor that the impending merger may shut down this plant.

I have asked section supervisors to schedule meetings with their teams, to
discuss what, when, how, and why this merger will affect each of you. Write
down any questions you have, and come to your meeting prepared to get the
facts.

Memo Writer Tips

1. Acknowledge that rumor mills do exist, but do so in a light, non-
   threatening tone.
2. Dispel the inaccurate information and present the facts, or detail
   what arrangements have been made to communicate the facts.
3. Don't belabor the point or alienate subordinates by scolding them
   for using (or abusing) one of the oldest forms of communication
   known to organizations.

Phrasing Alternatives

PARAGRAPH 1

I am writing this memo to present you with factual information about our
"rumored" move to the Minneapolis area.

This memorandum, contrary to what the "rumor mill" may say, will outline
the details of the new classification study results.

Getting Equipment Inventoried

TO:

FROM:

DATE:

SUBJECT: EQUIPMENT INVENTORY

Please inventory all office equipment in your department by 5:00 P.M., Friday, January 15. Provide the following information for each piece of equipment (see note below) in your section:

- year purchased
- type
- model number
- serial number
- condition (excellent, satisfactory, defective)

Your input will help us determine next year's equipment needs more accurately. Thanks for your help.

OFFICE EQUIPMENT: typewriters, word processors, computers, monitors, printers, adding machines, calculators, desks, chairs, file cabinets, bookcases.

Memo Writer Tips

1. Be specific about the type of equipment to be inventoried and the date the inventory is to be completed.
2. Define what you mean by "equipment."
3. Tell your reader why the inventory is necessary.
4. Provide your reader with an inventory form, whenever possible.

Phrasing Alternatives

Paragraph 1

Conduct an inventory of all repair tools in your area and return the results to me by Friday, June 10.

This year's equipment inventory will begin on June 15. Someone from the facilities department will be visiting your work area during that week.

PARAGRAPH 2

Thanks for helping me get an accurate count of our machinery.

Your cooperation in preparing your inventory report is appreciated.

GETTING EQUIPMENT REPAIRED

TO:
FROM:
DATE:
SUBJECT: EQUIPMENT REPAIR

The micrometer in Engineering Lab #3 needs repairs. Please send someone to repair this equipment today.
    Thanks.

Memo Writer Tips

1. Explain what kind of equipment is in need of repairs and, if possible, what kind of repairs you believe are needed.
2. Let the reader know when you would like to have the repairs completed.

Phrasing Alternatives

PARAGRAPH 1

Our microfilm reader (Serial #S-19844) is on the blink. Could you send someone to repair it as soon as possible?

Please have someone in maintenance take a look at the printer on Barb Walter's desk. For some reason, it's not printing properly. Thank you.

Repairs are needed on the Novak bookkeeping machine in my office. Please have someone look at it today. We're right in the middle of a billing cycle and need the machine fixed ASAP.

GETTING SUBORDINATES TO COMPLETE REQUIRED FORMS

TO:

FROM:

DATE:

SUBJECT: EXPENSE VOUCHER FORM

You submitted your receipts for your Dallas trip (3/14) but failed to complete the necessary Expense Voucher Form. Your request for reimbursement cannot be completed until you have done so.

Please complete the form (sample and blank form attached) and return it to my office in order to expedite your claim.

Thank you.

Attachments

Memo Writer Tips

1. Tell the employee what form needs to be completed and explain why this is necessary.
2. Attach a sample of how the form should be filled out, if necessary.
3. If a deadline is involved, let the employee know when the completed form is due and to whom the form should be returned.

Phrasing Alternatives

PARAGRAPH 1

Please complete Form #99-1 (petty cash reimbursement) and return it to my office no later than Friday. Checks will be cut on this date, and your request cannot be processed until the form has been completed.

Your healthcare benefits claim will be submitted as soon as you have submitted a copy of Form 303 (attached). Claims cannot be processed without this form.

Forms are "necessary evils." I need a completed W-4 form in order to include your hours on the 9/14 payroll run. Please complete the form and return it to Room 204 by noon tomorrow.

HANDLING A SUBORDINATE WHO DISAGREES WITH A DECISION

TO:
FROM:
DATE:
SUBJECT: IMPLEMENTING THE CANE DECISION

In follow-up to our meeting today, I know you weren't quite satisfied with the decision I made to have both you and Jean make the Cane presentation. Be assured that I made this decision because you have the accounting expertise, while Jean has excellent presentation skills and is also familiar with the ins and outs of the medical research industry.

Together, I thought the two of you would make a much more convincing presentation than either of you would alone. Though you don't agree with my decision, I know you'll do everything you can to get this account.

Memo Writer Tips

1. Acknowledge that the subordinate does not agree with the decision you have made.
2. Briefly explain why you made the decision and close by disclosing your confidence in the fact that the employee will carry out the decision even though he/she does not agree with it.

Phrasing Alternatives

PARAGRAPH 1

Even though you disagree with the construction estimates I presented today, I'm certain my figures will prove to be correct in the long run. Instead of dwelling on who's right, let's just get the job done. If you turn out to be right, I'll be the first to admit it.

You've been assigned to head the audit review team, in spite of your objections. You have the experience to conduct this audit, and I'm confident you'll lead the team without any major problems. Thanks for carrying out this responsibility even though you don't like doing so.

Moving Harry Stern to the marketing group just makes sense at this time. I heard your objections and took them into consideration, but trust me, I have a better overall picture of the operations than you do and am sure this is the best move under the circumstances.

PARAGRAPH 2

Work with me on this. The entire department will benefit in the long run.

I know you're professional enough to implement a decision, even one you don't agree with. Feel free to tell me, "I told you so" if you're proven right in the future.

I think Harry Stern's the best applicant for the position. Though you don't agree, I hope you'll support me in my choice and make Harry's transition to this department as smooth as possible.

HANDLING A SAFETY VIOLATION

TO:
FROM:
DATE:
SUBJECT: SAFETY STANDARDS

Welders must always wear safety goggles while operating their torches. While I was on the floor yesterday, I noticed two operators working without protective eye covering.

Safety standards may seem unnecessary, since all of you are experienced workers. But, believe me, these standards have been designed for YOUR protection. Let's continue to do a quality job, but let's do it safely.

Memo Writer Tips

1. Point out which safety rule has been violated.
2. Including information about how you came to know about the violation gives your reminder more "teeth," but avoid phrases like, "it has come to my attention."
3. Threatening employees is not likely to get the results you want. This memo should sound as though you're confident they'll comply.

Phrasing Alternatives

PARAGRAPH 1

Protective shoe covers must be worn at all times on the processing floor. I had to remind three handlers to wear this safety gear yesterday.

Bulk mail bins should be pushed, never lifted. This will prevent back and leg injuries.

PARAGRAPH 2

Safety standards protect you. Please follow them carefully.

Adhere to safety procedures at all times. Failure to do so may result in lost time and lost wages.

INSPIRING WORK ON AN URGENT PROJECT

TO:
FROM:
DATE:
SUBJECT: RUSHHHHHHHH PROJECT

Sorry to "put you under the gun" again, but I need the figures on the Amorti account within the next two days. Without them, we may not be able to hang on to their account.

You always manage to come through in the clinches, and I'm counting on you to do it again. If you need someone to cover your own accounts till this project's completed, let me know right away.

Memo Writer Tips

1. Say what you need and when you need it, but acknowledge that you're asking for extra effort.
2. Explain why you need the work in a hurry. People often work more quickly when they fully understand the ramifications of failing to do so.
3. Offer assistance IF you are able to provide it.

Phrasing Alternatives

PARAGRAPH 1

I would appreciate it greatly if you could rush the review of the merchant files and get them to me by tomorrow noon.

Would you please process the film marked "urgent" right away. I know you're already behind in your work, but I need these photos to show to the client at our morning meeting.

PARAGRAPH 2

You can always be counted on to work quickly and efficiently. Thanks for your help once again.

Thank you for lending your assistance in this crisis. You are a real asset to this department.

ITEMS IN SHORT SUPPLY

TO:
FROM:
DATE:
SUBJECT: SUPPLY SHORTAGE

We're quickly depleting our supply of form-fed computer paper. What we have must last through the end of the month. I'll have to ration the available supply until our order comes in.

Please take only what you need. We should have new stock no later than February 20.

Memo Writer Tips

1. Let employees know what item is in short supply and when new supplies can be expected.
2. Tell them what procedure you'd like them to follow with existing supplies.

Phrasing Alternatives

PARAGRAPH 1

I'll be dispensing the last of the computer diskettes we currently have available this week. If you need diskettes, pick them up in my office. New ones should arrive within 10 days.

Our stock of legal pads is just about gone. Holly will be distributing what we have left, and when those are gone, we'll just have to "make do" until our new order comes in, some time around the first of the year.

I've completely run out of Form J-221s. Do you have any extras you could spare until the printing office releases its new edition?

MAKING A HIRING RECOMMENDATION TO PERSONNEL

TO:
FROM:
DATE:
SUBJECT: HIRING RECOMMENDATION

Margaret O'Bannion is my choice for the Marketing Representative position. While the other applicants are qualified, Margaret has the mobile telephone sales experience I think this position requires.

Since we need this person yesterday, I hope you'll be able to speed up the process so Margaret can start by Monday, July 15. Thanks for all your help. You guys did a super job.

Memo Writer Tips

1. State who you'd recommend for what position.
2. If possible, be definitive about why you chose this candidate over other applicants. In the event one of the other applicants questions your decision, this memorandum may be used to document your choice.
3. Say when you'd like the applicant to start.
4. Build bridges with your personnel department by thanking them for the work they've done.

Phrasing Alternatives

PARAGRAPH 1

I recommend we hire Mr. Lance Smith for the equipment operator position. He has five more years of experience than either of the other two applicants.

Please notify Ms. Helen Craft that she has been selected to fill the scheduler position in our department. Her previous background in conference planning made her the obvious choice for this job.

PARAGRAPH 2

I'd like her to begin work by July 31. Thank you for your assistance.

See if he can begin work on September 3rd. I'd like him to begin then so he can train with Dirk for at least two weeks.

MOVING THE OFFICE OR SECTION

TO:
FROM:
DATE:
SUBJECT: OFFICE MOVE

Your section will be moved to Suite 406 over the weekend. Please meet with your employees and complete the attached floorplan. Leave it with my secretary before you leave on Friday.

Have employees label their boxes, furniture and equipment with the stickers provided by the movers. Sketch how furniture should be arranged on the floorplan; correspond numbers on the sketch with those you've affixed to the furniture.

By working together, we can make this move as painless as possible. I'm sure you'll enjoy your new space.

Memo Writer Tips

1. Tell when the move is to take place.
2. Describe the procedure employees should use to identify furniture and equipment.
3. Since people generally become territorial about their workspace, reassure them that the move will go smoothly and be beneficial.

Phrasing Alternatives

PARAGRAPH 1

You will be moved to Room 304 on Monday, as planned. Facilities staff will move your equipment. Let them know where you want items placed in your new office.

All offices will be moved to Troy Towers, 18th and Grant Streets. The move will begin on Monday, September 14, and everyone should be in the new building by September 21.

PARAGRAPH 2

Label your equipment with the stickers provided by the movers. Your supervisor will show you a diagram of the new floorplan.

Packers will label and pack material on Friday. The move should be complete by the time you arrive for work on Monday morning.

PARAGRAPH 3

The new facilities are attractive and spacious. You'll be very comfortable there, I'm sure.

You'll begin a new week in new surroundings. Your efforts can help make this move a smooth, pleasant one.

PARKING IN ASSIGNED SPACES

TO:
FROM:
DATE:
SUBJECT: ASSIGNED PARKING SPACES

People, park in your assigned spaces. Beginning Monday, the license plate numbers of cars in unassigned spaces will be written down. Owners will be asked to leave work, move their cars, and make up the time involved.

We went to great lengths to mark and assign parking spaces so we could avoid these problems. Please extend the courtesy to your fellow employees of parking your car in its designated space. Thank you.

Memo Writer Tips

1. Get right to the point. Employees know they are breaking the rules, so they're probably just waiting for you to take action.

2. Be clear about what the consequence of their actions will be, and then follow through.

Phrasing Alternatives

PARAGRAPH 1

Please park your vehicle in the space assigned to you. Ample parking exists if everyone uses his/her designated parking area.

Visitor parking spaces are reserved for guests of the company. Do not park your vehicle in these spaces.

Vehicles parked in Drexel Industries reserved spaces will be ticketed and towed. Park your car in the spaces designated for Judson, Inc.

PARAGRAPH 2

Please respect the rights of your co-workers by parking in your assigned space.

Violators will lose their reserved parking spaces and be asked to park in the all-purpose lot.

RELAYING INFORMATION ABOUT SALES PROSPECTS

TO:
FROM:
DATE:
SUBJECT: SALES PROSPECTS

Add the following names to your prospect list:

1. Allied Precast, Inc. Contact Jake Dewitt 333-4455
2. Continental Forms Co. Contact Angela MacFarlane, 448-3178
3. Universal Preforms, Inc. Contact Leonard Atwood, 758-1098
4. Macallister Concrete, Inc. Contact Florence Jones 777-8889

CREATE YOUR OWN TEMPLATES

Consider creating a file, either on your computer, or on paper, of various memos you've written, or that were done by someone else and you found particularly well-written. From a business standpoint, time is wasted sitting in front of a terminal writing essentially the same memo over and over again.

Keep prototypes on hand to cut down the time and focus on the details instead of worrying about the phrasing. You can even categorize them according to your needs: "Work Orders," "New Hire," "Office Social Event," "Moving an Office," "New Phone Numbers," "Rush Order,"—whatever fits your individual needs. By working with phrases you're comfortable with, or that you know your boss already likes, you know you'll be on safe ground. Be sure to edit each memo carefully, however, so old information doesn't make it onto current versions.

A lot of recycling goes on in the business world, and there's nothing wrong with it, as long as it's not outright copying.

Allied and Macallister are interested in delivered pre-mix concrete at prices less than $6.95 per square foot. Continental and Universal want forms. They're satisfied with their current supplier, but you may be able to sway them because the supplier has been late on several key deliveries.

All these firms are in the process of bidding on major projects, so a call this week would be right on target.

Memo Writer Tips

1. List the prospects by company, contact name and phone number.
2. Include information about any special requirements or tips that will make a sale more likely.

Phrasing Alternatives

PARAGRAPH 1

I thought you might be interested in this list of sales prospects:

Here are some sales prospects for your files:

REQUESTING ADDITIONAL PERSONNEL—PERMANENT

TO:

FROM:

DATE:

SUBJECT: REQUEST FOR PERMANENT NEW-HIRE

Request you initiate hiring of one full-time order-filler for my department. I need the person by the end of the month but will take the help whenever I can get a qualified person on board.

Use the job description I gave you for the last person we hired. Thanks.

Memo Writer Tips

1. Let the person who will be doing the hiring know what category of employee you want to hire.
2. Provide a job description, if one is not already on file.
3. Let them know when you would like the new-hire to begin work.

Phrasing Alternatives

PARAGRAPH 1

Please begin search and screen procedures for a Clerk-Typist II in the Contracting Division. I need someone yesterday but will take a qualified applicant as soon as you can find one.

I need a permanent, full-time licensed practical nurse in urology. A job description should be on file in your office. I need the person by September 12.

Could you advertise and screen for a printing press operator for my department as soon as possible. John Lee will be leaving at the end of the month, and with the backlog of work we currently have, I need someone right away.

REQUESTING ADDITIONAL HELP—SHORT TERM

TO:
FROM:
DATE:
SUBJECT: SEASONAL HELP REQUEST

I will need three (3) additional gift-wrap clerks during the holiday season, November 30 to December 31, 19—. Please advertise for the positions, forward a list of qualified applicants to me, and I will interview as soon as you can get some names to me.

Thanks for your help.

Memo Writer Tips

1. Say what kind of help is needed and for how long.
2. Briefly explain why you need the additional short-term help.
3. Close by thanking the reader for his/her assistance.

Phrasing Alternatives

PARAGRAPH 1

Please begin hiring for a six-month contract for a Nurse Practitioner for my office. Judy will be taking a six-month leave of absence, and I'll need someone as soon as possible to replace her. Judy's last day of work is April 12, and I'd like to get someone at least two weeks before then, so the new person can be properly trained.

The warehouse operation will need two (2) forklift operators for the period 4/6–6/30. This will help me complete inventory and close out the books for the end of the year. Whatever help you can give in getting these people on as soon as possible will be appreciated.

Contact a temporary agency and find a clerk-typist for the drafting department as soon as possible, but no later than May 11. I need someone to prepare invoices and to other clerical duties so we can process our standing orders. Thanks.

REQUESTING EQUIPMENT

TO:
FROM:
DATE:
SUBJECT: EQUIPMENT REQUEST

Please send a portable ventilator to the nurses' station, 3rd floor, by the start of the 3 P.M.–11 P.M. shift.
     Thanks for your assistance.

Memo Writer Tips

1. Specify what equipment is needed and by when.
2. Thank the reader for his/her cooperation.

Phrasing Alternatives

PARAGRAPH 1

Housekeeping needs a floor buffer for this evening's crew. Please deliver it to the storage room, 4th floor, by 5:00 P.M. Thanks.

Could you deliver a memory typewriter to the customer relations department by 9:00 A.M. tomorrow. We have a new typist starting and need this equipment so he'll have something to work with.

Equipment is needed in Room 304, Section 4. Our x-ray machine went out on last night's shift, and we need a replacement.

REQUESTING EXPENDABLE SUPPLIES

TO:
FROM:
DATE:
SUBJECT: SUPPLY REQUEST

The Legal Department needs the following supplies by Thursday, May 9, 19—:

1. 10 reams 8fi″ × 11″ bond paper, white
2. 6 boxes #2 pencils

3. 3 boxes felt-tip pens, black ink, fine

4. 6 packages 8fi″ × 14″ ruled legal pads

Charge the supplies to cost center number 23459-4456. Thank you.

Memo Writer Tips

1. Let the supply department know which department needs the sup-plies by when. Your "as soon as possible," may be different from theirs.
2. List the supplies. Include quantity and a description of the items. Lists are easier to read and will often prompt speedier results.

Phrasing Alternatives

PARAGRAPH 1

Please deliver the following expendables to data processing by Friday, June 4:

I need the supplies listed below by October 14. Thanks.

REQUESTING INFORMATION FOR THE SECOND TIME

TO:
FROM:
DATE:
SUBJECT: SECOND REQUEST

This is my second request for your quarterly report, originally due last Friday. Please make sure you get the report to me by Friday, May 12, 19—. The quarter-ly sales figures cannot be computed without your input.

If you cannot meet this deadline, call me today.

Memo Writer Tips

1. Notice the word "I" is conspicuously absent from this memorandum. This helps to shift the responsibility from the writer to the worker whose information is late.

2. The memo explains why the figures are needed and opens the way for the writer to make the reasons for delay known.

Phrasing Alternatives

PARAGRAPH 1

Please send the inventory list—due last Thursday—to me no later than 5:00 P.M. tomorrow. The final inventory cannot be completed until your list is in.

This is the second time you've been asked for the draft of the Comtex User Manual. Make sure you get it to me by this afternoon.

PARAGRAPH 2

Call me if you feel you cannot comply with this second request.

Let me know when you can provide information.

REQUESTING TIME SHEETS*

TO:
FROM:
DATE:
SUBJECT: TIME SHEETS

Time sheets for the period ending April 15 must reach the payroll office by April 18, 12:00 noon. Any time sheets received after this deadline will not be processed for the April 30 payroll run.

---

*This memorandum was written by a payroll clerk for a construction company.

> **Memo Writer Tips**
>
> 1. State the period ending date for time sheets.
> 2. Tell when the time sheets must be delivered to the payroll office and what the consequences will be if they are not.

Phrasing Alternatives

PARAGRAPH 1

I need all time sheets for part-time employees no later than 8:00 A.M. Friday, August 1 for processing. Please forward your time sheets to my office by then.

Checks for November 30 will be run on November 21. All time sheets must be in my office by then. If they are not, employees will not receive payment for that pay period until the next payroll period.

Please remind your employees that their time sheets need to be completed and returned to my office by Friday, June 3. Time sheets received after this date will be processed for the June 30 paycheck.

REQUESTING TECHNICAL ASSISTANCE

TO:
FROM:
DATE:
SUBJECT: TECHNICAL ASSISTANCE REQUEST

Word processors need additional Wordspeak software training. While the tutorials provide the basics, training targeted at our specific functions is required.

The following companies can provide the training we need:

Vendor	Hours	Cost
Acme Computer Training	40 hours	$195/participant
Compuworld	40 hours	$175/participant
Universal Software	60 hours	$295/participant
Avon Community College	80 hours	$125/participant

I suggest we contract with Avon Community College because they are the only vendor who agreed to tailor training to our specific needs. Training could begin within 30 days, and the total cost would include training development costs.

Could I have your decision by Friday, December 18? The new equipment, though installed, cannot yield maximum results until we provide adequate training for our personnel.

Memo Writer Tips

1. Tell who needs what kind of technical assistance.
2. Explain why technical assistance is needed.
3. To make the decision easier, do background work on potential vendors and costs, if appropriate.
4. Finally, suggest a possible vendor and explain why this company can supply the technical assistance you need, if necessary.

Phrasing Alternatives

PARAGRAPH 1

Could your department provide me with technical assistance on getting our computers up and running?

Your technical expertise is needed as we reinstall the ceiling wires in the new wing.

PARAGRAPH 2

Though we received basic training from the manufacturer, there are still a number of features we do not understand how to operate. I have surveyed the operators in my section, and a list of the features they need help with is attached.

None of our installers is certified to rig the wires according to code. The last time we attempted to install the, all our work had to be torn out when the building inspectors found code violations.

PARAGRAPH 3

Let me know when you could provide us with technical assistance, how long you think it would take, and how much it would cost. If you cannot help right now, please send me the name of a contractor whose work you trust.

Your help would really come in handy. Any labor costs would, of course, be paid out of our departmental budget.

RESCHEDULING AN APPOINTMENT

TO:
FROM:
DATE:
SUBJECT: RESCHEDULING OUR APPOINTMENT

Can we reschedule our Thursday appointment for Friday at 2:00 P.M.? The regional manager will be in the area on Thursday and wants me to meet him at our Flora Park store.

In this instance, no news is good news. If this time isn't convenient for you, call my secretary and we'll see what else we can work out.

Memo Writer Tips

1. Mention both the current meeting day and the day and time you'd like to meet. Phrasing your request as a question will probably net you a response right away.

2. Explain why you must reschedule the appointment.

3. Give the reader information about what action to take if the appointment can't be rescheduled.

Phrasing Alternatives

PARAGRAPH 1

I would like to reschedule our Tuesday appointment (8:00 A.M.) for Wednesday at the same time. My return flight from Boston won't arrive until Tuesday at 6:00 P.M.

PARAGRAPH 2

Let me know if this time is not convenient.

RESPONDING TO AN EMPLOYEE'S SUGGESTION

TO:
FROM:
DATE:
SUBJECT: SUGGESTION

Your suggestion for revamping the check processing procedure could, potentially, save the company considerable time and money. After the review committee has studied your suggestions carefully, I will let you know whether, how, and when your suggestion can be implemented. You will be contacted if the committee has additional questions.

Thank you for taking the time to suggest this new procedure. Efforts that go above and beyond your work requirements are always appreciated. Expect to hear from me within the next two weeks.

Memo Writer Tips

1. Make sure you respond to employee suggestions within two to three days.
2. Outline what will be done with the suggestion.
3. Thank the employee for submitting the suggestion.
4. Let the employee know when he/she can expect a reply. This way, you can avoid unnecessary phone calls, and the employee won't wonder about the status of his/her suggestion for weeks.

Phrasing Alternatives

PARAGRAPH 1

Thank you for suggesting a new method for logging incoming mail. When I've had a chance to study your recommendations and talk to other mailroom personnel, I'll let you know whether your system will be implemented.

Employee suggestions are always welcome. The ideas you have for stream-lining our credit analysis methods will be studied closely.

PARAGRAPH 2

I should make a final decision within the next 30 days.

You will be notified about the results of this study within 14 days.

RESPONDING TO A VERBAL/TELEPHONE INQUIRY

TO:
FROM:
DATE:
SUBJECT: TELEPHONE INQUIRY

As we discussed this morning, the figures for the Coscow Account are attached. If you need additional calculations, let me know.

Attachment

Memo Writer Tips

1. Review what was discussed in the verbal or telephone conversation.
2. Provide the reader with the information that was requested.

Phrasing Alternatives

PARAGRAPH 1

In follow-up to your questions, the budget for the Heathfaire Construction project is $1.3 million dollars. So far, construction costs are well under budget. and the job is proceeding on schedule.

Attached is the information you requested last week. If you need anything else, just let me know.

The relocation is scheduled for March 8. I wasn't sure of the date when we spoke this morning. If I can help in any way, don't hesitate to let me know.

REVAMPING A FAULTY DECISION

TO:
FROM:
DATE:
SUBJECT: CORRECTION

Hindsight is always 20-20. Therefore, I am changing the implementation date of the new billing procedure to September 1. We simply don't have enough time to provide all employees with adequate training, and your objections pointed this out to me.

I think this new date will allow us to introduce the new system more efficiently and void costly errors.

Memo Writer Tips

1. Admit that an error was made and state what it was.
2. Tell what the change in decision will be and when the change is to take place.

Phrasing Alternatives

PARAGRAPH 1

Okay, I made a mistake. I thought two people could process incoming insurance claims just as quickly as three, but I see that I was wrong. Go ahead and hire a new claims clerk.

The new tracking procedure I initiated last month was obviously done without thorough study of the results. Therefore, I am asking you to adopt the old procedure until the "bugs" can be ironed out of the new system. Thanks.

Hotel customers are complaining about the new room-service hours of operation, just as you said they would. Let's institute the old hours until further notice.

PUT IT IN WORDS—AND PICTURES

Depending on your company's policies, you might consider adding visuals for your memos' attachments section. Organizational charts, for example, help the reader navigate the decision-making process better, or help sort out who's responsible for what task. Well-presented diagrams and charts help bring staid numbers and statistics to life. Flow charts let readers see how progress is being made across time.

Well-crafted visuals help the reader retain information better, and make your written points clearer. Don't worry, you don't have to be an artist, either. Today, there are a variety of computer software programs available to make the task easier. Some are geared specifically to producing business visuals. Most spreadsheet programs, for example, have the capability to create top-notch graphs, charts, and other visuals. If you're writing about complex subjects where it's easy for the reader to get lost, this may be just the solution you're looking for to get your points across.

SENDING F.Y.I. (FOR YOUR INFORMATION) MEMOS*

TO:
FROM:
DATE:
SUBJECT: F.Y.I.

Attached is a copy of the proposed training schedule for employees in your branch, for your information. If you have questions, let me know.

Attachment

Memo Writer Tips

1. This is a brief memo used to cover some attachment or information you'd like the reader to have.
2. Let the reader know what the information is and where additional details can be obtained, if necessary.

---

*This memorandum was written by a clerk-typist in the training section of a governmental agency.

Phrasing Alternatives

PARAGRAPH 1

Here's something F.Y.I. Let me know what you think about it.

For your information, the following statistics outline the costs we've projected on your latest project.

Picked this up at the annual convention. Thought you'd be interested.

SOLICITING EMPLOYEE SUGGESTIONS

TO:
FROM:
DATE:
SUBJECT: EMPLOYEE SUGGESTIONS

All employees are asked to provide me with suggestions about which computer system will best meet our graphics need. Drop whatever suggestions you have in the suggestion box or send me a note outlining your recommendations.
I'll need your input no later than Friday, January 21. Thanks.

Memo Writer Tips

1. Tell employees what suggestions you would like and what you intend to do with this information.
2. Let them know when the suggestions are needed.

Phrasing Alternatives

PARAGRAPH 1

A suggestion box has been placed in the cafeteria. Any recommendations you have for saving money or improving operations will be greatly appreciated.

I need your input about the purchase of the new standardized processing equipment. Get your suggestions to me by next Friday, before we initiate purchase. Thanks.

Your suggestions regarding the qualifications for the new banquet sales manager are needed. Hall Franklin in Sales and Marketing would like to get our input before the position is announced. We've had problems in the past and think you can provide valuable input to keep us from making the same mistakes again.

SURVIVING A HIRING FREEZE

TO:
FROM:
DATE:
SUBJECT: HIRING FREEZE

A year-end deficit prevents us from hiring any new personnel until next fiscal year. This will pose a major challenge for many departments, especially those for whom additional positions had been budgeted.

Thank you for continuing to produce quality work, in spite of this temporary personnel shortage. Our difficulties should ease when new funds become available July 1. Until then, know your extra effort has not gone unnoticed.

Memo Writer Tips

1. Announce the hiring freeze, give a brief explanation for it, and indicate when it might be lifted.
2. Acknowledge the fact that this poses an additional burden on personnel, but call it a challenge (to be overcome), rather than a problem (one that can't currently be solved).
3. Use the body of the memorandum to "stroke" employees holding up under trying conditions.
4. The use of "we" and "our" make the hiring freeze a joint challenge, rather than the isolated problem "I" or "you" would connote.
5. Close on a positive note.

Phrasing Alternatives

PARAGRAPH 1

Until further notice, no new personnel can be hired to fill existing vacancies. Actual revenues did not match projections.

A hiring freeze is necessary until the reorganization of management ranks has been completed.

PARAGRAPH 2

Your quality work is appreciated. I'm certain it will help us get through the next two months.

I am as disappointed as you that this action had to be taken, but until additional funds are available, we will have to maintain current levels of production with existing personnel.

THANKING ANOTHER DEPARTMENT

TO:
FROM:
DATE:
SUBJECT: THANKS FOR YOUR COOPERATION

We could never have gotten the newsletter out on time without your assistance. Thank you for all the hard work you put in on it. If we can ever return the favor, just let us know.

Memo Writer Tips

1. Let the other department know what they did that you appreciate.
2. Thank them for their help and offer future assistance, should they need it.

Phrasing Alternatives

PARAGRAPH 1

Thanks so much for helping us fill our vacancy ahead of schedule. If I can ever return the favor, just let me know.

Please extend my sincere thanks to each member of your department for the overtime they put in to close out this fiscal year. We could not have finished our work on time without your help.

I thank you for loaning us your van for transportation to last weekend's conference. Your help enabled me to get our staff there on time. Just let me know when I can return the favor.

TOO MUCH WORK, TOO FEW WORKERS

TO:
FROM:
DATE:
SUBJECT: PERSONNEL SHORTAGE

Because of my backlog of work and shortage of personnel, I will not be able to prepare the report you requested before August 1. By then, I should have additional personnel on board and should have our end-of-year work completed.

Thanks for your patience during this shortage.

Memo Writer Tips

1. Spell out specifically who/what is short and how this shortage will affect production.
2. Let the reader know when circumstances should improve.

Phrasing Alternatives

PARAGRAPH 1

All the claim agents in my section have been working 10-hour days for the past three weeks. In spite of this, we have been unable to clear out our backlog of claims. We will continue to work overtime until all claims have been processed and hope to have this accomplished by October 1.

A 35 percent increase in orders and a shortage of personnel have resulted in a 7-day delay in filling requests. My people are working as hard as they can, but until we get additional help, our 3-day order cycle will be delayed.

THE TRANSMITTAL MEMORANDUM

TO:
FROM:
DATE:
SUBJECT: COST ACCOUNTING PROJECTIONS

Attached for your information are the projections you requested on the Nash Consulting Job (#458). If you need additional information, just let me know.

Attachment

Memo Writer Tips

1. The transmittal memorandum is a cover memorandum used to send reports, data, computer printouts, and other information.
2. The purpose of the transmittal memorandum is to briefly let the reader know what information is attached.

Phrasing Alternatives

PARAGRAPH 1

Recommendations for improving the process we use to maintain quality control operations is attached. Please review them and return them to my office within two weeks. Thanks for your input.

I am sending you copies of the Overton file, as you requested. This file will document the transactions we have already had with Overton and should provide you with the information you need to determine whether or not we should continue doing business with them.

The following documents are enclosed, as per your request:

1. A list of qualified applicants.

2. A copy of the job announcement.

3. Proposed interview questions.

4. Names of others who might serve on the interview panel.

Call me if you need other information.

UPDATING SUBORDINATES

TO:
FROM:
DATE:
SUBJECT: UPDATE—TELLER INTERVIEWS

I have screened 54 applications for the teller trainee position. Eight candidates will be interviewed on Wednesday, November 4.

After these interviews, the two best candidates will be selected, and I'm hoping we can hire these people by November 15.

Thanks for covering during this personnel shortage.

Memo Writer Tips

1. Let employees know what you're updating them about in the first sentence.
2. Detail what progress has been made.
3. If there are a number of details, list or bullet each.

Phrasing Alternatives

PARAGRAPH 1

I wanted to update you on the progress that's been made so far about our upcoming move to new offices.

Contract negotiations have been taking place for the past two weeks, and I wanted to let you know what progress has been made so far.

I've been reviewing the suggestions you made for making your work area safer, and I'd like to update you on the status of your requests.

PARAGRAPH 2

The lease for our new offices should be signed by Friday of this week. The offices will have to be remodeled slightly to meet our needs. We'll probably be moving during the week of October 3.

Concessions have been made on the hourly rate. The union wants an eight percent increase, and management has agreed to a four percent increase.

So far, these steps have been taken:

- A safety captain has been appointed for your area.
- Equipment has been rearranged.
- Safety goggles have been ordered for all personnel.

I am still working with several of you to develop safety presentations for all workers in the unit.

WELCOMING A NEW EMPLOYEE*

TO:
FROM:
DATE:
SUBJECT: PERSONNEL ANNOUNCEMENT

Atworth Development Corporation is pleased to announce that effective July 15, 1989, Mr. Conté Perez has joined the corporation as Manager of Finance. In his new position, Mr. Perez will be responsible for the analysis and coordination of all financial affairs of the corporation.

Mr. Perez is a graduate of the Horton School of Business and, most recently, was a consultant for Peter Rubloff and Associates.

Please join us in welcoming Conté to our staff.

Memo Writer Tips

1. Announce when the new employee will begin.
2. Give the new employee's job title and briefly describe what his/her duties will be.
3. Include a one-sentence description of the new employee's past work experience.
4. Invite the members of the organization to welcome the new employee to the staff.

---

*This memorandum was written by the Vice-president of Finance of an educational corporation.

Phrasing Alternatives

PARAGRAPH 1

I am happy to announce the appointment of Harriet Larson to the position of Senior Consultant. Ms. Larson will begin work with the company on February 1. She will oversee the work of consultants.

Please welcome our newest employee, George Havier. Mr. Havier will begin work on Monday, July 5 and will supervise our collections department.

Our new telemarketing representative will begin work on March 22. Hazel Reed, with more than 10 years of telemarketing experience, will make a fine addition to our staff, I'm sure.

PARAGRAPH 2

George comes to us from Knowles, Hamblin and Associates, one of the premier accounting firms in the city.

Ms. Larson has a B.A. from DeWitt University and a M.S. in Information Management from Brighton College. With 15 years of expertise in this area, I know she'll bring a vast wealth of expertise to our company.

Hazel was recently promoted and is being transferred from the Houston office. There, she supervised a staff of 55 and received last year's Outstanding Employee award.

PARAGRAPH 3

Welcome, Hazel.

Take a moment to meet Mr. Larson and welcome him to our office.

I know you'll make George feel right at home.

WRITING A MEMORANDUM FOR RECORD*

TO:
FROM:
DATE:
SUBJECT: MEMORANDUM FOR RECORD

Gene Callis, my supervisor, called me in to his office today at 8:15 A.M. He told me he was "writing me up" for being five minutes late to work this morning.

When I asked about the five-minute "grace period," he said, "This is the second time you've been late in the last two weeks, so the grace period doesn't apply to you." When I asked him why other members of the department had been more than five minutes late, but had not been written up, he said, "Don't worry about them; just worry about getting yourself here on time."

I signed the counseling statement and left his office, but I told him, "I'm signing this but I don't agree with it."

Memo Writer Tips

1. Memoranda for record are used to document conversations or situations that occur in your workplace, situations you don't want to forget.

2. When you want to document the specifics of a conversation, be sure to write a memorandum for record. You may think you'll remember what happened, but you will not be able to remember details weeks or months after the incident has occurred.

3. Write this memorandum as soon after the incident occurs as possible.

4. Write specific details of what happened and use quotation marks to indicate the exact words spoken by the parties involved.

5. Your memorandum for record becomes a permanent record of information you may need at a later date.

---

*This memorandum was written by a Contract Specialist for the federal government.

Summary Points

- Good memos don't meander. They get to the point in the very first sentence.
- Details count. Make sure you have your facts straight. Start with the most important information first, then work your way down.
- Follow the Memo Writer Tips carefully; they offer excellent general advice you can apply to your own situations.
- Use highlighting devices like "bullets" to make information stand out.
- Never forget to praise people for a job well done.

CHAPTER 3

WORK PERFORMANCE MEMOS: REAL-WORLD EXAMPLES

The marketing person you hired is really making sales soar. He's become quite an asset to your division. You want to tell him as much in writing so there's a permanent record, but don't have the words. Meanwhile, the person who handles regional sales has been slacking-off and you want to send him an unambiguous signal: shape up, or ship out. Again, you know how you might say it, but the words just don't seem to flow on paper. This chapter will help you tremendously.

Business at its most basic, like many other endeavors, is about human interaction. Dealing with individuals in person can be hard enough, committing yourself to writing is especially difficult when phrases can be misinterpreted, and you're not there to explain what you mean. Employees crave praise, and want to be acknowledged for a job well done. Managers, however, must also maintain standards and discipline and occasionally write memos that are difficult to phrase. These are the memos employees are loathe to receive.

Making sure the phrasing is just right so as not to offend, or appear over solicitous on the other side, is a delicate art. The model memos listed below excerpted from Cynthia Barnes' *Model Memos for Every Business Occasion,* offer excellent templates for the busy manager who must often write about performance issues from everything including accepting a resignation, praising a job well done, documenting tardiness, announcing an award, and so on. Each memo comes with tips that should always be kept in mind when writing in your own words. They also offer alternative phrases that show different routes for finding the phrase that works best for you.

MODEL MEMOS ABOUT WORK PERFORMANCE ISSUES

Once everyone knows what work gets done by whom, HOW that work gets done becomes the critical factor. If employees work hard and well, a memorandum can applaud their efforts. When workers are doing their jobs, but could be doing more, a memorandum might motivate them to put forth extra effort. When employee performance is substandard, the talk you have with the employee about improving work habits can be followed up by a memorandum that outlines corrective action.

Exemplary work performance needs attention. Who won an award or a contest? Who met production or sales goals? Who satisfactorily completed probation with the company? Who's the employee of the month? Who's marking another anniversary date with our agency?

Routine work performance issues must be communicated: time for performance appraisals, time to resign and move on, time to follow up on work that has deadlines.

Unsatisfactory work performance issues demand attention, as well. Use the memoranda in this chapter to warn an employee whose "moonlighting" has begun to affect job performance. Document a counseling session with an employee or document your counseling session with your boss. Follow up on a customer complaint and explain, in writing, why discourteous treatment and inefficient service can't be tolerated. Address problems of excessive absenteeism or tardiness. When you need a written record of poor job performance, use one of the model memoranda in this chapter to help you make your case.

The model memoranda in this chapter can help you make it clear HOW the work in your organization should be or has been done.

ACCEPTING A SUBORDINATE'S RESIGNATION

TO:
FROM:
DATE:
SUBJECT: ACCEPTANCE OF RESIGNATION

With regret, I accept your resignation from your position as Marketing Manager. You leave behind an impressive record with the company.

I know I speak for all of us when I wish you continued success with your new position. If I can ever be of any service in the future, please don't hesitate to contact me.

Memo Writer Tips

1. In the first sentence, accept the resignation and name the position from which the employee is resigning.
2. Include at least one sentence commending the employee for his/her contributions to the company.
3. Wish the employee well in future endeavors.

Phrasing Alternatives

PARAGRAPH 1

Your resignation from your Radiology Technician position is accepted.

I am sorry to see you go, but realize your need to move on. Your resignation is accepted, effective March 14.

PARAGRAPH 2

You will be difficult to replace, and your hard work will be missed.
I applaud your exceptional contributions to the organization for the past three (3) years.

PARAGRAPH 3

On behalf of all of us, good luck and best wishes.

Congratulations on your appointment at Radion Corporation.

I wish you continued success in your career.

ANNOUNCING A PERFORMANCE REVIEW

TO:
FROM:
DATE:
SUBJECT: ANNUAL PERFORMANCE REVIEW

I have scheduled the following appointments for annual performance reviews:

Jan Slokam	Monday, December 3, 8:00 A.M.
Phil Tolbert	Monday, December 3, 9:30 A.M.
Michelle Jones	Monday, December 3, 11:00 A.M.
Leslie Richard	Tuesday, December 4, 8:00 A.M.
Arthur Hammond	Tuesday, December 4, 9:30 A.M.
Annette Osborn	Tuesday, December 4, 11:00 A.M.

I have to complete all performance reviews by December 10 and submit them to the personnel office. I look forward to discussing your work performance for the past year with you, to identify your strengths and areas that may need improvement.
We will meet in my office.

Memo Writer Tips

1. Tell employees when and where their performance reviews will be conducted.

2. Outline a schedule if you have several employees to review.

3. Add a positive comment bout the purpose for the performance review process.

Phrasing Alternatives

PARAGRAPH 1

Please plan to meet with me on Friday, June 1, to review your performance for the past year. Meet me at 9:00 A.M., my office.

Performance review time is once again upon us. The evaluation process is an important one, as salary increases and promotions are based upon the results of annual performance appraisals. Your review will take place Tuesday, January 14, 10:30 A.M., in my office.

Annual performance reviews will begin next week. Yours has been scheduled for Thursday, May 24 at 11:00 A.M. We will meet in my office.

PARAGRAPH 2

Come prepared to discuss the contributions you've made during the past year. I am anxious to discuss how well you've performed since your last appraisal.

Annual performance reviews are an important part of our continuing efforts to upgrade performance and create a solid work team. I look forward to discussing your production efforts with you.

We will have the opportunity to determine whether or not the goals we set last year have been met. Getting feedback about performance helps us all do a better job.

ANNOUNCING AN AWARD

TO:
FROM:
DATE:
SUBJECT: TOP PRODUCER AWARD

Harry Beckman has been chosen to receive the Top Producer Award for fiscal year 19—. As lead salesperson in his department, Harry established 52 new accounts and exceeded sales goals by 43 percent.

Harry will receive his award at this Friday's recognition banquet. Join me in congratulating Mr. Beckman on his fine work and outstanding sales record.

Memo Writer Tips

1. Put the names of the recipient and the award in the first sentence.
2. Briefly explain why the award has been given.
3. Include information about presentation ceremonies.
4. Close by congratulating the recipient and encouraging others to do the same.

Phrasing Alternatives

PARAGRAPH 1

This year's Faculty Member of the Year is Janice Calgood, Social Sciences Professor.

I am pleased to announce this year's Management Excellence award winner: Mr. Avery Smith.

John Jones, Chief of Research and Development, is this year's Outstanding Employee award recipient.

PARAGRAPH 2

Mr. Beckman's software design has earned the company well over $5.6 million dollars.

Mark's unit consistently exceeded production goals by 35 percent.

Marsha Menton's efforts have positively affected employee relations and have improved communication throughout the organization.

PARAGRAPH 3

Congratulations, Harry, on your outstanding performance. I know your colleagues will personally take the time to congratulate you, as well.

Stop by Jane's office and congratulate her on receiving this prestigious award.

This honor, in small part, symbolizes our recognition of your excellence, and we all send special congratulations to mark this significant achievement.

ANNOUNCING A CONTEST WINNER

TO:
FROM:
DATE:
SUBJECT: "SKY'S THE LIMIT" CONTEST WINNER

Ms. Margaret Slokam has won the "Sky's the Limit" sales contest. Along with topping the charts with $51,000 in monthly sales, Margaret also designed an effective sales logo and slogan.

Margaret will receive a $500.00 cash bonus and a weekend stay for two at the Retreat Inn in Vail.

Congratulations, Margaret, on a job well done.

Memo Writer Tips

1. Name the contest and the contest winner.
2. Spell out why the winner won.
3. Tell what the reward will be, as an incentive to others in the department.
4. Congratulate the winner.

Phrasing Alternatives

PARAGRAPH 1

Our monthly promotion contest has been won by Mr. Martin Coil.

The winner of our Hawaiian Luau contest is Harry Phillips.

I am pleased to announce the winner of the Trailblazer Contest: Ms. Margaret Slokam.

PARAGRAPH 2

Martin sold more than $45,000 worth of goods last month.

As contest winner, Harry sold 65 new policies last quarter.

More than 35 new accounts were opened by Margaret during the past 60 days.

PARAGRAPH 3

For his outstanding performance, Martin will receive an all-expenses-paid trip for two to Oahu.

Harry will get a $1,000 cash bonus.

In addition to a weekend for two at the Kinnerly Lodge, Margaret will receive a $50.00 per month salary increase.

PARAGRAPH 4

Join me in congratulating Martin on his significant accomplishment.

On behalf of the company, congratulations on your contest win.

Congratulations are certainly in order. You've done an outstanding job!

ASKING AN EMPLOYEE TO COMPLETE A SELF-APPRAISAL*

TO:
FROM:
DATE:
SUBJECT: ANNUAL WORK PLAN

Call Lisa sometime during the next two weeks to schedule an appointment to review your annual work plan. Use the attached form to discuss your (1) accomplishments for 19—, (2) goals for 19—, (3) goals for personal/professional career development, and (4) concerns or recommendations for improvement.

Memo Writer Tips

1. Let the employee know when the performance appraisal will be scheduled. Include where it will take place.
2. Include instructions for completing the self-appraisal form.

Phrasing Alternatives

PARAGRAPH 1

Please complete the attached self-appraisal form and bring it with you to our appraisal conference: Monday, June 2, 3:00 P.M., room 202.

In preparation for your annual performance review, you need to fill out the attached self-appraisal form. I will schedule a review conference for you in the next few weeks.

A complete performance review process includes an employee's assessment of his/her performance as well as that of the supervisor. An appraisal form is attached. Please bring your completed form to my office on Monday, May 18, 1:00 P.M. We'll have the opportunity to compare assessments of our performance then. I look forward to a constructive, profitable discussion.

---

*This memorandum was written by the Dean of Instruction of a college.

COMMENDING AN EMPLOYEE FOR A JOB WELL DONE*

TO:
FROM:
DATE:
SUBJECT: JOB CLASSIFICATION STUDY

One of the most important projects that employees can be involved in is to have input into a job classification system. I have been very pleased with the work that has been done by your group and know that the quality of our system will be much better as a result of your efforts. We expect to have the revised system in place in early 19—.

For all of your hard work, I extend to you a heartfelt thank you.

Memo Writer Tips

1. Outline what job the employee(s) has(ve) done and why it is important to your organization.
2. Thank the employee for doing a good job.

Phrasing Alternatives

PARAGRAPH 1

I want to commend you for taking the initiative to track the flow of paperwork in our department. Your work will save us a lot of duplication of effort.

Our supply system has needed to be revised for quite some time. The new system will make it much easier for people to get the supplies they need, when they need them.

PARAGRAPH 2

Please accept my sincerest congratulations on a job well done.

Your efforts, above and beyond the call of duty, are commendable. I thank you.

---

*This memorandum was written by a Human Resources Specialist for a municipal government agency.

COMMUNICATING ABOUT SUBSTANDARD PRODUCT QUALITY

TO:
FROM:
DATE:
SUBJECT: DEFECTIVE BRACKETS

Brackets in Lot #40 are defective. They should be able to withstand 40 pounds of pressure, but quality control has informed me these brackets barely handle 30 pounds of pressure.

These brackets will have to be melted and reforged, in order for them to meet specifications. I want someone assigned to check samples from each 100 brackets off the line.

Costly errors like this cannot be tolerated. Discuss the problem with your personnel and make sure we don't have this problem again.

Memo Writer Tips

1. Be specific about what the product is and why it is defective.

2. Discuss what corrective action is to be taken, and remind the subordinate you don't expect this problem in the future.

Phrasing Alternatives

PARAGRAPH 1

Quality Control has reported a 32 percent error rate in data entered in your section.

The switches produced on Friday, January 4 are not firing properly.

Page 3 of the newsletters printed last week for the Marketing Department is blurred.

PARAGRAPH 2

Take the following corrective action today:

• Inspect the remaining computers in that shipment.

• Return any found to be defective to the line.

• Supervise, personally, any reworking required.

Ship the customer a new batch, Express Mail, no later than 5:00 P.M. today.

Pick up the defective chairs and deliver new ones.

PARAGRAPH 3

Our customers expect quality products from us, and I intend to deliver. Let's see to it this doesn't happen again.

We are known for our quality manufacturing, and such substandard production costs us money, time, and reputation. Monitor production carefully so that this does not happen again.

We can't afford such costly mistakes, and I expect this problem will be corrected immediately.

COMMUNICATING ABOUT INEFFICIENT SERVICE

TO:
FROM:
DATE:
SUBJECT: LATE DELIVERY

Magnusson Office Supplies called yesterday to complain that the order they were promised for January 14 was not delivered until February 3. Magnusson is one of our best customers and has been doing business with us for more than 10 years.

I assured them this problem would not reoccur and gave them a 2 percent discount on the order. Follow up with a letter of apology and make sure this doesn't happen again.

Memo Writer Tips

1. Describe, specifically, what the inefficiency was and, if possible, when it occurred.
2. Affirm the customer's right to receive efficient service.
3. Close by spelling out what corrective action is necessary, and reaffirm your position that incidents of inefficiency must be corrected.

Phrasing Alternatives

PARAGRAPH 1

Neimeyer Company ordered 50 boxes of photocopy paper on February 12, but received 50 boxes of stationery instead.

Why were Mr. George Olman's (Case #33457) laboratory test results lost?

Hamilton and Associates called for price quotations three days ago, but no one has yet returned their call.

PARAGRAPH 2

All customers are entitled to receive their orders—per their specifications—on time, and in good condition.

When orders aren't filled correctly and quickly, we lose money—and the respect of our clients. When respect is lost, we don't get their orders.

In a highly competitive field like ours, clients choose us because they have come to expect our efficient service. They expect it, and I expect we'll give it to them.

PARAGRAPH 3

Call them and offer our sincere apologies for the mix-up. Let them know this was a one-time mistake, one they can expect will not happen again.

Enroll in the January 31 Customer Relations course offered by the training department. Call Jan Rutledge at EXT. 431 for additional details.

You normally function so efficiently; this complaint took me completely by surprise. I know this problem won't surface again.

COMMUNICATING ABOUT DISCOURTEOUS TREATMENT OF A CLIENT*

TO:
FROM:
DATE:
SUBJECT: CITIZEN COMPLAINT

Last Wednesday, Councilwoman Johnson called to find out why two patrol cars were parked side-by-side and why the officers sat in their cars, talking for 10 minutes. Dispatcher Lori Hood took this call.

Lori told the councilwoman, "I don't know; I'm not out there." The conversation lasted for more than 15 minutes, when the dispatcher finally turned the call over to the Watch Commander.

It was clear from listening to the recording that Dispatcher Hood was very rude to Ms. Johnson. I discussed this incident with Lori at length, and she has promised that it will not happen again. Since Lori is an excellent employee, and this is the first incident of this kind, no further action seems warranted.

Memo Writer Tips

1. Describe the incident involving discourteous treatment in detail. Make sure your explanation focuses on facts, rather than speculations.

2. Affirm how important it is to maintain positive relationships with customers and clients.

3. If you are writing to your superior, tell what action has been taken, and reassure your boss that such an incident will not happen again.

4. If you are writing to a subordinate, use this memorandum as a follow-up to your verbal reprimand, reiterating what action has been/will be taken. Make it clear that discourtesy will not be tolerated.

---

*A Communications Supervisor for a police department wrote this memo.

Phrasing Alternatives

PARAGRAPH 1

An irate customer called yesterday to complain that she was put on "hold" five times, transferred to three different departments, and then finally "hung up on" by the last person to whom she spoke.

Yesterday, I received a letter from a Mr. George Hagelthorpe, regarding discourteous treatment he received while shopping in our menswear department on November 15, 19—.

Ms. Selma Jordan called yesterday to complain about the treatment she received on May 22, as she was trying to get current values on her stock portfolio.

PARAGRAPH 2

I have discussed this matter with the employee in question, and he says the caller became verbally abusive, prompting him to terminate the call. While this in no way excuses his discourtesy, it does, in part, make his case that he was not wholly at fault.

Maintaining the positive regard of our customers is our number one priority. Without them, none of us would be employed. You might consider this fact the next time you are tempted to act rudely to a customer.

Rudeness to clients cannot be tolerated under any circumstances. In future, let your supervisor handle the call if you feel you cannot manage the client in a friendly, courteous way.

PARAGRAPH 3

Because of the serious nature of this infraction and the fact that this is not the first time customers have complained about Ms. X's treatment, Ms. X is being suspended for three days without pay. I have informed her of her suspension and warned her that any future maltreatment of customers will result in her termination.

The employee has written a letter of apology to the client, and a letter of reprimand has been placed in her personnel file.

I expect we will have no further episodes of discourteous treatment of clients. Such acts can never be rationalized, under any circumstances. See to it that this never happens again.

CONGRATULATING A PEER ON A PROMOTION

TO:
FROM:
DATE:
SUBJECT: CONGRATULATIONS

Congratulations on your recent promotion to Retail Services Manager. You've really worked hard this past year, and no one deserves the promotion more than you.

Accept my best wishes for your continued success.

Memo Writer Tips

1. Extend your congratulations, including the name of the new position.

2. Include at least one sentence that covers why you think the person deserved the promotion.

Phrasing Alternatives

PARAGRAPH 1

Way to go, Jim. I just heard about your upcoming promotion to Regional Vice-president.

No one could be more pleased about your promotion to National Sales Rep.

Accept my heartiest best wishes on your promotion to Executive Assistant.

PARAGRAPH 2

Keep us the good work!

On behalf of all my staff, we wish you the best.

Good luck in your new position; I know you'll do well.

CURBING MOONLIGHTING

TO:
FROM:
DATE:
SUBJECT: OFF-DUTY WORK POLICY

Guidelines for work during off-duty hours are included in the employee handbook. Generally, the "moonlighting" policy does not restrict such work, unless the off-duty work affects on-the-job performance.

In the past 30 days, you have been tardy for work three times and have called in sick twice. While you assured me that your part-time job would not interfere with your work here, it would seem that your moonlighting is, indeed, beginning to affect your performance.

This is your primary job, and you are expected to be here every day, on time, and ready to work. If your attendance problems persist, we will need to review the issue of your off-duty work.

Memo Writer Tips

1. Explain, specifically, why you are addressing the issue of moonlighting with the employee.
2. Refer to any policies or guidelines that may exist about this issue.
3. Tell the employee what action you expect him/her to take and how you may handle the situation if the problem(s) persists.

Phrasing Alternatives

PARAGRAPH 1

The Employee Handbook outlines specific policies regarding moonlighting.

The policy about off-duty work is clear.

Are you familiar with the policy regarding moonlighting?

PARAGRAPH 2

Moonlighting is acceptable as long as it does not have a negative impact on your work here.

Working off-duty jobs is strictly prohibited.

In most instances, employees can work other jobs, as long as they maintain acceptable performance here.

PARAGRAPH 3

Recently, you have been so exhausted that you almost fell asleep on the job on at least two occasions.

Your moonlighting seems to have made it difficult for you to get here daily and promptly.

Your production has fallen well below standards since you began work on your part-time job.

PARAGRAPH 4

I'm sure you realize how important it is for you to give this job your primary focus. Let's discuss the problems you've been having and resolve this issue once and for all.

Obviously, you cannot give optimal effort to both jobs. If you do not curb your moonlighting, you are in danger of having to choose which job you prefer.

Your moonlighting has begun to jeopardize your employment here. Unless you can resolve these problems, you will need to decide whether the benefits derived from your part-time employment warrant the problems you are currently experiencing on your primary job.

DOCUMENTATION FOR TERMINATION ACTION

TO: FILE
FROM:
DATE:
SUBJECT: WORK RECORD—HAROLD SANFORD

3/8/—	Mr. Sanford was 15 minutes late for work. Did not call in. (9:10 A.M.)
3/11/—	Harold called in sick; said he overslept. (9:18 A.M.)
3/19—	Harold asked to leave work one hour early; said he had a family emergency. (4:18 P.M.)

3/20/—   Counseled Harold. Told him he needed to report for work each day, on time. Harold said he "had some personal problems," but would "get my act together."

3/22/—   Harold called in sick; said his car wouldn't start. (9:00 A.M.)

3/26/—   Harold took two hours for lunch without asking for annual leave. When I asked him why he'd taken so long for lunch, he said he "got caught in traffic." (2:30 P.M.)

Memo Writer Tips

1. In the event you must terminate an employee, you will need documentation of the poor performance that led to the termination.

2. Record each incident as it occurs. Complete sentences are not necessary.

3. Include dates and times.

4. Provide as much specific information about what occurred as you can.

DOCUMENTING AN EMPLOYEE COUNSELING SESSION

TO: FILE
FROM:
DATE:
SUBJECT: COUNSELING SESSION—JANICE OWENS

ITEMS DISCUSSED

I had a counseling session with Janice Owens on Tuesday, July 3, 19—, at 2:00 P.M. The following items were discussed:

1. Janice's frequent absences from work (five days in the past month).

2. Janice's missed deadlines in the Woodward and Keystone reports.

3. Janice's confrontational communication style. She has had arguments with three other employees in the department during the past two weeks.

EMPLOYEE RESPONSE

1. Janice said her child has been ill, and she has had to miss work because of this. She assured me should would make every effort to get to work every day on time.

2. Janice said she could not get the figures from the research department, and she could not finish the reports without them.

3. Janice said she was been under considerable pressure lately and that this had probably contributed to her "short fuse."

SUPERVISOR REPLY

1. I suggested Janice make arrangements for childcare so she would not have to miss work again. She said such arrangements have been made.

2. I told Janice to let me know when she found herself unable to meet a deadline. I suggested I might be able to help her get the information she needed. She agreed.

3. I directed Janice to speak to each of the three workers, apologize to them, and explain why she had lost her temper.

4. I referred Janice to the Employee Assistance Program.

Memo Writer Tips

1. Outline what topics were covered in the counseling session, as well as when the session took place.
2. Record the employee's responses.
3. Include any suggestions you made, and record what the employee said in response to these suggestions.
4. Be as specific as possible.

DRAFTING A RESIGNATION

TO:
FROM:
DATE:
SUBJECT: RESIGNATION

With regret, I will be resigning my position as Medical Technologist, effective Friday, February 24, 19—. I have accepted a position as Laboratory Chief at Montview Community Hospital.

Thank you for your assistance and support during the past four (4) years. If I can help you find a suitable replacement, let me know.

Memo Writer Tips

1. State what position you are resigning from and the effective date of your resignation.
2. Give a reason for your resignation and keep it positive. Now is not the time, regardless of the circumstances, to "burn bridges."
3. Thank your present employer for assistance and support and offer to help with screening applicants or training a replacement, if you are inclined to do so.

PUT IT IN WORDS!

Although study after study shows that most people in business prefer to hear news—good or bad—in person from their boss, the role of the memo in addressing work performance issues is still very important. A memo is neither a trophy for a job well-done, nor a "pink-slip" for inferior performance. It's the next best thing to verbal acknowledgment—physical proof.

Praising an employee with a pat on the back at the water cooler is great, but having written words that can be filed and proudly passed around is much better. In that same vein, warning employees about bad performance and putting them on notice in writing helps make your case airtight to those above you. They know where you stand, they know what you expect of them, and they know what must be done to remedy the situation.

More than a few legal cases have gone to trial because an employee was under the false impression that "all was well" and there was "nothing to worry about." By putting your concerns in unambiguously written memos, you are creating a veritable "paper trail," that can head-off a lot of confusion, and perhaps needless management, or even legal, headaches down the line.

Phrasing Alternatives

PARAGRAPH 1

Please accept this memorandum as my resignation from my position as Manager III. Friday, June 22, 19—, will be my last day of work.

Regrettably, I must resign from my job as Mailroom Supervisor, effective Friday, January 17, 19—.

As of Friday, August 6, 19—, I am resigning as Policy Analyst.

PARAGRAPH 2

While I have enjoyed my employment at XYZ Corporation, I feel now is the time to pursue other career goals.

My spouse is being relocated to Spartan, Tennessee.

Barton Electronics has offered me an excellent position with their company.

PARAGRAPH 3

You have helped make my tenure here a successful, productive one, and I thank you for your assistance over the years.

The support and encouragement you have give me for the past two years have been greatly appreciated.

I appreciate the help you've given me during my employment with XYZ International.

HANDLING EXCESSIVE ABSENTEEISM

TO:
FROM:
DATE:
SUBJECT: FREQUENT ABSENCES

Each member of our work unit is an important part of the team. That's why even a single absence affects the overall functioning of the work unit.

During the past 30 days, you have been absent eight (8) times. This seems to me a bit excessive. We have spoken about your attendance problem in the past, and while you assured me you would correct the problem, your excessive absenteeism persists.

Expecting others to continually make up for your absences is unfair and cannot be tolerated. Accept this as notice that if you are absent again, disciplinary action will be taken, and termination proceedings may begin.

Feel free to call me or come by my office if you wish to discuss this matter further.

Memo Writer Tips

1. Some positive statement about the necessity of being at work may start the memo off on a positive note.

2. You should then give specifics about the number of absences the employee has had.

3. If this has not been a persistent problem, warn the employee about the attendance problem; set up a time to discuss the situation face-to-face.

4. If this is a recurring problem, a more severe tone is warranted, and you should tell the employee what disciplinary action you plan to take.

Phrasing Alternatives

PARAGRAPH 1

You are an essential part of our work group, and your absence makes things difficult for us all.

Regular attendance, except for legitimate absence, is required of all personnel.

Each employee must do his/her job efficiently if the work group is to perform successfully.

PARAGRAPH 2

You have been absent 14 times in the past 30 days; this is not acceptable.

You have developed a pattern of absenteeism, by missing work 10 times in the past 20 days.

Your excessive absenteeism—9 of the past 20 days—cannot be tolerated.

PARAGRAPH 3

After our original discussion, you agreed to change this pattern. Still, the problem exists. If you cannot get to work regularly—every day—you will be fired.

When I spoke to you about this problem initially, you made a commitment to report for work every day. Since you have not kept your part of the bargain, I must begin termination action.

You said you would not be absent again when we discussed this issue, but your excessive absenteeism has continued. You are suspended without pay for five (5) days.

HANDLING EXCESSIVE TARDINESS

TO:
FROM:
DATE:
SUBJECT: EXCESSIVE TARDINESS

Productive employees make reporting for work on time a habit. You, on the other hand, seem to have made tardiness a regular occurrence. You have been late for work six (6) times in the past two (2) weeks, an unacceptable record of tardiness.

If you are having specific problems that make it impossible for you to get to work on time, I want to know about them. In any event, your September 15 paycheck will be docked for the time you were late.

Memo Writer Tips

1. If you like, begin the memo with a statement about how important it is to get to work on time.
2. Outline, specifically, how many times the employee has been tardy.
3. Ask the employee to make you aware of any extenuating circumstances that may be causing these difficulties.
4. Close by telling the employee what corrective action you expect to be taken and what the result of failure to do so will be.

Phrasing Alternatives

PARAGRAPH 1

Each employee is responsible for getting to work every day—ON TIME. Attendance records show you've been late for work three (3) times this week.

Reporting for work promptly each day underscores an employee's commitment to his job and his co-workers. Why have you been tardy for work four (4) times in the past twenty days?

If a job is important, then coming to work on time is important, as well. Your excessive tardinesss—six times in the past two weeks—has not gone unnoticed.

PARAGRAPH 2

You can either get here on time or look for another job.

This excessive tardiness will not be tolerated, and unless your attendance pattern improves, you will be suspended without pay for at least five (5) days.

If you continue this pattern of excessive tardiness, dismissal will be the result.

IMPROVING PRODUCTIVITY

TO:
FROM:
DATE:
SUBJECT: PRODUCTIVITY

For the past three (3) years, your work record has been one of the best in our department. Lately, however, some of the letters you have typed have been sent out with errors, phone messages have either not been taken or have been misplaced, and several key contracts have yet to be prepared for signature.

This substandard performance is certainly not representative of the work you are capable of doing. If you have some personal or work-related problems that are affecting your work habits, I'd be only too happy to discuss these with you.

Your work record has been one of the best in the department, and I trust you will take whatever steps are necessary to correct any deficiencies in your performance right away.

Memo Writer Tips

1. Begin the memo on a positive note, by saying something positive about the employee's past performance.
2. Outline examples of the employee's substandard performance.
3. Offer to discuss why productivity has not been the best.
4. Close by encouraging the employee to take appropriate corrective action, and discuss what you expect the employee to do.

Phrasing Alternatives

PARAGRAPH 1

I have always been able to count on the fact that you would do your work and do it well. However, in the past month, some problems with productivity have surfaced.

You are a valuable and productive employee in this division. Is there some reason your recent performance has not been up to standards?

Anytime a job needs to be done well, Travis Smith is the one who gets it. Recently, however, your work has not been handled as quickly or efficiently as it might have been.

PARAGRAPH 2

The McKenney Project is now behind schedule. There must be some reason for this recent change in your performance. I'd like to know what it is.

Several payments to vendors are 90 days past due. I am always available to talk to you about problems you might be having.

The budget forecasts were due two (2) weeks ago, and this seriously delays the preparation of next year's projections. Let's discuss the situation and work out a way to resolve it.

PARAGRAPH 3

I know you'll get back on schedule and bring your performance up to standards.

You know what production standards are, and I'm sure you'll work hard to meet them once again.

I'm confident your productivity will improve right away.

INITIATING COMPLAINT FOLLOW-UP

TO:
FROM:
DATE:
SUBJECT: COMPLAINT FOLLOW-UP

Just this morning, Ralph Netcam of Randolph Enterprises called my office to complain that the shipment promised him for January 1 has not yet been delivered.

Find out what is causing the delay and notify Netcam when he can expect his shipment. Be sure to offer our apologies for this foul-up.

Memo Writer Tips

1. Outline what the complaint is, when it was received, and from whom.
2. Direct the appropriate employee to take whatever action is necessary to resolve the matter.

Phrasing Alternatives

PARAGRAPH 1

Attached is a complaint from Mrs. Teresa Richmond, Delbert Industries. Apparently, there was a mix-up made in her order.

I just spend a half-hour on the telephone apologizing to a Mr. Hank Simms for the rude treatment he says he received from one of our operators.

Justin Cruz of Network Corporation claims they were overcharged $591.00 on last month's bill.

PARAGRAPH 2

Follow up on this problem and resolve it today. A letter of apology would be an appropriate response.

Research the complaint and let me know what actually happened. I want to get back to the client by 5:00 P.M. today.

Can you determine what actually took place and call the customer to smooth things over?

INCREASING SALES PERFORMANCE

TO:
FROM:
DATE:
SUBJECT: SALES PERFORMANCE

Your sales goals, based on the size of your territory and the past purchases of your clients, were fixed at $42,000.00 per quarter. Actual sales for the past quarter were only $34,000.00. This represents the third quarter this year where your sales goals were not met.

We all know the market fluctuates, and there are a number of reasons why sales drop from time to time. I'd like to know why your sales performance has fallen off in recent months and what we might both do to turn this situation around. You're an able sales rep, and I trust your figures for next quarter will improve.

Memo Writer Tips

1. Your memo will have more "teeth" in it, if you can state specifically how much sales performance has lagged.
2. Offer to provide assistance and close by telling the sales person you expect improvement.

Phrasing Alternatives

PARAGRAPH 1

Your sales performance has been less than optimal for the past three months. Sales in your region have decreased 14 percent.

You're one of our finest sales personnel, which makes me wonder why you haven't made sales quota for two months. Sales volume on your route was $4,000 less than projections.

You're obviously putting forth the effort, but not making the sales. During the past 90 days, your sales have declined to 22 percent below quota.

PARAGRAPH 2

Let's sit down and discuss why sales have been so difficult to generate in your region. I'm confident this temporary lull will be corrected within the next 60 days.

I've asked your Sales Manager to work with you for the next 30 days. I look forward to figures that either meet or exceed goals next month.

If additional training would help, let me know and I'll schedule you for the next training session. As an experienced sales rep, you know how to get the sales; go do it.

INFORMING AN EMPLOYEE ABOUT DISCIPLINARY ACTION

TO:
FROM:
DATE:
SUBJECT: DISCIPLINARY ACTION

Efforts to improve your performance and correct your poor attendance record have failed. Accept this memorandum as official notice that your case has been submitted to the Discipline Review Board for further action.

Their next meeting is scheduled for Monday, August 11, 19—. Following this meeting, you will be notified about what disciplinary action will be taken. Until that time, you are to report to work as scheduled

---

Memo Writer Tips

1. Inform the employee why disciplinary action is being taken, what the process will be, and when the employee can expect to know what action will be taken.

Phrasing Alternatives

PARAGRAPH 1

The following disciplinary action is being taken. Effective June 15, 19—, you are suspended without pay for one week.

You were officially warned that if your production did not improve, disciplinary action would be taken. You are being demoted to Technician II, beginning Monday, July 11, 19—.

Since you have chosen to ignore previous warnings about your deficient performance, disciplinary action is now in order. You will be suspended with pay, beginning immediately, until a thorough investigation has been done. At that time, you will be informed of your status.

MEETING PRODUCTION QUOTAS

TO:
FROM:
DATE:
SUBJECT: PRODUCTION QUOTAS

Congratulations on once again achieving assigned production quotas. Turning out both quality and quantity is no easy task. It doubtless took extraordinary effort on each team member's part.
Thanks for a job well done.

Memo Writer Tips

1. Congratulate the reader for meeting production quotas.
2. Affirm the hard work you're sure went into this effort.

Phrasing Alternatives

PARAGRAPH 1

You again exceeded production quotas this month. Making these goals took considerable time and effort.

Please accept my sincere thanks for meeting your production quota. I'm certain this could not have been achieved without hard work and maximum output.

Your diligent work and effort have paid off in fulfilled production goals. This accomplishment could not have been made without concerted effort on your part.

PARAGRAPH 2

I applaud your achievements.

Accept my sincere thanks for an outstanding job.

Pass my congratulations along to each member of your section.

MEETING SALES GOALS

TO:
FROM:
DATE:
SUBJECT: SALES GOALS

Congratulations on putting forth the effort needed to meet your sales goals this quarter. Such consistent achievement did not go unnoticed. You're a valuable member of our sales team, and I'm confident you'll continue to meet or exceed sales goals in the months ahead. Way to go!

Memo Writer Tips

1. Congratulate the subordinate for making sales goals.
2. Add a sentence that affirms the hard work needed to achieve this goal.
3. Thank the employee and encourage him/her to continue to meet these standards.

Phrasing Alternatives

PARAGRAPH 1

You've made sales goals this quarter—OUTSTANDING. Without top sales skills, this would not have been possible. Keep up the good work in the weeks and months to come.

I just wanted to applaud your making sales goals this month. Consistently meeting sales goals is a sure mark of sales ability. You've done an excellent job. Thank you.

Allow me to congratulate you for making sales goals this quarter. Thanks for a job well done. Meeting sales goals month after month keeps us in business.

MOTIVATING A PROCRASTINATOR

TO:
FROM:
DATE:
SUBJECT: MEETING DEADLINES

Why put off until tomorrow what needs to be accomplished today? I expected your report on the Lofton Project last Wednesday.

I know you've done some of the work on it, and I also recognize how busy you've been these past few weeks. You just need to make the time to finish the Lofton report.

Have it on my desk by the end of the week. If you can't let me know why today.

Memo Writer Tips

1. Procrastinators often put things off to defy established guide-lines. Threatening them, therefore, is only likely to produce more procrastination.

2. Take a light approach. Specify what work needs to be done and when you expect it. Use an encouraging tone.

Phrasing Alternatives

PARAGRAPH 1

The figures on the Abbingdale venture were due on my desk last week, but for some strange reason, I've yet to receive them. Make some time this week to complete the project.

Where are the statistics you promised me last Thursday? This task is easy for you and should not take long to finish, once you've made the time to get at it.

PRIVACY ISSUES

Many companies today have e-mail on their computer systems. E-mail is fast becoming an effective way to circulate memos across major companies saving time and printing costs. But privacy is not always assured. "Mailboxes" can sometimes be accessed by a variety of parties. In cases where you must address an employee's poor work performance, it may be better to send a hard copy sealed in an interoffice envelope labeled "private" than to risk having the memo fall into the wrong hands electronically. As a rule of thumb, if it's a sensitive topic, the old-fashioned way is still the best way to go.

The old procrastination "bug" must have bitten again, just when I desperately need those forecasts for Mr. Waterman. I'll expect them by Friday, along with an explanation today if you don't think you can get this done.

MOTIVATING SUBORDINATES UNDER PRESSURE

TO:
FROM:
DATE:
SUBJECT: BID SUBMISSIONS

The deadline for bid submissions is rapidly approaching, and I know you must be feeling the pressure. Thanks for all the hard work you've done so far. I'm confident you'll meet this deadline, and I appreciate your efforts.

Memo Writer Tips

1. Acknowledge that you know the employee is under pressure and reiterate why.
2. Encourage the subordinate by expressing your confidence in his/her ability to finish the task, and thank the employee for his/her diligence.

Phrasing Alternatives

PARAGRAPH 1

As the deadline for end-of-year reports approaches, I know you must be feeling the pressure. Be assured your hard work is appreciated. I know you'll finish this project on schedule.

The auditor arrives next week, so I know your department is under a great deal of pressure right now. I'm confident all accounts are in order.

Don't let the deadline on the Forbes account get you down. You were given this task because you always make deadlines in time, on time, every time.

PARAGRAPH 2

Know that your hard work is greatly appreciated.

Please accept my thanks for your diligent efforts. Keep working at it; I know you'll complete the project on schedule.

RECOGNIZING EMPLOYEE ANNIVERSARY DATES WITH THE COMPANY

TO:
FROM:
DATE:
SUBJECT: ANNIVERSARY DATE

Congratulations on the completion of your third year with the company. You are a valued employee, whose diligent efforts have made you an invaluable asset to our firm.

Here's hoping you'll celebrate many more anniversary dates with Langley Associates.

Memo Writer Tips

1. Congratulate the employee on the anniversary, specifying how many years the employee has been with the company.

2. Include a positive statement about the employee's work, and close by letting the employee know you expect him/her to be around for years to come.

Phrasing Alternatives

PARAGRAPH 1

Please accept my sincere congratulations on your 5th anniversary date with Jetts Enterprises. Productive employees like you make us a successful company.

Ten years have passed quickly; congratulations. Your contributions to this organization during that time have been exemplary.

On behalf of the company, I extend my best wishes to you for the completion of eight years of service. I'm certain you'll celebrate many more productive years here.

PARAGRAPH 2

Thank you for years of dedicated service.

RECOGNIZING SUCCESSFUL COMPLETION OF PROBATION*

TO:
FROM:
DATE:
SUBJECT: CERTIFICATION OF SIX MONTHS' SERVICE

I would like to take this opportunity on behalf of the Mayor and City Council, City Manager and the Career Service Board to congratulate you on the satisfactory completion of your probationary period. The Career Service Board will certify you in your current position and bring you under the protection of the Career Service system at the Board's next meeting on July 5.

Satisfactory completion of your probationary period will be, I hope, the first of many accomplishments in your career with the City.

Memo Writer Tips

1. If formal approval was required, tell when and how this occurred.
2. Congratulate the employee for completing the probationary period.
3. Add a sentence that wishes the employee a successful tenure with the organization.

---

*The Personnel Manager for a municipality authored this memorandum.

Phrasing Alternatives

PARAGRAPH 1

Congratulations on the successful completion of your probationary period with the city of Galveston.

Accept my best wishes on the successful completion of your probationary period with McKnaughton, Inc.

You have successfully completed your probationary period at Lebold Corporation. Let me be the first to congratulate you.

PARAGRAPH 2

I hope this will be the beginning of a rewarding, successful career with this agency.

Let this be the first in a series of successful accomplishments with our organization.

As a full-time, permanent member of our team, may you have many more successes in the years to come. Again, congratulations.

RECOMMENDING A PROBATIONARY EMPLOYEE FOR FULL-TIME EMPLOYMENT

TO:
FROM:
DATE:
SUBJECT: FULL-TIME EMPLOYMENT RECOMMENDATION

Ms. Janice Hanover is hereby recommended for full-time, permanent status as Medical Technician I. She has successfully completed her probationary period.
  I recommend she be certified effective January 1, 19—.

Memo Writer Tips

1. Recommend the employee for permanent status, naming the position.
2. Include any effective dates and/or information about salary increases.

Phrasing Alternatives

PARAGRAPH 1

I hereby recommend Mr. Harvey Smith for full-time, exempt status. Mr. Smith has successfully met the requirements for Telemarketing Representative.

I certify the successful completion of probationary period for Ms. Sharon Boyd and recommend full-time, permanent status, effective Monday, January 10, 19—. Successful performance has been documented.

Accept this as official recommendation for the granting of career status to Mr. Michael Overstreet, effective at the end of his six months' probationary period, February 14, 19—. Mr. Overstreet has passed probationary requirements and will make a valuable addition to our housekeeping staff.

PARAGRAPH 2

His probation ends March 3, 19—, and I recommend full-time status be granted the following working day.

Please initiate a $.50/hour increase, effective pay period ending August 1.

Draft necessary paperwork for presentation at the Personnel Board's next meeting, October 15.

RECOMMENDING THE DISMISSAL OF A PROBATIONARY EMPLOYEE

TO:
FROM:
DATE:
SUBJECT: DISMISSAL RECOMMENDATION—Lawrence Green

I recommend Lawrence Green (Janitor I) be dismissed immediately. He is a probationary employee hired on August 3. After three months on the job, he is still unable to perform even basic tasks. I have provided additional training, but Mr. Green just doesn't seem to have the skills we need.

A record of his work performance to date is attached.

```
┌─────────────────────────────────────────────────────────────────┐
│                         Memo Writer Tips                          │
│   1. Say you want the probationary employee dismissed.            │
│   2. Briefly discuss why and include documentation, if needed.    │
└─────────────────────────────────────────────────────────────────┘
```

Phrasing Alternatives

PARAGRAPH 1

Lois Markham, a probationary Community Relations Specialist, should be terminated, effective Friday, March 15. Seven community residents have made complaints about Ms. Markham. Each of these complaints has been researched, and the citizens were found to have legitimate complaints in each case.

I am recommending that Mr. Everett Hawkins, a probationary telemarketing representative, be dismissed at once. Mr. Hawkins has admitted he falsified his records.

PARAGRAPH 2

I have counseled Ms. Markham four times, but there has been no improvement in her job performance. In our last counseling session, I told Lois that any further complaints from citizens would result in her immediate dismissal.

Since falsifying call records is grounds for immediate termination, Everett Hawkins's final check should be prepared today.

RECOMMENDING A SUBORDINATE FOR EMPLOYEE OF THE MONTH*

TO:
FROM:
DATE:
SUBJECT: EMPLOYEE OF THE MONTH NOMINATION

We would like to nominate David Hawthorne, Communications Supervisor, for the November Employee-of-the-Month Award, in recognition of his achievements and contributions to the city and the police department.

---

*The police department administrators wrote this memorandum.

David has been instrumental in developing and carrying out various projects that have resulted in more efficient operations within the department. He has also shared his expertise in communication skills through workshops conducted for supervisors and managers of various city departments.

Through his direction, guidance and managerial skills, he has enhanced the role of the Communication Specialists. He has also developed a positive rapport between the operations and communications units of the department.

Mr. Hawthorne is a highly respected, dedicated employee and a definite asset in both the city and this department.

Memo Writer Tips

1. In the first paragraph, name the employee and the award for which he/she is being nominated.

2. In paragraph two, outline why the employee deserves the award.

3. Conclude by affirming the employee's value to the organization.

Phrasing Alternatives

PARAGRAPH 1

With pleasure, I nominate Gladys Stackhouse for the October Employee-of-the-Month award.

Mr. Frank Overton is my recommendation for the July Employee-of-the-Month.

Please accept this memorandum as my nomination for Ms. Julie Hampstead for the September Crew Member-of-the-Week.

PARAGRAPH 2

Gladys has designed a new record-keeping system that will save the company approximately $12,900 per year. In addition, she has worked tirelessly to revamp data entry procedures.

Four customers wrote letters last month commending Frank for his courteous, prompt service, He is a real team player who gets along well with both his superiors and peers. Such great customer relations skills cannot go unrecognized.

Julie operated her department $15,000 under budget for the fiscal year. Her management expertise has created an effective working group in her unit. Her group has consistently met or exceeded quotas for the last quarter.

PARAGRAPH 3

Gladys's exemplary service makes her an ideal candidate for this award. He work reflects well on her and on the company.

Mr. Overton is a model employee who is deserving of this award without a doubt.

Such a valuable member of our organization deserves this kind of recognition. I hope you will give this nomination every consideration.

RECOMMENDING TERMINATION

TO:
FROM:
DATE:
SUBJECT: TERMINATION RECOMMENDATION—Judy Block

I am recommending termination of Judy Block, copywriter trainee. Ms. Block's work has been consistently unoriginal. In addition, every piece of copy she has written has had to be revised by another copywriter. Her work contains glaring grammatical and spelling errors. Judy Block does not have the writing skills necessary to perform her job satisfactorily.

Her work performance record, including documentation from counseling sessions, is attached.

Memo Writer Tips

1. Say you want the employee terminated.
2. Briefly explain why.
3. Include documentation.

Phrasing Alternatives

PARAGRAPH 1

I recommend Art Jones, Draftsman II, be terminated immediately. The errors he made on the Gilchrist blueprints cost us a major construction project. This makes the second major job we have lost because of Jones's inaccurate drawings.

Please initiate termination action for Alonzo Weathers. Mr. Weathers has proven he is not dependable. During the past month, he as been late for work nine (9) times and has called in sick seven (7) days (documentation attached).

REPRIMANDING A SUBORDINATE FOR MISSING A DEADLINE*

TO:
FROM:
DATE:
SUBJECT: PERFORMANCE REVIEW

You have been requested on several occasions to return your performance review to my office. The last request was June 22, at which time you stated that it was at your home because you were making comments on it. I directed you at that time to return it. To date, you have not returned it and have not indicated a reason for not doing so.

I am directing you to bring your review to your weekly meeting with me on Tuesday, June 28, 19—.

Memo Writer Tips

1. Stick with the facts on this one, so the reprimand doesn't end up sounding like an attack on the person involved. Outline what deadline was missed and any other pertinent facts in the case.
2. Spell out clearly what the employee is to do to rectify the situation. Be sure to include specific dates, times, and so on.

---

*The Director of Administration for a metropolitan transportation district prepared this reprimand.

Phrasing Alternatives

PARAGRAPH 1

The deadline for submitting input on next year's budget proposal was last Friday. I have yet to receive yours.

Your department newsletter should have gone to the printer's no later than August 15. Why didn't it?

I expected the report you were asked to prepare by June 15 and was disappointed when I did not receive it.

PARAGRAPH 2

Projection schedules are important deadlines and must be met. Failure to do so results in significant setbacks for not only your department, but the company as a whole.

Surely you realize how important deadlines are.

You explained why you could not prepare the report by the target date and were granted an extension. So why the continued delay?

PARAGRAPH 3

You are directed to finish the report and have it on my desk no later than Friday, August 15, at 3:00 P.M.

Delays such as this prevent progress and cannot be tolerated. Get your work to me by this afternoon.

I will expect that analysis by 2:00 P.M., January 4. Don't disappoint me again.

WARNING AN EMPLOYEE ABOUT SLEEPING ON THE JOB

TO:
FROM:
DATE:
SUBJECT: SLEEPING ON DUTY

Sleeping on the job will not be tolerated—period. You are being paid to perform a service, one I'm sure you cannot do while you are asleep.

Any further reports like this will result in your dismissal.

Memo Writer Tips

1. Since sleeping on the job is a serious infraction, come right to the point in this memo.

2. Be sure to let the employee know what consequences will result if he/she continues to sleep on the job.

Phrasing Alternatives

PARAGRAPH 1

On July 22, you were found asleep on duty. Sleeping on the job carries severe penalties, including suspension and/or dismissal.

Sleeping on the job is a serious violation of company rules. Though this is a warning, another violation will result in immediate termination.

I received a report that you were discovered asleep on your June 14 watch. You will be fired on the spot the next time you are found sleeping on the job.

WARNING AN EMPLOYEE ABOUT UNSATISFACTORY PERFORMANCE

TO:
FROM:
DATE:
SUBJECT: WARNING AN EMPLOYEE ABOUT UNSATISFACTORY PER-FORMANCE

Certain problems with your performance have arisen, including the following:

1/3/89	Reporting for work 30 minutes late without calling
1/6/89	Errors in balance sheet detected and returned for correction
1/15/89	Mid-month budget report submitted late
1/17/89	Insubordination noted in counseling session with supervisor

These incidents represent serious problems with your performance, and counseling does not seem to have corrected them. If your efforts do not improve significantly by your next quarterly review, termination action will be initiated.

Memo Writer Tips

1. Problems with performance are generally a very ticklish situation. Be sure to keep adequate documentation, including dates and times when an employee was advised about problems.
2. In this memo, list the specific performance problems.
3. Inform the employee what corrective action, if any, is to be taken and what the consequences will be if performance does not improve.

Phrasing Alternatives

Paragraph 1

Deficiencies in your performance have been noted in the following areas:

Your work is below standards in the following ways:

Your work has not been satisfactory for these reasons:

Paragraph 2

A corrective action plan has been outlined for you, and your work will be reviewed each week for the next 30 days. If improvements are not noted, I will be forced to terminate you.

Suspension without pay is the next step, should these problems go uncorrected.

You will continue to be employed as long as satisfactory progress is made toward improving these deficiencies.

Summary Points

- Managers use carrots and sticks in their written communications too. Superior work should be acknowledged. Inferior work pointed-out with warnings to improve.

- When addressing poor performance, it is critical you have your facts straight. Keep a journal or a log so you have irrefutable evidence, and your writing does not a appear to be an ad hominem attack.

- For memos such as alerting an employee to excessive tardiness, it is a good idea to begin on a positive note. Talk about how critical it is for team members to work as one unit, for example.
- When terminating an employee, it is important to include as much documentation as possible to back up your case. Be precise.

Chapter 4

Handling Delicate Issues: Real-World Examples

Nightmares. Management nightmares. Two employees who barely talk to each other, racial epithets that could lead to even worse trouble, an employee who shows up drunk, a sexual harassment suit by a frightened executive assistant, a worker who appears to be abusing drugs. Something's got to be done, and done fast. The task falls on your desk and you have to be the voice of management committing itself to writing.

These are the memos everyone dreads writing—but they must be written. It is always a good idea to seek the advice of legal counsel before committing yourself in writing on particularly sensitive issues. There is no substitute for solid legal advice. If you already have that advice, or feel you are on solid legal grounds, the memos listed below offer excellent ideas for themes, structure, and phrasing and for writing memos that meet your firm's individual needs.

These particular types of memos often require a precision of language and thought that most other memos don't necessarily require. Therefore, it's particularly important to pay close attention to the phrasings suggested and the Memo Writer Tips listed below. Your best course of action is always to involve your legal department at some phase of the writing before even a single piece of paper is distributed. In these circumstances, it is always good business practice to err on the side of caution then to fire-off a memo quickly and deeply regret it later.

Model Memos About Sensitive Issues

Writing about sensitive issues challenges even the best business writer. This challenge involves choosing the best words, phrasing them in the most appropriate tone, and conveying what may often be disturbing messages without disrupting operations or placing yourself in legal jeopardy.

The model memoranda in this chapter target a variety of sensitive topics. Whether you're writing a memorandum to announce a strike action, informing employees about drug testing, discussing incidents of racial discrimination, dealing with charges of sexual harassment, or reprimanding an employee for alcohol abuse on the job, the memoranda in this chapter provide you with a framework for communicating your ideas and decisions.

Of course, legal counsel will provide you with definitive guidance about how to handle some of these situations. Your organization also likely has policies to guide you in your decision-making when sensitive topics are concerned. Add information about your firm's policies to the model memos in this chapter, but realize these models do not take the place of adequate legal advice. They can, however, offer you the words, phrases, and structure you need to write memorandum about sensitive issues.

ANNOUNCING A STRIKE ACTION

TO:
FROM:
DATE:
SUBJECT: STRIKE ACTION

Since agreement cannot be reached with management regarding the renewal of our Contract Agreement, a strike action has been authorized, beginning at midnight, January 15, 19—.

Arbitration will continue in an effort to resolve our major demands:

1. A pay increase of 7.8 percent.

2. The option of childcare or childcare-referral benefits.

3. Employer-paid medical insurance.

When we have resolved these issues, the membership of Local 271 will once again provide the excellent level of service previously furnished to the company.

Memo Writer Tips

1. Address when the strike is to begin and reiterate the demands of the striking employees.

2. Say under what conditions you will return to work.

3. Make it clear that the strike is the last resort, that you would prefer to return to work as soon as the issues at hand have been settled.

Phrasing Alternatives

PARAGRAPH 1

A strike vote has been taken on the members of Local 261, the Electrical Workers of America. Since management is not willing to compromise and at least consider the demands we have put forth, we have no alternative but to strike, effective midnight Friday, March 14, 19—.

Until the issues before management can be satisfactorily resolved, the membership of Local #242, the United Plant Workers of America, will be on strike.

Members of Local 1456, Construction Workers of America, are on strike, pending negotiations on our work contract.

PARAGRAPH 2

The existing demands on the table include (1) safe work conditions, and (2) a pay increase of $.56 per hour.

Binding arbitration should be able to resolve the issues of work hours, pay benefits, and promotional opportunities for employees.

We are ready to return to work as soon as we come to agreement on the $2400.00-per-year salary increase we are seeking for our members.

ANNOUNCING MANDATORY DRUG TESTING

TO:
FROM:
DATE:
SUBJECT: DRUG TESTING

In our efforts to maintain a safe work environment, we must ensure that all employees are drug-free. To this end, we are announcing a mandatory drug testing program, to become effective on Monday, July 1, 19—.

Under this policy, employees will be randomly asked to provide urine samples on the premises, which will then be analyzed by Colton Laboratories. Reports of such tests will be held in the strictest confidence, and employees will be notified when a positive drug test occurs.

Such tests are authorized by the agreement you signed when you were hired by the company. If you have any questions about this policy, contact the personnel office at ext. 809.

Thank you for your cooperation.

Memo Writer Tips

1. Let employees know when drug testing will begin and why this policy has been implemented.
2. Tell them what process will be followed during drug testing, and assure them that test results will be confidential.

Phrasing Alternatives

PARAGRAPH 1

Our mandatory drug testing program will begin on Monday, March 15. Since employees handle potentially hazardous materials, the company has the responsibility of protecting all its employees by maintaining a drug-free workplace.

The lives of passengers are in your hands. Only through peak performance and mental and physical health can their safety be assured. For this reason, no employee can be allowed to operate a vehicle while impaired by drugs. Mandatory drug testing will be implemented, effective Monday, January 14, 19—.

PARAGRAPH 2

Details of the testing program will be outlined at an upcoming meeting. Test results will be strictly confidential and will be used only to refer employees to appropriate drug rehabilitation programs, when necessary.

The attached pamphlet explains the drug testing program in detail and provides you with specific information about how and when testing will be carried out. Test results will be returned to me, and I will distribute these results to employees. Strict confidentiality will be maintained at all times.

Drug testing will involve the following steps: . . . I can assure you that your drug test results will be made known only to me and to you.

PARAGRAPH 3

Contact the Human Resources Division should you have questions about how this policy will affect you.

Jan Hopper in personnel (ext. 102) will be happy to answer any questions you might have about the drug testing program.

Refer any questions about this testing program to your immediate supervisor.

DIFFUSING A MALE/FEMALE CONFRONTATION

TO:
FROM:
DATE:
SUBJECT: CO-WORKER COOPERATION

During the past several months, you and Hal Jones have had a number of conflicts about what seemingly would be work-related issues. I have been called upon several times to settle these disputes. While, on the surface, they would seem to be issues related to the projects you are working on, what I find when I look more closely is a situation caused by the fact that one of you is a woman and the other is a man.

I think that when you sit down and really air your differences, you will find many of them have their roots in the stereotypical roles assigned to males and females in the larger society. Since this company is interested, however, in maximizing employee potential, no matter whether that potential belongs to a man or to a woman, you will simply have to find a way to settle your differences.

While the two of you are trying to find common ground on which to base your working relationship, the company is losing valuable time and money. I would be happy to facilitate a problem-solving session in which we delve more deeply into the problem at hand and move on to resolve this issue.

Please call my office as soon as possible to set up an appointment to resolve your dispute, once and for all.

Memo Writer Tips

1. Sex bias is a very sensitive issue, indeed. Make it clear in your memo that you have determined the problem at hand to be based on these issues.

2. Outline a plan of action or agree to play a mediator role in order to resolve the differences.

3. Make it clear that operations cannot be hampered by differences between or among employees based on the issue of sex.

DISCIPLINING AN EMPLOYEE FOR SUBSTANCE ABUSE

TO:
FROM:
DATE:
SUBJECT: SUBSTANCE ABUSE

On Saturday, February 15, 19—, you reported for work while under the influence of drugs, a clear violation of company policy. Effective immediately, you are suspended from duty without pay for the next 14 days. Contact the personnel office before you leave work today, so that they may refer you to drug counseling and rehabilitation services.

     You are a valued member of our operation. However, any further incidents of this nature will lead to immediate dismissal (Section 1, Paragraph 14, of the Employee Handbook). I hope you will seek the treatment necessary to overcome this problem.

Memo Writer Tips

1. Provide the employee with specific information about when the infraction occurred. You must be sure of your facts before you can even begin to address this problem. Cite what day the employee reported for work under the influence.

2. Spell out what disciplinary action is being taken.

3. If your company has services designed to treat alcohol and drug abuse problems, refer the employee to these services.

Phrasing Alternatives

PARAGRAPH 1

When you came to work on Friday, August 8, you were obviously under the influence of some kind of substance. When I confronted you, you admitted that you had used drugs prior to coming to work. The nature of your work requires you to function at peak mental capacity, and substance abuse on the job is cause for immediate termination.

Your work performance has been seriously hampered by your continuous incidents of reporting for duty under the influence of illegal drugs.

Substance abuse cannot be tolerated. Since you were under the influence of drugs last Wednesday evening when you came to work, disciplinary action will be taken.

PARAGRAPH 2

You are terminated from employment with Avery Enterprises, effective today. Under company policy, reporting for work under the influence of drugs leaves you no grievance rights or other avenues for continuing employment with us.

You are, therefore, suspended for 10 days without pay. You will immediately enroll yourself in a drug rehabilitation program, and any further occurrences of this kind will result in immediate dismissal.

A counselor from our Employee Assistance Program will contact you to arrange drug counseling services. If you refuse such counseling, you can no longer remain in our employ.

PARAGRAPH 3

I regret that this action must be taken, but the safety and welfare of your coworkers demands that every employee work drug-free.

You are directed to make use of all services available to you, in order to rectify this problem. Should you refuse, you leave me no alternative but to fire you immediately.

I hope you can resolve this problem and return to work drug-free. You have been a valuable employee, and I hope you want to continue working here.

EXPLAINING A DEPARTMENTAL ERROR TO A SUPERIOR

TO:
FROM:
DATE:
SUBJECT: DEPARTMENTAL ERROR

Last month, the central accounting office changed its computer program for pay-roll processing. When this change was made, some of the stored information was not transferred to the new data base. Consequently, several errors occurred in employee paychecks: (1) medical benefits were not deducted, (2) annuity deduc-tions were not made, and (3) errors occurred in federal withholding calculations.

Each of the employees affected has been contacted, and this error has been explained. My staff has been working overtime to input all missing data, so that corrections can be made on the August 30 payroll run.

Had I double-checked the information before paychecks were run, this would not have happened. There is no excuse, but I can assure you that I have implemented a verification system that will ensure this does not happen again.

Memo Writer Tips

1. Explain the error in as much detail as possible.
2. Explain why the error occurred, being sure to take ultimate respon-sibility for it, if that is appropriate.
3. Tell how the error is being corrected.
4. Give an assurance that you have implemented proper procedures to make sure the error does not recur.

Phrasing Alternatives

PARAGRAPH 1

Several departments have been without essential supplies for the past 14 days, because some purchase requisitions were filed though the orders had not yet been placed.

The customer calls you received about billing errors have been researched. This billing error occurred because customer bills were calculated using an incorrect discount formula.

The food and beverage orders for the upcoming conference will have to be filled by another supplier since the original vendor was never given an order confirmation.

Paragraph 2

These supplies will be given rush priority and will arrive no later than the end of this week.

The correct formula has now been programmed into the computer, so all future bills will be calculated correctly.

The new vendor has assured us that adequate food and beverages will be available for the conference dinner.

Paragraph 3

I will personally supervise any future transactions to make sure this does not happen again.

Please accept my assurance that the problem has been resolved, adequate training has been instituted, and this situation will not arise again.

I can assure you adequate steps have been taken to resolve the matter.

Explaining an Employee Error*

TO:
FROM:
DATE:
SUBJECT: ERROR IN AIRLINE RESERVATIONS

I made an error in ordering tickets for your Dallas to Nashville flight on August 5. Instead of booking you on a non-stop flight, I booked you on a flight with three stops.
New, first-class travel arrangements have been made.

---

*This memorandum was written by a reservations clerk.

Departure:

Comstock Airlines,   Flight #46
                       Leaves Dallas   August 5   1:00 P.M.
                       Arrives Nashville   5:10 P.M.

Return Flight:

Comstock Airlines,   Flight #112
                       Leaves Nashville   August 7   2:42 P.M.
                       Arrives Dallas   6:23 P.M.

Thank you for bringing this error to my attention. Enjoy your trip.

Memo Writer Tips

1. Explain what error was made and why.
2. Take responsibility for the error and explain how it has been corrected.

Phrasing Alternatives

PARAGRAPH 1

The brochure you ordered, "Excellence in Education," has a number of typographical errors in it.

Instead of scheduling the staff meeting for Conference Room B, I put the meeting in the 4th floor conference room, which is already occupied on that date.

Dave Kendall was to have reported to Maxwell Company to repair their telephone system on January 15 at 3:00 P.M. Because of an error on the dispatch form, he reported to the wrong address.

PARAGRAPH 2

If you will return the proofs of the brochure to the printing office, we will proofread the document again, make necessary corrections, prepare a second set of proofs for your review—at no additional cost.

I regret any inconvenience the room assignment may have caused you, but I can assure your future assignments will be double-checked.

I have called the customer to explain what happened. Their equipment has been repaired, and they have been given a 20 percent discount on their bill to make up for the error. In the future, dispatchers will read addresses back to customers, to make sure dispatchers record the correct address.

HANDLING A DISCRIMINATION COMPLAINT

TO:
FROM:
DATE:
SUBJECT: DISCRIMINATION CHARGE

I have received and reviewed the discrimination complaint you made regarding your supervisor, Mr. Edward Timmons. As per company policy, all allegations will be thoroughly investigated by the Equal Employment Opportunity Committee, whose next meeting is scheduled for Friday, October 10, 19—. This committee will take approximately 30 days to interview parties involved and render its decision regarding your complaint. The decision of this committee is final and binding on both parties.

Let me assure you that this company is committed to equal opportunity for all employees, regardless of race, ethnic background, or national origin. Allegations of discriminatory practices are taken very seriously, and violations of equitable treatment policies, if found, are not tolerated.

Expect to hear from this office no later than November 11. Thank you for bringing this situation to my attention.

Memo Writer Tips

1. Follow company policy and directives when handling allegations of racial discrimination.
2. Acknowledge that the complaint has been received and review what steps will be taken to investigate the complaint.
3. Let the complainant know when he/she can expect to hear the results of the charges.
4. Assure the complainant that all necessary action will be taken to resolve the matter in a fair and equitable way.
5. Seek legal advice if necessary.

Phrasing Alternatives

PARAGRAPH 1

Your complaint of adverse action based on racial discrimination has been received and is currently being investigated.

I have received your racial discrimination complaint. Be assured that the necessary steps are being taken to thoroughly research and investigate this matter.

I want to assure you that the complaint you recently filed (Complaint #22-46) alleging actions of a discriminatory nature will be dealt with in the most fair and equitable way possible.

PARAGRAPH 2

Section 29, Paragraph 3, of the Policy and Procedures Manual outlines the steps to be taken next. You can expect to know the results of this process no later than November 4.

After a thorough investigation of the charges by an impartial party, you will be notified of the results of the investigation within 30 days.

The thorough investigation of this matter will take approximately 45 days to complete, at which time you will be notified of the decision made by the Complaint Review Panel.

PARAGRAPH 3

Our agency prides itself on its commitment to equal hiring and promotional practices, and any violations of this process will be dealt with swiftly and fairly.

This organization does not condone or tolerate racial and ethnic discrimination, and when charges such as yours are brought, we take those charges very seriously and want to resolve the matter as expeditiously as possible.

You can be certain that if racial discrimination practices can be substantiated, every effort necessary to eradicate these practices will be taken.

Handling a Sexual Harassment Complaint

TO:
FROM:
DATE:
SUBJECT: SEXUAL HARASSMENT ALLEGATIONS

Your recent charges of sexual harassment are disturbing. An investigation into the allegations was begun today, and the results of that investigation should be available within 30 days.

During that time, you are being reassigned to the Pathology Laboratory, pending the outcome of these investigations. This should alleviate any reprisals that might result from filing such charges.

Be assured that this company neither condones nor tolerates violations of its fair practices policy. Your allegations, if substantiated, will result in whatever steps are necessary to rectify the problem, including criminal prosecution if it is warranted.

Memo Writer Tips

1. Follow the established practices for dealing with issues of sexual harassment.
2. Acknowledge the receipt of the complaint and explain to the employee what steps will be taken to resolve the issue.
3. Let the employee know when he/she can expect to receive the results of the investigation.
4. Assure the employee that sexual harassment will not be tolerated.

Phrasing Alternatives

Paragraph 1

I have received and am in the process of reviewing your charges of sexual harassment.

Any charge of sexual harassment is taken seriously and evaluated thoroughly.

Your sexual harassment complaint has been received and is being processed by this office.

PARAGRAPH 2

Your Employee Handbook outlines the steps to be followed when such allegations are made. As outlined there, you will be notified of the findings of the investigating body within 45 days.

Both employees involved will be interviewed, as will other employees who may have witnessed inappropriate actions. Following this, the Fair Practices Task Force will evaluate the complaint and all pertinent testimony and make a decision about the charges. Their decision is binding and will be rendered in a hearing to be held no more than 60 days from the date of the initial complaint.

The charges you have made will be thoroughly investigated and, if corroborated, will result in appropriate action. You should hear something in the way of findings no more than 30 days from now. If you have questions in the interim, feel free to contact me.

PARAGRAPH 3

Harassment under any circumstances is a serious and disturbing matter and will be dealt with harshly.

This company values all its employees and makes no decisions based on matters of sex or race. The fair practices doctrine of the company will be upheld.

I can assure you that everything possible will be done to get to the bottom of this matter. Even the perception of sexual harassment episodes is something our organization can ill afford and will not tolerate.

HANDLING PREJUDICE AGAINST MINORITIES

TO:
FROM:
DATE:
SUBJECT: RACIAL INCIDENTS

A disturbing practice of using racial slurs and telling racial jokes has begun to develop. While this agency cannot control the opinions of its workers, it can control the actions of its workers. Any display of racial prejudice which hampers the work efforts of employees is strictly prohibited. The intimidation and/or harassment of minority employees of this firm will not be tolerated.

A series of racial awareness seminars will be conducted over the coming month. Each and every member of this plant WILL attend, and each and every member of this plant will work together harmoniously without any further incidents of racial bigotry or harassment.

I hope I have made myself VERY clear. Learn to work together or find work elsewhere.

Memo Writer Tips

1. Episodes of prejudice are certain to occur in the workplace and must be dealt with quickly and forthrightly.
2. Let employees know where the company stands as far as racial incidents are concerned.
3. Make it clear what the consequences of continued racial problems are.
4. If necessary, schedule workshops or meetings to discuss this issue. The memorandum serves as simply a reminder since problems this serious cannot be dealt with on paper alone.

Phrasing Alternatives

PARAGRAPH 1

Several members of minority groups have made complaints to me about your use of racial slurs and epithets. Let me assure you that such conduct will not be tolerated.

I take a very hard line when it comes to even the perception of unfair or harmful treatment based on race. Any behavior that interferes with the productivity of employees will be eliminated immediately.

You will refrain from any further behavior that demeans the character and background of the racial minorities employed by this organization.

PARAGRAPH 2

I will be closely monitoring the conduct of workers in your section, and let me assure you any further racial incidents will be dealt with swiftly.

You will report to me weekly on the progress you are making in resolving racial problems.

I cannot believe that you made those remarks, and I know that you will not make them again.

PARAGRAPH 3

This agency operates on a policy of fair treatment for all its employees. Either adhere to this policy or suffer the consequences of continued violations.

I am certain you will want to follow the equal treatment guidelines set forth by this organization.

I do not want to revisit this issue again. See to it that I don't have to.

MAINTAINING OPERATIONS DURING A STRIKE

TO:
FROM:
DATE:
SUBJECT: STRIKE—COVERAGE OF WORK DETAILS

Local 242 has announced a strike, effective at midnight tomorrow night. All managers will report for duty to handle operations during this strike. Managers should begin advertising for temporary workers, to replace those on strike.

I am confident a new agreement will be reached soon. In the interim, thank you for helping to make operations go as smoothly as possible.

Memo Writer Tips

1. Tell when the strike action is effective.
2. Let managerial personnel know what their duties and responsibilities will be during the strike action. In many cases, this may involve a specific list of personnel by name and their assigned tasks.
3. Thank the employees for managing operations during the strike.

Phrasing Alternatives

PARAGRAPH 1

A strike is slated to begin on Monday, September 3. Schools will be closed until this action can be resolved. All principals and assistant principals are to report to their schools as scheduled. During this time, you will be expected to answer telephone calls and inquiries from parents and community members.

Negotiations have not yet been reached on the nurses' new collective bargaining agreement. If a strike does occur at midnight on April 1, each of you will be called upon to do whatever is necessary to ensure the care of patients.

A strike of Local 65 seems unavoidable at this time. Supervisors will report for duty at 12:00 noon on Friday if this occurs, and work assignments will be distributed at that time.

PARAGRAPH 2

The attached roster lists the work assignments of supervisory personnel: . . . Your efforts during this emergency are greatly appreciated.

I want to extend to you my warmest appreciation for your efforts to keep us operational during this crisis.

Thank you for your assistance. Hopefully, this strike will be over soon.

RESOLVING A DISPUTE BETWEEN ANTAGONISTIC SUBORDINATES

TO:
FROM:
DATE:
SUBJECT: CO-WORKER COOPERATION

My repeated efforts to resolve the differences between you and Jamison have been largely unsuccessful. Report to my office on Monday, June 4. The three of us will sit down and work out a plan that will allow the two of you to work together. If we cannot do that, then we will have to discuss reassignments or other steps that may be taken to resolve this matter. See you Monday.

Memo Writer Tips

1. Subordinates who do not get along is an issue that should be resolved in a face-to-face conference.
2. Use this memorandum to announce what steps you are planning to get the workers to cooperate.
3. Make it clear that you expect them to work out their differences.

Phrasing Alternatives

PARAGRAPH 1

Your inability to work harmoniously is beginning to affect the overall operations of your section. This cannot be tolerated. I am giving you one more chance to sit down and discuss your differences and develop a plan that will allow you and Mr. Hanrahan to function in a cooperative spirit. I'll expect a report within two weeks on the outcome of your negotiations.

The differences Ms. Curry and you have are costing us time and money. Get your differences resolved and get on with it. If not, I will be forced to take measures to resolve this situation myself.

I have scheduled a conference on Wednesday so that you, Ken, and I can discuss the problems you are having working together. Draw up a list of your differences, as well as a list of potential solutions to these differences and bring them with you. We will meet at 3:00 P.M. in my office.

STEERING A SUBORDINATE TO THE EMPLOYEE ASSISTANCE PROGRAM

TO:

FROM:

DATE:

SUBJECT: EMPLOYEE ASSISTANCE PROGRAM

Our Employee Assistance Program offers a variety of counseling services aimed at helping employees with financial, personal, or stress challenges. I'm enclosing a copy of the brochure that outlines these services for your information.

Many of these services are provided either free of charge or on a sliding-fee schedule, based on your ability to pay. Your use of these services is strictly confidential.

I know that you have been under a great deal of stress lately and encourage you to take advantage of the assistance available through this program.

Memo Writer Tips

1. Don't put the employee on the defensive by beginning this memo by talking about the employee's problems. Simply outline the services available through the assistance program and enclose other pertinent information that details the services.

2. Tell what kind of services the program offers and what the costs, if any, are.

3. Reassure the employee that confidentiality will be used to allay any fears the employee may have about using the services.

4. Close by saying you hope the employee will use the services, and include what led you to write this memorandum.

Phrasing Alternatives

Paragraph 1

Many fine problem-solving opportunities are available through the company's Employee Assistance Program (details enclosed).

I recognize that our employees work here as whole persons. The problem is, their personal lives can sometimes influence their on-the-job performance. For this reason, the company has contracted the counseling services available through its Employee Assistance Program.

Look over the information I've attached about our Employee Assistance Program. You may find the personal, confidential counseling services offered by licensed professionals helpful.

Paragraph 2

The initial consultation is free, and the other counseling sessions are offered at a reduced rate to company employees. All information discussed in these sessions is held in strictest confidence.

Employees can avail themselves of top-notch counseling at significantly lower rates than would be available if they sought out these services on their own. Using these services would be in no way reflect negatively on their work here, since all dealings with the EAP company are strictly confidential.

Services are provided on a sliding-fee scale, and your confidentiality would be maintained throughout.

Paragraph 3

I suggest you look into the services provided by EAP. They may be able to help you get through a difficult period in your life.

Use these services if you think they'd be helpful.

I know you've been having some problems lately, and I think EAP might be able to help.

SUMMARIZING LABOR NEGOTIATION PROCEEDINGS

TO:
FROM:
DATE:
SUBJECT: UPDATE ON LABOR NEGOTIATIONS

Negotiators met with the leadership of Local 42 again today and there is the status of those negotiations:

1. Management offered a 4.3 percent pay raise; labor maintains its 7.8 percent raise demand. Progress is being made on this issue, however.
2. Labor agreed to drop the request for two additional paid holidays per year.
3. Some progress was made on the issue of healthcare benefits. Labor proposed that the company pay 80 percent of these benefits and employees pay 20 percent. Management is proposing a 60/40 split of these costs.

Meetings will resume tomorrow at 6:00 A.M. I will keep you up to date on proceedings as events occur.

Memo Writer Tips

1. Let the reader know when meetings occurred.
2. Outline each point of negotiation and summarize what progress has been made on resolving each issue.
3. Let readers know when they can expect the next update.

REMEMBER, YOU'RE ALWAYS ON THE RECORD

When speaking to the press, it's always a good idea to assume that everything you say is on the record. Try this exercise: imagine your words spelling out a headline. When it comes to sensitive issues like sexual harassment, warning an employee about substance abuse or alcoholism, try a similar exercise: imagine your memo being read in a courtroom, because that's exactly what just might happen. Will it pass the test?

Our legal system places much weight on physical evidence such as letters, memos, and other documents. It is therefore imperative to make sure all the legal requirements are met. Other considerations should also be kept in mind: Does the memo make your company look like it is solving the situation properly, or does it portray an unflattering image? Does it adequately reflect the concern your company has for this matter, or is it just bland boilerplate? Remember, the other side will be paid to make your side look bad. Step aside briefly from your current role, and try reading it anew as a disinterested party.

The best course of action is always to check with your legal department on such matters early. Depending on how your firm operates, you may want to draft the memo first and run it by legal, or have them draft it first. Remember, be proactive and follow the rules precisely.

Phrasing Alternatives

PARAGRAPH 1

Here is a summary of negotiations held on Monday, August 24:

The list of union demands and the status of negotiations with regard to each are as follows:

Little progress has been made in the labor dispute as of 10:00 P.M. today. Management presented its latest proposal, but labor rejected it completely. No new negotiations have been scheduled.

PARAGRAPH 2

Negotiations will continue through the night, and I'll prepare another update tomorrow morning.

Union membership is expected to vote on the latest package this evening. I will report the results of that vote as soon as they become available.

WARNING AN EMPLOYEE ABOUT DRINKING ON THE JOB

TO:
FROM:
DATE:
SUBJECT: DRINKING ON THE JOB

This is a warning that if you report for work while intoxicated again, you will be dismissed immediately. Drinking on the job cannot be tolerated, and this policy has been discussed with you twice before.

I assume that if you value your continued employment with this company you will come to work alcohol-free.

Memo Writer Tips

1. Follow your company policy about handling incidents of this nature.
2. Make it clear to the employee that drinking on the job will not be tolerated.

Phrasing Alternatives

PARAGRAPH 1

You are terminated immediately for drinking on the job. Previous discussions about this have not corrected the problem, and we can no longer keep you in our employ.

I have reason to believe that you were drinking on the job last evening. Though I cannot prove it, I will be watching you closely, and if I can find proof, you will be terminated immediately.

Summary Points

- Legal counsel is your best source for the proper phrasing of memos that might involve future litigation.

- Do *not* write ad hominem attacks. When dealing with an employee whose performance is under par, it is important to be able to document your words with solid facts.

- When writing about an error, it is important to be forthright and honest, but be sure to explain *what specific steps* are being taken to remedy the situation.

- With problems such as racial discrimination, or male-female conflicts, it is better to attack the problem sooner than later. Memos should appropriately reflect your level of concern.

SECTION TWO

SPEECHES

INTRODUCTION—WRITING AND DELIVERING CROWD-PLEASING SPEECHES

Speechmaking is rapidly becoming an important part of the businessperson's life. If you've ever visited the convention centers of major cities like New York, Chicago, or L.A.—or even smaller locales for that matter—you know the sheer number of business conventions, conferences, panels, and special business events that take place everyday. Public speaking is at the center of each of these events, and someday, it may well be you who will be the center of public attention.

While not all of us are like former Chrysler Corporation Chairman Lee Iacocca who had a staff of more than ten professional speechwriters, at various points in your career you will likely be asked to give an address. Your best bet is to be *prepared*. Perhaps you'll be asked to serve as Master of Ceremony at a local United Way or Chamber of Commerce fund-raiser. Maybe you'll be picked to serve on a panel at a business conference, make a statement to the press, address a visiting school group, or just deliver an "impromptu" pep talk to employees. Odds are, at some point, you will be asked "to say a few words."

Yet for many people, public speaking can be a potentially harrowing experience because either they don't know what to write, or they are afraid of speaking before an audience—sometimes both. This section will de-mystify the whole process. In Chapter Five, we detail the basics of speechmaking: how to structure your address, which words to use, which words to avoid, how to deal with nerves, how to survive a faux pas, and more. Can't get started? Groping for that perfect opening line that will have the audience fixated on your every word? Chapter Six details excellent openers and closers for whatever subject you're addressing.

Much like politicians, great businesspeople take advantage of speechmaking opportunities to motivate "their troops." Chapter Seven provides actual speeches you can use or incorporate into your own speech for whatever your motivational needs, whether it's urging greater cooperation from top to bottom, getting departments to stop fighting, urging employees to innovate, and more.

WRITING AND DELIVERING A SPEECH: THE BASICS

You've been chosen to make the big presentation. You'll be standing in front of hundreds employees to deliver the good news about the latest acquisition. It's your big chance to be seen by upper management, and you know it. But instead of seizing the moment, you're seized with fear. "I've never written a speech before in my life! What do I do?" "What are the right words to say?—For that matter, what are the *wrong* words?" "How can I calm my nerves on stage?" "What if I make a mistake in front of all my colleagues?" Relax. This chapter should put some of your worst fears about speechwriting and public speaking to rest.

As an executive, you know public speaking is increasingly an integral part of the business world today, whether it is in front of employees, colleagues, stockholders, the media, or the local Chamber of Commerce. Mastering these key skills can help you build poise, confidence, and give you the exposure you need to help boost your career.

In this section, excerpted from Prentice Hall's *How to Say It Best,* author Jack Griffin describes the nuts and bolts of putting a speech together, how to use humor to your advantage, how to rehearse your lines, what to do if you do make a mistake, how to pace your presentation, and other subjects. Each section offers useful tips for every business professional—from the nervous first-timer, to the more experienced businessperson who's delivered more than a few *bon mots* throughout his or her career.

ARCHITECTURE

Most books on writing and on that special application of writing called speech writing begin with a prescription for structuring the composition of the piece. After all, you can't build a house without working from a plan.

But a speech is not a house. Really, it is an extension of something that we human beings do every day: communicate. So I began this book not with abstract instruction on the theory and practice of speech architecture, but with the real occasions that demand real speeches. Now that you've—presumably—plunged into at least some of those examples, you might find it helpful to step back and look at the principles that guided the construction of the speeches.

Veteran speechwriter Joan Detz, in her *How to Write and Give a Speech* (St. Martin's Press, 1984), boils the process down to two pairs of principles. Want to write a good speech?

1. Make it simple.

2. Make it short.

Want to write a *great* speech?

1. Make it simpler.

2. Make it shorter.

Not all good speeches, let alone great speeches, are simple and short. But you can't go wrong if you at least begin the process of planning and writing your speech from these principles. I'd alter Ms. Detz's advice this way:

1. Make it as simple as an enlightening treatment of the subject will allow.

2. Make it as short as an enlightening treatment of the subject will allow.

The same writer also introduces a time-honored "formula for a successful speech," the origins of which have been attributed to a wide variety of speakers and speech writers:

1. Tell them what you're going to tell them.

2. Tell them.

3. Tell them what you've told them.

Unfortunately, if you try to follow this formula literally, you will create a very boring speech. You also run the risk of sounding as if you are *telling* your audience what to think. A good speech does, of course, inform, persuade, move to action—in short, create thoughts or a certain mind set. But it does not *dictate* thought. It guides your listeners. It makes it possible for your audience to think the thoughts you want them to have, to reach the desired conclusion for themselves. It is no accident that, when we are particularly impressed by a speech, we use a metaphor so commonplace that we no longer think about what it really means. We say that the speech *moved* us.

An effective speech *moves* us to a desired mental or emotional place. It does not thrust that "place" upon us or force us, kicking and screaming, to it. It moves—motivates—us to that place seemingly of our own volition.

With this caution in mind—move, don't shove—the simple formula given here is nevertheless a good point from which to start thinking about your speech. Be aware that the spoken word is the most ephemeral of all communication. A speech consists of sound waves that move through the air only to vanish as soon as they are produced. In a speech, you cannot develop the subtlety and complexity of exposition available to the writer of a printed text meant to be read, reread, studied, and underlined, and consulted again as often as necessary. Make the simplest points your subject will allow. Make them as simply and as directly as your subject will allow. Begin as clearly as you possibly can. Develop the subject as clearly and as unambiguously as possible in the body of the speech. Then conclude as definitely as your subject will allow, taking the opportunity to underscore your point of view.

In 1687, Sir Isaac Newton formulated the First Law of Motion, the principle of inertia, which holds that a body at rest remains at rest and a body in motion remains in motion at a constant velocity as long as outside forces are not involved. An analogous principle seems to apply to human behavior. Just as an extra effort is required to coax a still body into motion or to alter the motion of a moving one, so the beginning of a speech is the most difficult part of the talk, both for the speaker and the audience. An extra effort is required to overcome the mental and emotional inertia that affects the speaker as well as the audience. How do you get into a speech? I won't presume to say that there are x number of ways, because somebody more creative than I will always be around to think of a dozen more. However, here are some opening strategies that have proven effective.

1. *Jump right in with a declaration of your subject:* "Tonight, I will speak to you about. . . ." Assuming your subject is of interest to your audience, this no-nonsense approach is quite effective.

2. *Jump right in with an offer.* The benefit—and the risk—here is that this approach is, quite frankly, a sales pitch. "I am here to tell you how to improve your life by at least 60 percent."

3. *Start with an anecdote.* The illustrative story is at least as old as Aesop. It works best when it is personal in origin; just think about how much money Andy Rooney of TV's *60 Minutes* makes with his autobiographical fables. Generally, the anecdote should be short and sharp. Avoid beginning with a shaggy dog story.

4. *Come clean.* Admit something about yourself or your qualifications. "I hate motivational speakers—people who get up and give you a pep

talk—so, let me admit to you that what I'm about to say is very difficult for me." This approach involves risk, but if you use common sense it can be an effective attention getter. Obviously, if you've come to address a gathering of dermatologists on the subject of acne cures, you should not begin by declaring your ignorance of skin disorders.

5. *Throw down a gauntlet—sort of—by challenging a common misperception or cherished belief.* "Ladies and gentlemen, I know that the Constitution guarantees the right to bear arms. But this does not make gun control unconstitutional." As with the "come clean" approach, this one requires careful judgment. You do want to shock your audience into "motion," at least mildly, but you do not want to begin by offending them or turning them off. The late movie director Sam Peckinpah was widely admired (and in some circles reviled) for the masterful way in which he orchestrated the violence of his often quite violent movies. Why go through the trouble of making an *art* out of violence? Because ultrarealistic violence would, according to Peckinpah, incite an audience revolt. "If I sent them running out of the theater, I've failed," Peckinpah observed. Don't begin so outrageously or offensively that you drive your listeners (figuratively or literally) from the room.

6. *Bond with your audience.* You are speaking to the Irish Cultural Club and you begin, "I'm proud to be Irish." What if you're not Irish? "My mother's father was Polish and my father's people all come from Russia, but right now, standing before all you lovely people, I wish to hell I were Irish."

7. *Turn the preceding strategy up a notch by beginning with an outright compliment.* "It is not every day that the most prestigious retailer's association in the state asks you to address them." The danger here is that audiences are likely to see through a phony compliment. Better be sincere.

8. *Start with a relevant bit of humor.* "There is a tombstone in a little cemetery in Georgia that bears a very interesting epitaph. It says: 'I *told* you I was sick.' I want to talk to you tonight about what it means to be right at the wrong time."

9. *Conjure with the title of your talk.* "I've titled my talk "Three Bags Full.' You have every right to ask: *full of what?*"

10. *Promise brevity.* Hard as it may be on your ego, there is no surer way to win the honor of your audience than to promise them imminent release—especially if your talk is only one part of a lengthy program. Just make sure that, having promised to be brief, you are.

After the beginning comes—what else?—the middle. There is more than one effective way to organize this, the body of your speech. The most useful methods tend to be the most natural.

- Chronology (a narrative of events from first to last)
- Cause and effect, or before and after
- Need and fulfillment, or problem and solution
- Emotional order—from what your audience will find most acceptable to what will most challenge their beliefs
- Dramatic order—from least intense to most (think of this in musical terms as building to a crescendo)
- From smallest or least to biggest or most

If your speech is primarily descriptive, figure out a logical way to break up your subject. For example, if you are talking about the results of a national sales survey, you might divide the nation into regions (Northeast, Southeast, Middle West, Middle South, and so on) and work from east to west and north to south. If you are describing an airplane, you might naturally start from the nose and end up at the tail. All else being equal, there is also that old standby, alphabetical order.

Whatever method of organization you use, you might also find it helpful—especially in a heavily descriptive speech or report—to begin the body of your talk by providing a verbal outline. "I will approach the subject in three parts: origins, development, and consequences." Then announce each part as you come to it. "First, to origins . . ." "Now we move on to development . . ." And so on. Unless you are a very skilled speaker, it is a good idea to telegraph these *transitions* from one part of your speech to another. Let's say you're presenting a problem-solution speech. You've explained the problem; now it's time to get to the solution: "This, then, is the problem. Now let's move on to the solution." Or perhaps you've structured the body of your speech in emotional order: "Up to this point, "I've been covering pretty familiar territory. Now, if you will, let's venture into the extraordinary, an area that may well strain your willingness to believe." Or you've gone from smallest to biggest: "These problems are significant, but by far the biggest problem facing us is. . . ."

A special method of organizing a speech is the extended metaphor. This takes still on your part and a certain mental agility on the part of the audience. Furthermore, inappropriately used, an extended metaphor quickly becomes strained, cloying, and unintentionally comic. But it can be a very useful device for explaining the unfamiliar in terms of the familiar—which is, after all, the primary purpose of a metaphor. For example, I had an English teacher who made crystal clear the very difficult and arcane distinction between ordinary language and the language of poetry. He explained that ordinary language was a match. It is struck, illuminates, then burns out and disappears. Having served its purpose, it is given no further thought. If someone asks you to "bring the cup, please," you do not stop to admire or ponder the language of the request. The words motivate action as the match creates light, but once the action has been performed, the words burn out and are—mentally—discarded. Poetic language, in contrast, is a gorgeous chandelier. Like the match, it also produces light. But it is treasured and admired for itself as well. John Keats's "Ode on a Grecian Urn" provokes much thought and invites admiration of its beautiful language.

More famously, philosopher-designer-ecologist R. Buckminster Fuller wrote and lectured on what he called Spaceship Earth, developing the metaphor of our planet as a spaceship, self-contained, self-sustaining, but vulnerable and finite. Using this metaphor, he counseled ecological and political responsibility. Another thinker of the period, media and communications theorist Marshall McLuhan, spoke of how television was transforming the world into a "global village." In many of his writings, McLuhan effectively developed the implications of this metaphor, speculating on what it means to live in such a village.

My English teacher's metaphor, like those of Fuller and McLuhan, was not only extremely helpful in communicating a complex idea by making an abstraction more concrete and explaining the unfamiliar in terms of the familiar, it also made an idea easier to retain and remember. That English class took place years ago, and it has been a long time since I read Fuller or McLuhan. The details of what they said and wrote are lost to me, but their metaphors remain vividly in my mind.

Beyond the very real danger that you or your audience can easily get lost in the metaphor ("can't see the forest for the trees," to cite a familiar metaphor), there is also the hazard of falling into what rhetoricians call the metaphorical fallacy. During the 1950s, for example, Red-baiting American politicians often said that Communism was a "cancer" on this country. This is a most compelling metaphor. Cancer is universally dreaded, crippling, and deadly. It spreads insidiously, takes over the body, then kills it. The cure? No halfway measures: major surgery. Extirpate it. Cut it out.

The trouble is that political beliefs and the human beings who hold them are *not,* in fact, cancers. But if you are swallowed up in the metaphor, it is all too easy to see them as such and to lose sight of their rights as human beings as citizens of a democracy. Doubtless, the Nazis found it convenient to think of those individuals they condemned to death camps as mere cancers on the Third Reich. Particularly in ideological speeches, organization through extended metaphor is powerful—and very dangerous—medicine.

For many speakers, conclusions are almost as tough as beginnings. One reason for this is faulty reasoning in the body of the speech. Ideally, your speech should "add up" to a logically justifiable conclusion. If the logic fails, it is time to rethink your assumptions.

Beyond the logical component of the conclusion is a small arsenal of rhetorical methods for ending the speech:

1. *End by referring to your opening.* "I began by stating such and such. I would like to conclude on the same note."
2. *Review the main ideas of your speech.*
3. *End with an anecdote or story that illustrates your main point(s).*
4. *End with an inspiring quotation.*
5. *End with a rhetorical question.* "Is this the kind of school board we want? Are we satisfied that we have the best school system possible?"
6. *End with a dose of reality.* "Nothing I've said here is the magic bullet that will cure all of our ills. But I know that, together, we can *significantly* improve the situation—now—and *vastly* improve it within five years."
7. *End with hope and optimism.*
8. *End with a call for unity and cooperation.*
9. *End with a call to action or thought.*

In addition to these strategies for bringing a speech to a close, bear in mind two principles that are important enough to be called rules:

1. *End briskly.* Once you've announced or rhetorically signaled that you are about to conclude, get on with it. Don't leave your audience waiting for the dropping of the proverbial other shoe.
2. *Summon up and concentrate whatever eloquence you have within you and use it here.* Use strong, direct language—and this, above all others, is the place for deliberately quotable phrases.

AUDIENCE GIVE AND TAKE

I am a music lover, and I have been most fortunate to have heard over the years some of the greats (as they say) Live and In Person. Two performers stand out: Vladimir Horowitz and Luciano Pavarotti. Well, why *shouldn't* they stand out?

These are two of the greatest musicians of our time—of *all* time. But, when I think of the experience of having heard them in performance some fifteen years ago now, it is not so much their exquisite music making that comes to mind, but that difficult-to-define quality called *stage presence*. Both of these musicians, in personality and performance style quite different from each other. had in common a certain magical rapport with the audience.

A kind of special aura, is, to be sure, a gift. I don't know that it can be learned, at least not fully. But once you become aware of the existence of such a thing, an ability to create a unique bond with an audience, you can begin to practice it in an effort to cultivate it within yourself.

Don't regard your audience as a mass, a screen of blank faces. They are people who want to hear you, to make contact with you, to communicate with you. Performers regularly speak of deriving energy from an audience. Tune in to your listeners as human folk, and you, too, can draw on this power.

It's not as mystical as it sounds. Begin by taking some practical, deliberate steps:

1. Use the first person: I, me.

2. Along with using the first person, adopt the active voice and eschew the passive. "I wrote the report" is a good, strong statement in the active voice. "The report was written by me" is a weak statement in the passive voice. The next step into the swamp of total anonymity would be to say "The report was written." Using the active voice puts you and your listeners in a world populated by living, breathing, *doing* humanity. The active voice makes people more important than actions or things. In contrast, the passive voice alienates listeners by serving up a murky world of beings whom we glimpse at best dimly, if at all. People take a back seat to acts and things. At its worst—as in the last example—people disappear altogether. Active voice not only greatly simplifies your sentence structure (passive constructions are more awkward and require more words and more complex syntax than active constructions), it builds a rapport between you and the audience, an "I" and "thou."

3. While using the first person in reference to yourself, address the audience as "you."

4. Snuff out stale and overblown oratorical phrases such as "I am honored to have been chosen," "Unaccustomed as I am to public speaking," "Let us address the major issues of the day," and anything else that smacks of artificiality.

5. Don't make your audience conscious of passing time. "I have three minutes left" will drive your audience to concentrate on their watches and the clock on the wall rather than on what you have to say in those precious three minutes.

In addition to these means of establishing warm relations with your audience, please consult "Body Language" and "Getting Personal" in this section.

BODY LANGUAGE

A speech is speech, right? That's why they call it a *speech*.

This is true enough for a tape-recorded discourse, but one presented in the flesh is a live performance, consisting of words as well as actions. It hardly comes as news nowadays that the body speaks its own language, and many books have been written on the subject since Julius Fast published *The Body Language of Sex, Power and Aggression* in 1977. Fine. Most of us are willing to admit that body language—our visible gestures and expressions—have some effect on how our verbal messages come across.

Some effect? A 1971 study by psychologist Albert Mehrabian (cited in Jeff Scott Cook's *The Elements of Speechwriting and Public Speaking* [Collier, 1989]) reveals this startling fact: When listeners judge the "emotional content" of a speech, they give greatest weight to facial expression and body movement (55 percent), followed by vocal qualities (tone of voice, etc. 38 percent), and only then to the words themselves (a mere 7 percent). It behooves the effective speaker, therefore, to devote some attention to his or her body language, at least to the extent of ensuring that facial expressions and bodily gestures are in harmony with the verbal message.

The one thing everybody knows about body language and speech is the importance of eye contact. We speak of a dishonest person as "shifty-eyed," and when we doubt someone's veracity, we'll ask him to "look me in the eye and sat that." Obviously, then, it is important to maintain good eye contact during the course of your speech if you want your remarks (as that most revealing and relevant phrase puts it) to be taken at face value. This shouldn't be too difficult, but, unfortunately, it often is. Why? There are mechanical, logistical, and psychological reasons.

Mechanical

Many of us find it difficult to read from a manuscript without taking our eyes off it. We fear we'll lose our place. Two things can help us get over this hurdle.

First, make sure that you type the speech neatly and legibly. See "Typing the Speech" later in this section for details. Another factor that contributes to legibility is adequate lighting at the podium; consult "lighting" in this section for a brief discussion. Also make certain that your microphone, if you are using one, is positioned comfortably—neither so low that you feel compelled to look down at it, nor so high that it interferes with your field of vision. Finally, even if you have completely written out your speech, rehearse it, practice it so that it becomes familiar; see "Reading, Memorizing, Rehearsing, and Winging It." Practice the technique of glancing down at your speech, absorbing a phrase or sentence, then looking up. The more familiar you are with what you have written, the more legibly you have typed it, and the better lighted it is, the easier it will be for you to look down, absorb, and look up with a natural, graceful rhythm.

Logistical

Even shy folk can train themselves to make eye contact in the course of one-to-one conversation. But how do you make simultaneous contact with twenty, fifty, a hundred or more pairs of eyes in a meeting room?

The answer is, you can't and you don't. Experienced speakers learn not to gaze out into a shifting—and highly distracting—sea of faces. Instead, they talk to one person at a time, making eye contact with that one person for a few moments—five to fifteen slow beats is a good measure—then moving on to another. This will have the effect of visually underscoring your credibility, enlivening the speech (nobody wants to hear a reader, head down, drone on and on), and establishing a bond of intimacy with the audience, who will quite accurately, get the feeling that you are speaking to them personally and as individuals.

I wear eyeglasses, and I can tell you that they do present a potential obstacle to maintaining eye contact. I make certain they are clean and tight fitting. Glasses that slip down your nose are annoying and distracting to you—and even more so to your audience, who has to watch the ticlike lifting of hand to face and who must anxiously anticipate the spectacles' falling to the podium or the floor (thinking, perhaps uncharitably, Well, at least, *that* would bring an end to this irritating speech). Don't do without glasses if you need them. Whatever problems they may cause are far less significant than the consequences of not being able to read your speech easily and smoothly. Nor should you be reluctant to wear your eyeglasses because you think they make you look old, infirm, or like a nerd. Most audiences do not equate glasses with age or infirmity, but with wisdom—a plus. As to looking like a nerd, it certainly is possible to select eyewear clumsy enough to match that ink-stained plastic pen protector you wear in your wrinkled white shirt—the one that has the little notches in the short sleeves. But there are a lot of other, quite fashionable eyeglass styles available as well.

There are two types of eyeglasses speakers should avoid. Bifocals (or trifocals) and half-frame reading glasses force you literally to look down your nose at your audience, giving your listeners the uncomfortable feeling that you hold them in contempt. Purchase full reading glasses at least for speech-making purposes.

Of course, you can sidestep the entire issue of eyeglasses by wearing contact lenses. But many people—myself included—cannot stand the thought (let alone the deed) of poking themselves in the eye with a piece of plastic.

Let's move out from the eyes to the face. The great silent film actor Lon Chaney, Sr., was billed as the "Man with a Thousand Faces." This instance of Hollywood hyperbole was actually an understatement. It has been calculated that each of us exhibits a range of at least *seven* thousand facial expressions. The difference between us ordinary folk and a Lon Chaney is that he, like other gifted and well-trained actors, learned how to command—consciously and at will—a wealth of the expressions available to him. Alas, few of us possess the natural ability to do the same; nor can we afford to invest the time and cash necessary to secure professional training.

This does not mean that you should neglect the matter of facial expression. The simplest positive step you can take is to smile more often than you are accustomed to doing. Obviously, this is not called for if you are delivering a eulogy on a dear departed friend or a report on your firm's impending bankruptcy. But, in most speaking situations, a pleasant smile is appropriate and certainly preferable to a grimace or a hard-set frown.

Beyond this, if you will be speaking regularly, you should consider videotaping some of your performances, or, at least, your rehearsals. Take the tape and view it—alone—once with the sound on and again with the sound off. Make careful note of any repetitive or distracting gestures or expressions. Work on ridding yourself of them.

Now, from the face to the body. Except for the middle period in the history of rock 'n' roll and the heavy-metal headbangers of today, it has always been possible to distinguish dance from random motion. In varying degrees, dance consists of prescribed or choreographed steps coordinated to music. Similarly, the experienced speaker learns to choreograph her movements to suit her message in order to facilitate communication. She retains only those gestures that are useful, while suppressing any that are random, nervous, distracting, or ticlike.

It is generally easier to take away than to create and cultivate. So begin by ferreting out any nervous gestures that afflict you and that you, in turn, inflict on your audience. Most common among the purposeless distractions are continuous hand motions, face rubbing, shoulder shrugging, adjustment of clothing, pacing, and most prevalent and most distracting, habitually shifting weight from one side to the other. Using a videotape, identify any of these and work on eliminating them. Once you've established a more or less clean slate by getting rid of what you don't want, think about developing some purposeful gestures. The goal, after all, is not to learn how to stand stock still and function as the human equivalent of a loudspeaker, but to use gestures to underscore, propel, and energize verbal language.

There is a long way and a shorter way to accomplish this coordination. The long way involves close observation of effective public speakers and even seeking professional speech coaching or acting lessons. I don't offer this alternative as a rhetorical extreme, but as a very reasonable option, especially if your livelihood requires frequent speaking. For most of us, however, the shorter course is the more practical. Most of us use our hands in conversation, especially when we are making an emphatic point. Moreover, we don't gesture idly, but purposefully, though without thinking about it. Try to achieve the same level of emotional commitment to what you are saying in a speech as you feel when you are talking to a good friend about something that has genuine meaning for you. Then let yourself gesture naturally and emphatically.

Elsewhere in this book, I have pointed out some basics of body language. They bear repeating here.

Adopt a firm but comfortable stance at the podium. (If you are short and the podium is tall, stand on a box or step to the side or in front of the podium). Practice good posture: stand upright. Be aware that crossing your arms in front of you suggests a closed attitude, as if you are resisting input from the outside. Placing your hands on your hips, in the manner of Benito Mussolini, communicates defiance. Avoid bringing your hands to your mouth; this conveys evasion. Running your hand across your forehead not only conveys evasiveness, but anxiety as well. While you should freely, naturally, but purposefully use your hands to underscore the verbal points you make, beware of pounding the podium or clenching your fists. Such gestures are not 100 percent taboo, but they must be used very, very sparingly. For gesturing purposes, it is generally better to keep your hands open or to make an open fist, in which only the thumb, index finger, and middle finger make contact at their tips.

CLOTHES

This is not the place to present a dissertation on "dressing for success." (As I type this, I'm dressed in blue jeans and a T-shirt—though, admittedly, there's no one else in the room.) But there are a few points universal enough to be made here.

1. Be yourself—unless you are (frankly) a slob or very, very strange.

2. Learn from the well-dressed sales executive, who aims to dress *just a little more* expensively than his client. You don't want to dress so impressively that you impress your audience as a "fat cat" or a "snob," in short, someone from an alien culture. The exception to this is if you are an investment broker (or the equivalent) speaking about or promoting investment. In this case, by all means, dress expensively, impeccably, but conservatively. In a money game, the proper clothes communicate confidence.

3. Avoid the bizarre or *outré*.

4. Avoid loud patterns and jarring color combinations. This is always important, but particularly crucial if you are appearing on television. Video equipment has a tough time digesting sharp contrasts, loud patterns, small patterns (checks, hound's-tooth, zigzags, etc.), and bright whites. For television, wear a light blue, light gray, or light tan (khaki) shirt in preference to white.

5. More important than the style of your clothing is its condition. It should be spotless, shirts freshly laundered and suits and skirts dry cleaned especially for the occasion.

6. Avoid wearing elaborate jewelry. It is visually distracting, and it gets in the way of the podium and the microphone. Lapel mikes are notorious for picking up the jingle-jangle and click-clack of pendulous jewelry. Shiny jewelry also reflects the bright lights of television, creating a distracting video "burn" that is the bane of studio engineers and viewing audiences alike.

7. To pick up on the first point, be yourself. Wear what makes you feel good about yourself. If that means going out and buying new clothes, a speaking engagement is a better excuse than most for doing just that. If it means donning something old and familiar, well, just make sure it's clean and pressed and in tip-top repair.

COMFORT

Let's face it. It may not be possible for you to get comfortable facing a hundred or more strangers and semi-strangers whose collective attention is focused on you. We'll deal with nerves under its own heading section; however, here is a checklist of steps to take to ensure as much comfort as possible:

1. Prepare. Nothing will make you more comfortable than adequate preparation.

2. Get a good night's sleep.

3. Don't go to the podium hungry (positioned low enough, a good lapel mike will pick up gastric rumblings very nicely), but don't fill up on unfamiliar food, either.

4. Limit your intake of coffee and sweets. If you are accustomed to having a cup of coffee to wake up, don't choose the occasion of your speech to break that habit, but don't load up on caffeine or processed sugar. These will raise your anxiety level. Drink too much coffee and you may actually feel buzzed, tipsy, and disoriented.

5. Wear clothing as comfortable as the situation permits. Avoid anything constricting—trousers, jackets, shirts, and shirts you've "out-grown," or tightly tied neckwear. Feeling neat and natty—feeling that you look your best—will also increase your level of comfort.

6. Go to the bathroom before you venture onstage.

7. See that you are provided with a pitcher of water and a glass. Fill the glass before the program begins.

8. To the degree possible, familiarize yourself with the lecture hall or meeting room. Make sure you know how to work all audio-visual equipment, including microphones and slide projection equipment. By all means, try to check out the podium lighting beforehand.

9. If it is within your power to do so, adjust the climate of the room for optimum temperature and ventilation. In a room that will hold fifty to one hundred persons, a temperature of 68 to 70 degrees is about right.

10. In general, do what you can to ensure the comfort of your audience: provide the proper climate, glare-free lighting, minimize extraneous noise, and furnish comfortable seating. The more comfortable your audience, the more comfortable you will be.

DICTION, PRONUNCIATION, AND GRAMMAR

If you must make your living in significant measure through public speaking, you should, as I suggested earlier, consider investing time and cash in professional coaching, both acting and voice. When the Warner Brothers' *Jazz Singer* sounded the death knell for silent films in 1927, Hollywood rushed its hitherto mute actors and actresses to diction coaches. After all, it wouldn't do for the Count of Monte Cristo to sound like one of the Lords of Flatbush. Similarly, I taught for some years at a small southern college specializing in preparing students for law and business administration. In the neighborhood of the college, a private diction coach prospered by promising to teach students how to overcome "talking southern."

It is commonly believed that a flat, "neutral" midwestern accent is best for the public speaker. "Least offensive, most desirable," diction experts say. I believe, however, that, regardless of your region of origin, the really important thing is to speak clearly, giving full value to each of your words and to each syllable within those words. To my ear, regional variations are not only permissible, they are even attractive; I don't go to New Orleans to eat the Styrofoam-packaged fast food I can get in New Jersey. It is possible, though, that your audience will equate some geographically influenced features of diction as evidence of poor education or lower economic origin. Nothing wrong, of course, with wearing a blue collar—unless you are speaking to a white-collar audience. Our democracy proclaims equality for all, but ours is hardly a classless society. Remember the lesson of George Bernard Shaw's *Pygmalion* (or its musical incarnation as *My Fair Lady*) if you doubt that diction greatly affects how you—and your message—will be perceived.

This is not the place to make a complete list of regional and socioeconomic habits of diction that will load you down with negative freight, but here are some of the more common locutions most likely to work against you:

ax for "ask"

d for *th* (dis for "this," etc.)

failure to pronounce the entire word ('n for "and," woulda for "would have," etc.)

heighth for "height"

in for *ing* (nothin' for "nothing," etc.)

pixture for "picture"

t for *th* (boat for "both," etc.)

Contractions (don't for "do not," etc.) make some speakers uptight. I don't object to them, because they lend a conversational touch to any speech. However, when you want to underscore a point, use the long form. "Merely hoping for the best isn't enough" is not as effective as "Merely hoping for the best is not enough."

In a single sentence, here is what you should do to ensure effective diction: First, purge your speech of the habits of diction that work against you, then take the more positive step of opening your mouth and slowing down.

Closely related to diction is pronunciation. Speakers of languages other than ours often express amazement at the range of pronunciation English allows as "correct." Modern dictionaries have given up much of their traditional prescriptive role as arbiters of correct pronunciation and, instead, "report" a range of pronunciation for a given word, even telling us that the order in which these pronunciations are listed is not intended to reflect a judgment as to which pronunciation is "preferred." Despite all this, it is certainly still possible to mispronounce an English word, and, let's be frank, doing so can make you sound dumb. Look up any word or proper name of which you are unsure. In your typescript, spell it out phonetically and, if necessary, indicate the accented syllables. If you are introducing other speakers, make certain you pronounce their names correctly. Check it out with them personally.

The harsh fact is that as an audience will not forgive poor diction or obvious errors of pronunciation, neither will they excuse grammatical clinkers. I don't have the space to provide a guide to grammar, but, fortunately, I don't have to. An excellent, concise, painless, and even pleasurable one exists that will give you all the guidance you're likely to need. *The Elements of Style,* by William Strunk, Jr., and E. B. White, published in paperback by Collier Books and universally known to writers and writing teachers simply as Strunk and White, is justly considered a classic.

If you use a computer to write your speeches, you might find some of the currently available grammar-checking software useful. These programs comb your manuscript, ferreting out and flagging any questionable sentences. Some of them even give you stylistic comments ("too wordy," "confusing," etc.). The flaw in some of these programs all the time and all these programs some of the time is that they flag *too many* sentences as questionable. If you are in a hurry, this can really try your patience. If you already lack confidence in your writing, this can shake you up even more. (The stylistic function of these programs is particularly finicky. If most of this software would choke on the likes of Faulkner, Fitzgerald, Mailer, and Styron, what will it do to you and me?) I suggest that, if you do use such programs, you use them in conjunction with Strunk and White or another solid guide to grammar and style.

"...I'D LIKE TO THANK..."

Where appropriate, early in your speech, it's often a good idea to acknowledge people present in the audience and any accomplishments you may wish to praise—especially if they emphasize themes in your address. Politicians use this technique very effectively to boost popularity and project an image of familiarity and closeness. "It's good to see Bob Dwyer here this morning. Congratulations on your *Employee of the Year Award*. It's also good to see Jane Bowman. Great job on the Amtex account—we're *all* proud! How about a hand for them both!" Although it takes a little extra time and research, it can yield tremendous benefits. The people being mentioned will always be extremely grateful—if not, outright flattered and surprised. Others will see positive reinforcement and acknowledgment for a job well done. One cautionary note: unless you are mentioning these people in the abstract, it's a good idea to make sure that these people are indeed in the audience when you mention them. Saying they're there, when they are not, can be embarrassing to say the least. If an assistant can't make a quick check for you, scan the audience beforehand, and be sure to cross-out quickly any mention of people who eventually did not show up. Everyone loves a little recognition.

Finally, a word on spelling. Who cares, you say, as long as *you* can read it? True enough, if you are sure that nobody else will ever see your manuscript. But what if you give your manuscript to a local newspaper for publication or to *Vital Speeches of the Day* or any of the other journals that regularly publish speeches? (See "Publicizing and Publishing" later in this section.) It is best to take the time to proofread your spelling. For those who compose on computer, I can unreservedly recommend the "spell-checking" software that is usually a part of the most widely used word-processing programs. These programs have gotten very good at finding errors. Otherwise, consult a good modern dictionary.

GETTING PERSONAL

Most novice speechwriters do everything they can to stamp out every last trace of humanity that may stray into their presentations. They avoid speaking in the first person, substituting "one" or, perhaps, the imperial "we" where "I" is called for. They use complex and tiresome passive sentence construction where the active voice would greatly simplify and vitalize their message. They never address the audience directly. They avoid all reference to themselves.

Throughout this book, I have suggested a strategy of getting personal—that is, speaking as yourself and speaking directly to your audience, communicating as one human being to another.

I have very little fear that my advice to get personal will result in a wave of shocking confessional speeches sweeping across the nation's Kiwanis clubs. However, do exercise common sense. By all means, whenever appropriate—by which I mean whenever it is genuinely meaningful to do so—speak from your own experience. Nothing is more powerful and commands more attention than one human being reaching out in direct communication to another. But beware of irrelevant personal details. Don't spill your guts when what's really required is the Annual Treasurer's Report.

The same principle holds true in addressing members of the audience. Beware of directing your speech to this or that individual or to a clique of friends. To be sure, you need not ignore audience members you know. If it relevant to your message, you may even make special reference to someone present. But don't turn your talk into a personal dialogue that excludes the majority of your listeners. Also avoid embarrassing individuals in your audience by making revelations about them they may not want to share or by coaxing them to say something they may not want to say or for which they may be unprepared. If you plan to call on Joe Blow to give an "impromptu" report on the progress of a project, work it out with him well in advance of your speech. Don't put anyone on the spot. It will be awkward for that person (who will hate you for it), for your audience (who will fear that they, too, are at risk), and for yourself (who will look sadistic and silly).

HECKLERS

Relax. This is largely a nonproblem. Hecklers are, fortunately, a very rare breed. Most speaking situations do not lend themselves to heckling, anyway. If hecklers are to be found anywhere, they are liable to show up at controversial or strongly partisan speeches or where liquor is served (nightclub comics *do* regularly contend with this sort of person).

Okay and great. But what if the unlikely does happen. What if you are beset by a heckler?

If the heckling is relatively innocuous—a hand upraised and waving as if the audience member is undergoing a flashback to his days as a second-grader—ignore it. Chances are, the hand will come down.

If the heckler is or becomes more insistent, especially if he speaks up, do not try to outshout him. Stop speaking, look him in the eye, and politely *ask* him to hold his question until after the speech. Most of that time, this will prove effective.

If the heckler persists, stop again, and speak to him again. This time, however, assert more control by framing what you say as a declaration rather than a request: "As I said, I will be happy to take questions *after* I have concluded my remarks."

Escalation at this point is unlikely, but it is possible. Now is the time to put the heat on the heckler. "I have been invited to speak here. *My* name is Mary James from Gordon and James, Inc. Suppose you tell us *your* name." Most hecklers crave anonymity and will back down. If, however, the heckling continues, it is time for you to stop, step away from the podium, and look at the person who invited you to speak. Let him deal with the heckler. Failing that, look out at your audience. Let them apply the necessary pressure. If everything fails, leave quietly and without demonstration.

HUMOR

To paraphrase Dr. Samuel Johnson's remark on patriotism, humor is the first resort of nervous speakers. Don't get me wrong, genuine humor is welcome in virtually any speech. Audiences love to laugh, and we all crave amusement. The trouble is that many speakers equate *humor* with *joke*, and, in the manner of the old-fashioned traveling salesman, hamhandedly graft a "good one" onto the head end of a speech to "soften the audience up." Irrelevant humor culled from joke books and "speaker's handbooks" instantly turns off any audience that possesses an ounce of sophistication.

Here are some serious rules for using humor in a speech:

1. Make sure it is relevant to your message—not just an add-on to kill time.
2. The more original the material, the better. Avoid canned jokes and off-the-shelf humor.

3. Avoid humor that offends, embarrasses, hurts, or humiliates anyone.

4. Avoid sexist, racist, or religious humor.

5. Avoid using humor to make a serious situation seem less serious. By all means, a speech delivered in or about a crisis should help put that crisis in a perspective that will allay panic and promote effective action. But an attempt to laugh off a problem or make light of a grave situation is not only ineffective, it is irresponsible, and it will certainly backfire on you.

6. If you are not adept at telling a story, you should probably avoid humor altogether. It will fall flat.

7. Unless you are a good comic storyteller, don't base your speech on laughs.

LIGHTING

You may not have a great deal of control over the lighting that will be provided at the site of your speech, but try to ensure that:

- *You as well as your audience have adequate light.* If you were a pop star or a rock act, darkening the hall and putting the spotlight on you would be a good idea. Unfortunately, in a speaking situation, a darkened room invites audience somnolence. It also prevents your listeners from taking notes, if they so wish.

- *The podium is provided with adequate light.* If you can't see your script, you can't read your speech.

- *Glare is minimized.* Close any window curtains behind you.

- *Lighting on you is flattering and comfortable.* Don't let spotlights blind you, making it difficult for you to read your speech or to make eye contact with the audience.

- *The room can be darkened adequately if you are going to use slides or overhead transparencies.* In this age of media saturation, the projection of still images is not very exciting. If slides and overheads are truly relevant to your talk, by all means use them. If, however, they are marginal, minimize their use. The less time you keep your audience in a darkened room, the less incentive you give them to drift into semiconsciousness or, indeed, a profound (and perhaps highly audible) slumber.

NERVES

The best advice I can give on the subject of nerves is just to get used to feeling scared. The butterflies in the stomach, the sweaty palms, the feeling of dread—the whole nine yards: just get used to them. These things are, after all, only feelings. Feel them, and get on with the speech.

You can also take steps to minimize the unpleasant aspects of anxiety. Read the chapter on "Comfort" in this section. Prepare and rehearse; nothing allays anxiety like confidence, and nothing builds confidence more effectively than competence born of preparation and rehearsal. Beyond this, understand that anxiety and the unpleasant sensations that accompany it are perfectly normal. Then sit down and make a list of what you fear. What are the worst things that are going to happen to you when you get up to speak? Look at the list, then evaluate it realistically. Your list may include:

- *The audience will laugh at me.* Why? What's so funny about you?

- *The audience will discover that I know nothing.* In twenty minutes? Anyway, if you know (or learn) enough about your subject to talk for twenty minutes or so, you've acquired a great deal of knowledge. If someone asks you a question to which you don't have the answer, tell him that you don't know, but that you'll look into it.

- *The audience will be bored.* Create a speech that interests *you,* and it is likely that most of your audience will be interested as well.

- *I'll freeze up or make a big blunder.* Prepare. Arm yourself with a good script or thorough notes. You may as if you're freezing up, but, unless you've made the mistake of trying to wing the whole affair, you have simply to remember how to read. This should give you the push you need, if you need it.

- *My voice will fail.* Have a glass of water ready. If your voice does crack, flash a knowing smile to your audience. It will endear you to them in all of your humanness.

- *I'll get sick or wet myself.* If these things happen to you with any frequency, consult a physician; there are medications to help. If such accidents have not occurred to you in the past, they're not likely to occur now.

After realistically appraising your fears, try some of the following to reduce the physical sensation of anxiety:

1. Understand that you will feel uncomfortable, but that such adrenaline-related sensations as sweaty palms; tight, dry throat; rapid heartbeat; weak knees; flushed face; and butterflies will recede or pass altogether once you are into the speech.

2. Take a walk before your speech. If possible and practical, step outside into the fresh air and the "real world."

3. Take a few deep, cleansing breaths.

4. Stretch and move.

5. If you have heart palpitations, try forcing a yawn or a few vigorous coughs. This often helps.

6. Mouth dry? Have some water or chew some gum. (Remove it before you speak, of course).

7. As soldiers obliged to stand at attention in the hot sun quickly learn, don't stand with your knees locked. Flex them slightly.

8. Avoid unusual quantities of coffee and food containing large amounts of processed sugar. These things may help to get you "up" for a speech, but a little too much will significantly raise your level of anxiety and reduce your ability to concentrate.

9. Avoid alcohol or (except on the advice of a physician) tranquilizers. These may or may not calm you. (Indeed, alcohol may have the opposite effect.) What they will almost certainly do is make you less alert, which definitely will not improve your performance. You are better off enduring some discomfort and, in fact, learning to use it to help you hone what athletes call their "competitive edge." (A note of extra caution: In your anxiety, do NOT be tempted to self-medicate by mixing prescription—or even nonprescription—drugs. And remember, combining alcohol with tranquilizers can put you to sleep, maybe even permanently.)

10. Bear in mind that, unless you are addressing a meeting of Sadists International, the overwhelming majority of your audience wants your speech to be a success. They are on your side. Really.

OFF-COLOR LANGUAGE, REMARKS, AND STORIES

Little needs to be said on this subject, but that little does need to be said. Whatever your feelings about the First Amendment to the United States

Constitution (as a writer, my sentiments on this topic are particularly strong) and regardless of your attitude toward acts of communication between and among consenting adults, off-color language, remarks, and stores have no place in any speech you are likely to give.

You are not a nightclub—or cable TV—comic. As far as smutty stories are concerned in public speaking, just say no. It is not only that you risk offending someone and thereby turn off part or all of your audience, but that, in imposing off-color material on your listeners, you risk treading on *their* rights. Sure, you have a right to free speech. But your listeners have a right not to be offended or embarrassed.

The question of what constitutes obscenity is subject to endless debate. One Supreme Court justice threw up his hands and simply declared that he couldn't define obscenity, but he knew it when he saw it. I would argue that there is one area of obscenity that, in a democracy, we cannot afford to dispute. Avoid language, remarks, and stories based on sexist, racist, or ethnically denigrating assumptions and ideas. These are obscene without question and, beyond question, absolutely unacceptable.

PUBLICIZING AND PUBLISHING

Here are some additional ideas for getting the most publicity mileage out of your speech:

- Give serious thought to a provocative title. The title should offer your audience (as well as the greater audience of TV viewers, radio listeners, and newspaper readers) something of value to them: "Talking Yourself into a Better Job," "It's 10 A.M.: Do You Know Where Your Children Are?" and so on.

- Make copies of your presentation available to your audience. Unless your talk is of a highly demanding technical nature, make sure you distribute the copies *after* your speech. You don't want a lot of people noisily fumbling through papers when they should be listening to you.

- Make use of your company's public relations office or the publicist associated with the organization that has invited you to speak. Give the appropriate person or persons a copy of your speech, together with an abstract and a resume. *Do not count on these folks coming to you.* Go to them with the material.

- Identify specialist and trade publications that will be interested in the topic of your talk. Invite representatives to the speech itself. Send them an abstract of the talk in advance. Immediately before or after the event, send a copy of the complete text. Take time to highlight with a bright transparent marker anything especially germane or quotable. Unless you know of a specific contact person, address the material to the editor or managing editor.

- Prepare a press release, which amounts to a strong abstract of your speech, and distribute it to the media, including community newspapers, local media, and local college newspapers. Try to get coverage of the speech itself. Immediately before or after the event, send a highlighted copy of the complete text to the appropriate editors or reporters.

Even after the immediate newsworthiness of the speech has faded, you can extend its life by distributing a self-published version of the text to key individuals in your field. With the availability of desktop publishing and inexpensive laser printers, you can make the document attractive and professional looking. You should also consider sending a copy to *Vital Speeches of the Day* (City News Publishing Company, P.O. Box 1247, Mount Pleasant, SC 29465), which reprints current speeches on a wide variety of topics. The newsletter-style publications is issued twice a month and is in the periodical collection of all major and many moderate-sized libraries, including school libraries. Other reprint outlets worth tapping are *Speechwriter's Newsletter* (407 South Dearborn Street, Chicago, IL 60605) and *The Executive Speaker* (P.O. Box 2094, Dayton, OH 45429).

Whenever you offer your speech for publication, make sure you send a clean and thoroughly proofread manuscript. These days, if you can, offer a keyboarded manuscript on computer diskette in addition to the "hard copy." This will save the publisher the labor of typesetting it from a manuscript, will minimize errors, and may serve as an added enticement to publish. You should also offer to read galleys or proofs—but you should not demand to do so.

READING, MEMORIZING, REHEARSING, AND WINGING IT

I was trained as a college instructor at a time when the emphasis was so heavily on spontaneity in the classroom that *lecture* became a dirty word. Once I actually started teaching, I soon discovered that students are not, in fact, turned off by lectures. What turns them off are poorly written, tedious, droningly delivered lectures. And this is not the only thing that turns them off. Misguided and ill-prepared stabs at spontaneity—*at winging it*—deeply offend students, especially those who are paying their own way through college. Confronted by a professor spouting random remarks, they feel cheated—and for very good reason.

I believe that my experience as a teacher applies to public speaking in general. Give up the idea that audiences are turned off by a well-written speech well read, that what they crave is unbridled spontaneity. Few of us have the gift of delivering spontaneity in a consistently interesting and informative manner. Why, then, expose our listeners to what we cannot do exceptionally well?

Unless you are a brilliant impromptu speaker, write your speech and read it.

Read it well, however. Writing out your speech does not absolve you from the responsibility of rehearsing it any more than possessing the score of a Mozart piano sonata absolves a concert pianist from practicing the work before performing it in public. Rehearsal will accomplish six things.

1. It will give you an opportunity to *hear* your speech before you commit it, irretrievably, to the public ear. Don't read it aloud for the first time with the purpose of congratulating yourself. Listen for anything that sounds awkward or that falls short or wide of the target. Make the necessary revisions—now. You should NOT attempt your first trial reading immediately after you have written the speech. Let the completed manuscript "cool" for at least a day—preferably two—before you try it out on yourself.

2. It will give you an opportunity to indicate points that should be verbally and/or visually emphasized. Mark these, just as a pianist would mark special places in his score.

3. It will identify any words you have a tendency to stumble over. If possible, substitute other words. If this can't be done, provide yourself with appropriate phonetic clues.

4. It will make you aware of the logical and dramatic rhythms of your speech. You'll appreciate where to slow down, where to pause, where to speed up, where to increase volume, and where to reduce it. Mark these places.

5. It will give you an accurate idea of the length of your speech. The rule of thumb is that each typewritten page consisting of about 300 words takes two minutes to deliver. But you never know for certain until you actually read the speech aloud.

6. It will get you accustomed to the piece, so that you will, to a degree, commit it to memory. This will make it easier for you to read with conviction and enthusiasm and without having to keep your gaze glued to the page under your nose rather than the audience in front of you.

Should you rehearse in private, in front of a friend, or before a small "rehearsal audience"? The easy answer is to do whatever you are comfortable with. My personal preference is to rehearse entirely in private. (Certainly, your first read-through should be done in solitude.) If I want the opinion of a friend or two, I give them the manuscript to read for themselves, since I find it unnatural and awkward to deliver a speech to one or two people sitting across a table from me. If you can gather together a rehearsal audience, you might try that technique. But I have never had the luxury of drawing on such a group, and I don't know any speaker who has.

There are wonderful speakers who insist on memorizing their entire speech rather than reading it. Garrison Keillor, the writer and host of Public Radio's "Prairie Home Companion" and other shows, delivers marvelous, elaborate, and lengthy monologues that he fully writes out and then fully commits to memory. If you possess a talent for memorization, by all means a well-delivered speech spoken without script or notes will greatly impress your audience. It's up to you. Just remember: there is no dishonor in reading a speech, as long as you read it well.

THE RIGHT WORD

The great French novelist Gustave Flaubert, author of *Madame Bovary* and a handful of other masterpieces, was famous for the slow and meticulous pains he took in order to find what the called *"le mot juste,"* the right word. *Madame Bovary* was the product of seven years' labor. The American librettist Oscar Hammerstein II, collaborator with Richard Rodgers on such musicals as *Oklahoma!* and *The King and I,* was similarly obsessive. It is said that he pondered a full two weeks over whether to begin the song that opens *Oklahoma!* with or without the "Oh" ("what a beautiful morning").

Few of us can afford to invest the kind of time available to Flaubert or Hammerstein, but any time we do invest in finding what Mark Twain called "the right word, not its second cousin" will be amply repaid.

There are no absolute rules for finding the right word, but, usually, the simplest term, the most concrete, the most vividly appealing to the senses is the strongest and best choice. Minimize the use of adjectives and various qualifiers while emphasizing solid verbs and nouns. Not "he shouted loudly," but "he roared." Not "they objected violently," but "they rebelled." Did she *win, triumph, conquer, or overcome?* I *understand* or I *grasp*? He *likes, loves, admires, appreciates, is fond of,* or *has an affection for?*

   You will certainly find it helpful to consult a good dictionary in your search for the right word. You will probably also find a thesaurus of some value.

SLANG

For linguists and etymologists, professional students of language, slang is a topic of endless fascination. It is difficult to define slang precisely (indeed, a symposium held in Paris during 1989 for the specific purpose of arriving at a definition broke up after several weeks without having reached a consensus), but the poet Carl Sandburg called it "language that rolls up its sleeves, spits on its hands and goes to work." At its best, this is certainly the case. For instance, the word *skyscraper* started out as slang, and the language offers no term more vivid to describe a building so sharp and tall that it seems to abrade the very heavens. The trouble is that it's difficult to tell in the heat of the present moment which slang terms will live long and prosper, moving from the periphery of generally accepted vocabulary to its mainstream, and which will wither and die or merely degenerate into quaintness. (Groovy, man. Like, far out.)

   Slang can enliven a speech or can date it—and, if you're not sufficiently hip (hep?) to the jive—it can date the speaker as well. Some rules of thumb:

- All else being equal, if you can find an effective, vivid word in "standard" (that is, mainstream) English to say what you want to say, use it in preference to slang.

- If you are comfortable with a slang term, chances are your audience will be as well. If the term makes you uncomfortable, why use it?

- Observe decorum. Don't appeal to diners at a $5,000-a-plate charity gala to "lay some more bread on us."

- Beware of ethnic slang. You run a very real risk of appearing to mock the group whose language you are borrowing. If you yourself are a member of that group, you run the risk of alienating those in your audience who are of different ethnic background.

- Slang is by no means synonymous with smut. However, as language "at an extreme position on the spectrum of formality" (to borrow the definition Tony Thorne gives in his marvelous *Dictionary of Contemporary Slang* [Pantheon, 1990]), slang does often encompass sexual and scatological taboos. Usually, these have no place in a speech that readers of this book are likely to give. (See "Off-Color Language, Remarks, and Stories" earlier in this section.)

- Slang is best employed sparingly, like a dash of tabasco, not served up as a main course. It can be very effective, especially to make a strong point in a speech otherwise framed in mainstream English.

SURVIVING MISTAKES

One of the most moving piano recitals I ever heard was by the late Rudolf Serkin, who delivered a luminous performance of the Beethoven *Waldstein Sonata* and the Schubert *Wanderer Fantasy*. During one of the innumerable virtuoso runs that make up the Schubert work, Serkin's fingers became audibly tangled, but he went on. When he rose from the bench at the conclusion of the piece, he acknowledged his error by good naturedly shaking his fist at the piano, evoking laughter from the audience, who, I can assure you, were nonetheless moved by the performance as a whole. It was a more revealing, more beautiful rendition of this piece than many other "perfect" versions I have heard played by other musicians before or since. The lesson is obvious: Deliver a good product overall, and you will be forgiven an error or two, even an obvious one. Moreover, just as Rudolf Serkin's audience did not attend his recital for the purpose of catching him in a blunder—as if waiting to pounce on that wrong note—so it is highly unlikely that your audience will have gathered for the express purpose of hearing you make a mistake. And if you do err, well, we all do. Acknowledge the gaffe and get on with the show.

Broadly speaking, there are three kinds of mishaps that may befall you when you speak.

1. Your tongue may trip. Don't try to cover this up. Doing so usually results in compounding the gaffe. Instead, pause. Smile. Start the sentence again and proceed.

2. You may experience "technical difficulties." A microphone may fail. A slide projector may break down. A guest speaker due at the dais may be stuck on the Turnpike. Again, don't try to cover up. Explain to your audi-

ence what has happened and what you are doing to remedy the situation or how you plan to carry on despite the problem. Do whatever you can to avoid making your audience wait, and don't blame anyone ("The audiovisual person should have . . ."), including yourself ("This wouldn't have happened if I had only . . ."). The best strategy, of course, is to take to heart that hoary old law of Murphy and assume that, if anything *can* go wrong, it will. Try to anticipate and prepare for technical difficulties: Have on hand extra projector bulbs and even a spare projector. Tell your guest speaker to arrive at 9 A.M., even though he won't go on until 10:30.

3. You may commit an error of fact. World War II veteran George Bush embarrassed himself early in his term as president when, in a speech, he gave the date of the Japanese attach on Pearl Harbor as *September 7, 1941*, and Mr. Bush's vice president erred so frequently that a small magazine was started just to publicize Dan Quayle's latest howler. If, in mid-speech, you realize that (as Mr. Bush put it) you "misspoke yourself," stop at a convenient point and correct your error. Don't try to cover it up, hoping no one will have caught it. And don't try to ignore it yourself. It will irritate and distract you throughout the balance of your presentation, prompting you into additional errors.

What if an audience member challenges a point of fact during a question-and-answer session? You should not react defensively, but neither should you plunge blindly into admitting an error. You should pause to hear your questioner out. If you are not convinced that you are in error, tell him and your audience that your sources indicate a different conclusion and that you would be interested in discussing the matter further with the questioner at the end of the program; alternatively, promise to investigate the matter further. If it seems likely to you that you are, indeed, mistaken, admit it—with an explanation: "You know, it is perfectly possible that you are correct. I was using figures based solely on the February study. You have had access to some additional information. I think this bears further investigation and discussion."

TYPING THE SPEECH

I knew a man who used to deliver sales presentations twice a year. He wrote out his speech, which is, of course, just fine, except that he really did *write it out:* in longhand, in pencil, or yellow legal paper. Up on the podium, the document was barely legible, and he would stumble through it in a manner both excruciating to watch and tedious in the extreme to hear.

Type your speech. At minimum, use a new, clean ribbon (preferably a black acetate ribbon rather than one made of fabric) and a clean typing element. Triple space the copy, leaving plenty of room at the top, bottom, and sides for margin space. Put four spaces between paragraphs.

Better than this is to use a typewriter equipped with the "speech-writer" type-face, a very large and very legible typeface designed expressly for speakers.

Better still, compose the speech on a computer and print it out on a laser printer using a 14-point sans-serif font. Always use upper and lower case.

Some additional pointers:

- Put your name at the upper right- or left-hand corner of each page, togeth-er with the name of the group to which you are speaking, the location of the speech, and its date.
- End each line with a complete word. Don't hyphenate, especially at the end of a page.
- Keep numbers together on a single line:

  Six hundred dollars   *not*   Six
                                     hundred dollars

- Spell out numbers, especially large numbers: Five billion, not 5,000,000,000. Never use Roman numerals.
- Best to end each page with a complete paragraph or at any other point where a natural pause occurs. In this way, shuffling a page won't cause you to introduce an awkward and purposeless pause.
- Number the pages clearly and boldly. (What if they fall to the floor?)
- Write out abbreviations with hyphens: PhD becomes P-H-D.
- Spell out difficult words and proper names phonetically, using a phoneti-cal system that has meaning for you.
- Underline words you wish to emphasize.
- Use an ellipses (. . .) to mark brief pauses. Use # or / / to indicate a longer pause of three or four beats. This is appropriate after a punchline or con-clusion, to remind you to allow your audience a few moments to react.
- Do not staple your speech together. Hold it together with a paper clip, which you remove when you read the speech.

- Carry the speech in a folder so that it will stay crisp.
- Prepare two or three spare copies. Carry at least two with you in separate places (say a suitcase and a briefcase). If possible, deposit one copy with a trusted friend who will be present in the audience.

USING FACTS AND FIGURES

If you think that statistics appeal only to nerdy number and crunchers, think again. We are a nation of number junkies perpetually hungry for statistics. This does not mean that your speech should indiscriminately reel off an endless stream of facts and figures. Use them selectively and in vivid context, but by all means, *use* them.

Just as you should choose your words with the goal of making your message as real, as concrete, and as appealing to the senses as possible, so you should use numbers in a way that maximizes their reality. What, you may ask, could be more real than numbers? Consider this statement, quoted in Jeff Scott Cook's *Elements of Speechwriting and Public Speaking*: "1988 inflation in Nicaragua has been 10,000 percent." Pretty impressive. But, as Cook pointed out, TV newsman Garrick Utley made it even more real in a report he delivered from Managua: "If America had inflation at the same rate as Nicaragua that past year, this pineapple that costs fifty cents would instead cost fifty dollars." Activate the numbers you use. Put them to work—instantly and dramatically.

Whenever possible, provide a context for facts and figures. If you declare that inflation is running 8.5 percent this year, point out that it was 7.5 percent the year before and has averaged out at 8.3 percent for the decade. Better yet, talk about what your dollar will buy today, compared to what it bought last year or ten years ago.

Where figures are likely to be controversial, cite your source—and make sure that it is, in fact, up-to-date and authoritative. If timely figures are unavailable, explain why. ("Since the Communist unification of North and South Vietnam, accurate figures on birth rates have been virtually impossible to obtain.")

To bolster your interpretation of statistics, you might draw on expert testimony. "What does a 10 percent rise in the rate of violent crime mean? Police Captain Rod Stark of the Village Police Department told me that his officers have investigated 230 more muggings, assaults, and rapes this year than they did last year, but that they have been able to solve only 1,850 cases this year as compared to 2,105 last year. More crime makes the police work harder, but less efficiently, and it leads, inevitably, to even more crime."

USING QUOTATIONS

A true story from my days as a college instructor: A student handed in a term paper on the philosopher Friedrich Nietzsche. I awarded it an F accompanied by the following comment: "This paper consists of approximately 1,800 words. Of these, some 250 are yours and the rest are Nietzsche's. Nietzsche passes. You don't."

Intelligently used, quotations are valuable adjuncts to a speech, extending its authority well beyond yourself and demonstrating that you are not shut up in an ivory tower, but that you are alive to the world around you. It is all too easy, however, to let quotations usurp your speech. Remember, it is *your* speech, and the words of others should be subordinated to yours. Beyond this caution, observe the following guidelines:

1. Keep the quoted material brief. Be selective. Don't distort the quotation, but do paraphrase the marginally relevant or dull parts and cut to the chase.

2. Work the quoted material organically into your speech. Not:

    President Dwight Eisenhower once said, and I quote "Farming looks mighty easy when your plow is a pencil and you're a thousand miles from a cornfield," unquote.

    But:

    President Dwight Eisenhower put it well by observing that farming "looks mighty easy when your plow is a pencil and you're a thousand miles from a cornfield."

    Use nonverbal cues or marginally verbal ones—a significant pause or a drop in the tone of your voice—to signal the beginning and end of a quotation.

3. If you use more than two or three quotations in a speech, make sure you draw from a variety of sources, especially if you are quoting material concerning a single subject. Not only will overuse of a single source bore your audience, they will come away feeling that they should be in the library reading your single source rather than listening to you give it to them secondhand.

4. Make certain you are quoting accurately and in context: "As Winston Churchill declared, 'Democracy is the worst system devised by the wit of man.' Nope! "Democracy is the worst system devised by the wit of man, except for all the others."

5. Sure, we all use books such as *Bartlett's Familiar Quotations,* but be advised to gain a least a modicum of familiarity with the actual source of any quotation you use. At least make sure you can correctly pronounce the name of the sage in question. (In my hometown of Chicago, everybody pronounces Goethe Street Go-ee-thee. But that doesn't make it right.)

VISUALS

Technical talks, speeches involving numbers, and discussions involving geography (for example, a presentation concerning zoning) greatly benefit from visual aids. These do not have to be elaborate. Third-party presidential candidate H. Ross Perot made a strong impression during his 1992 campaign by appearing on television with simple but effective hand-drawn bar graphs and pie charts. The object is not to impress your audience with audio-visual hardware (in this age of big-screen televisions, VCRs, and high-resolution color computer monitors, that's pretty difficult to do in any case), but to subordinate the visuals to the speech, using them only as a graphic underscore to our words. When you are talking about market share, for example, a handy pie chart gives added meaning to the figures you're rattling off.

The visual aids you are most likely to use are flip charts, overhead transparencies, slides, videotape presentations, and visual handouts.

Flip charts are the simplest. Unless you are a quick-draw artist, prepare your illustrations in advance, using the best-quality and biggest flip chart you can find. And note that these really *should* be illustrations, not just figures. Use graphs, pie charts, and the like to help make numbers come alive. Here are some additional guidelines:

- Make sure the lecture hall or meeting room will be equipped with an appropriate stand for your flip chart.
- Limit yourself to one graphic per page.
- Arrange your graphics in the precise order your speech requires.
- Leave a blank page between graphics. Do not flip to the graphic until you discuss it. Then cover it with the intervening blank page until you get to the next point requiring a graphic. You want your audience paying attention to you, not studying an out-of-synch illustration or anticipating what you're going to say next by examining the graphic for your upcoming point.

- Stand to one side of the chart and do not fall into the trap of directing your speech at *it* rather than the audience.

- Make sure that the terms you use in your speech are the terms that are written on the chart.

Overhead transparencies serve a function similar to that of the flip chart. The transparencies are easy to prepare and have the virtues and vices of the flip chart's graphic simplicity. What can go wrong?

- As with any projector, the bulb can burn out. Make sure spares are available.

- Unless they are clearly numbered, the transparencies can easily get out of sequence.

- The machine, which is equipped with a fan, may make a loud and distracting noise.

- The light from the overhead projector may be irritatingly bright, especially if your graphics are very simple. Dim the room lights only as much as is necessary for legibility on the screen. Usually, an overhead projector does not require a significantly darkened room—unless you are trying to project the image from too great a distance. Turn off the projector between transparencies, especially if there is a long pause between them.

- As with a flip chart, show our graphic only when you have reached the appropriate point in your talk. Do not keep the image on screen after you have finished discussing it.

Preparing good slides used to require the work of a professional. To be sure, professional photographers and graphic artists can still be employed effectively to produce top-quality slides, but if you are a good amateur photographer or know how to make use of computer graphics programs to create material that a specialized service bureau can transfer to slides, you can produce excellent 35-mm visuals on your own.

- Carefully coordinate the choice and order of the slides with your talk. You will be tempted to choose more slides than you need in a mistaken belief that the audience will find them entertaining. In fact, even very good slides cannot compete with the other kinds of graphic stimulation readily available to our audience in the form of television and movies. Use the fewest slides you need to get your message across.

- Even though the slides for a presentation are usually arranged in a "carousel" tray, number each of the cardboard mounts, just in case they fall out of the tray.

- As with flip charts and overhead transparencies, do not project the slide until you are ready to discuss that particular image. Unless the projector has a blackout feature, include opaque blanks in the carousel between each image so that you can remove the image from the screen when you have finished discussing it.

- Make sure that the room can be darkened adequately. Slides that are barely visible or washed out because of room light make for a most irritating and tedious presentation. Also make sure that the projector bulb is of sufficient wattage to cover the distance between the projector and the screen.

- Although slides do demand a darkened room, minimize the amount of time during which your audience is plunged into darkness. Depending on the time of day or evening (and, perhaps, the blood alcohol level of your listeners), a darkened room may well induce slumber.

Although presentation-quality video is expensive to produce, some speeches benefit from it and others virtually require it. Training seminars, documentary progress reports, and the like may consist of your live introduction, the presentation of the video, then your conducting a question-and-answer period. In general, it is difficult to subordinate a video of more than fifteen minutes' length to your talk.

Handouts can reproduce material presented visually during the speech or may include additional, supplementary graphic material. Usually it is best to distribute handouts at the conclusion of your speech rather than before beginning to speak. If you distribute the handouts early, you are inviting your audience to look at them instead of giving their full attention to you. It is very difficult to talk to a crowd of bowed heads and against a noisy background of shuffling, shifting papers.

In addition to two-dimensional graphics, you may find three-dimensional props quite useful. If you are demonstrating a new product or if you are speaking to children, a prop may be an absolute requirement.

- Hide it until you are ready to use it.

- If the thing has working parts, make sure they work. This is especially true if you are demonstrating a product you are trying to sell.

- If possible and appropriate, make the prop available for hands-on audience examination at the conclusion of the speech.

VOLUME, TONE, AND PACE

Oratory is by its very nature louder than normal conversation. Even if you are using a microphone, you must speak up and project your voice. The goal is not to shout, but to bring your voice up from a place inside you that feels deeper than the origin of ordinary conversation. How do you know if you are speaking loudly enough? You should feel that your voice is resonant and sustained when you speak. It should not sound strident, but verge on the musical. It should sound and feel impressive to you.

Anxiety tends to work against volume. When you are scared, your breath comes faster and more shallowly. Sustained speech at higher than normal volume requires measured and deep breathing. So what do you do when you are nervous? Will your voice come out thin and squeaky? Not necessarily. It has been my experience—and other speakers have shared similar experiences with me—that if you force yourself to begin at the required volume, the demands your voice makes on your heart and lungs and nerves will help these systems work for you. The great American psychologist William James once declared that we do not run because we are afraid, but that we are afraid because we run. The nasty thing about an attack of nerves is that if feeds on itself. You feel anxious, so your heart starts to beat faster, your palms sweat, and the pit of your stomach is invaded by butterflies. In turn, these physical sensations make you feel more anxious. But just as the physical aspects of anxiety can increase the emotional intensity of anxiety, so the physiological changes brought by oratory at a sustained and substantial volume actually reduce those physical and emotional symptoms. In short, yes, your anxiety may make it more difficult for you to speak loudly and evenly, but exert the effort to speak at the required volume and the sensations that accompany anxiety will likely be reduced.

Tone of voice is harder to control than volume. Some of us have smooth voices, others harsh. Some speak in the lower registers, others up high. If you feel that the quality of your voice presents a problem and you plan to do a good deal of public speaking, it might be advisable to look into professional voice training. But almost anyone can make some improvement on his own.

- Unless you have a deep voice to begin with, pitch your voice slightly lower than normal. Listeners tend to associate credibility and authority with a relatively deep voice. This is true whether you are a man or a woman.

- Unless the sentence is a question, do not end on a rising note. Many speakers (more women than men) end declarative sentences on an up-pitch, as if the statement were meant to be interpreted tentatively. This undermines your authority and, over the course of a speech, is also quite irritating. Try to end declarative sentences on a low tone without, however, trailing off in volume.

- Audiences find prominent nasality very annoying since, over the course of a speech, it begins to sound like whining. Speaking slowly and consciously lowering the pitch of your voice should minimize an unwanted nasal quality. If you suffer from allergies or chronic breathing problems, consult a physician.

Finally, the matter of pace. Ninety-nine percent of the time this an be addressed in two words: *slow down.*

Anxiety, a desire to get the speech over with, and a benevolent inclination to avoid boring an audience all tempt you to deliver your speech at the rapid conversational rate of about 200 words per minute. This is much too fast for public speaking. True, it will get you through the speech faster—though you are also much more likely to trip and stumble over words and sentences. Rapid reading will not make the speech more interesting, however. Your audience will find your words more difficult to follow and almost impossible to enjoy. Speak fast enough, and they will be downright irritated, offended by what strikes them as an unprofessional and even impolite presentation—as if you don't even want to give then the time of day.

Slow down. The maximum rate of speed you should reach is about 150 words per minute. This means that it should take you about two minutes to get through a conventional, double-spaced, typewritten page of manuscript. (If you type the manuscript as recommended in "Typing the Speech"—using 14-point type and triple spacing—you will get through a single page in one minute.)

To be sure, don't slow to a crawl that your audience will find excruciating. And be aware that a faster pace is appropriate to some kinds of speeches: a sales *spiel* should proceed at a livelier pace than a funeral oration. But if, like most of us, you tend to rush through a speech, inscribe in large letters on each page of your manuscript a self-instruction to "slow down."

CHAPTER 6

GREAT OPENERS AND CLOSERS FOR SPEECHMAKERS

Your boss has given you a plumb assignment: give a speech at the next sales meeting on results in your region. No problem. You know the facts cold. Sales are up 42 percent. You know how each member of your staff has performed, you can rattle-off all the new clients you've acquired as if they were Mantle's batting average. Guess what? That's ninety percent of the speech right there. You know the body of the text already. Once you have that down in typical speech form, it's time to put a frame around your masterpiece.

"Oh no! I know exactly what I have to say, I've said it a million times to my staff, I've even regaled my wife with what I have to say, but I'm no public speaker. How in the world do start this thing? More importantly, how do I bring it in for a perfect three-point landing that my boss will notice?" What you need are transition phrases to get you started—and finished—with flair.

You do this already in everyday conversation. You don't immediately launch into a discourse on the latest acquisition. If you're like most people, you usually start with a couple of sentences to make the transition. Maybe a line about last night's ball game, a comment about the weather, some nicety. Speechmaking is somewhat similar, but there's not that sense of intimacy with your audience as there is when talking with one or two other people. You're addressing several people, and odds are they don't know you personally. Dianna Booher's *Executive Portfolio of Model Speeches for All Occasions* offers some excellent suggestions on how to put a frame around your own words, with ideas on humor, calls to action, self-effacing comments, breaking the ice, and so on. As with other prototypes offered in this book, you can adjust the writing to your individual needs—just the right phrase you need for just the right occasion.

OPENINGS

General Icebreakers

Good evening. Thank you for inviting me and putting me on the program in such a favorable time slot. At this early stage in this game you are still alert and expectant of great things to come. We're 15 seconds into the program now. So far, so good.

¤

Thank you very much. No, I know that most speakers say "thank you" to the audience at the end of their speech, but since I'm sort of a backward person anyway, I thought I'd start out that way. Thank you—if you want to hear that right up from so you don't miss it. I appreciate very much your efforts in . . .

¤

Hello. My name is _____, and I'll be your emcee tonight. Maybe I better define that role before I fill it. You do know what emcee normally stands for, don't you? Master of circuitous tripe. That is, in between the speakers, they usually apologize for the boring ones and exaggerate about the upcoming ones. Well, I'm not going to have to fill that role tonight because the speakers we have need no apologies and no exaggerations. You'll come to your own conclusion that they are all superb.

¤

After being hit on the head by a mugger, a traveler found himself wandering the streets of (city) completely addled. He approached a passer by, "Sir, excuse me, but could you tell me where I am?"

"Sure, you're right in front of a McDonald's playground."

"Oh," the traveler responded, "You must be a senior executive in a large corporation."

Flattered, the man nodded. "How did you know that?"

"Well, your information is typical—accurate but rather useless."

I'll do better for you today. I want to give you some useful how-to's on . . .

¤

When I asked (name of meeting planner) how long I should talk, she said for me to take as long as I wanted—but that you would leave at 8:00. If that's the case—and obviously it must be, from the looks on some of your faces—I think I'll get started right away. I'd hate for you to stop listening before I finish speaking.

¤

As I began to prepare what I wanted to say tonight, I started to jot down some key ideas about [insert details about speaking topic]. But then the list got pretty long, so I decided to leave off the "nice to know" things and just concentrate on the "must know" things.

But then the list was still a little long, so I started thinking about your frame of mind at this time in the program and what would really be essential information after a week of meetings, several airline hassles, jostling around on the expo floor, and lots of spicy food.

So trying to keep all that in mind, I decided that the thing you would most like to hear is about ten minutes. No more than ten minutes of anything. So here goes . . .

¤

The old proverb that states, "Blessed is he who has nothing to say and who refrains from saying it" does not apply to me on this occasion. I have something of utmost importance to say. I just hope to say it well. I'll be straightforward. My message is simply this: . . .

¤

Very late the other night I was having trouble with a particular software program for my home computer and called the support hotline. And the person who answered "Hello" was only the night security guard.

I explained my whole problem to him: "I need a quick answer before this software drives me crazy. After I get the NET screen, I get a "bad command" message. I don't need a special mag card for that utility, do I?"

There was dead silence on the phone. And I mean I was frustrated. I think I probably shouted back into the phone to him, "Don't you know anything about your own software?"

"Listen," the guard said to me. "I just told you all I know about computers when I said 'hello.'"

Well, that's exactly how I felt when your program chairman called me to tell me your program theme this year. So I'll dispense with an attempt to seem literate on the subject of X, and I'll go to something I do have a little expertise on. And that's . . .

Recognition of Distinguished Guests (See also "Introductions.")

Chairman _____. Members of _____. Family members. Honored attendees. Friends.

¤

Welcome and thank you for coming. It's great to stand before such a distinguished and beautiful audience. And rarely do I get to say that not having the privilege of speaking to predominantly female groups. And looking out over this crowd, I can say one thing for sure. Anybody who says this is a man's world is probably not too bright about other things either.

¤

I want to recognize one especially distinguished guest tonight. In this industry, his name has truly become a household word. He has been the catalyst and converter for [insert]. The (type) industry owes him its future. (Name), would you please stand and accept our gratitude.

¤

(Name) is with us tonight. Were I to list (name)'s contributions to our profession and community, the credits would be longer than those that roll across your latest movie screen. You've read them everywhere, so I won't repeat them tonight. Let me just say we're honored that you're here.

¤

The letter after (name)'s name sound like alphabet soup. Ph.D. CPS. CPAE. CPE. But I'll try to translate all those distinguished titles into proper English: This is one successful tycoon. Give him a hearty welcome.

¤

Don't you like suspenseful movies, those that keep you on the edge of your seat? Don't you like the part where the detective or the private eye cleverly gathers all the suspects and interested parties in one room and then suddenly reveals the true killer? Or the movies where, right to the very end, you don't know which of the nice guys will win the girl?

Well, I feel much the same way tonight. I could turn to several of you gathered here—(names of distinguished guests or honorees for award)—and say "You did it." Or, "You won." Or, "You have been successful." "You have done what it takes to make a successful career and a successful company." The rest of us have the utmost respect for your talent and your achievement.

¤

I take great pleasure in introducing our distinguished guest tonight, (name). Her responsibilities are many and heavy. Among them, she is totally responsible for [insert], [insert], and [insert]. With great respect and admiration, I present to you (name).

Self-Effacing Comments

I was certainly relieved to see this auditorium fill up at the last minute. The president and I both arrived early, talking about what to expect tonight. When he said that you usually had about 200 people and there were only four people here, I got a little worried. In fact, I just asked him outright, "Did you announce that I was going to address the meeting tonight?"

"No," your president assured me, surveying the empty audience. "But it sure looks like word leaked out, didn't it?"

Well, never mind. What I have to say is good for ten or 10,000.

¤

Great. After listening to all of those wonderful things just said, I know exactly how a waffle feels when somebody smothers it with syrup.

Well, never mind. I've always had a sweet tooth. Just let me enjoy it. As you can imagine—where I'm concerned—such introductions are rare.

¤

That meager applause didn't bother me. I've had the wind knocked out of my sails before. In fact, when the program chairman introduced me at an engagement last week, she said "We have only one speaker today. So, when he is finished speaking we can sit back and relax and enjoy ourselves because the rest of the program is going to be entertainment.

¤

Thank you, (name) for those gracious remarks. About the only thing you didn't say about me was that I was born in a log cabin. And you were right. I wasn't born in a log cabin. But my family did move into one as soon as they could afford it.

¤

Thanks, (name) for that introduction. If I'd known I was going to be that good, I'd have gotten here earlier to get a better seat.

¤

Thanks for such an introduction. I think the three most difficult things in the world to do are these:

1. Hanging on to a bucking bronco
2. Eating melted ice cream with a fork, and
3. Living up to that flattering introduction you just gave me.

¤

I think I should warn you at the outset—I'm just a mediocre speaker. But there's a bright side to that. You never know when you have a bad day.

¤

I know some of you had doubts about my being here tonight. The state of my health and all. In fact, after I sent in the photo they used in the publicity brochure, someone from your office called, quite concerned. She said, "Mr. (name), if you look like your photo, are you sure you're well enough to accept this invitation?"

¤

Before I get into my talk, I just want to remind you that I come free—no fee attached. And you usually get what you pay for. That reminder out of the way, let's talk about . . .

¤

Speaking on the designated topic, I feel a lot like the bureaucrat who addressed a group of farmers about the governments' policy on drought. After the program was over, the speaker asked a farmer in the audience how he thought the talk was received by the rest of the group. The farmer answered. "You did okay, but a good hard rain would've done a heck of a lot more for us."

Likewise, I don't know what I'm going to say that will lessen the impact of [insert]. But I'll do my darnedest.

¤

I noticed that some of you were already yawning before I got up here. But I'm not offended. On the contrary, . . . I take it as a compliment. In expectation of my talk, you were yawning to take in more oxygen to the brain so that you'd be more alert. So, if you yawn, as I get further into the talk, don't worry about it— I'll just talk with more fervor.

¤

Thank you for this opportunity to address you as a group, I've always loved motivational speakers, and now I am one. In fact, I still remember the first really superb motivational speaker I ever heard—(name). He encouraged us as new employees just embarking on our career to improve the world—to go out and establish a sound financial policy for business and for government, and to eliminate poverty and crime in the world. As you can see, the results speak for themselves. So, I feel fully capable of motivating you to do likewise today.

¤

That was such a glowing introduction I hardly recognized myself. But didn't it sound good? I can't wait to hear what I'm going to say.

¤

You know, you're lucky this is an after-dinner speech. They say that hearing is considerably dulled by eating—I suppose that nature's way of protecting us from boredom.

¤

I'd like to introduce myself—you'll see me listed on the program before you. I'm "speaker pending." If my talk's interesting enough, they'll fill in the real name later.

¤

You've heard of "Who's Who" listing. Who's Who in Science. Who's Who in the Arts. Well, I'm more in the category of "Who's He?"

¤

Some of you have probably spent a lot of time tracing your family history, your roots. But I never did like research. So I just decided to offer to speak somewhere and let the meeting planner and newsletter editor do that research for me. I that introduction, you've just heard and read more about me than I knew myself. You did a fine job, (name). Thank you. May I have a copy to send to my folks?

¤

Thank you, (name), for that wonderful introduction. Praise has many effects on man. It makes a wise man modest, but a fool more arrogant. Now, listen, up, you dunderheads, and I'll tell you how to set the world straight.

¤

Hello. That was a wonderful meal, and I see some of you are still sipping your coffee. You may want to put those cups aside, however, now that I'm speaking—the caffeine may keep you awake.

¤

They say a prophet is not respected in his own country. Well, I'll have to admit that's so in my case. My own company sometimes has a less-than-high regard for my abilities to forecast the future in our industry. And as I was rubbing my Pet Rock, drinking my New Coke, and listening to my quadraphonic sound system, I tried to figure out the problem about credibility. Nevertheless, I have a few ideas to share about the future. . . .

¤

I want to begin by welcoming each of you and especially those of you I know personally. I only wish that my family could have been here. My father would have really enjoyed that introduction. My mother would have believed it.

¤

Thank you, (name), for allowing me time on the program. I promise to be brief—no matter how long it takes me to get my ideas out.

¤

Hello. I want you to know that I take speeches and pre-meeting promotional literature very seriously. In case you don't recall, your invitation promised, "The lunch will be delicious, the networking opportunities excellent, and the program brief." I can handle brief.

¤

As you may know, you don't pay speakers to address your group. And, of course, that's fine with me as long as I know your money is going elsewhere for a good cause. (Name of meeting planner) did offer me a small honorarium, which I refused. And she seemed rather happy because she said that you all contribute individually before each program. You'll be happy to know that she put the honorarium intended for me back into the group's fund. She said that contribution would bring you pretty close to your total goal—for a coffee pot.

¤

For those of you whose sense of guilt got you out of bed this morning after such a long week, I offer my admiration.

¤

I'm going to speak today about [insert program topic], and you're going to listen. I hope you don't finish before I do.

¤

As I stand before you, I can't help thinking about the man who was killed in a recent flash flood. He made his way to heaven, and at the Pearly Gates he was asked to give his case history—to tell the story of how he died and came to heaven. This he obligingly did. St. Peter thought the story so interesting that he asked the new arrival if he would agree to give a talk to the other angels in heaven, telling them all about the flood and his demise. The newly arrived resident of heaven was very much flattered, and he immediately accepted the invitation. As he flew away, a kind young angel tugged at the sleeve of his robe and said, "Sir, I think I ought to tell you that Noah will be in the audience."

That's exactly how I feel about addressing you this morning—a roomful of Noahs—on the subject of . . .

¤

Yesterday as I thought of this talk, I grew a little panicked because I know how valuable your time away from the job is. Taking out my notes, I tried to eliminate everything that you might already know about [insert topic] and concentrate on just the few important insights I might be able to add to your considerable knowledge.

So, in conclusion, . . .

¤

Thank you for allowing me this slot on your program. A keynote, after-dinner speaker. I'm flattered. Up until this meeting, I was just an after-snack speaker.

¤

Good evening. I appreciate the opportunity to address a group such as this, my peers in the industry. If I don't seem larger than life, it's because I'm not. But try to keep in mind that it's not I who speaks, but life within me. And believe me I've had an eventful life. I chose to make my own mistakes . . . to learn by doing rather than simply observing others' experiences.

¤

When I was first contacted about this speaking engagement, I got the impression that your conference organizers were searching for more than a chief executive officer. They were also obviously looking for someone who could adequately—and perhaps even eloquently—address the very complex topic of total quality in the American workplace. Naturally, I was quite impressed with my selection as keynote speaker . . . until someone told me the story of two little old ladies walking through a cemetery. They spotted a tombstone that read: "Here lies John Smith—a chief executive and a quality expert." One lady looked at the other and said: "Isn't it a shame they have to put two people in one grave."

Well, I *am* a chief executive. . . . But I'm really not sure about being an expert on quality.

—Marshall McDonald
President, FPL

¤

My parents didn't have much formal education, but having seen my report cards, they would catch the irony of my offering counsel to a roomful of Ph.Ds— and in chemistry, no less!

—Richard K. Long
Director of Corporate Communications
Dow Chemical

¤

I'm reminded of the fellow who was once introduced at a similar luncheon meeting as the most gifted businessman in the country—evidenced by the fact that he had made a million dollars in California oil.

When he rose to speak, he appeared a bit embarrassed. The facts as reported were essentially correct, he said, but he felt compelled to state that it wasn't oil, . . . it was coal, . . . and it wasn't California, . . . it was Pennsylvania, . . . and just to keep the record straight, it wasn't a million, . . . it was a hundred thousand, . . . and it wasn't me, . . . it was my brother, . . . and he didn't make it, . . . he lost it.

Matters of fact aside, though, I'm grateful for those kind words and for this opportunity to talk with you today.

¤

Before I start, I'd like to assert that I'm better than sunshine. Pardon me, but I just feel the necessity of saying that. After the last time I spoke, I heard a nice little lady walking out with her husband say what an inspirational speaker she thought I was. And her husband turned to her and snapped, "Thirty minutes of bright sunshine would have done me more good."

Well, that hurt my feelings, and I just want to remind you that the sun isn't out today. So there's no use making a comparison.

¤

Let me say at the outset that I'm considered a very good speaker. In fact, at my last engagement as the crowd was leaving, several came by, shook my head, and told me how much they had enjoyed the talk. Except for one old geezer. He shook his head and told me it was the sorriest speech he'd ever heard. Talk about embarrassed. I was. But then the president made me feel a lot better. He overheard the comment and rushed over to assure me, "Don't give that comment a second thought. That guy's a half-wit. He's never had an original thought in his mind. Just repeats what he hears everybody else saying."

¤

I'm really pleased that you invited me to speak in such nice surroundings. The accommodations and acoustics are wonderful. Not like the last place where I spoke. There was so much hall noise and interruptions that I couldn't even hear myself. Of course, a couple of attendees assured me that I hadn't missed much.

¤

I think it's important that you get to know me—my personality and all—before I start into my real speech. And, of course, in this kind of a situation, it's a little difficult to get to know each of you intimately. So maybe I'll just tell you a little about myself. I'm kind of a "life-of-the-party" type. But then I guess that gives you a pretty good idea of how dull the parties I attend are.

¤

I feel that I should warn you—you're guinea pigs tonight. Yes, I'm trying out some new ideas and I'd like your honest feedback when I finish. To tell you the truth, I'm thinking of writing a book on this subject, and I'd like to have your opinion after I'm finished. I've already talked to a publisher, who once commented to the press that every public speaker has a good book in him. When I phoned him to talk about my particular subject and expertise, I reminded him of his earlier remark. And he reaffirmed that belief: "I'm still sure that's true that every speaker has a book in him—and I think that, in your case, that's where it should stay."

¤

I've been selected as your speaker. You're my audience. It's my job to talk to you and it's your job to listen. If you finish before I do, let me know.

Auspicious Occasions

Good morning. This is a very important day for all of us. In a few minutes, after this ceremony, you will no longer be "just a group of employees." [Or, "you will no loner be in the XYZ Building." Or, "you will no longer be employees of (company), but of (new company name)."] Instead, you will be part of a much larger purpose [or mission or organization].

. . . HOW DO YOU GET TO CARNEGIE HALL? . . .

People who are used to public speaking usually have a treasure trove of classic openers and closers in their head. Politicians, business executives, and other high-profile individuals are usually past-masters of approaching the podium and delivering a seemingly effortless presentation. Unless you're extremely gifted, or have taken acting lessons, it's a lot more difficult for the rest of us.

Here are some tips that might help. If you're having trouble with the opening and closing of your speech, forget about it for awhile. Concentrate on writing the body of the text—after all, that's the majority of the speech anyway. When you're comfortable with the bulk of the text, sketch out some opening and closing lines on colleagues and friends. See what they think. When you've got the lines you like best, incorporate them into the text. It takes time. Even experienced speechwriters go through countless drafts and revisions.

True, some people make it look like their openers and closers are spontaneous. Many are, and if you're good at it, do it. But if you're like most of us, script it out and try memorizing the opener and closer so you at least project the *image* of spontaneity. There is nothing worse than being on stage and freezing because you can't think of a way to start your talk. It may be a crutch, but it can help make you a star public speaker.

¤

As you listen to these text comments, I hope you'll take them to heart because they come from my heart. For all of us, this day is of monumental importance. It marks the beginning of . . .

¤

We gather today at a turning point of our careers and our organization. We need wisdom, foresight, commitment, and patience to tackle the formidable task before us. That task is to . . .

¤

Welcome. This is a day of progress and growth. . . . Of giving and receiving . . . Of celebration and fear . . . Of zeal and commitment . . . Today is the occasion of . . .

¤

Today marks an anniversary. (Number) years ago we numbered our membership in two digits. We administered a budget of $X. We boasted completion of our first community project. Today, (number) years later, our membership has swelled to (number). Our budget stands at $X. Our organization has just completed its (number) service project to the city. Like all anniversaries, such victories demand celebration. Let's pause and give ourselves a hearty slap on the back.

¤

Today demands the attention of the entire city. Struggle. . . . Pain. . . . Patience. . . . Victory. These are the phases we've passed through to get to our present occasion. This morning I'm proud to announce to you . . .

¤

What occasion could get the attention of an entire industry? What progress could arouse the curiosity of old-timers who've "seen it all"? What novelty could trigger the curiosity of neophytes to the field? Answer: Today we are unveiling our . . .

¤

Today is an emotional one for many of us. And emotion is never something I've been ashamed to show. Emotion melts ignorance into knowledge, . . . gives passion to persuasion, . . . turns mediocrity into growth. I'm talking, of course, about the . . .

CLOSINGS

General Closes

Thank you for your attention today. The nodding heads, the smiles—it's very evident some of you are into assertive listening, and I've appreciated that. Good night and good work.

¤

I wish you all good health, great happiness, and glowing success in whatever situation you find yourself.

¤

Thank you for attending tonight. The concern you have show by your presence has been a very meaningful gesture to all those involved. On their behalf, I again say thank you.

¤

Well, there you have it—my news, my philosophy, my experience. It's up to you to improve on it—and I hope you will.

¤

Now comes the hard part—it's time for you to think. I ask that you think briefly about [insert]. That you think hard about [insert]. And finally that you think creatively about the future. With all my best wishes. The rest is up to you.

¤

Have a good night and a good life.

¤

I hope we've grown together tonight in our sharing and in our understanding of this situation. Voicing the issues has certainly brought us closer to resolution.

¤

As so many before me have added to my life in similar ways, I hope I've added to yours in some small way. God bless.

¤

I don't think I'll ask for a show of hands of those who can now explain all the intricacies of (subject). But if you're still confused, at least I hope it's because of a broader knowledge base. Thank you for your patience on this complex issue.

¤

I want to close by expressing my appreciation for your participation tonight. Your encouraging nods. . . . Your questions. . . . Your examples. . . . You have made my job very pleasant and I thank you.

¤

If there's one thing we in this room can all agree on, it's that you've done an excellent job of sharing your feelings with each other. I hope I've been equally enlightening with new information you'll find useful. Let's thank each other.

¤

I want to say thank you for your time and your emotional energy in listening to what I've had to say. Please continue to give it some thought. That's all I can ask.

¤

Thank you for your generosity in allowing me this forum today to share my ideas with you. I trust that we'll both reap some benefits from the exchange.

¤

Thank you very much for the recognition you've offered me by inviting me to address you tonight. With sincerity I say that it has been an honor for me.

¤

As we celebrate together, let's remember that tonight is more than an event. We are part of a much larger process—a process of learning, growing, creating. I look forward to what the future holds for all of us.

¤

The food has been good, the networking better, and the program best. I thank each of you who've had a part in making this a memorable evening. Have a safe trip home.

¤

Thank you for your enthusiastic attention—at least, it has seemed that way from my vantage point. I hope I've helped to make the path a little clearer and the future a little brighter.

¤

This event has been our way of saying thank you for your commitment to the organization and your caring—so freely offered to the community. We hope you and your families have enjoyed the evening. Thank you for sharing with us on this occasion.

¤

After this last half hour, I simply can't identify with a former Congressman of mine. After one of his political rallies, a constituent came up to him and said, "Mr. Congressman, I've heard you talk for almost an hour now, and I still don't know where you stand on the issue."

"Fine," the Congressman said. "It took me two days to write it that way."

It took me almost as long to prepare for tonight, and, unlike the Congressman, I've intended to be *very* clear. This issue is important to me and to you.

¤

Let me remind you of the father who always wrote a note to the teacher on his son's first report card each semester. "The opinions expressed by this child are not necessarily those of her father's side of the family." The opinions I've expressed tonight are not necessarily those of my entire organization; they are my own. But I hope you'll agree that each of us must make up his or her own mind about these issues and then express those opinions to influence whomever we can. Change is inevitable.

¤

Let's never look back unless we're planning to head that way.

¤

In closing, all I ask is that you consider thoughtfully the ideas I've shared. Mull them over while you're waiting in line at the supermarket check-out or sitting in traffic. Ideas have a way of growing on you. I hope this one will take deep root and have a significant impact on your future.

¤

In thinking of our heritage and what I've tried to say here tonight, remember your spelling. *American* ends with four profound and prophetic letters, "I can."

KNOW THY AUDIENCE

There are a number of hard-and-fast rules to writing. This is one you should never forget. When opening or closing a speech, there is always the temptation to insert some humor to lighten the occasion a bit. A joke or two, a self effacing remark, a comment about the emcee, and so on. If you're like most people who sit through speeches, you appreciate these light interludes. But be careful. One person's joke can be another's offensive remark. Without getting into a debate about the current "political correctness" movement, plain common sense tells you to avoid remarks which could be construed as racist, prejudicial, or otherwise potentially offensive when telling opening or closing jokes. If in doubt, try them out on someone for a second, or even third, opinion.

While everyone loves a good laugh, remember, not everyone will share your sense of humor.

Calls to Action

Your attentive support has made my job rather easy tonight. I've tried to share four ways to [insert]. In return, I hope you'll spread the message to your colleagues and friends.

¤

I know that we've all been told that there's nothing much we can do about the situation. Many of us may feel like the little girl who kept standing up in the front car seat. Finally, her mother pulled the car off onto the shoulder of the road and yanked the child down in the seat, fastening her into the seat belt. The little girl pouted and then after a minute snapped at her mother, "I may be sitting down, but in my heart I'm still standing up."

Well, I identify with that feeling. This situation has us sitting down, but in my heart, I'm still standing up. And I'm asking that each of you stand up with me. I challenge you to find a way to change things at every opportunity.

¤

As I see it, we're all in this together. We're at a decision point as a group and as individuals. We can sit and think. Or we can band together and act. I prefer to act. How about you?

¤

I've not really said all I want to say on this subject, but I'm going to stop because my plane takes off in exactly two hours. However, I hope you'll take off on these ideas immediately—within the hour. Tell a friend.

¤

Thank you for your invitation, your attention, your support. All that remains is your action.

¤

I'm tired of hearing the same answer to every question: "It depends." If you, too, are ready for some straight answers, demand them. I encourage you to get vocal every chance you get.

¤

Together we can accomplish great things—things more important and more meaningful than I've even outlined here tonight. You will be the final source of those good ideas. You will be the driving force that launches us in the right direction. More power to you.

¤

Together we can accomplish great things—things more important and more meaningful than I've even outlined here tonight. You will be the final source of those good ideas. You will be the driving force that launches us in the right direction. More power to you.

¤

Write. . . . Phone. . . . Fax. . . . Throw a tantrum in the middle of the street. . . . But do *something*. Your job depends on it.

Self-Effacing Comments

From the looks on a few faces, I think you're about through with my talk. All you have to do to get me to sit down is to start clapping. . . . Did I hear someone applaud? Thank you. (Be seated.)

¤

(Glance at your watch.) My, my, how time flies when you're having fun talking . . . and philosophizing . . . and telling people how to set the world straight. Here it is, already eight fifty-eight and three quarters. Let's call it a night.

¤

Well, I'm finished with what I had planned to say. Before I sit down, does anybody have a present for me? I don't mean to be presumptuous or anything, but at the last place I spoke they gave me a new stereo system. Well, not exactly. They gave me an extension cord and said that the next time they invited me back, they'd give me the stereo to go with it. (Glance around.) No gift? Well, thanks anyway.

¤

In wrapping up my talk, let me say that I'm a little disappointed about tonight. There are two people in the audience—former colleagues of mine whom I'd asked specifically to attend to give me their opinion on the talk. Both have gone to sleep. But then I guess sleep *is* an opinion. Maybe I'll just keep polishing on this talk before I wake them.

¤

Well, it's ten o'clock and you're still here. (Glance at meeting planner.) (Name), I don't know what to do now. You see, here was our plan. If you were still here after dinner, (name) was going to talk about [insert]. Then if you were still here at eight, (name) was going to talk about [insert]. Then if you were still here at nine, I was supposed to give you my views about (subject covered). And then if you were still here at ten—we didn't discuss what to do then. But, not to worry, I have a wallet full of grandbaby pictures. And in the trunk of my car I still have slides from our Colorado vacation. Oh, . . . I see there's a little shuffling around now. Maybe we'd just better wrap this up without the extras.

¤

Let me say in closing that I hope you couldn't tell I ate before I spoke. A former pastor of mine always used to refuse a meal when a parishioner offered it, saying "no thanks," because he had to preach later. And more than once I heard members of our congregation say that as far as they were concerned he might as well have eaten. Well, I didn't eat. How was it?

¤

I want to close by sharing one little theory I have. To me, the mark of a gentle, considerate person is that he or she listens attentively to someone with very limited knowledge tell him what he already knows a lot about. Thank you for being so considerate tonight.

Summary Points

- Speeches should be framed by an opener and a closer. This eases the audience into what you're going to say, and signals politely when it's coming to an end.
- Audiences like self-effacing comments from speakers. Use them where possible. Speakers who take their introductions too seriously often don't connect with the audience.
- Don't let endings drag. Don't say, "In conclusion . . ." and then speak for 20 more minutes.
- Don't forget to always give credit where credit is due; acknowledge people by name.
- End your speech on a high note: an appeal to our better side, a reminder of what the company is all about, why the firm is headed for greater profits, and so on.

CHAPTER 7

RALLYING THE TROOPS: MOTIVATIONAL SPEECHES

Whether you've been in management for 35 years, or joined the firm last month, you know that one of the greatest responsibilities any manager faces is motivating the troops. When sales are down and spirits are low, a motivating speech can help boost sagging morale and turn a bad quarter into a record-breaking streak. When the year-end competition with the other division is coming close to the wire, motivating your troops to give 110 percent is just what they need to put them over the top. Employees expect it. And it's your job to do it well.

Isn't this the very essence of leadership? Political figures urge us to greater heights, generals motivate their troops to perform beyond the call of duty, sports coaches urge their players to give it everything in their fiber, managers do much the same. Through example and well-said words of encouragement, managers can get the most from their employees for whatever tasks lay ahead. While you may be a pro at pulling someone aside and giving them a pep talk in private, maybe you're a little nervous about repeating that performance in front of two people or a group. You're not alone. As you well know, what works well with one individual does not necessarily work in front of a crowd.

Worry no longer. Dianna Booher's *Executive Portfolio of Model Speeches for all Occasions* contains a number of pre-drafted motivational speeches on a variety of topics including: asking for greater productivity, urging greater interdepartmental cooperation, improving customer service, and reaching business goals, among others. In addition to some excellent phrasing which you may use as you see fit, each speech is preceded by useful information including: intended audience, overall message, tone, and timing.

Obviously not every phrase will fit your firm's exact needs. You will need to add or delete as appropriate. Yet the speeches below are complete so that you have a veritable treasure trove of ideas at your fingertips on how to motivate employees to achieve their fullest potential.

Motivational Speeches

General Guidelines

- Express appreciation for what the audience has already achieved or contributed.
- Focus on one objective, and prefer to make only one primary point in any given speech. Then illustrate that key point with several supporting details, statistics, or anecdotes. It's better to make one point well with several memorable illustrations than to present several key points and have none of them remembered.
- Call for a specific action. Don't leave your audience with the feeling of fluff: "What did he say?" Instead, give them specifics about changes, improvements, or goals to which you want them to aspire.
- Be clear and direct—even about the negatives.
- Use a "we're in this together" approach.
- Be upbeat in your tone; express confidence in the future rather than condemnation for the past.

To Express Appreciation for Work Done

Audience: employees, civic associates

Message: Each of you, in your own way, has contributed to our success.

Tone: informal

Timing: 3 minutes

We've finished. . . . The pressure's off. . . . We've been successful. . . . So who gets the glory? I'm here tonight to say, not me. Not management. But you. Each of you.

So how did we motivate you to do such an excellent job? To pull off such a feat? *We* didn't. You motivated yourselves. The difference between ordinary and extraordinary is that little *extra*. And each of you has contributed that little extra to make a big difference. They say that one of the greatest sources of energy is pride in what you're doing. You displayed that extra—that energy, that pride, that commitment.

You can't pay somebody enough for that.

(Name) rescheduled the vacation she'd been planning a full year in order to be here at the crucial decision time. . . . You can't pay someone for that.

(Name) spent (number) weekends out of the last (number) at the office, redesigning plans that we found necessary to change for various phases of [insert details]. . . . You can't pay someone for that.

(Name) dropped out of her night class at the university to devote the extra time it took to get her end of the project started. . . . You can't pay someone for that.

People in the (name) department put in (number) hours of overtime during the last two weeks to complete the paperwork. . . . You can't pay people for that.

(Name) spent days listening to completely unjustified, unreasonable demands from the public. She did it without losing her poise and her perspective. . . . You can't pay someone enough for that.

(Name) postponed surgery to avoid being away from the office during their crucial phase of the project. . . . You just can't pay someone enough for that.

So many of you have made similar sacrifices. You just can't pay people enough for that. So what *do* you do? Well, first you hope these individuals, and others like them, gain an inner satisfaction from a job well done. You hope their coworkers recognize and value their sacrifices and dedication. You hope their families reaffirm their commitment to personal excellence. In short, you hope other people recognize the qualities that make them unique.

Yes, as a management team, we hope that, in some small way, each of you, who has shown such commitment to your job, feels pride in our joint success and in your individual contributions. As British educator and social commentator John Ruskin so aptly observed, "The highest reward for a man's toil is not what he gets for it but what he becomes by it."

But you can't pay someone enough for that kind of attitude, for that kind of hard work, for personal sacrifice of time and emotional energy. We can only say a small "thank you" and hope each of you understands the gratitude we feel. You have our respect.

Audience: employees, civic associates

Message: I commend you for your hard work and your support.

Tone: informal

Timing: 5–6 minutes

You may have met a couple like this: The husband and wife have been married for about 40 years, but the wife grows increasingly unhappy. After all her efforts to communicate her feelings to her husband she finally gives up on resolving the conflict herself. So she persuades her husband to go with her to their minister for counseling. The minister asks the husband what he sees as the problem in the relationship, and he details his wife's growing solitude and grumpiness. Then the minister turns to the wife and asks her what she identifies as the difficulty.

"My husband never tells me he loves me," she answers.

"What do you have to say about that?" the minister probes with the husband. "Are you aware that a woman frequently needs to be told that she's loved?"

The husband looks downright insulted. "I told her I loved her the day we got married. If I ever change my mind, I'll let her know."

Even if you don't identify with that couple in your personal life, you may in your corporate life. After all, when we recruited you here at (company) we told you that you were special. And in your periodic performance appraisals, somebody pats you on the back.

So why tell you again how much we appreciate you? Well, someone put it like this: "Appreciation is like an insurance policy. It has to be renewed occasionally."

Today we want to extend the coverage—for years to come. My purpose is simply to tell you that we think you're doing a maximum job with minimum recognition. The equipment we've been using has not exactly been state of the art. The customer's specifications and instructions are not always what anyone would call lucid. And the potential for profit on this latest project will probably be minuscule.

But you've given it your best—regardless. You've had a great attitude about everything we've asked you to do. You've performed well under pressure deadlines with near perfection. You've accomplished something we can all be proud of. Without you, we'd soon find ourselves without the talent necessary to compete and survive.

As part of our efforts to show you our appreciation, we have begun a company newsletter in which several of you will be highlighted in the coming months. Let us know who's doing what where so we can get our editorial crew out to interview them and share their expertise with the whole company.

You can contact (name and department) to pass on your suggestions for this recognition. With those referrals, you'll be doing the newsletter editor, the spotlighted employee, and the rest of us a service. Great work deserves recognition and emulation.

And we want to continue to receive your input on how we can do a better job for our customers—both internal customers and external customers. You know best what it takes to get your job done and where the wastes are. You can tell us best what changes still need to be made and in what areas you can contribute more. You can tell us best what we need to do more of and what we need to do less of. Your input has a direct impact on our bottom line.

We appreciate your concern in all these ways: your enthusiastic spirit, . . . your creativity, . . . your attention to detail, . . . and the sound business sense needed to make this corporation profitable.

As you help us meet our business goals of profitability, we can in turn help you meet your personal and family goals of job stability, . . . good salaries, . . . and a satisfying sense of accomplishment.

Although I won't play the part of the out-of-touch husband, I am sincere when I say that you as individuals are uniquely important to us. You've worked hard with great results and we appreciate it. Keep up the good work.

TO INCREASE PRODUCTIVITY

Audience:	employees, civic associates
Message:	We need to do more at a lower cost with fewer people.
Tone:	motivational, informal
Timing:	18–20 minutes

Asking me to talk about productivity is like asking third-world countries to apply for a loan; persuasion just isn't part of the picture. I preach the subject with the fervor of a tent revivalist. It's *practicing* the message, however, that's the hard part. But practice, it, we must.

I want to begin by raising a few questions, and then outlining a few answers we've stumbled onto. Perhaps—and we're really hoping on this one—you can add to our answer list.

First the questions: What's happened to our capitalistic system here in the U.S.? It's still suffering from a bad hangover after years of celebrating technological superiority. Granted, our businesses have not ordered their burial plots, but neither are they well enough to do calisthenics.

What has changed—that we Americans now have to concern ourselves with productivity and quality?

I remember Saturday afternoon shopping sprees in the local variety stores as a child. I'd sidle up to my mother and show her my selection for the dollar she'd given me for being "good." She'd look carefully at what I'd picked out. . . . And if she turned the label over and saw "Made in Japan," the verdict was always, "Put it back. That's no good. It'll tear up before we get home with it." Today, the reaction of mothers is just the opposite. "Made in the USA" has meant shoddy while the Japanese have surpassed us in everything from radios to microchips.

Why did it all happen?

For one thing, bureaucracy buried flexibility. Policies and procedures took precedence over ideas. Assumptions about our technological superiority smothered creativity and technological advancement. In other words, smugness settled in for smartness.

Then there was the energy crisis. . . . Then the recession. . . . Then inflation. . . . Then scandal in high places. . . . Then our drug war. . . . Then our literacy problem. . . . While we were and are fighting these fires, the Japanese have been outworking us. Their products have cut into our profit in most of our basic industries.

But the tide has been turning.

We're a competitive group as Americans. You've heard it said that people always root for the underdog. Well, we ourselves have become the underdog in the economic competition around the world. And American workers have started rooting for themselves. To put it succinctly: We were up against the ropes, but we didn't go down for the count. In fact, we're responding well to the challenges.

Now here's where you come in.

All of us individually have the power to produce. You, as well as I, know that there's a difference between working every day and simply having a perfect attendance record. We want to find those people who are giving it their all—day after day after day. We want to reward them and promote them. We want each of you to get excited about carving out a future here—not just whittling away the time.

You are our economic advantage in winning this competition. You have much to contribute in making this a better, safer country. The question is: How badly do you want to win? How much do you want to find a way to do your job better? Can you find a way to do it cheaper? Can you come up with an idea that's both better *and* cheaper?

Our pledge to you is to give you an environment that will make you comfortable in reaching your highest potential. We want to do everything possible to eliminate any obstacles to team effort and spirit. We want you to understand that the only long-term security for any of us in American business is innovation and cost-effectiveness.

We want to attract, retain, and reward people who are sold out to excellence in every way. And, in turn, we'll provide you with security and any retraining you need to climb to your highest potential. We guarantee you that if you work yourself out of a job, we'll find you another, better place. One more in line with your creative talents. In other words, we not only want your good ideas, . . . we expect them.

You are our biggest asset. Although we can't go to the bank and borrow against you, you will show up on our balance sheet. In the years ahead, you'll be the difference between profit and loss. And we want to ensure your personal ownership in the success you foster.

So, together, how do we get the job done?

Well, productivity simply means working smarter, not harder. It means completing a task with fewer ergs of energy. . . . Or less raw material. . . . Or less machine time. . . . Or less paperwork. . . . Or fewer worker hours. . . . In other words, we need you, our extraordinary people, to find ways to make extraordinary tasks just ordinary after all. I'm finding a lot of people around here capable of doing just that.

Work smarter, not harder. We're starting to do that again in America. As Ann Landers would say, "We woke up and smelled the coffee." We're once again inventing new products and new processes that will continue to raise our whole standard of living.

Specifically, here's what we're asking you to do to work smarter, not harder.

1. We want you to use our technology to its fullest. What products and processes can we improve with our know-how?

2. We want to reduce the number of people it takes to do a job. That's a sensitive issue, of course, and our plan is to cut our workforce through attrition rather than layoffs. But believe me, you don't have to put off thinking until someone voluntarily leaves or retires. If you work yourself out of a job, there'll be a better one waiting for you, one that can fully use your talents and expertise.

3. We want you to help us redesign our products to make them easier and faster to ship out the door. And even more importantly, to make them exactly what the customers want to buy at a price they want to pay.

4. We want you to become motivated to give it all you've got—to do more work in less time so that you receive the personal benefit of a higher paycheck based on higher profits.

Let's translate these into a more specific to-do list:

We have to talk to each other smarter. We need input from all of you—from those of you who service our elevators to those who prepare our annual stockholders report. From those of you who design our (product). We want our vendors to talk to our buyers. We want our engineers to talk to our accountants. We want our sales reps to talk to our service technicians. We want you to share your goals and your obstacles to those goals. It's only with widespread collaboration that we can spark each other's creativity.

We have to measure smarter. Do we know where the waste is? Do we know where to cut? Admiral Joseph Metcalf had this to say upon discovering that some of our largest Navy frigates carried as much as 20 tons of paper and file cabinets. "I find it mind-boggling," he said. "We don't shoot paper at the enemy."

Neither do we here at (corporation) shoot paper at our competitors. But we have enough of it to do some serious damage—to ourselves. We've got to measure what we're doing now against where we're going, so we'll know when we arrive.

For years, management teams have asked ourselves and our workers how much we could save if we bought this or that software. If we accessed this or that database. If we hired this or that consultant. And you know what? We couldn't find out. The savings didn't show up on any radar screen, computer printout, or bank statement. We wanted a PC on everyone's desk, but we didn't know how to pinpoint its impact on the bottom line. And those who hold the purse strings—ultimately our stockholders—keep nagging us with their questions.

Consequently, we have to learn to measure. We need to count how many unnecessary files we keep on employees and projects. We need to count how many invoices we have to prepare before we get the numbers right. We need to know how many times the average monthly project reports have to be rewritten before they're clear. We have to measure everything we do so we know where the waste is.

But the real improvements will come when we can *do* something *about* the waste. When we can cut invoice handling to once rather than twice. When we can write the research report clearly the first time without having to ask an editor to interpret and rewrite for us. In other words, we have to understand that being busy can no longer pass for being productive.

Another to-do on our list, besides talk to each other smarter and measure smarter: We need to market smarter. We need to go to our customers and show them the value they're getting for their dollars. We need to tell them what is costs us to build thus-and-so, and then ask them what feature they don't think is worth the cost. We need to ask them what they want first—then figure out a way to make it better and faster than the competition. We have to do that to hold the line on prices and make our customers profitable in their own businesses. In our narrowing economic circle, we're going to have to hold hands.

Another item on our to-do list: We need to educate ourselves smarter. Once upon a time, we Americans had all the great ideas in the world. Then the rest of the world followed our lead and began to think. They've come up with some good ideas while some of us have taken a long recess. Individually, we have to realize that education never stops. Formally, we are putting our budget where our mouth is and increasing the number of training opportunities open to you through the company.

But individually you can build your own productivity power base by reading magazines, journals, and books. Then those research efforts and those training classes have to be translated to practical processes and products the customers want and need.

Another to-do: We have to dream smarter. You've heard it said that some people entertain ideas while others put them to work. We want you to be in the last category. People are finding new ways to do their jobs every day. We have to continue to look for new ways to do things rather than to settle for "this is the way it's always been done." The best way has to win over the old way.

We have to focus smarter. We have to work with direction and good aim. Our left hand has to know what our right hand is doing. We have to eliminate duplication of effort and research. We have to focus on one task at a time. Step by step, task by task, day by day, and month by month, the little completed tasks turn into big completed projects. The quickest way to do *any* task is to do *only* that task. Productivity is concentration and focus.

We're building quality smarter. Doing it right the first time means doing it faster over the long stretch. If you cut out all the costs of poor quality—the cost to do something over, . . . the scrap and waste, . . . the service cost for things that don't work right, . . . the supplier rejects, . . . the auditors and the inspectors—then you simply have to be increasing productivity.

We have to lead smarter. People of our generation are better educated and informed. They think creatively for themselves. They ask "Why" when told what to do. They want more than a paycheck from our payroll; they want a sense of satisfaction from contribution. So we have to stimulate ourselves to think productively.

We want to give you the freedom to use your intelligence and internal motivation to our advantage in thinking of better, faster, cheaper ways to do things that are assigned. Your smarter thinking means our better production. Your skill, ingenuity, and use of the newest technology will determine how well we hold down costs and raise our quality.

To repeat: We have to talk to each other smarter. To measure smarter. To market smarter. To educate ourselves smarter. To dream smarter. To focus smarter. To build quality smarter. To lead smarter.

As with many new management ideas circling the globe, after all is said and done, . . . much is said and little is done. But this productivity issue I've been discussing is more than a new slogan—more than the latest management fad.

We are in earnest. This way of thinking—increased productivity—has to become part of our company culture. It has to be more than a hobby; it has to be our work lifestyle.

To produce more, we have to see further down the road—to long-term quality and savings. Only as we get that big picture will we cope with tomorrow's challenges and harness its opportunities. Yes, it is hard work out there. But Americans of the past have never been afraid of hard work. Especially when we know what we want and how to get it. As your management team, we're determined. We hope you're ready to climb into the driver's seat with us and take off for the game. Winners eat free.

To Cut Waste/Expenses

Audience: employees

Message: We have to do more with less.

Tone: motivational, instructional

Timing: 12–14 minutes, depending on insertion of expense details

Einstein once said, "My mind is my office." Now, that's low overhead.

There's no doubt that with employees like him on our payroll, we could reduce day-to-day expenses. But don't worry—we're not going to ask you to clear out your desk and work in your mind. Instead, we're going to ask you to clear out your mind and work at your desk—productively.

You've heard a lot in the last two decades about increasing office productivity. I say you've heard a lot about it because you as a group have been doing more with fewer people for several years now. That's the story from the smallest firms in the U.S. to our Fortune 500 colleagues. U.S. companies globally have had to do some belt-tightening to compete with the Japanese.

And I do mean belt-tightening—that's what you do in a recession. In a depression, you have no belt to tighten. And when you have no pants to hold up, that's a panic. Well we're not in a panic yet; we do still have a belt.

But we want you to be aware of more than one way to get things done—the cheaper way.

The late Malcolm Forbes claimed that the answer to 99 out of 100 questions was money. But maybe not in our case. Maybe productivity is.

In other words, learning how to produce the same quality products and services with less will result in more—more productivity and more profit for the future. That's our goal.

But we can say this for adversity—people stand up to it. That's more than we can say for prosperity. When there's plenty of water in the well, we waste it. When the well goes dry, we learn the real value of water. We build character. We see what kind of employees and managers we really are.

In past difficult times, you've stood up to adversity. You've hung in there with whatever it took to get the job done. That's why we're confident that if you have the right information and a plan of action, you'll continue to improve the way we work.

So, I want to give you the scouting statistics before we get to the game plan. These numbers should give you a framework for understanding our strategy.

[Insert statistics on some of your monthly or annual costs to emphasize the magnitude of the troublesome expenses.]

Now here's the game plan to bring such costs under control.

We are learning to get the work done with fewer people. Through our early-retirement incentives, we've had volunteers to take their bonus payouts and leave. With the fewer people remaining, we've given our managers wider responsibility and control. We're learning to delegate downward. And we're now in the middle of eliminating nonessential tasks and other wasteful expenditures of time, energy, and money.

That's where you come in.

First, we want you to look at the expense of pushing paper. Governmental studies show that we white-collar workers spend 50–70% of our workday on paperwork. Reading it, writing it, analyzing it, responding to it, filing it, maintaining it, and retrieving it.

I encourage you to get rid of the unnecessary paperwork on your desk and mine. Information is power, but information comes in many forms other than paper. We don't need 17 copies of the same information floating around in four different report formats. Get off other people's distribution lists and get them off yours. Experts tell us that we'll never look at 85% of all the paper we stick in our files. We don't need to confirm every telephone conversation in writing. We don't need to write memos to protect ourselves in case somebody down the line fouls up. We don't need to draft a formal cover letter when a Post-It note will do.

Look at those weekly status reports. Those routine trip reports. Those reams of computer printouts. Those two-page forms filled out and filed in triplicate.

Could the work get done without them? What processes could we eliminate? What actions could we cut out of the loop? I challenge you as managers and individual employees to find out what goes where and why in your department. What comes in? What does out? What would happen if we stopped sending this or that?

The computer was supposed to create the paperless office. Instead, it simply added to the paperwork pile. We can now edit so easily that writing has become a pastime. And with the stroke of a single key, we can send copies to the world, snowing everyone with paper.

Most our work should get done *in spite of* the paperwork—not *because of* it. Ignore what you can and see if it won't just go away. Paperwork usually begins as a cure for a mild case of forgetfulness or distrust. But quickly the cure becomes worse than the disease. Paperwork threatens to devour our time and our budget.

Eliminate the unnecessary.

Second, we want you to take a hard look at your travel expenses. Before you hop on a plane, consider what you would do in person that you couldn't do by phone or letter or fax. And when you do have to fly, consider the off-peak hours and discount fares. Even with penalties when we have to cancel at the last minute, we usually come out ahead with advance purchases.

And a hidden cost of travel is human "downtime." Here's how you can make travel time more productive: Take along a reading file—all those journals that you've been meaning to get to. Pack your laptop or your dictaphone for those long layovers and missed connections. Do your strategizing and planning processes while you're away from office interruptions.

A third cost we want you to scrutinize is meeting time. Count noses around the conference table and multiply that half-day meeting by the average salary of those in attendance for some idea of how much the meeting is costing in lost productivity. Could you get the information out in another way? If the purpose of the meeting is just to inform, could you write a memo instead? Now, that would be a meaningful, money-saving memo.

Meetings are appropriate for brainstorming and problem-solving with a special goal in mind. Meetings are appropriate for negotiating details and gaining buy-in from your colleagues. But consider eliminating those for the purpose of simply informing.

Fourth, we want you to consider unnecessary telephone expenses. Check your watch before you dial. Could you wait until cheaper hours? Could you leave a complete message so you don't have to play telephone tag? Could you let someone's assistant help you rather than making four call-backs?

Fifth, we want you to consider the use of office supplies. A $2 binder here. A $10 ribbon there. Fourteen highlight pens left open to dry out around the training room. A ream of paper with coffee stains. It's the little things that add up to that astronomical cost of supplies I mentioned earlier, (number) dollars every year.

So there you have our strategy for eliminating the nonessential and performing the essential most effectively: Reduce paperwork. . . . Control travel expenses, using travel "downtime" well. . . . Eliminate unnecessary meetings. . . . Monitor your telephone habits. . . . Make do with less around the supply cabinet.

The tendency in times of cut-backs and belt-tightening is to whine because we've been taught the squeaky wheel gets the grease. But in times of difficulty, it gets the ax. If we can't find a way to do the job with less money, we may find that we can't do the job at all.

We don't want to have to put the ax to anything in its entirety—not our benefits, . . . not our travel, . . . not our training programs, . . . not our jobs. Instead, what we want to do is just prune the whole tree a little so our entire operation will bloom next season.

Our goal is to save everybody's job, yet to be able to turn a profit for our shareholders—and that includes many of you who are participating in our employee stock-purchase plans. You have a double motivation to work lean and mean.

As you well know, there are two ways to put money in your pocket—earn more or save more. We'd like to do both. And in our present industry's downturn, we think it's a lot easier to save more than earn more. We hope you'll agree. And we welcome your ideas on doing more with less.

You will make the difference. When a company faces upturns or downturns, the willingness of its employees to accept the challenge makes the crucial difference. Your attitude will be contagious.

Thank you for your hard work. . . . For your commitment. . . . For your continued confidence and support. Together, we can trim our fat and still enjoy a profitable dessert.

To Communicate Up and Down the Corporate Ladder

Audience:	employees
Message:	Clear communication builds credibility and the bottom line.
Tone:	motivational, light
Timing:	14–15 minutes, depending on insertion of details about employee-involvement plans

---

ABOVE ALL, BE SINCERE

Motivational speeches must come from the heart. They must be convincing. Put yourself in the shoes of your audience. A boss who drones on without any hint of sincerity is not likely to win many converts. However, a boss who speaks from the heart, who knows his people can do better, and shows genuine feelings, is more likely to get what he wants.

This leads to a difficult question. Should you *read* a speech, or just give one extemporaneously? The answer is: it depends. It depends on the forum, it depends on the audience, and it depends on your own comfort level with public speaking. The most ideal scenario is a speech off the top of your head—unrehearsed and straight from the heart. Of course, for most of us, that's just not in the cards. The next best thing may be to carefully outline what you're going to say, have your choice quotes ready, know your power opener and power closer, and read as little of the speech as possible.

This allows you to "connect" with your audience by showing more eye contact and less "sticking to the script." It may take practice though. Do it in front of a mirror or a friend or colleague to make sure the points get across, and your timing is correct. At the very least avoid looking like this is a chore you would rather not be doing. Get them psyched. Get them enthusiastic. Get them ready to join you wherever you want to take them.

You ask a teenager who is having problems with his parents to explain the difficulties. He'll respond with something like this: "We just don't communicate."

You ask a professor about why those in his class aren't making the grade and she'll respond, "They just don't communicate well."

You ask a married couple whose marriage is on the skids about the cause of their difficulty. They'll respond with, "We just don't communicate anymore."

My thesis is that the whole world is in a mess because we don't communicate. Students don't listen to the teachers. Politicians don't listen to the taxpayers. Suppliers don't listen to the customers.

We're not communicating. And I can't think of anything more vital to our organizational health than communicating—and communicating well.

A friend of mine tells this story about her elementary-age daughter. The mother came home from work one chilly fall afternoon and found her little girl sitting out on the patio, wrapped up in a big sweater, with her head buried in a library book. She went to the door and called out, "Honey, what are you doing, sitting outside reading when it's so cold?"

The little girl looked up, "Well, my teacher told us that if we wanted to be good students we should do a lot of outside reading."

I'm afraid that's been the story around (company) too often. Between management and employee. . . . Between Engineering and Marketing. . . . Between Service and Sales. . . . We're just not communicating all that well.

So what I want to talk to you about today is your communication style and mine. About what's happening. And how we can improve it. First, here's what I see happening.

We're not talking to each other *at all*. Many of us are retreating into our offices and writing memos about things that could be more clearly communicated and negotiated face to face.

Second, we're ignoring all the formal channels of communication—meetings, face-to-face discussions, internal correspondence—and opting to listen to the grapevine. Not that the grapevine isn't a viable rope—it's just that it's going to hang someone if we're not careful.

And finally, we're building paranoia because we're withholding information that everyone has a right to know. Management has a right to know that we've discovered a better way to get something done. And employees have a right to know the why behind decisions and policies.

That's the problem summary. So what's the solution? Talk more. . . . Listen more. . . . Match behavior to words.

Personally, I used to have a communication style a lot like Calvin Coolidge. One Sunday night after he returned home from church, his wife asked him what the preacher had talked about. The president answered in a word: "Sin."

His wife probed further. "What did he say about it?"

The president thought a minute and then responded, "He's against it."

That used to be my communication style. Not a word to spare. Say what you mean, mean what you say. But I've wised up a little since then. I've realized that the effect of my words alone are minimal in conveying my message.

Communication experts tell us that only 7% of our message comes from the actual words. The other 93% of our impact results from our voice quality and our appearance. In other words, our tone and our body language. That's the personal dynamic of one-on-one communication.

Now consider what I've just said in light of our organization as a whole. Multiply that 93% impact by the number of employees around here to see what's going on. You'll notice that a lot more gets communicated . . . than gets spoken.

How? Just as is the case personally, we as an organization sometimes communicate more by what we *don't* say. We communicate by our selection of what information to pass on and what to hold back. We communicate by what policies we enforce and which we ignore. We communicate our values by what behavior we expect and what behavior we reward on the job.

You've just heard my first point. Communication and the lack of it up and down the corporate ladder involve much more than talking. We communicate by appearances, by actions, by policies.

The second intriguing aspect of communication is that it needs to flow in all directions—upward, downward, and laterally—to be true communication. A one-way flow is a monologue. A two-way flow is a real dialogue.

You'll appreciate this communication dynamic a little more with this illustration used in many communication classes. Instructors often divide the class into two teams and assign some project to both groups, such as building a model with sticks or Lego blocks.

But the two groups play by different rules. One group leader must give all the directions without any feedback from the group. The audience can ask no questions. But the second group leader follows no such restraints. His group is allowed to stop him at any point for a repeat of something he said, for questions, for clarification or illustrations.

Well, no doubt you know how this exercise turns out. The group that gives the leader some feedback—tells him when his instructions are unclear and asks questions—does a much better job at the task. Such exercises are a real eye-opener for participants.

And the exercise pinpoints a major organizational problem. When communication flows only one way, we're in trouble. We're misunderstood. We're ineffective.

People don't make friends, . . . make enemies, . . . make a marriage, . . . or make a living without the effort involved in talking and listening to others. Yet for all its importance, communication doesn't get much formal attention. Perhaps because everybody talks, we assume that communication comes as naturally as breathing. It's not until we get communication hiccups that we decide to pay a little attention to the specifics.

Well, we've got the hiccups at (company) and we're paying attention to the cause. One of our primary goals in this coming year is to open up the ears and mouths of management and employees alike to get messages flowing both ways.

And flowing correctly:

You may have heard about the farmer who stopped by the barn to see how his new roustabout was doing on the job. "Where's the horse I asked you to have shod?" he asked the new employee.

"Did you say 'shod'? I though you said 'shot.' I just buried it."

Like the farmer and the roustabout, we all can probably recall a few such miscommunications. And the consequences may have been more serious than a dead horse.

Those hurt profitability.

So, in the next few months we intend to improve our communication. We intend to put a process in place that will help you as employees analyze your jobs and suggest improvements to us. We expect to generate more involvement from you. And we intend to make managers better listeners.

Here's how the process will work:

[Insert details about your plans for the employee-involvement program.]

We've learned, however, from other companies' experiences that such an employee-involvement plan won't work if people view it as an empty gesture. As I mentioned earlier when talking about the 7% impact of our words, we won't communicate our earnestness in seeking your solutions with our words only.

We'll communicate our commitment to this program by the priority we give it in allowing on-the-job time for your analysis and follow-up of problems and proposed solutions. We'll communicate our commitment to this program by grabbing excellent ideas generated from the program and acting on them quickly. We'll communicate our commitment to this program by rewarding those good ideas and those people that communicate them.

Having this program printed in a little booklet is easy. Having this program happen on the ground floor is difficult. But we're committed to communicate.

We're going back to our basic assumptions. At (company), we hire the very best people. When you get the job, it's because we assume you have certain talents and abilities. That we can trust your judgment. That you can decide how to carry out your assignments without step-by-step instructions. If we hadn't made these assumptions, we wouldn't have hired you.

So we're going back to our basic assumptions. You are very capable people to whom we're trusting our profits. We want to hear from you. We *need* to hear from you. We're *committed* to communicating with you. And we want that same commitment from you.

In short, we want you on the front line of corporate warfare with our competitors to improve on Silent Cal's style.

Now we know good two-way communication won't happen overnight. It won't happen next month. But it will happen, a few conversations at a time. A few meetings at a time. A few suggestions at a time. And I promise the effort will be worth it to you—in personal satisfaction on the job and in corporate profitability that affect us all.

To Cooperate Among Departments

Audience:	employees
Message:	We're partners, not opponents.
Tone:	motivational
Timing:	14–15 minutes, depending on insertion of details about team-building plan, appraisals, reward systems

Playwright Henrik Ibsen wrote, "A community is like a ship; everyone ought to be prepared to take the helm." My version is: "A *corporation* is like a ship; everyone ought to be prepared to take the helm." Everybody ought to have a compass.

Some of us share an attitude with the cartoon character Snoopy. He and Linus are standing on top of Snoopy's doghouse when the cat scurries away with Linus' blanket. "That cat has my blanket," screams Linus. "How are we going to get it back?" Snoopy looks puzzled, "We?"

For years, American corporations thought that competition was the key to outstanding performance within the doors of the organization. Get everybody to compete for their bonuses, their commissions, and their jobs, and, the theory went, they'll scramble with the ball. They'll get fired up and achieve, achieve, achieve.

But that's not was has happened. That competitive spirit has fostered jealousies and resentment, low morale, and low productivity.

Harvard professor and author Dr. Rosabeth Moss Kanter has dubbed these competitive environments "cowboy" management. Cowboy management makes competition, rather than cooperation, a virtue. Cowboy managers and employees like to get out there in the wilderness with a few trusty pals and no restraints. They practice survival of the fittest for their product, service, idea, or department. But research has shown that this kind of competitive environment has *not* been effective.

At (company), sure, we want to race against the clock to get the product to market. Sure, we want to go up against our competitors' proposals to our customers. Sure, we want to race against our own track record of performance for increased productivity.

We need to compete against the rising tide of economic troubles. We need to compete with the Japanese and the whole Pacific Rim. We need to compete with (name of competitor's organization).

But what we *don't* need . . . is to compete with each other.

Comedienne Lily Tomlin once quipped, "We're all in this alone." But here at (company), we shouldn't be.

In short, we benefit from a cooperative, not a competitive, attitude between people and departments. And on some occasions, we may not even be aware that we're working against each other.

Let me tell you a little story about (name of marketing manager) and (name of engineering manager). [Be sure to use names of well-known company leaders here who do get along well.]

It seems that (George) was having a horrible time carrying some heavy boxes of books when we moved in to the building here. In fact, just as (George) walked by (Mark)'s desk, (George) threw his back out, dropped the box of books he was carrying, and fell to his knees with excruciating back pain.

So (Mark), being such a helpful, compassionate sort of guy, offered to finish moving the boxes while (George) went to the doctor for x-rays. When (George) got back to work, (Mark) ran into him in the front lobby. "I finished moving all the boxes in and have the books all on your bookshelves for you."

(George) smiled. "Thanks. And I appreciate your help. . . . But I was trying to move them out to my car to take them home."

As I said earlier, similar things have been happening too often lately between departments here. Unintentionally, maybe even unknowingly, we are doing or undoing each other's best-laid plans.

If you don't believe we're interdependent, watch what happens to a conference room chair when one leg falls off. Now, the outside world may not know that our conference room chair has a leg missing. And our competitors may not know the chair has a leg missing. But I'll guarantee that the person who tries to sit down in the chair will know there's a leg missing.

When departments around here are vying to see who gets credit for the idea and the results, we'll know it. Because things will get really lopsided. People won't sit in those positions for long. And those around them will be moving away because they don't want to be nearby when the chair falls apart. That's a good picture of what happens when departments don't cooperate. Everybody just stands to the side to see what happens. We have a circus, but nobody's laughing.

Team-building can't be just a program around here. It's got to be a way of life. Of course, everyone pays lip service to teamwork. "He's a team player," we say. Or the referral letter says of the applicant, "She makes a real contribution to the team." Believing in teamwork is like believing in apple pie and motherhood. We believe in it, but we haven't always practiced it. That practice is not automatic.

Oh, yes we have processes for teamwork such as profit-sharing, employee stock-purchase plans, and quality circles. These processes and plans *should* foster a team spirit because the reward is based on our pulling together as a team to make a profit—a profit that goes directly into our pockets. The idea is that since we have team ownership, we should jointly feel responsible for our company's problems and profits.

But those processes don't always lead to the team spirit on the job every day. And that's the issue here.

To carry the goal of teamwork day to day, we're changing the way we evaluate what you do. We're no longer going to evaluate and reward on the basis of building a departmental empire. Instead, our performance appraisals and our reward systems are going to rest on a much broader base. We're going to look at the management of complex, interdepartmental tasks and teamwork efforts. We're going to reward those people who mentor and groom their employees to assume more responsibilities elsewhere. We're going to reward those people who spend time on buy-in and compromise rather than ultimatums and stalemates.

We want to sponsor team players, not referees.

Let me ask you mentally to take a scorecard and rate yourself on your team-building skills.

Do you consider people in other departments as your internal customers? And are you as eager to please them as our sales reps are to please our external customers?

Do you value consensus on decisions? Are you willing to take the time to gain buy-in from those who must contribute and make your idea work?

How are you at listening? Do you evaluate and act on feedback from other groups?

Do you look for ways to communicate your goals and problems to those in other departments who can help?

Do you fear that offering suggestions across department lines will foster resentment rather than resolutions?

How did you do on that quiz? . . . Teamwork isn't easy. Ask any member of Congress. Ask any pro ball team.

So we want to offer some coaching help—some goal posts and a game plan to get the ball between them.

Here is (name) to give you the details of that new plan:

[Call on the responsible person to speak, or you yourself incorporate details of training programs for team-building skills or new appraisal or reward systems that foster teamwork. Then conclude the other individuals' talk or your own with the following comments.]

According to author Robert Allen in his book, *The Challenge,* "A network saves legwork." We need a network of people who talk to each other and who help each other, who solve problems together and who produce together.

And it's up to us as management to give you the framework and the systems to become a real team. You've heard our plans. We're eager to put them to work. We think you're the players we need to take us to the bowl game. We're betting our paychecks on it.

To Change or Take Risks

Audience:	employees
Message:	We must accept change and take risks. Failure will not be punished.
Tone:	motivational
Timing:	13–14 minutes, depending on insertion of anecdotes about past risk-takers in the organization

Most of us grow up asking ourselves, "Am I normal? Can I run as fast as the other kindergarteners?" In high school, the question becomes, "Am I normal? Can I get a steady date?" In college, the question becomes, "Am I normal? Can I make the grades?" In the corporate world, the question becomes, "Am I normal? Can I get the job and do the job?"

Well, let me answer all the questions at once: To *change* is normal. To take risks is *not.* We've heard the old saying that nothing is constant except change. Our interest rates change. . . . Our clothes change. . . . Our cars change. . . . The face of our workforce changes. . . . Our politics change. . . . Our philosophies change. . . . Even our cultures change.

Change has become the status quo. Think of that. Change is the only thing that's the same. That's normal.

But to take risks, . . . well, that's . . . risky.

It's risky to get too enthusiastic about new ideas. Someone has observed: "We have never learned to support the things we support . . . with the enthusiasm with which we oppose the things we oppose."

We're vocal about the status quo. It works—at least to some degree. But we're much more vocal about new ideas that we count as risky. After all, risky can mean wrong.

You've heard it said that two wrongs don't make a right. Well, that may be true when you're talking ethics. But in matters of productivity and quality, two wrongs may very well lead us to right. We need people who are not afraid to be wrong occasionally . . . in order to increase our chances of being right most of the time—when it counts.

I repeat: What's normal? The normal reaction to a new idea is to think of reasons it won't work. But we can't afford that normal reaction. The greatest risk of all is to take *no* risks.

But risks require courage. It takes courage to think creatively about what if. . . . It takes courage to break through barriers. Frederick Wilcox put it like this: "Progress always involves risk; you can't steal second base and keep your foot on first."

We have some great examples of risk-taking in the corporate world. CEO Roberto Goizueta risked changing Coke's formula to increase market share. Allen Neuharth risked profits and reputation to start *USA Today,* because he believed there was a market for a new type of newspaper.

We've had our own risk-takers here at (company). Our founder was a risk-taker, for example, when

[Insert details about how the company's founder began the business.]

But our first CEO and president wasn't the only risk-taker. There have been others blazing risky trails.

[Insert anecdotes of other company figures who have taken risks in organizational decisions—with new product lines, new plant openings or closings, changes in packaging or policies, and so forth.]

If you study our company's past record, I think you'll agree that risk-takers have always been around—our own variety of movers and shakers.

Try your hand at this rhyme or brain-teaser from former Citibank Chairman Walter Wriston: "If wages come from work, . . . rent from real estate, . . . and interest from savings, . . . where do profits come from? . . . The answer is that profits come from risks."

We agree. And we intend to set a climate for constructive change and risk-taking. We intend to applaud, not undercut, risk-takers. We intend to provide recognition and reward rather than rules and reins.

So here are our principles for dealing with change and taking risks. We want you to see change not as an obstacle but as an opportunity:

One, do your homework—collect the available information and analyze it. Notice I said "available information." No one will ever take a step if we wait for *all* the information to come in. It never does. Waiting for all the market studies, . . . waiting for all the reports, . . . waiting for all the numbers, . . . is simply delayed decision-making. The risk-taker uses the numbers that are available, . . . analyzes them, . . . and then acts.

Two, recognize that inaction in staying with the status quo can be as risky as action in trying something new. The concept is as old as the Bible and the parable of the Ten Talents. The landlord gave three servants money for investing while he was away in the far country. The man with the ten talents risked them by investing and returned them with ten additional talents upon his master's return. The one given the five talents did the same. But the third man feared the risk. He buried his money in the ground and then simply returned the sum upon the landlord's return. Was he commended for his security-conscious action? Hardly. The angry landlord took away what he'd protected so well and gave it to the ten-talent servant who had proved he knew how to take a calculated risk.

To repeat: Maintaining the status quo can be a costly mistake.

Three, take action. You may find that you can't get all the sign-offs you need before the opportunity has passed. You may find that the market has moved on before the research has been completed. But if you've collected the available information and weighed the risk of the status quo against the change, act. We'll support you. We don't punish mistakes.

Four, admit mistakes. This is not contradictory to what I just said. Taking risks doesn't always result in profit. Never mind that.

Admitting mistakes has to be a way of life as much as risk-taking. It took Coke about 78 days to bring back its old formula as Coca-Cola Classic. But admit their mistake they did, rather than further anger their loyal customer base and lose more market share. Admitting mistakes and then going to work to reverse them is a natural part of risk-taking.

Let me list these steps again: One, do your homework—collect the available information and analyze it. Two, calculate the risk of maintaining the status quo against changing something. Three, take action. Four, admit mistakes. That's what we're *encouraging* you to do.

No, more than *encouraging*. We *expect* you to take risks.

And in response to that risk-taking attitude we're encouraging and expecting, our policy is going to be . . . explain, . . . train, . . . and then refrain. We're going to *explain* what our goals are. We're going to *train* you to do your job. Then we're going to *refrain* from controls that make you fit the norm.

In other words, we're going to change the meaning of normal. To us, normal won't mean "conformity." Normal will mean "different."

Today's environment—as fast-changing as it is—requires risk-taking. Companies large and small, new and old—companies like ours—have to risk to grow. Businesses do not win by letting marketing research studies, short-term profit reports, and fearful employees dictate the future.

CEO of Phillips Petroleum C. J. Silas has summed it up this way: "We've exchanged *free* enterprise for *frightened* enterprise. Some people fear being unprofitable. Some fear going to court. Some fear embarrassment. Some fear rejection."

But we don't. At least here at (company), we fear inaction and stagnation more.

Yes, it takes courage to change, to risk. Taking risks means moving forward while others are waiting for better times. Taking risks means moving forward while others are waiting for proven results. Taking risks means moving forward while others are waiting for applause on their past performance.

Yes, it takes courage to change, to risk. But then we have never aimed to hire the normal employee. We hire only the abnormal, . . . the extraordinary, . . . the excellent.

To Improve Quality

Audience:	employees
Message:	Here's what quality means specifically at our company. We need your commitment to build quality in, not add it on.
Tone:	motivational
Timing:	23–24 minutes, depending on insertion of anecdotes and details about quality control issues at your company

---

"ON THIS DAY . . ."

Here's a technique that public relations professionals use all the time often with great success. When picking the day to deliver your motivational speech, look carefully at the calendar. Perhaps you'd like to tie it to a significant date in history or in the company's own history. "Twenty years ago this week, our company was on the brink of foreclosure, when a bright young manager saw the way out. . ." "Today is the 5th anniversary of the launching of the XYZ widget. In those past five years, this company has grown to heights unimaginable just a short half decade ago . . ." "Thirty years ago today, Vince Lombardi was facing Superbowl defeat when. . . ." "Fifty years ago, Winston Churchill faced the possibility of seeing his country overrun, until he appealed to the people with blood, sweat, toil, and tears."

People mark anniversaries and important dates all the time. Birthdays, weddings, major holidays. They serve as times to remember and reflect. They also serve as excellent springboards from which to ask for excellence from those who work for you.

I want to talk to you for a few minutes about quality and elephants. Someone has said, "An elephant is a mouse built to government specifications." We've built a few elephants around here over the history of our company, and not necessarily for the government. Some of the specifications were ours. And, to give you the bottom line on this subject, I guess you could say we've found building elephants to be an unprofitable product line.

According to Aristotle, "Quality is not an act. It is a habit." Although we're not staging a hanging for our few acts of omission or commission—our mistakes— we are determined to ingrain the quality habit. It's no longer enough to make the *most* products or the *greatest* array of products; we have to make the *best* products.

And quality doesn't just have to do with products.

Here's the way we define it at (company). Improving quality involves all our activities: Products and services. . . . Customer relations. . . . Management style. . . . Human-resource policies. . . . Community-involvement projects.

Quality is nothing but . . . continued attention. Continued attention to everything. Every nut and bolt. Every product packaging and coat of paint. Every process and policy. Attention to detail.

In fact, that's the nature of business in general, says John L. McCaffrey:

> The mechanics of running a business are really not very complicated when
> you get down to the essentials. You have to make some stuff and sell it to
> somebody for more than it cost you. That's about all there is to it, . . . except
> for a few million details.

Those details are in your hands. As someone has said, "Every job is a self-portrait of the person who did it. Autograph your work with excellence." You are our quality control. Individually and collectively. Attention to detail will produce profit or put us out of the market.

What kind of detail? Let's translate all this talk about quality into specifics. To some people, quality means "being American" or "using common sense" or "being ethical." Vague generalities.

Although quality is easy to talk about in generalities, it's difficult to define in specifics.

Think for a minute about what the term quality means to you: The lonely Maytag repairman? Exxon's "quality you can count on"? AT&T phones that don't fall apart?

Or maybe you think of what it is *not:* Like "guaranteed" hotel reservations and airplane seats that are not? The full-service gasoline station that isn't? Department-store clerks who answer "I don't know—that's not my department"? Or, maybe "The computer's down again—we can't give you that information"? Or how about the bank teller's "You'll have to get at the back of the line, sir"? Quality can't always be measured in widgets per hour or durability alone.

So let's define it specifically and broadly:

With internal policies, quality means: Are our employees happy with their work environment and benefits? How many people do they have to talk to when they need to get a problem straightened out? How much paperwork do they have to shuffle to get their insurance claims filed and paid? How many forms do they have to fill out before they can arrange for a payroll deduction? Can they come to work in a pleasant, comfortable environment? Do we make it easy for them to handle their family responsibilities as well as their job responsibilities?

With regard to management style, quality means: Does your manager tell you what the department's goals are? Doe she or she give you feedback about how you're contributing to those goals? Does the manager set realistic deadlines on projects? Does your manager provide you with the necessary training to do your job? Does the manager follow through on promises. Do you get rewarded for your contributions?

With community involvement projects, quality means: How many of our employees contribute their talent and time to community efforts? How many hours do they devote? Does the community view us as a willing corporate citizen or one that has to be cajoled into contributing? What projects have we participated in and with what success?

With our internal customers—say, the people in Public Affairs—here's what we mean by quality: Do they get the information they need from Data Processing on time? Does it make sense? How many times do they have to ask for an interpretation of the computer printout? Does the VP—the internal customer—get the results of an internal audit in a form that he or she can read? Is it timely information?

These are the definitions of quality with internal customers.

In customer relations, here's what we mean by quality: How many times does the phone ring before we answer it? How long does the customer have to wait on the phone or in person to talk to one of our reps? How many people does the customer have to tell his or her story to in order to get some action? Are we courteous? Are we reliable when we say we'll do something? How easy is it for the customer to buy from us? How often do we make billing mistakes? Do we ship fast enough to meet the customer's expectations? Do the products arrive in good condition?

With products, we're talking about these quality issues: Does the product work as the instructions say it will? How often does it break down? How many times does the customer have to call us to ask an operational question? How long will the product last?

Journalist Russell Baker has classified things into three scientific categories: Those that don't work to begin with, those that break down, and those that get lost. We plan to eliminate all three categories from our product line.

These are some pointed, difficult questions to ask ourselves. But ask we must. All of these are the essence of the vague term "quality." The specifics. . . . The details that we need to handle effectively to be productive and profitable.

No matter how vague we may think the term "quality," our customers don't. They define it specifically, but subjectively: To one, quality may mean, "It won't break when I drop it on the floor." To another, it means, "It doesn't fade when it has been sitting in the sun." To another, it means, "It will print faster than anything else on the market." To still another, it means, "It will impress my colleagues and friends."

However they define quality, customers are "hopping mad," as my grandmother used to say, when they don't get it. Here's a letter to the editor published in *Newsweek* form Michael J. Cohen, New York:

Don't you get it—you big cheese, decision makers, production whiz kids? We consumers are not fools. We want fine design, good quality and long-lasting products. Foreign—read Japanese—products are designed, produced and marketed to respond to those wants. Until American manufacturers wake up to the fact that we consumers are entitled to the very best, we have every right to use our good taste and shopping skills.

Whatever the customer's subjective definition, we have to define quality to mean all those things I've just mentioned.

Quality goes in after the necessary and practical features are already assumed as part of the design.

Someone has been laughing at the customer's expense. Have you heard this riddle? How can the competition make money selling their products so cheaply? Answer: They make their profits repairing those products.

When I first read that quip, I laughed. Later it wasn't so funny. That's been the story in the U.S. at too many companies over the last 20 years. As a consumer, it hurts me to think about the broken gadgets and widgets that I've trashed after a few uses because to get them repaired was more trouble or expense than to buy a new one. There's got to be something unethical in all that—not to mention unprofitable in the long-term.

In fact, there's a big connection between quality and productivity—that's why so many industry journal articles lump them together. David Kearns, chairman and CEO of Xerox, believes that "one-fourth of all work in American industry is done to correct errors." Now, that's expensive.

You've heard the question before: "If you don't have time to do it right the first time, how will you ever find time to do it over?" Another pertinent question might be, "If you can't afford to build in quality the first-time around, how can you pay someone to add it on later?"

Here is William A. Foster's definition of quality, written almost a century ago: "Quality is never an accident; it is always the result of high intention, sincere effort, intelligent direction and skillful execution; it represents the wise choice of many alternatives."

Foreign competition has shown that low cost and high quality are not mutually exclusive terms. Making things right the first time eliminates waste and increases productivity over the long haul.

A recent survey by the American Electronics Association revealed that although 85 percent of respondents had undertaken a quality-improvement effort, fewer than one-third could document significant improvements in quality and productivity.

But these studies showed something else. Most of these quality programs had been designed for "after-the-fact" quality. Finding and correcting errors in things that had already been made. That's expensive. That's why we're aiming to build the quality in up front—not add it on.

I want to outline our framework for building quality in. Within the next few weeks and months, you'll be hearing a great deal about these quality-assurance programs:

[Insert an overview of the new programs you plan to implement.]

In other words, the quality race is a marathon—not a 50-yard dash to the finish line.

The Strategic Planning Institute's research on 3,000 businesses has shown that as quality increases, so does productivity, . . . market share, . . . customer satisfaction, . . . profitability. To put it simply: Quality pays its own way.

Someone has said, "It's better to deserve honors and not have them than to have them and not deserve them." We may not have won any worldwide titles for our products—I don't know that there are any except for the bottom-line title. But we ourselves will know the quality's there. And our customers will know—that's what really counts.

Well, you may be saying, we do pretty well. We already handle 99.9 percent of the details well. Isn't that enough? That's a good question. Here's how quality consultant Jeff Dewar of QCI International would answer that. He argues for a goal of zero errors or defects with a few analogies. If we accept 99.9 percent perfect as our goal, we'd have to accept the following conditions:

- 2 unsafe plane landings per day at Chicago's O'Hare Airport
- 16,000 pieces of mail lost by the U.S. Postal Service every hour
- 22,000 checks deducted from the wrong bank account every hour
- 20,000 incorrect drug prescriptions each year
- 32,000 missed heartbeats per person per year

That puts our total quality goal in perspective. Our aim is perfection in every way every day. We don't want to build more elephants.

We can't let ourselves work in circles. We hit the market with a new product—like our (name of product). It's successful. That builds pride and confidence. That confidence and pride relaxes our attention to detail. That let-up in attention to detail produces problems. Those new problems in quality destroy our confidence. It can become a circle—a circle that we want to break.

You may have known some people who don't want it good—they just want it Tuesday. We've got to break that line of thinking.

Quality is everyone's responsibility. That's not a new statement or idea, but one worth repeating often. There is no job so simple that it cannot be done wrong. I don't know about you, but some mornings I have problems tying my shoelaces so that they stay tied. But we don't want to let the simple things trip us up. Simple things such as how we

[Insert details about a few specific, "small" things that need to be done right in your organization.]

In other words, we need to question ourselves on every task—just like the second-grader who questioned her teacher while they were on a class trip to an art museum. They stopped in front of an abstract sculpture. And the second-grader asked, "What's that?"

The teacher answered, "It's supposed to be a galloping horse."

"Well, why isn't it?" the second-grader wanted to know.

We need to be asking ourselves similar questions about our tasks and products. Why aren't they what they're supposed to be?

Customers see a big difference between almost right and right, between good and best, between so-so and superior. That difference is what we want to manufacture around here.

Journalist Sydney J. Harris has observed: "An idealist believes the short run doesn't count. . . . A cynic believes the long run doesn't matter. . . . A realist believes that what is done or left undone in the short run determines the long run."

I'm a realist. Quality in the short run determines our long-term profit. Customers often forget how little we *charge* to do the job. But they remember how *well* we do the job.

I'm not a prophet, but I have a prediction. In the years ahead, technology won't win the war. Even those companies who are the first to develop certain technologies will lose their advantage in time. Everybody will follow the leader and eventually develop the same products. The competitive difference will be the people who attend to the quality.

That's you. You will be our decision makers on quality. Every day. With every detail.

To Improve Customer Service

Audience: employees

Message: You each represent our company to the customer; you have the power to win or lose customers for us.

Tone: motivational, light

Timing: 23–25 minutes

You may have seen this advertisement used by a training consulting firm: Two colleagues are talking about a particular company and one says, "Their product is fine, but their customer service is a joke." The second person responds, "Oh. Well, then, who would you recommend?"

The implication? Good product is not enough. Customer service is what people are buying. And anyone who thinks customers aren't important should try doing without them for a period of 90 days. When someone says to you that pleasing a customer is hard, ask them, "Compared to what?" To having to find new ones? Believe me, it's a lot harder to get new customers than to treat the ones we have right.

And we've all read a lot about that lately. From Tom Peters, from Lee Iacoca, from Buck Rogers. But let me get a little more personal. I want to tell you a true story about two friends of mine who recently moved. A rather long story. But I think you'll identify with it.

Like the proverbial average family which moves every five years, Mike and Marsha got the itch to mow a new lawn. Finding the house of their dreams, they applied for a loan with Mortgage Company X, which guaranteed in-house loan approval within 30–45 days.

"Will I need a CPA-prepared financial-worth statement since I'm self-employed?" Mike asked. "If so, I want to get it now rather than slow up the process somewhere down the line."

"No problem," the loan officer answered. "If you keep your own books, your statement is good enough."

A few days later, the loan officer called to say she had lost the VA eligibility certificate. Could Mike and Marsha supply another? They did. A few days later the loan officer phoned to say that they would, after all, need their CPA to prepare a statement. He did. Mike and Marsha waited.

Finally approval came. But two hours before closing, their realtor called to say there would be no closing. Without notice, the mortgage company had decided to renege on their interest-rate commitments not yet in writing and "to relieve from duty" all loan officers at that location. Others were flying in shortly from headquarters to hear customer complaints. But no one there thought to call Mike and Marsha to let them know the closing had been canceled. A couple of days later they "permitted" Mike and Marsha to quietly take their loan package to another institution. They ran.

But that was just the beginning of their experience with customer service—or lack of it. They pulled out the home-furnishings catalogs. Custom window covering came from Department Store A. The master bedroom woven-wood was two inches too short and two inches too narrow. Someone didn't measure or record the dimensions correctly. Would Marsha mind if the designer just sprayed a chemical treatment and "yanked" the window covering down? Mike and Marsha agreed. It didn't work. The department store refunded the money and my friends were only out the four-week delay.

They called Store B. Humming to herself while the installer hung the second woven woods, Marsha dreamed of privacy in the bedroom. But the installer came down the hall shaking his head. "You wanted a double-pull wood, Ma'am? I'm afraid the factory made a mistake. Or someone copied down your order wrong. I'm going to have to send this back."

On Store B's second delivery, Marsha was afraid to look. "Ma'am," the installer said, "you're not going to believe this, but they made the same mistake. It's the same one we sent back." They got the correct window covering six weeks later.

Store C delivered a brass bed for their daughter's room. One hole for the frame was drilled higher than the other. "But it is a $34 special," the salesclerk reminded Mike on the phone. Mike drilled a lower hole.

The master bedroom brass headboard, a more expensive variety, Mike and Marsha didn't dare leave for a delivery truck. The salesman promised to send it to Package Pickup while they pulled the car around. He did and they did. In the bedroom light, after Mike and Marsha had unloaded the headboard with (literally) gloved hands, they saw the scratches. Headboard to footboard. Yes, the salesman said on the phone, they could return it if they brought it back immediately. The sales clerk "had a feeling" Package Pickup would be careless with it. "They do it all the time," the clerk assured them. It was the only headboard of its kind in stock.

The following Saturday Store D delivered the new washer; the old one, in its 12th year, had washed its last load a week earlier. On its first spin cycle, a smoky scent filled the house. The repairman said it couldn't possibly have a burned-out motor. It did.

After only two tries, Store E delivered the fireplace screen (without the screws) and a dinette. They had delivered both to the old billing address rather than the one carefully printed on the contract under "Deliver To."

"Be glad to give you a refund on the fireplace screen if you want to bring it back," the clerk said. Was it worth the 45-minute trip across town? Mike found the screws at the corner hardware store and made do.

The garage-door opener they bought as an unassembled do-it-yourself kit. After installation the remote controls didn't control. The store owner promised to have the manufacturer send new ones. They came ten days later, COD for $62. After refusing the delivery, Mike phoned the store again. Ownership had changed hands, and the assistant office manager "didn't know" about honoring the old guarantee. Old guarantee? Eleven days? Mike took the opener off the garage door and returned it anyway. How could they refuse eyeball or eyeball? They did.

"If you'll come back tomorrow when the repairman will be around to see that you haven't damaged the controls when you installed it, we'll see about a replacement," the new owner offered. After they made a second 45-mile trip the following day, the repairman verified that the remote controls never controlled. Their refund was uncheerfully given.

Now you're asking: Had my friends been singled out for this persecution? Believe me, they'd begun to wonder. Was the rest of the world faring any better? Not even their daily newspaper could tell them; the assistant who took the address change by phone argued that their street was nonexistent. Four days and two lengthy direction sessions later, they got a paper at their new address.

So much for the outside world. But could they make contact? Now, Mike and Marsha had always been ones to get mail. But the second week after their move when mail dwindled to "Dear Occupant" circulars, a trip to the old address produced approximately an eight-inch stack of first-class mail.

Yes, various clerks responded, the Post Office did still have the change-of-address notice on file. But frequently a sub was on the route and possibly nobody had told him to forward the mail. The supervisor promised to "take care of it personally." Four months and numerous phone calls later, Mike resorted to removing the mailbox from the pole.

But anticipating such "disruption of service," they had planned early phone installation: One month before M-Day, they called to have telephone service transferred and asked for a cost estimate. A "marketing specialist" promised to call back because their order was quite "complicated." After hearing nothing for two weeks, Marsha phoned again. The representative apologized for the delay and promised to give the order "her personal attention." Marsha asked if the phone rep could give them an assigned number. Which she did, insisting, of course, that the number couldn't be guaranteed until installation. Relying on the "96 percent chance" that the number would work, Mike used the number in a national ad for his consulting business. The next day, the phone rep called back to explain that she'd made a mistake in assigning the number and figuring the charges. So much for an ad that reached the public.

Four weeks later, the installer phoned. He wanted to know where Marsha was. The installer was at the new residence to hook up the phone and the house was empty. Marsha told him about the reschedule due to Mortgage Company X's shenanigans, giving him name, date and hour of rescheduling. The installer had never gotten the word, he insisted. According to his assessment of the situation, "Somebody" fouled up. Marsha rescheduled installation for a week later.

Marsha waited in the new, cold, empty house for the installer to arrive between 8 A.M. and 5 P.M. At 4:55, he showed up. The phone worked, but the answering service would take another five days. Thank goodness for at least one inefficiency; the phone company had failed to put the transfer tape on their old number. We, in the outside world, could still contact them.

Fifty-four days after their original order request, my friends had a working telephone. Rejoicing, they phoned us with the correct new number. But when Mike tried to dial the downtown library, he couldn't. Had the phone company done what he suspected? Yes. The operator verified that they had indeed installed a limited suburban line instead of the metro service Marsha had ordered.

Two days later, the phone bill arrived for one month's service. Since the phone had been working for only 46 hours, Mike called to complain. "Not to worry," the assistant told him. She would adjust the bill and send a corrected copy.

A week later Customer Relations called to ask about "the manner in which their recent order had been handed." Was it worth 15 minutes to tell her? Marsha decided that it was, giving the Customer Relations rep names and dates. "This is my job," she gushed, "to catch problems like this. I'm going to give this to my supervisor for his personal attention and he'll get back to you immediately."

A disruption-of-service notice arrived. Marsha phoned to say that she had never received a corrected bill. "We'll make a note not to disconnect, then," the representative promised, "so don't worry." They did.

Two days later, the phone wasn't working; their line was crossed with another number. The phone company corrected that problem 12 days later.

And no one ever called back from Customer Relations. . . .

You're smiling. No, I take that back. Some of you are crying. It's all too familiar, isn't it? The frustration of getting products that don't work, . . . of getting poor service, . . . of telling people who don't listen, . . . of telling companies that don't care.

And in most cases, the *problem* is not the problem. It's one's *attitude* about the problem. Well, whatever it takes to make the customer happy, our attitude at (company) is going to be to get it done.

We don't want to be one of those companies Mike and Marsha dealt with. We've got to learn from the mistakes of others—we can't stay in business long enough to make them all ourselves.

We're *not* going to be one of those companies that think selling is enough.

Starting today, (date), I want to go on record with my number-one priority: customer service.

We don't want a customer to walk out of here mumbling: "This isn't really the color I wanted." Or: "This really will be difficult to use." Or: "I wonder if that sales rep's going to be here if I have to return this thing." Or: "I paid enough for this (product); you'd think they could at least help me get it to the car." Or: "The salesperson didn't have the foggiest idea how this works."

Never do we want to hear our customers mumble something like that. Or even *think* it.

So how can we achieve that goal? I can't. Oh, I'll do my part by setting policy that supports you all the way. But the key to our success will be you. Each of you individually.

In the moving fiasco of my friends, any one employee who cared could have turned the tide.

What if the loan officer had gotten around to putting the interest rate in writing, as she'd promised? Or had bothered to phone to say that the house closing had been canceled?

What if the draper designer had taken correct measurements?

What if the rep in Package Pickup hadn't banged the brass headboard around?

What if the inspector had noticed the fireplace screen was missing screws?

What if the new manager where they bought the garage door opener had gladly offered a refund without Mike having to make two trips across town to prove his point?

What if the newspaper rep who handled new subscribers had asked for directions?

What if the mail carrier had cared enough to check out a situation where mail remained in a residence box for four months?

What if the telephone installer had double-checked his installation orders and given the customer a clue about when he would arrive?

What if the customer service supervisor had cared enough to follow up when the rep discovered Mike and Marsha's phone horror stories?

What if . . .?

What if . . .?

What if businesses saw themselves as the candidate and saw the customers as the voters? In a real sense, that's the situation. Customers vote with their dollars.

Mike and Marsha shouldn't have had to go through a nightmare to move into their dream house.

Our customers shouldn't have to be hassled to get what they need when they phone us or walk into our place of business.

You are on the front lines. You see fiascoes like Mike and Marsha's waiting to happen. Today, I'm asking you to become the customer's advocate. You, as a (company) employee, practice the golden rule: If you wouldn't want it done for you, don't do it to our customers. Take the initiative; go the second mile. If that means making an extra phone call or two, do it. If that means replacing the product, do it. If that means working overtime, do it.

Customer service is an idea whose time has come. Customer service keeps us in business. Our attitude isn't going to be the problem. Your attitude—those of you who are on the front lines with customer contact—your attitude toward the customer will be our key to success. That's what our market is buying. That's what we're selling.

You know, as John McCaffrey observed, "The mechanics of running a business are really not very complicated when you get down to the essentials. You have to make some stuff and sell it to somebody for more than it cost you. That's about all there is to it, except for a few million details."

Those "few million details" are in your hands.

To Reach Goals

Audience:	basic, civic, or social groups
Message:	You need personal and career goals to become successful.
Tone:	motivational, instructional
Timing:	13–14 minutes

You've heard it said that the road to hell is paved with good intentions. Let me twist that a bit: The road to *achievement* is paved with good intentions. We call them goals.

If you don't know where you're going, any road will get you there. So it's not enough just to "start out" in your career; you have to know where *you're* going personally and where *we're* going as a company.

"There's no point in carrying the ball until you learn where the goal is." At (company), we tell new hires right from the beginning that they have to let their managers know what their career aspirations are. Do they want to get into management? Do they want to stay in a technical field? Do they want to be a specialist? Or do they want to be a generalist? We have to know where their goal line is—and they have to know ours—so that we know who to give the ball to and when.

But then talk is cheap. Everybody talks about goal-setting. We have corporate mission statements and objectives. Department goals. Sales quotas. But really what's their value? An old proverb from India sums it up like this: "No one was ever lost on a straight road." And you'll have to admit it, some companies have gotten lost in the global race for quality products.

Something like 90 percent of all products launched in the U.S. are failures. Our success rate at (company) is (number) percent—better than the average. And we're always looking for ways to improve those odds.

So why don't *people* set goals as methodically and frequently as corporations? Fear. Not having goals covers up for failure. We don't have to face failure if we have no yardstick. If we don't do much, nobody—including ourselves—knows. People without goals drift.

The most important thing about a goal is to have one. Goals focus our attention.

I like the story about the old man who was trying to lead a contrary donkey down the road. A passer-by stopped him and commented on the way the donkey was behaving. "Oh, I can make him do anything I want him to with just a kind word," the owner said.

"Doesn't look like it to me," the other sneered.

"Sure, I can," the owner said. Whereupon he climbed off the donkey, picked up a two-by-four beside the road, and clobbered the animal on the head, then explained to the onlooker. "I simply have to get his attention first."

Goals get our attention. Losers stay busy doing things. Winners concentrate on planning before they ever make a move. For people who don't give attention to long-term goals, the future is any time after tomorrow. But the future has a habit of suddenly becoming the present. And some 40-, 50-, and 60-year-olds are still asking themselves what they want to be when they grow up. To repeat: Goals make us focus.

So what are the characteristics of good goals?

Well, first, good goals are set by decision, not default. You have to set the long-term goal early on in any project. Have you ever started out for a Sunday afternoon drive with a friend without a particular destination in mind? And after a mile or two the conversation began to go like this:

"Where do you want to go?"

"I don't know—where do you want to go?"

"How about to Tony's for dinner?"

"Well, we already passed that highway."

"Okay, how about a game of golf?"

"The best golf course is all the way across town."

"Well, then how about a movie?"

"Hmmm. It's 2:45—everything's already started now."

I can tell by the nods, you've had some of those Sunday afternoons. John R. Noe, in his book *Peak Performance Principles for High Achievers,* sums up the experience like this: "By the time we are ready to make the big decisions, the options have been narrowed by our little choices along the way. If we do not focus our goals, our lives will be controlled by haphazard decisions."

You've heard it said that not deciding . . . is deciding. In goal-setting, the same is true. Late goal-setting is not really goal-setting—it's recapping after the fact.

The second characteristic of a good goal is that it's a big goal—one worthy of your efforts. Someone has said that if you intend to succeed beyond your wildest expectations, you have to have some wild expectations. A few people wake up every day to go out and slay dragons. Most are satisfied to chase lizards.

If you're an "average" performer, don't set your sights on "above average." Look at "excellent." Whatever the average, look at what your colleagues would term as "reasonable" goal and then double it. That would be worth working for. That would be worth achieving. Consciously or unconsciously, you always get what you expect. So the secret to success, it seems to me, is to raise your expectations, to set goals worthy of your effort.

And don't let fear that you won't reach big goals keep you from setting them. Here's what author and management consultant Peter Drucker has to say about that fear:

> Objectives are not fate; they're direction. They are not commands; they are commitments. They do not determine the future; they are means to mobilize the resources and energies of the business for making of the future.

Oliver Wendell Holmes agreed: "The greatest thing in this world is not so much where we are, but in what direction we are moving." Unless you set big, worthwhile goals, you'll never move beyond your current abilities.

The third characteristic of a good goal is that it has a completion date. Goals are dreams with deadlines. Always put a deadline on your goals, because deadlines wake you from your dreams to bring you to the reality of achieving them. Sleepwalkers don't get around very well—at least not without a lot of bumps on the shins.

When talking to the authors of the bestseller *Thriving on Chaos,* Fred Brooks, a System 360 Chief Designer at IBM, had this to say about the lack of setting corporate goals: "How does a project get to be a year behind schedule? . . . One day at a time."

Set five-year goals. Ten-year goals. Six-month goals. Without deadlines for their achievements, goals are simply "pie-in-the-sky" plans.

A fourth characteristic of good goals is that they are followed up by a plan of action. The how. Will Rogers quipped, "Even if you're on the right track, you'll get run over if you just sit there." You've got to put the how-to to the goal. If you plan to switch careers, what new training will you need? Where can you get it? What college or corporate course?

If you plan to raise funds for a civic memorial, how? Which contributors do you want to reach—individuals or corporations? Do you want to use a direct-mail campaign or a fund-raising dinner? Or both? Goals are not good without plans of action to bring them into reality.

Successful companies have elaborate plans. You wouldn't dare to go to work for them if they didn't. "Buy low, sell high. Collect early, and pay late," says educator and author Dick Levin. Sounds good in theory, but we'd be in trouble if we depended on a paycheck from companies that didn't have a more complete game plan than that. Without plans, the only way businesses run is downhill. The same is true for individuals and organizations such as ours. We need specifics to be successful.

A fifth characteristic of good goals is that they can be broken into specific short-term steps and completion dates. Maximum achievements are the result of minimum steps. A big house is built with one little nail at a time. A suit is sewn one seam at a time. A business is built one employee at a time.

Next, good goals are written goals. Committing them to writing makes them real for you. You can review them. Modify them. Commit their accomplishment to others. They're constant reminders of where you've decided you want to be at what point in your life.

Finally, good goals generate excitement. The late Malcolm Forbes said, "Men who never get carried away should be." Don't be afraid to show your commitment—some might even call it fanaticism—about reaching a goal. If you're kicking and screaming about reaching or not reaching a goal, at least we all know you're alive.

Let me run those by you once again. How to set good goals:

- Set them by decision, not default.
- Set big goals.
- Add a completion date.
- Develop a plan of action.
- Set short-term steps and interim completion dates.
- Write them down.
- Get excited about them.

Norman Vincent Peale may have oversimplified it, but I don't think so. He said, "Plan your work for today and every day, then work your plan."

If you don't start, it's certain you won't arrive.

To Be Ethical

Audience: employees

Message: We want everything you decide to do in this company to be ethical.

Tone: motivational, instructional

Timing: 8–10 minutes, depending on insertion of details on policies

My topic this morning is ethics. Just how far our society has come on business ethics was brought home to me recently in reflecting on this incident about a neighborhood teenager looking for a part-time job. He was asked to take one of those integrity tests before the supermarket would hire him to sack groceries. At dinner he confided to his parents: "I'm kind of worried about that test they had me take today. They had questions like: Have you ever taken drugs? Have you ever cheated in school? Have you ever stolen money from your parents? Have you ever stolen anything from a schoolmate or an employer? When I started answering 'no' to all those questions, I started worrying that they'd think I was lying because I sounded too good to be true."

The student got the job. But where have we gotten to when our teenagers feel uneasy about being too honest to get a job!

Unfortunately, too many businesses grab today's headlines for the wrong reasons—their unethical behavior rather than their new technology. Executive extravagance at the expense of shareholders. . . . Insider trading scandals. . . . Corporate espionage involving trade secrets. . . . Overcharges and kickbacks on contracts. . . . Price-fixing. . . . Illegal disposal of chemicals. . . . Patient infringements. . . . Warranties that aren't.

Of course, these are not typical of *all* businesses—not typical of even the *majority* of businesses. But the point is—they *are* typical.

Allen I. Young, general counsel at Price Waterhouse, points out in their *Price Waterhouse Review* the fraud and dangers in what is termed "cute accounting" or "loopholing." If caught, the people who lie in these ways can always point out a chapter and verse in accounting literature that, they claim, led them to such erroneous thinking. Their rationalizations, however, rarely wash with the IRS because they know they are following only the letter of the law rather than the substance.

Why do we have to pass policies and establish procedures on ethics? Isn't just plain old-fashioned honesty in vogue any more? It hasn't been for quite some time. According to Winston Churchill, "A lie can run around the world before the truth can get its boots on."

But besides an inner code of morality, there's a bottom-line reason for our interest in ethics. In the experience of most CEOs—or at least among those who voice their experience to others—unethical behavior sparks a failure mode that runs throughout the entire company. All the way to the bottom line, given enough time.

The Greek poet Sophocles admonished: "Rather fail with honor than succeed by fraud." And the Greek sage Chilon put it like this: "Prefer loss to a dishonest gain; the one brings pain at the moment, the other for all time."

So there are two overriding reasons for our concern with ethics: A basic moral code that we value and subscribe to. And a common-sense law of business—credibility with our customers and long-term profitability.

This morning, I want to highlight some of the key areas where we have concerns:

[Insert details about specific policies and procedures that have ethical implications.]

Speaking of ethics in general, C. J. Silas, CEO of Phillips Petroleum, says, "Improving our corporate credibility is something that merits a strong effort. It will take substantive, structural work—not just a quick paint job."

Summary Points

- Express confidence. Do not appear dour or defeated.
- Always acknowledge the audience for achievements to date.
- Focus on *one* objective.
- Be direct about what you expect. Set benchmarks.
- Lay out a precise pathway. Give your audience an idea of what is expected of them and *how* they can get there.
- Remember the phrase, *we're all in this together.* . . .

SECTION THREE

INTERPERSONAL COMMUNICATIONS

INTRODUCTION—IT'S NOT ALL TALK!
INTERPERSONAL COMMUNICATIONS

What's a chapter about interpersonal relations doing in a book about communications? What would it not be doing in such a book? That's the better question. While you can take the word "communications" to mean the act of writing or speaking, communications is much more complex. When you get right down to it, virtually "everything" communicates.

Think about it. What does the suit that you put on this morning say about you? If you're dressed well and make a sharp appearance, it says you respect your work, and fit in with firm. What about how you greeted those above you? Do you show the level of respect someone in a position of power deserves? What about talking to colleagues? Are you distant, or do you foster a general feeling of camaraderie needed work together effectively? Do you hold back at staff meetings because you're afraid to express your ideas, even though you know you're creative? Do you project a positive attitude toward the boss, or are you more likely to seem distracted and negative? Do you let other people finish their thoughts before speaking, or are you quick to interrupt? All of this "communicates."

It doesn't take a written memo to demonstrate a lack of rapport with the regional sales department in front of your boss. You don't need to give a speech to show that you're a team player. There are a variety of ways to express any number of thoughts using both verbal and nonverbal language that telegraph feelings, emotions, and desires. And since people are often quite good at "reading between the lines," you must be particularly attentive to yourself as an entire package of "communications" or "signals"—not just what you write down, or present formally, but what you say or do in those moments when you're not "on stage."

This section will provide you with excellent insights and tips to help you improve the more nonformal types of communications you engage in everyday. It will help give you an edge in business, with the boss, colleagues, supplies, contractors, or with whomever you may work.

Can you afford not to improve in these areas? While it is true that good memo writing skills will ultimately reflect well on you, and the ability to deliver a great speech or presentation will likely very much advance your career. If you are not able to survive in an office environment, you'll not likely last long enough to demonstrate those skills. Remember, businesses are social organizations. Not "social" in the sense of "free-time" or "leisure," but social in the sense of being comprised of individuals who must interact with one another cooperatively toward a common goal. Whether that goal is increased profits, larger markets share or greater dividends, the bottom line for every company is that all employees—from the highest to the bottom—must strive to work as harmoniously as possible, not just for the sake of creating a pleasant work environment, but for the sake of increasing the odds that these business goals will ultimately be achieved.

If you've been wondering how you can impress the boss, ask him or her for a raise, work with difficult colleagues, handle criticism constructively, or any number of day-to-day issues that often are the most important communications that go on in an office, this section will unquestionably be useful to your career.

CHAPTER 8

MANAGING YOUR RELATIONSHIP WITH YOUR BOSS

Whether you love your boss and can't imagine working for anyone else, or you simply don't get along with the person, your boss is perhaps the most important person in your life outside of family and friends. Think about it. Without him or her, you would not be able to have the current lifestyle you enjoy, you would not have your current income, you would not be able to define yourself by your career. The bottom line is that you just might be out of a job if it weren't for your boss. Again, can you think of anyone more important to you outside of friends and family? Not likely.

Yet, how much investment have you made in improving and maintaining a positive relationship with your employer? Have you really sat down and thought about it? Have you honestly assessed where you stand vis-à-vis your boss, where you should be, and how you plan to get there? If you haven't, this may be a critical chapter for you. Excerpted from Muriel Soloman's *What Do I Say When . . . A Guidebook for Getting Your Way with People on the Job,* this chapter features a self-diagnostic quiz you can take to assess where you are today, and four excellent strategies to help map a course to where you want to be tomorrow.

As with many other forms of communications, style often counts as much as substance. It's not always what you say, but *how you say it* that makes the biggest impact. This is especially true in interpersonal communications where nonwritten and nonverbal cues often play a tremendous role in creating the image your boss has of you as an employer. Once you've completed the insightful quiz at the beginning of this chapter—remember, be honest, or you'll only be cheating yourself—pay careful attention to the practical tips she offers. They provide real-world advice to anyone eager to impress their boss with enthusiasm, professionalism, and verve.

FOUR STRATEGIES THAT FAVORABLY SHAPE THE BOSS'S PERCEPTION OF YOU

Quiz: Are You Impressing the Boss?

Fill in your own report card. No one else will see this, so be perfectly honest in grading yourself on how well you're coming across to impress the boss. "A" means you're doing great; "B" is okay, but could be better, "C" says you want to improve in that particular area.

	A	B	C
1. You communicate major skills top executives look for—seeing the broad picture, making quick decisions, and getting results.	( )	( )	( )
2. You think of yourself as a product to be sold, a total package to be merchandised.	( )	( )	( )
3. You appear secure and don't resort to extremes to call attention to yourself.	( )	( )	( )
4. You practice speaking by listening to yourself on recorded tapes.	( )	( )	( )
5. You can be forceful without being dogmatic.	( )	( )	( )
6. You avoid quick, jerky moves, sitting on the edge of your chair, and other body language that shouts you are feeling nervous.	( )	( )	( )
7. You speak politely to everyone, having the same manner for the messenger as for the manager.	( )	( )	( )
8. You use office gatherings to make important contacts and you talk there knowing higher-ups are observing you.	( )	( )	( )
9. Your conversation is animated, showing a high degree of energy and physical fitness from following good health habits.	( )	( )	( )
10. You maintain visibility by speaking up at staff meetings on agenda items you've carefully studied.	( )	( )	( )
11. You gain notice by submitting to the company newsletter, joining the speakers bureau, or working on the boss's pet project.	( )	( )	( )

12. You remember to phone or write notes of appreciation
    and congratulations. ( ) ( ) ( )

13. Your frequent smile says you are obviously getting
    satisfaction and pride from your work. ( ) ( ) ( )

14. You propose concrete plans to back up your
    enthusiasm. ( ) ( ) ( )

15. You always appear to be in control of yourself,
    avoiding talk about your personal problems around
    the office. ( ) ( ) ( )

16. You accept the blame without making excuses when
    one of your subordinates goofs up. ( ) ( ) ( )

17. After being blamed for your boss's mistake, you wait
    until the boss is calm and rational to objectively
    discuss alternatives. ( ) ( ) ( )

18. You express excitement and eagerness to accept a new
    assignment or challenge. ( ) ( ) ( )

19. You hear the boss's constructive criticism as a
    compliment, knowing he wants you to improve and
    stay with the company. ( ) ( ) ( )

20. You indicate how your proposals relate to company
    priorities. ( ) ( ) ( )

21. You ask guidance from the one person in the office the
    boss most respects. ( ) ( ) ( )

How to Say What the Boss Wants to Hear

Don't hold your breath waiting to be discovered. When looking at all the employees, all your boss sees is a sea of faces. You have to wave your potential and anchor his attention on you.

Here are four strategies to help your boss see you in a more favorable light.

- Create the illusion of success
- Maintain visibility to the boss
- Present a positive attitude
- Sell your ideas

CREATE THE ILLUSION OF SUCCESS

Part of impressing bosses is smoke and mirrors. What you are is not nearly as important as what they think you are. They draw conclusions from the way you speak, move, and look. If you present the image of confidence and competence and convey a sense of mission—knowing you're meant to do something and committed to getting it done—you show you're willing to pay your dues. You needn't be the smartest one in the office as long as you're viewed as one who grasps the whole picture, makes quick decisions, and gets results.

Improving everyday speech as part of your total package. Some people who work diligently don't advance. They never think of themselves as a product, an entire package to be merchandised, yet their bosses notice things other than their job performance. Everyday speech plays an important part in that perception.

> **TIP:** How you speak is more important than what you say. Pick out a few role models among people the boss admires. Study their speech, notice when they're quiet, figure out why they impress you.

Strategy. Your objective is to express yourself more effectively. Tape record talks with friends to hear for yourself how you're coming across to others, concentrating on areas needing improvement.

Fern is anxious to move up. Her work is excellent, she's well dressed, exuberant, expresses her thoughts well, enunciates clearly, but her everyday talking is holding her back. She has to leave her four-letter words at home even though her colleagues laugh at her dirty jokes at meetings.

What to say. Fern has to slow down, quiet down, and stop monopolizing every discussion. She also has to practice being forceful without being dogmatic by substituting softer language.

Fern: "You make a good pont, but statistics show . . ."

"It seems to me the only logical conclusion is . . ."

After listening to her taped conversations, Fern recorded imaginary conversations, redoing them until she was satisfied with the tone and pace. Within a few months after her transformation, Fern was suddenly "discovered" as a rising star. Marketing yourself means perpetually polishing your skills and seeking better ways to express your thoughts.

Letting body language tell what you're not saying. Your boss will catch clues if you aren't saying what your actions suggest. Your expression, eyes, tone of voice, shrugs, and other gestures are dead giveaways.

> **TIP:** To appear more confident, imitate the way successful people glide smoothly and move decisively. They sit and stand erect and self-assured in contrast with those who slouch and sway.

Strategy. Your objective is to let your body language say you can succeed at whatever you try. Hold your head up, straighten your backbone, and practice acting as though you already are successful.

Jerry makes quick, jerky moves and sits too close to the edge of his chair. He might as well have a sign across his chest reading "I am very nervous."

How to say it. Jerry practiced at home before his mirror until he learned how to sit comfortably and still lean forward a little to show that he's listening carefullyand to make a point. He concentrated on looking at his reflection without glancing away and controlling the hand gestures he hadn't been aware of before.

Sounding animated draws your boss to you. An animated, excited quality works like a magnet to draw your boss to you. Your smile is a magnet because it says you like being there. Your boss believes your exuberance when you declare without a trace of doubt in your voice, "I know I can do it. What a great idea! Let's get going."

> **TIP:** Sounding animated requires a high level of energy. Increase your supply with good nutrition, exercise, relaxation, and by flowing with the tide. Don't squander your energy. Either resolve annoyances or stop steaming about things you can't control.

Strategy. Your objective is to be perceived as enthusiastic about your work. You can get yourself excited and experience more energy by celebrating little "successes."

1. Develop your own system for rewarding yourself after you complete each major segment of your assignment.
2. Conserve your energy and enthusiasm by changing negative reactions into positive words.

Irene was clever but overly cautious, annoying everyone with her wimpy comments ("Although we agreed, I believe we should think about this some more before we implement it.") As a result, she became the target of barbs from colleagues—delivered in front of the boss.

What to say. Irene agreed to reward herself at the end of each segment of her work by devouring a luscious, forbidden brownie with her coffee. I also suggested that she imagine herself protected by a plastic shield from which piercing remarks would bounce off instead of penetrating. She learned not to accept negative comments, but to rebuff them with a smile and a simple

"You may be right."

With much self discipline, Irene managed to restore her confidence and vitality. She displayed her new animation at office gatherings, introducing herself, expanding her contacts, talking enthusiatically about her work. An executive was so impressed with her team spirit that she was offered a promotion.

Maintain Visibility to the Boss

Except in a very small office, your boss won't necessarily know everything you are doing. To impress the boss who doesn't know, get your name or your face in view as much as you can. Be where the boss is reminded of you or your work, however, this approach will backfire if you are blatant or become a pest. Use finesse.

Getting noticed by speaking at meetings. Rather than complaining about boring meetings and wishing your boss were a better planner, help the boss while setting the stage for winning attention by asking politely:

"Boss, do you think we could have an agenda for our staff meetings, distributed the day before, so that we'd be better prepared to discuss the issues?"

Now you can do your homework and take a more active role in the discussion. Most people will *not* do much advance studying. If you do, you stand out. By reviewing issues and formulating questions that put problems in better focus, you signal invaluable leadership that your boss will surely hear.

Getting noticed by volunteering. Ideally, volunteering combines satisfying your desire to serve with receiving some benefit in your work. For instance, chairing a charity fund-raiser and getting the committee to identify you with your firm when they publicize the event. A boss is usually impressed to learn that you're promoting the company's image.

> **TIP:** Realistically, you have limited time for extracurricular activities in the office. Select carefully, looking first at whatever project the *boss* thinks is important.

Strategy. Your objective is get the boss's favorable attention while you're doing some good for someone else.

1. Volunteer for the boss's pet project. Create an opportunity for higher-ups to notice your organizational and motivational skills.

2. Volunteer for projects that let you learn a skill or meet new people, such as coordinating the office picnic, blood drive, or United Way sign-up.

Merle completed her agency's speakers bureau training which helped her personal development and put her inn a position to make friends for her agency all over the community. Her question was: How could she make sure the boss heard about her volunteer activities?

What to say. I told Merle to fold this information into casual remarks gently.

Merle: "Boss, when I was speaking yesterday to the chamber of commerce, they appeared very excited about our new project. They asked me to find out from you if . . ."

The boss was intrigued with Merle's initiative. Volunteering also may provide you with an opportunity to send thank you notes to co-workers who help you. They receive these so infrequently, you'll automatically be spoken about kindly— little tidbits that get back to the boss.

Getting noticed by talking through company channels. Assess company channels open to your self-expression. For example, watch for a photo opportunity about your unit's work for the company newsletter or annual journal and suggest a succinct quote or call to suggest a potential news story.

> **TIP:** So few employees bother to take advantage of existing channels, you'll probably find our offer, contribution, or statement very well received.

Strategy. Your objective is to become more aware of existing channels that can help you win approving nods from your boss.

1. Send carefully calculated comments to the letters-to-the-editor column of the company bulletin, newsletter, or magazine.

2. Offer to coordinate the program at an official company conference or after-hours function.

3. Join influential committees and offer to draft reports.

Kerry submitted a one-page article to the company monthly, offering suggested changes to cope with a personnel problem. He hit on certain aspects of the retirement plan that were bothering many other employees. This resulted in a task force being forumulated which let to change in the regulations. Even though his article was unsolicited, it was controversial with company-wide interest, a combination newsletter editors look for.

More important to Kerry was the boss's reaction. Vi, his director, came up to him soon after publication and said:

Vi: I've got to keep my eye on you, Kerry. You have some really good ideas."

Getting noticed by promoting yourself.   You can also create new opportunities. If you had an experience that could help others, contribute your findings to professional or trade journals. Your boss reads them. If you're an expert on some subject, speak before community groups. Accept an office in a community organization. Your boss will hear about you.

TIP: Your objective is to blow your own horn with subtle, inoffensive, muffled toots. Hide your boasting beneath compliments you pay others. ("You know Hope is terrific. She could have taken all the credit for that cost-saving idea, but she shared it with me.") When attending out of office lunches, meetings, seminars, and conferences circulate, "work the room," and expand your external support network.

Strategy

1. Broaden your contacts and exchange information. You may meet people who'll put in a good word to your boss or make you an offer.

2. Publicize your professional accomplishments.

3. Be a good loser—utilize a rejection as an opportunity.

Carla was feeling down because Warren, her boss, refused the proposal she submitted. I told her being a good loser this time may help her get what she wants next time.

What to say.   I suggested an upbeat comment.

Carla: "Warren, I very much appreciate your considering the downtown proposal. I understand why it isn't timely, and you've helped me focus on our current priorities. Thanks again."

Warren: "I'm so pleased to hear you say that, Carla. It was evidently a good learning experience for you. Don't be discouraged. Feel free to show me your next idea."

Opportunities for self promotion are everywhere if you're alert to them. A frequently used technique is to convert the spoken compliment into a tangible asset. After someone lavishes praises to you about your fine work wishing there were some way to show appreciation, you say in a very modest tone:

"Well, there is something you could do that could help me. Would you consider dropping a note or calling my boss? As department head, he would surely appreicate knowing you thought your case was handled well. And I certainly would be grateful to you."

Telling you is nice for your ego, telling your boss is good for your career.

Present a Positive Attitude

Having a positive attitude is as important to you in the office as a hammer and nails are to a carpenter. You always have the choice of being happy about your work or being miserable. Often you determine how your day will go. You are able to control many actions that are self-defeating such as staying off the phone for personal calls. You also can control smiling easily and often, and being pleasant to be with.

Stay professional—don't discuss personal problems. No one's interested in every detail of your private life. If baring your soul and your sorrows is all you contribute to conversations, you'll find yourself alone because you make other people feel uncomfortable. It is especially bad to tell your boss more than your boss wants to know.

TIP: Talking openly about personal matters may jeopardize your advancement. It takes too much time away from work, and your boss may figure if you speak so openly about private matters, you probably can't be trusted to keep your mouth closed about company developments.

Strategy. Your objective is to have your boss consider you dependable. Talk as if you are always in control. Don't discuss your personal problems unless you have to be excused for an emergency.

Although Sybil's boss is fond of her, Cecile has grown impatient constantly hearing about Sybil's drawn out divorce battle, chronic allergies, and her son's troubles.

Sybil: "Carl is being totally unreasonable and spiteful. I don't know if we'll ever be able to work out a settlement and . . ."

Cecile: "I know you're upset, Sybil, but we really have to get these reports out."

What to say. Sybil has a definite need to talk out her personal problems, but personal matters should be exchanged between close personal friends or family members. Such discussions are out of place in the work place.

What to say when you are having a really bad day. It's difficult, but it's smart to be congenial even when you'd like to give in to a rotten mood. We all have our troubles.

TIP: Every type of work has its moments of tedium. If you'll get these out of the way first, when you're having a bad day, you can be looking forward to more exciting parts as you proceed.

Strategy. When you have troubles, your objective is to separate yourself from the rest of the world until you're ready to make unemotional, rational decisions. Find a quiet spot to get away for a while.

Willie was having a really bad day. Thee was no door to close so that he could be undisturbed, and he desperately needed a little time and space to bounce back. He didn't want to take out his anger on his colleagues or tell his boss where to put the job.

What to say. Willie asked Dale to take his telephone calls, turned his chair around blocking entry to his desk, and hung a sign on it:

"I need 15 minutes alone and then I can talk to you."

Willie used this time to figure out why he was so upset and what options were open to him.

Taking credit and taking blame. Good or bad, whatever happens in your unit is your responsibility and you are accountable to your boss. You get the credit; you take the blame. You can prevent some mistakes by paying closer attention to alarm bells that go off in your head when, for instance, you start to turn in an assignment and feel something is not quite right. Double-check for accuracy.

> **TIP:** When you make a mistake, or some one under you does, admit this to your boss. Own up immediately before it's perceived as a cover up and even minor blunders are blown out of proportion with dire consequences.

Strategy. Your objective is to correct errors and acknowledge good work within your sphere.

1. When admitting responsibility, recommend ways to keep the error from recurring.

2. Modestly share in the credit for causing something to get done. When reporting accomplishments, mention subordinates who carried them out.

Dean had given Maury instructions that were perfectly clear, but Maury blundered. There was no time to correct the mistake before Dean's boss had to be told. He had to hear it from Dean.

What to say. Dean came right to the point and stuck to the point of this meeting:

Dean: "Boss, I wanted you to be aware of a problem in my unit. Evidently, I didn't make my instructions clear enough and one of my workers didn't . . . It's too late to correct this blunder, but I think we can prevent such a thing from happening again if we were to change the system so that . . . Does that meet with your approval?"

We all love to listen to confessions because we all make mistakes. Most people are quick to forgive if you are genuinely anxious to atone. But you must mean it when you say you're sorry, and you must say it right away.

What to say when it's not your fault. Sometimes it's not anyone's fault. The building was evacuated because of a bomb scare and you didn't finish your work on time. What good is it to dwell on a calamity? When you're a success, you flip. When you flop, mop up the tears and go forward.

Face disappointments realistically. Use boners as building blocks. Decide what you can learn from the experience and let your sense of humor help you bounce back. Stop to muse when you get a bruise. Then brush off and rush off to do it better. Include your evaluation and recommendations with your report. Those involved will listen to the lesson.

What to say when it's your boss's fault. You're invaluable if you can catch ahead of time any mistakes the boss may make. If told to do something that doesn't make sense, restate it in your own words to be sure you understood correctly, politely pointing out your concern.

However, sometimes, the boss needs a scapegoat and you're it. Whatever you say you're in a no-win position, even if you convince him that he caused the error. Keep still. Later, when he's calm and rational, you can discuss the alternatives objectively.

What to say when you can't keep your promise.   When you find you can't keep your promise, make other arrangements and inform the person you are disappointing, especially if that person is your boss. If you can't produce on time, do the responsible act without waiting for a lecture on incompetence.

> "Boss, I found it necessary to make alternative arrangements in order to get the work done that you need by this afternoon. When I saw I was tied up in an unanticipated delay, I called Shirley and asked her to prepare the report you requested. I hope that's OK with you."

Speaking graciously even under pressure.   Another way to present a positive attitude is to show you're anxious to get started on an assignment. Express pleasure in being asked to do something you know will help the company.

TIP: If you think you might snap at your boss when under pressure to produce, remember your job was created to give back-up, make work easier, and make the boss look good.

Strategy.   Your objective is to keep calm when asked to do the impossible. Suggest an alternative or ask your boss to prioritize.

Kirk had planned to do something other than prepare a report that his boss now wanted done right away. Kirk's annoyance was evident.

> **Kirk:**   "Boss, you told me to be at Honker's office this morning to go over the summary. I can't be in two places at the same time."

What to say.   Regardless of his protests, Kirk will eventually do what the boss wants. How much better if the boss sess him as a willing assistant.

> **Kirk:**   "Boss, I'll be glad to. Is it all right if I delay the summary with Honker until I finish the report?"

Look at each directive as something the boss needs. Don't argue, help figure out how to get it done.

Accepting the boss's criticism with appreciation.   When your boss criticizes, listen gratefully without getting defensive. The boss probably wants you to get ahead and is trying to help you.

> **TIP:** Instead of making excuses, try it the boss's way. Your objective is to learn from your mistakes.

Strategy. Release the negative emotions you feel when you make a mistake. Vent your feelings to a good friend, get rid of the anger and disappointment you're holding onto, then examine the situation with your boss.

For two weeks Lee worked to get an account that fell through. He's been walking around with his chin on the ground, snapping at everyone. Colleagues who empathized with him at first are annoyed that he hasn't tried to pull out of his gloom. His boss put the matter in focus.

Charlotte: "If you had taken a different approach, Lee, it might have worked. For example, if you had . . ."

Lee: "Yes, but if I had done that, it would have been just as disastrous because . . ."

What to say. Being argumentative won't help. Accept the criticism.

Lee: "Thanks, Boss, that's certainly another way to look at it."

Be glad your boss cares enough to show you a better way.

SELL YOUR IDEAS

Keep your finger on the company pulse. Use your antennae to spot subjects that are in the air. Think about where the company is probably heading. Analyze recent statements by the CEO so that you can zero in and relate your work to company priorities.

Relating your proposal to company goals. As long as you can tie your idea to stated objectives, go ahead and present it. To have the head honchos see you as an idea person is even more important than having your idea accepted. Just remember that the boss is only interested in achieving the objectives defined for the company.

> **TIP:** You can trigger innovative thoughts. As you read newspapers, magazines, books, and journals, or listen to TV and radio, glean ideas from the media that you can adapt to fit your needs. For instance, you can reword an appeal in a video commercial to enhance your board room presentation. If you borrow directly, credit the source.

"IT'S A SMALL WORLD AFTER ALL"

Perhaps this has happened to you (I hope not). You're at a conference and there is a coffee break between presentations. You strike up a pleasant conversation with someone else and it turns out you know someone in common. Instead of holding your fire, you launch into a description of how terrible this person was to work for. You give details of what this person was like both as a boss and an individual. A few days later, word gets back that that person heard what you said and is deeply offended.

There are quite a few sins in business. This is one of the worst. Former President Ronald Reagan used to joke about the Republican Party's "Eleventh Commandment": "Thou shalt not speak ill of fellow Republicans." Well, it's good advice for business too. The world is much smaller than you think, and the last thing you want to do is speak ill of a boss and have word come back to you that they found out. Not only that, but even if he or she never hears what you said, you are presenting the image of being a person who can't be trusted with confidential information. After all, if you speak so freely about other people in negative terms, what's to stop you from doing the same about your current boss, or your current firm. If you want to create the right impression, hold your fire, swallow your pride and don't speak openly even if egged-on. You'll be a lot better off in the long run.

Strategy.   Your objective is to come up with new ways to meet current needs. Demonstrate the value of your proposal. Document data to back up your estimates. Specify projected benefits to the company.

Mona was in stiff competition to get funds allocated for her proposal. I told her to think as though she were the persons doing the allocating. Why does spending money on her project get them closer to where they want to go? How?

What to say.   Forthright, factually, and unemotionally Mona presented a complete picture including anticipating obstacles.

Mona: "We'll be able to save $10,000 and eliminate 120 work hours while creating good will for the company. I do foresee running into a little difficulty with training, however that can be handled by . . . I've prepared and attached a proposed budget for your consideration."

Stand in the top executives' shoes. Talk their language and give them all the information they need to make an objective decision.

How to submit your plan without an invitation. In companies where departments are invited to submit program improvement requests prior to budget hearings, enterprising employees submit unasked-for proposals whenever they've developed their thoughts.

TIP: Test the water before you dive in. Don't announce prematurely what you're working on. At this point you don't want to be encouraged or discouraged, you're after the facts.

Strategy. Your objective is to sell your idea yourself and not have it interpretated by someone who can't do it justice. You can also team up with someone as knowledgeable and enthusiastic and preferably with more clout.

Oscar was convinced his plan would increase production, improve morale, save time, and cut costs—everything top management could ask for. His complete proposal acknowledged problems as well as benefits. He reasoned how the company would lose out if the idea was not accepted. His boss seemed to like it, but was non-committal.

What to say. I suggested that Oscar explain the plan at the next level instead of having his boss do it.

Oscar: "Boss, I know you will want to talk this over with the executive commitee. Would it be possible for me to be with you when you do?"

Boss: "That's a good idea. You can explain it better than I can and answer their quetsions."

When you can present your plan better, try to do it yourself and avoid the middleman.

Giving more clout to your suggestion. A few additional pointers:

1. *Find the person your boss most respects and listens to*

   "Frank, I'd like to ask your advice about an idea I think could help us with . . ."

2. *Get guidance.* Follow suggestions exactly. Try to make this person your mentor who'll carry the ball. You'll get your credit soon enough.

   "I'm glad you see potential. How do you suggest I proceed?"

3. *Call on those you've helped in the past*. They know they owe you one.

> "Wanda, would you look over this proposal coming up for discussion and let me know if you can support it? Thanks. I really need your support."

Planting the seed in your boss's mind. You plowed the ground and planted the seed of an idea. It often takes three months to grow. Sure enough, three months later, the boss comes in very excited. ("Gee, a great idea popped into my had while I was driving to work . . .")

TIP: It's great if the boss subconsciously adopted your idea as his own. You know your thinking is on target.

Strategy. Your objective is to win approval for something important. Help your office move in a positive direction and you'll eventually get credit for it.

Jody wanted her boss to be receptive to the nucleus of an idea without waiting three months for the idea to germinate.

What to say. Here's a faster approach.

Jody: "Boss, I got this idea from something you said at the meeting . . ."

"As you suggested the other day, Boss, I have a little outline on how we can . . ."

"Boss, as a follow-up to our discussion this morning, it occurred to me that . . ."

Without acknowledging it as your idea, the boss subconsciously knows it is and forms a favorable impression of you.

* * *

To impress your boss, stop being part of the herd and be heard. Sell yourself beyond job performance. Consider your appearance, manner of speech, attitude, energy, and innovations when talking to your boss.

SETTING THE STAGE TO ASK FOR A RAISE

Quiz: Are You Prepared to Ask for an Increase?

Check the alternative you'd be more apt to choose. An interpretation of your choices follows:

1. You want the boss to be aware of all that you're doing,
    (a) but you do nothing for fear you'll appear pushy.
    (b) unrequested, you send him a copy of all but your routine work.
2. You see only two alternatives, both undesirable. You
    (a) weigh them again to choose the less objectionable.
    (b) you re-examine the dilemma and try to expand your options.
3. You and a cohort have had a running feud, and you
    (a) counter her distortions with some mud of your own.
    (b) suggest being civil to each other lest you both get fired.
4. The office grapevine is often a tip-off of what is to come. You
    (a) obviously want no part of office "gossip."
    (b) feed the grapevine information about your work.
5. You would like to get legitimate personal publicity, but all your work products are team efforts. Therefore, you
    (a) cannot get individual credit.
    (b) become expert in one aspect of your field to earn recognition.
6. To impress the boss, you do extra curricular work,
    (a) volunteering for everything the boss mentions.
    (b) limited to the boss's pet projects.
7. Your job title doesn't describe your tasks. You
    (a) accept this, content to constantly explain your role.
    (b) risk anointing yourself with a more descriptive working title.
8. Before asking the boss for a raise, you
    (a) tell how hard you work and why you need the money.
    (b) list your major achievements during the past year.
9. You base how much of a raise you ask for on
    (a) how much you actually need
    (b) your research of your job's national and local pay range.
10. Their counteroffer is much less than you can earn elsewhere. You
    (a) accept it to save yourself the trouble of moving on.
    (b) continue negotiating, not accepting less than a predecided minimum salary.

Interpretation.   If most of your answers are a's, you take the easy way out. Your focus is limited—you don't see beyond the ways in which *you* are affected. Because of this narrow vision, sometimes you fail to appreciate your worth to others and therefore don't try to convince them how good you really are.

If most of your answers are b's, you have an assertive but acceptable manner. You are practical and base your actions on how you and everyone else involved would be affected. You plan tactical ways to advance your career.

How to Lay the Groundwork Before Asking for a Raise

It is not working hard that propels you upward or gets you a raise, but working hard on whatever the boss thinks is important. Reinforce the good impressions you make by spinning a web of support. Others give this to you gladly if you feed in information effectively and if you're a team player who pitches in when needed before you are even asked.

Although you are sure you deserve a raise, before you go rushing into the boss's office, be certain you have laid a solid foundation by

- Attaining a good reputation
- Using office politics
- Meshing your goals with company goals

ATTAINING A GOOD REPUTATION

The boss wants to know that you're consistent and steady. You impress the boss by doing a little more than you have to. Maintain your own professional standards and refuse to turn in sloppy work, either produced by you or your subordinates, because the assumption is that messy work means a messy mind.

Informing the boss that your work is consistently good.   In the entertainment field, you remember that actor's last role; in sports, the player's last game. In business, your boss remembers your last assignment. Frankly, you can't survive on past triumphs. You're only as good as your last effort or, as some wag observed, the difference between a halo and a noose is eleven inches. Therefore, when you do something well, you want to be certain to inform your boss about it.

> **TIP:** When you can't talk to your boss, attach a brief handwritten note to your report. ("I know this is something that interests you—note last paragraph, page 2.") By frequently telling your boss the status of your tasks, you enable your boss to be accountable when asked how things are going in your division. You create a reflex action—the boss associates your name with accomplishment.

Strategy Your objective is to find some way to keep your boss apprised of your good work.

1. Relate your work to the boss's goals.

2. Veil your part beneath a compliment to the effort of your team.

Hilde sends her boss copies of all nonroutine matters, but wanted to know how she could be sure he reads any of it and knows of her nice work.

What to say. In reporting to your boss, there are three words to remember: enthusiasm, modesty, and brevity.

Hilde: "Boss, I know you'll be pleased to hear the meeting went well. We had good teamwork and the association appeared genuinely receptive to the ideas we suggested."

Hilde can paste another gold star on her chart. What she did well reflects well upon the whole company. She can afford to be generous in praising her entire group since she's the one who molded a few individuals into an effective team.

Getting unsolicited commendations. Being able to move quickly and decisively without holding up your peers and meeting your deadlines are among the best ways to get them spouting spontaneous, unsolicited commendations about you to your boss.

> **TIP:** Vital information sent through interoffice mail can get buried in an In Basket. It is better to personally hand deliver your memos or send a dependable messenger.

Strategy. Your objective is to follow the Golden Rule when dealing with colleagues. Be considerate of the time and effort your peers expend and they will show you more consideration. This also will result in nice reports about you getting back to your boss.

At 10:00 A.M. Margie called Sherrie for some attendance figures she needed that afternoon. Sherrie assured her she'd have them before lunch, but then ran into a problem.

What to say.   After promising something for a specific time, call back immediately:

Sherrie: "Margie, getting those figures you want will take longer than I thought. Is 2:00 P.M. too late to get them to you?"

Acting responsibly earns you a good reputation.

Volunteering before you're asked shows you're a team player.   Consider exchanging a little bit of freedom for a little bit of security. Give up a little of your time to get a little better reception. By joining whatever is happening around the office, *gladly* doing more than you have to, you cause the word to spread that you're a member of the club.

STRIKING A BALANCE

A few cynics reading this book may say, "I understand what you're saying. Of course, it's important to present the right image in front of the boss, but aren't you just asking me to be subservient or even obsequious in front of him?" Not at all. Bosses are usually quite good at recognizing people who are trying to "cozy-up" to him or her for the sake of "scoring points" from those who genuinely reflect enthusiasm and energy for the work.

No one likes a teacher's pet. They're almost always shallow and transparent in their desire to impress those above them. They stand out for all the wrong reasons. But if you're like most people, you work hard, you enjoy what you do, and you also want a little acknowledgment from the boss. Unless you know how to "package" yourself, you won't necessarily get what's coming to you. Therefore, it's important to strike a balance between being seen as eager to please and competent and secure in the work you're doing. To paraphrase an old public relations term, "it's just as important to sell the steak as it is the sizzle."

> **TIP:** Consider it an opportunity when you have the chance to help someone. You never know how or when you will be repaid. Helping someone now is one way to pay back people who helped you before. Just don't go overboard and volunteer for everything without finishing your own work or your boss may conclude you lack both organizational skills and the judgment to decide what's important.

Strategy. Your objective is to demonstrate to the boss that you're always available to help the department. Anticipate what's needed and volunteer to do it before the boss requests it.

Shelly has been studying her boss's list of priorities and she doesn't have to be nudged to accept any assignment. Color her reliable. But more than that, she's learned to foresee what her boss wants done—sometimes before Melissa, her boss, does.

What to say. In the following exchange, note how Shelly stepped up and volunteered before she was asked.

Melissa: "Shelly, the top brass are making noises about reducing the operating costs of each department by ten percent. If we're forced to take an across-the-board cut, how will services in your division be affected?"

Shelly: "We're operating pretty close to the bone, but I know how important it is to maintain our current level of services. Why don't I work up a few alternatives for you to consider. I'll have them for you in the morning."

Being a team player also means going beyond what you and your boss need and seeing what might help your colleagues and your department. For instance, prepare and circulate a succinct report on accomplishments or information exchanged at out-of-office meetings and conferences you attend. Also volunteer to report briefly at the next staff meeting.

Using Office Politics

If you want to get ahead, hang this sign on your wall as a constant reminder: "Only Make Friends." You can't afford any enemies. From your clerk to your CEO, treat each person with respect. And treat everyone alike. In *Pygmalion* (adapted as *My Fair Lady*), George Bernard Shaw expressed it like this: "The great secret, Eliza, is not having bad manners or good manners or any other particular sort of manners, but having the same manner for all human souls."

Mending fences before it's too late.   Professionals know that vilifying any-one, even the most obnoxious, is not an option. There are precise and proper ways to deal with incompetence and more effective ways to handle dirty deal-ing. Name calling isn't one of them. Once you get a negative reputation, it will take months of controlling your every action to try to reverse it and you may not succeed.

TIP: You needn't become buddies with a former enemy. You should try to bury the hatchet someplace besides each other's backs. Getting along with colleagues is a vital skill when you're being considered for advancement.

Strategy.   Your objective is to patch up any hard feelings that may exist between you and a colleague. Take the first step, explaining that it is mutually beneficial to become friends again and not risk a bad reputation.

Neva and Wilbur have had an ongoing argument about office procedure. Neva believes Wilbur is out to undercut her at every corner and she may be right. She complained to some of his staff who seemed to sympathize with her plight, but they went right back and reported to Wilbur that Neva was saying nasty things about him.

What to say.   This situation can only fester into full-scale warfare. It's not worth it. I suggested that Neva tie a handkerchief on a ruler, wave her little white flag at the door to Wilbur's office, smile, and ask to discuss it.

> **Neva:**   "Wilbur, how about calling a truce? Let's sit down and talk about our problem."
>
> **Wilbur:**   "OK, Neva, I think this *is* getting out of hand."

Wilbur welcomed the opportunity because, as Neva learned later, he had gone to the boss with the problem. But he miscalculated. Their mutual boss goes berserk when she hears about personal feuds and told Wilbur to straighten it out or he and Neva would both be gone.

How to use gossip for your advantage.   You can't avoid office politics or keep out of it. Just being in the office makes you involved. Others will talk about you because it's the nature of the group to discuss the players. So you might as well give them something positive to pick up from your casual remarks than leaving them to their own conclusions.

> **TIP:** Use the grapevine. Unless you read tea leaves, you never know who says what to whom about you, so be friends with everyone. A promotion doesn't always go to the most qualified, it may go to the most politically adept.

Strategy. Your objective is to manage the information about you that's fed through the grapevine. Casually mention what you want passed along to anyone who might spread the word to your boss.

Oliver's supervisor, who was asked to draft a speech for the boss, turned in Oliver's work as his own. The boss loved it. Now Oliver wants the boss to know that it was he who wrote the speech and that he's capable of pulling together good information quickly. How could he do this without disparaging his supervisor?

What to say. We decided the safest route was through the boss's assistant.

> **Oliver:** "My fingers ache from all that research I did preparing the speech the boss is giving this afternoon. But I know he's going to do a great job. He has such charisma . . ."

The assistant was quick to inform the boss that it was Oliver who had actually written the speech. For the next talk, the boss asked the supervisor to delegate the assignment to Oliver.

Listening and speaking up when needed. Besides feeding information into the grapevine, you have to gently pull information out. While you have your nose to the grindstone, keep your ears to the ground. Listen to what's going on around you and you'll find many opportunities to be helpful or even save the day.

> **TIP:** Do a small favor and win a friend. Be quick to pick up the cue when you hear a colleague needs a helping hand. At that moment a minor problem seems enormous. Come to the rescue. ("I've pulled emergency duty this weekend and it's my wife's birthday. She's going to have a fit!") You offer to exchange weekends. No big sacrifice for you, you've won eternal gratitude.

Strategy. Your objective is to keep alert and quickly sift through all the talk surrounding you. Sort the information you hear into three categories—for immediate use, for later use, and for the disposal.

Kevin heard Joy predicting to anyone who'd listen that a new procedure would prove defective.

Joy: "Just you wait. When they start with that new 30-day requirement, there'll be an epidemic of flu excuses in this office.

What to say. Reading the storm signals, Kevin intervened by offering the boss a positive suggestion.

Kevin: "Boss, to avoid a morale problem, we may need to do a better job of explaining the new 30-day regulation. Why don't we get a small committee to suggest how to do this? Maybe Joy would be a good one to chair it?"

Kevin helped avert a potentially serious problem by listening and speaking up.

Helping your mentor sound better. Mentors are in the position to help you develop your skills, make the right contacts, and generally guide you in your upward climb. Quite often they want to help simply because they like you. Or it may be their way of reciprocating for assistance they received on the way up.

The best mentor may be your own boss, but caring goes both ways. Anticipate the boss's problems, offer solutions, and double-check your facts. Suggest ideas that make the boss look and sound better. Then you feel at ease asking the boss for advice and guidance.

Sharing resources and solutions with your personal network. While networking often applies outside your office where members attend professional or trade meetings to share solutions for the same kinds of problems, there is also networking, both formal and unorganized within your office. It boils down to being a friend and, in return, having a friend, and showing sincere interest and pleasure when your friend succeeds. Then your colleagues will trust you and listen to what you say. Don't keep your career ambitions a secret from them if there is any way they can assist you. Seek their advice. Those who are in a position to do so will put in the right word where it counts.

> **TIP:** Keep a contact file. Get a small alphabetical index card file to record names, addresses, phone numbers, and comments about contacts you've made or want to develop.

Proclaiming yourself a more fitting title. Drama students have it drummed into their heads that there are no small parts, only small actors. It's the same way with any role in your company. The job grows to the limits of your insight and imagination. Be careful not to upstage anyone and the rest of the crew will be glad to see your part become as big as you can make it. If your job classification is meaningless even to those within your organization, try anointing yourself with a new *working* title.

TIP: Your opportunity may come as a soft tap instead of a loud knock. Grab the chance to do extra work if that lets you learn a new skill you've been wanting to master. Most supervisors are pleased when their subordinates take initiative.

Strategy.   Your objective is to make the most of your job and to see its potential as a stepping stone. Study your operation for better, faster, cheaper, more effective ways to do anything related to your job.

Doug, a program analyst in the Grants Administration Section, decided to call himself "Assistant to the Grants Administrator" because this better described his actual work.

What to say.   When his boss questioned the new title on the correspondence, he explained:

Doug: "Boss, most people don't understand what a program analyst does. I did this to clear up the confusion over how I could be of service to those contacting the office. Is that all right with you?"

Of course he would have backed off if the boss objected. The following year Doug shortened the title to "Assistant Grants Administrator." Even though Doug crowned himself (and this has nothing to do with the salary negotiation other than more accurately describing what he really does) everyone in the company began to think of Doug as having been promoted. When you sense the time is right to take the initiative, act on it.

MESHING YOUR GOALS WITH COMPANY GOALS

Before asking for a raise, link your personal objectives with the specific company needs you can best meet. Listen carefully when your boss talks, observe which projects the boss authorizes expenditures for, or where extra staff and other movable resources are concentrated. If you are going to be paid more by the company, you have to give the company something it particularly wants in the way it wants it. Working painstakingly is not enough to merit a raise unless you are spending your time on the boss's priorities.

Matching the boss's style when presenting your case. Bosses have their own way of handling situations. Study your boss's style so that you can present your case in a manner the boss will accept. Some pick apart every possibility, methodically sorting facts before choosing. Others go for the desired result:

"Spare me the analysis and details. I only want to discuss general strategy."

Some are impatient to get going:

"Look we already know what works. Enough talk. I want action."

Some bosses are synthesizers. They ask few people on the same team to prepare the exact same report, each not knowing the others are doing it. Hearing them out together is not meant to embarrass anyone but to assemble the pieces of each report closest to what the boss is looking for.

Determine your boss's style so that you'll know how much to include or leave out of your talk.

Acknowledging the boss's priorities. Before you prepare your pitch, understand the company's point of view. It really doesn't matter that you can't manage on your present salary, or your daughter needs an operation, or your old car keeps breaking down and you must get some other transportation. The main obligation of the boss, a nice person who'd like to help, is not to you but the company. The only questions from the top are:

1. "Why do you think you're worth more to us than we are now paying you?"
2. "How does investing in you benefit the company?"

Asking for more money can be intimidating. Being rejected is worse. To overcome this fear, you have to be convinced your work is worth more.

If it's been a thorn in your side waiting for the raise you feel should be given you without your even asking for it, your resentment will affect your work. Deal with this by preparing a presentation that tells the boss what the boss needs to know.

Preparing your pitch. Before you ask for a raise, determine what's going on in your company and in your job market, and how much you think your work is worth. Can your company afford the raise? Must requests be in at set times such as three months before final budget? Will your cohorts also be asking for a raise? What is the going pay range or your type of job nationally and locally?

TIP: After gathering national and local data, compile a one-page Pay Rate Chart on your type work. This, together with a crisp report of your Achievement Highlights over the past year, gives you something concrete to discuss with your boss.

Strategy. Your objective is to be persuasive, to sound confident, business-like, and believable.

1. Based on national and local data, decide in advance the minimum salary you'll accept, the minimum amount you feel you're worth and can earn elsewhere.

2. List recent accomplishments—specific ways you helped cut costs, increase sales, and so on.

Ava, an executive assistant, has been at the same job nine years, always getting excellent ratings. She just learned at a national conference that others doing the same kind of work make considerably more money and she's understandably upset. We developed a plan of action:

1. To learn the going pay range for her particular job, she obtained figures from her professional association and from her company's personnel department. She learned the pay scale for jobs similar to hers.

2. To see what's currently available locally, she combed the newspaper want ads and called a few employment agencies.

3. To examine the possibility of carving a new position for herself with a bigger salary, she listed additional duties assumed this year without a raise, analyzing how important these are to her boss.

To speak to her boss with conviction, Ava had to appear assertive. She had to study her options:

- Keep working here if the minimum raise is refused. Will her pride let her work for less?

- Quit if she doesn't get a salary increase. Are there other employers waiting for her in the wings?

- Keep working here if the raise is refused while secretly seeking other employment. Does she depend on uninterrupted income?

What to say. Ava rehearsed her talk with a close colleague, trying to think the way their boss does and trying to anticipate every possible question and response.

Ava: "He'll say, it's company policy to give raises only when . . . and I'll say, but isn't it also company policy to acknowledge . . ."

Friend: "I agree your work is worth another $5,000, however $2,000 is the absolute limit . . ."

Ava: "Since we agree my work is worth another $5,000, surely you'll understand that a $2,000 increase is not sufficient. Why don't we split the difference at $3,500?"

Friend: "If I give you a raise, it'll have a domino effect we can't afford."

Ava: "I know you can't afford across-the-board raises, but don't you want to motivate the special people like me who get you the results you want?

Friend: "Ava, your work is very good, but there's no room now for you to advance."

Ava: "I don't mind waiting a while to advance if we can discuss additional fringe benefits and eliminating weekend work."

Delivering your request for a raise.   Here are a few reminders:

1. *As your boss for a few uninterrupted minutes.* You want to be sure your timing is right.
2. *Talk in a strong voice.* Keep calm, unemotional, no whining or crying. Remember to be pleasant and conversational.
3. *Start with a friendly greeting.* Be brief and get right to the point.

"Boss, I've come here today to talk to you about my raise."

Because you've practiced, you can sound enthusiastic although your heart does flip-flops. It's acceptable to glance at your notes, but keep looking the boss in the eye. Watch the eyes and other types of body language. The boss slowly wiping his eyeglasses, for example, is probably thinking about the point you just made—keep still a moment. Drumming fingers on the table or playing with a key ring indicates impatience—go to the next item.

Extracting valuable lessons from the boss's comments.   Whatever the result of your request, you've alerted the boss that you want to move up and you will be watched more closely.

If you got the full raise, congratulations! If you negotiated a compromise you can live with, such as extra benefits, that's great too. If the rejection had nothing to do with you personally ("I'm sorry, you're already at the top step in your classification") then do what you can, such as immediately working on getting reclassified.

If, however, you were turned down without good reason, don't slam the door on the way out. Just walk away without bluffing or threatening to quit and say,

"Thanks for your time." or

"I understand you can't do anything now. I'll think about what you said and get back to you."

TIP: It may definitely be to your advantage to look for another job, but keep that your secret for a while. If you slam the door at this time, how are you going to open it again to ask for a reference in three weeks when you're ready to give notice?

Strategy. Your objective, besides the raise, was to learn as much as you could about where you stand. Note the boss's responses so that you can consider the options when you get back to your desk.

Neelie was disheartened because her boss Jay had just rejected her request for a raise. In his doing so, however, she learned quite a bit of helpful information. The boss disclosed areas in which she should improve.

What to say. Neelie accepted the criticism and restated it in a positive way.

Jay: "You're doing more than your job. You're trying to do someone else's job, too."

Neelie: "I admit I try to be helpful. I'll be back in three months to prove to you I've toned down."

If you understand why the raise could not be given you now, you can concentrate on making an indelible impression for next time. You have incentive to work even harder, with belief in yourself that next time your request will be granted.

* * *

In essence, your getting a raise is not based on your needs or even on the amount of work you do or how well you do it. The decision hinges on your ability to communicate to the decision-maker how valuable you are in helping your company achieve its desired results. If you are perceived as a rising star, others will want to help you.

Summary Points

- Part of impressing your boss is creating the *impression* of success. Success badly communicated will not be seen as success in your boss's eyes.

- View yourself as a total package. You're not just the work you hand-in, you're a person who communicates any number of messages both verbally and nonverbally.
- Always project an image of confidence. If you're confident in yourself, people will be confident in you.
- Know when and how to take credit—and blame as well.
- Avoid getting too personal. It tends to make people uncomfortable and may jeopardize your advancement.
- It's O.K. to promote yourself. It's a mistake to brag, however.

CHAPTER 9

BUILDING A LOYAL WORKFORCE: SIMPLE STEPS

We've covered how to make sure your boss maintains a high impression of you and your work. But what do you do when *you're* the boss? What do you do when *you* are leading the team? What communications skills are required? How do you inspire loyalty and confidence from those down the corporate ladder? As a manager, you will be called upon almost daily to deal with situations requiring you to effectively communicate your intentions to those under you. If you think about it, it may be *the most major challenge of management:* nurturing loyalty among your staff through effective communications.

Just as using verbal and nonverbal skills to impress the boss can help your career, using a different set of verbal and nonverbal skills can help you maintain a loyal team willing to follow you anywhere. Whether you're a natural-born leader, or you've risen to the challenge, there are right and wrong ways to manage your communications with employees. And while it is obvious that people are individuals, and don't always respond to the same signals, there are certain motivators and techniques you can use to lay the right groundwork for a healthy working environment.

Muriel Solomon's *What Do I Say When . . . A Guidebook for Getting Your Way with People on the Job,* excerpted below, offers excellent tips on how to inspire loyalty from your staff, beginning with a diagnostic quiz that should help assess where you are now, and where you should be going. Four key elements are addressed: making yourself accessible; being clear about expectations; giving motivating feedback; and adding a touch of *panache* to your directives. Also, be sure to follow the tips, they're very practical for today's busy manager.

FOUR SURE-FIRE WAYS TO NURTURE LOYALTY FROM YOUR STAFF

Quiz: How Loyal is Your Staff?

Choose the answer to each question that best fits your situation. The interpretation of your choices follows.

1. The emotional climate in your office is
    (a) predictably harmonious
    (b) tightly controlled
    (c) encourages critical comments

2. Before asking your staff for suggestions, you
    (a) say the best suggestions will be considered
    (b) imply the best suggestions will be used
    (c) promise the best situations will be used

3. After your staff has come up with suggestions, you
    (a) promise to take them to your boss—eventually
    (b) request they reduce their ideas to writing
    (c) feel you needn't report your boss's reaction to your staff

4. In giving directions to subordinates, you
    (a) depend on facial expressions and gestures
    (b) spell out what you mean to convey
    (c) ask workers to restate them in their own words

5. When it comes to goals and objectives, you tell your staff
    (a) the company and unit aims
    (b) to develop objectives in line with the company's and unit's objectives
    (c) you'll help them write their objectives

6. To improve job performance, you
    (a) frequently make specific comments
    (b) offer to help after the worker does something wrong
    (c) accept or reject sloppy workmanship depending on the reason

7. When a blunder occurs in your unit, you
    (a) explain it wasn't your fault; you didn't know about it
    (b) shoulder the blame, no matter who was at fault
    (c) promise to catch the culprit

8. When you delegate tasks to subordinates, you
    (a) maintain rigid control to guard against error
    (b) delegate only easy tasks where error is unlikely
    (c) allow them to make mistakes

9. You tell those working under your subordinates

    (a) to go first to their supervisor who'll come to you if necessary

    (b) to go first to their supervisors, then to you

    (c) come directly to you, bypassing their supervisor

10. Your idea of adding a personal touch is to

    (a) use competition, prizes, and special award programs

    (b) send each employee a printed Christmas card

    (c) distribute ten-year service pins

Interpretation

1. Unless workers are free to express, question and disagree, it's your unit, not theirs. Tight control and continuous harmony don't instill loyalty.

2. You mislead if you imply or promise the best suggestions will be used. All you can promise and all they should expect is for the idea to be considered.

3. Their loyalty erodes if you don't keep your promise or report back. Getting ideas in writing sharpens their thinking and reminds you to act.

4. When subordinates feel you truly want them to do well, you build lasting loyalty. The message from (a) is indifference; (b) may be insufficient; (c) meets their needs.

5. Neither (a) or (b) meshes their personal goals with company/unit goals. Helping them produce clear, dated, measurable objectives increases their allegiance.

6. They won't trust you if you're inconsistent or wait to catch them. Give professional, caring feedback immediately, specifying what's wrong and how to improve it.

7. Subordinates feel loyal and respect leaders strong enough to own up to blunders in their unit and smart enough to prevent it from recurring.

8. Both (a) and (b) are stifling. By freeing them to make mistakes and learn through new situations, you show your faith in their capabilities.

9. You, too, must obey the chain of command. If you don't give your assistants this support and respect, why should they be loyal to you?

10. Make work more enjoyable. Managers who show showmanship by utilizing competition usually have devoted followers and productive workers.

How to Inspire Personal Dedication from Your Team

You've tried to develop loyalty to the company because if your workers don't believe in what they're doing, you may as well give up. Instead of selling the company, they won't perform well or will be constantly bickering.

Tell them how their personal goals (security, prestige, achievement, and so on) dovetail with company goals. You give them a sense of accomplishment, explaining that even the most routine job is an important peg in the whole operation. All workers want to feel their being there makes some difference.

At the same time, you want to develop their loyalty to you. By offering to share the planning, problems, and progress, you demonstrate you are there for each other and that your subordinates are important to you. Even if they are a little short on devotion to the department, if they're dedicated to you, their leader, that's a solid motivational footing. Without it, your unit can be unbalanced. And the larger the unit, the louder the crash if the walls come tumbling down.

Try these four ways to plant and nourish personal loyalty.

- Make yourself accessible to complaints
- Be perfectly clear about what you expect from your staff
- Give motivating feedback
- Add fun, flair, and style to your directives

MAKE YOURSELF ACCESSIBLE TO COMPLAINTS

When you're feeling smug because you've heard no complaints, that's the time to worry. It's human nature to gripe. But to bring up a problem, your people have to know you allow respectful disagreement. Show your interest, open your door, and establish set times such as every morning 8:00–9:00 A.M. or Friday afternoons after 2:00 P.M. when you are available for feedback.

Glean important information from hostile comments. For you to succeed, you need your workers to succeed. *Only through them* do you achieve the results you want. Therefore, instead of seeking a win-lose solution, go for a win/win outcome, something everyone can feel good about. You're not worth your salt unless you allow and listen to the peppery comments of hostile workers. What are you afraid of—a little progress? Your objective is to maintain enthusiasm at a high level.

> **TIP:** Remembering to talk to subordinates you promised to get back to shows you care and eliminates resentment. Whether your entries are on huge desk pads or small daily calendars or "Talk to . . . Date . . . Regarding" sheets, have some set procedure for follow-up talks.

Strategy

1. Talk in an open, conciliatory manner to subordinates with whom you're at loggerheads.

2. Design and adhere to a system that keeps everyone informed of latest developments.

Kevin had had several screaming confrontations with Bart, his production chief, and knew he had to try another tactic. Yelling wasn't working.

What to say.   Kevin acknowledged that he needed a direct, nonconfrontational "What's bothering you? Let's talk about it" approach.

Kevin: "Bart, I know you're angry. I truly want to hear what you have to say about the new system. Don't pull any punches."

Bart: "Kevin, your new method is terrible. It's slowing us down far too much. The only way it could work is to alter the . . ."

Kevin: "Thanks, Bart. That idea deserves careful consideration. I will get back to you as soon as I can. By Friday for sure, so keep cool."

The result was a compromise that both agreed was an improvement. More importantly, this established the pattern of a boss willing to hear opposing opinions.

How to respond after a blow up.   Being accessible and open lets you defuse and often solve problems before they escalate. If you don't discuss a problem, your subordinates bottle up their frustrations until they explode. Your *objective* is to help your employees become productive again.

> **TIP:** People who take pride in their work need to get satisfaction by expressing their ideas on how to improve quality and procedures. If denied this opportunity, their hostility grows and you lose out on good ideas.

Strategy

1. Stay calm and let irate workers get it off their chests.

2. Soothe wounded feelings by working with them on the problem.

3. Point out the mutual benefits to your helping them.

Bart wasn't the only contender for the title of discontent employee. Kevin told me he felt like he'd been hit by a tornado when Chris, his assistant, blew his stack.

Chris: "This place stinks. You aren't supposed to use your mind. You use a procedure manual to tell you what to say, when to say it, what to do, and even what to feel. And don't dare feel anything else or the whole company is thrown out of whack. I'm wasting my time on this job."

What to say. This needed a calm and caring response.

Kevin: "Chris, you're obviously at the end of your rope. You know we all appreciate the fine work you do, and if you're tied up in red tape, let's untangle it. "Of course we're here to make money, but it's also vital you feel good about your work. When you're more productive, there's more profit which, in turn, pays for our raises and greater security. We're all going up on the same elevator. Now what can we do to straighten things out?"

Remember, your workers wouldn't get so hot under the collar if they didn't care. Let them know you're playing on the same team.

How to ask your people for their ideas. Periodically, get away from your desk to talk to people in the field for information independent of what your top lieutenants feed you. You'll stop hailing the status quo and start listening to new ideas and better ways to do things.

Your objective is to let your staff know you want to consider their suggestions affecting their work and to create a climate that encourages such contributions. If you don't ask, they won't offer. They may think you'll resent their ideas or that they'll look foolish or uninformed.

TIP: Reinforce your request to hear their ideas. Offer prizes, rewards or recognition for the best suggestions. Invite a different small group of your staff to lunch with you every couple of weeks to fill them in on new happenings affecting the company and to listen to their concerns. This is an excellent way to get good feedback. You may also hold regularly scheduled weekly staff meetings at which you solicit solutions for specific problems.

Strategy. Establish the ground rules.

1. Ask for their succinct, specific ideas in writing. Explain that seeing their ideas on paper sharpens their thoughts and helps them spot potential problems. This also gives you a tangible reminder to take upstairs.

2. Tell them their recommendations are suggestions to be considered and you really want to hear them. They may or may not be accepted, but each one will be carefully reviewed and you'll let them know the result.

3. Promise to alert your boss to any suggestions that encompass other departments, and that you'll be sure to credit the source of the idea.

Eleanor did everything right when she openly asked for her subordinates' ideas and arranged a meeting to discuss them. Her staffers excitedly came up with concrete suggestions. But it backfired because Eleanor dropped the ball. Follow up is as important in responding to employee suggestions as it is with employee problems. Later, Eleanor heard comments like this:

JoAnn: "Eleanor, I believe I was sloughed off. You never told me the reaction of the front office to my idea."

What to say. Eleanor knew it would be more difficult for her to elicit suggestions next time unless she dealt with the situation honestly.

Eleanor: "I'm sorry, JoAnn. It was my fault that I failed to report your good suggestion. To prevent this mistake from recurring, from now on we'll follow a new procedure: (1) . . . (2) . . . (3) . . ."

It's not enough to ask your subordinates for their ideas, you also need to spell out your procedures for considering them.

BE PERFECTLY CLEAR ABOUT WHAT YOU EXPECT FROM YOUR STAFF

As the dramatist Goethe wrote, where we stand isn't as important as the direction in which we're moving. Your workers need to know exactly where *you* are moving—and in which direction you're headed—before they have confidence in the boss they're to follow.

Give precise directions. If your people aren't doing what you've told them to do, take a hard look at the way you're giving directions.

TIP: Say what you mean to convey. Don't depend on facial expressions or gestures that can be misinterpreted or seem to contradict your words.

Now take the following steps:

1. *Spell out the details in writing for the tasks to be accomplished and each person's duties.* Clearly define the goals, responsibilities, lines of authority, manpower, equipment, money, materials, deadlines, and whatever else is required.

2. *State your directions in plain English with each employee.* Level with them about exact deadlines to avoid constant checking. In a tone that denotes authority and understanding, tell them what's involved, why they're equipped to do it, and why you think they'd want to.

> **Candice:** "I want you to handle the Stapleton matter. I know Mrs. Stapleton has been a pain, but you're the best presenter I have and this will give you a chance to develop your research skills."

3. *Invite their questions and then ask them to restate the directions* you've given to make sure they understand.

Spell out measurable performance objectives to build allegiance. This combined verbal/written approach also works well when you want to set performance goals for the staff in your department.

TIP: Agree in advance on what is expected. When the assignment is completed, you need a reference that plainly tells you if the goals were achieved. Your objective is to agree on the *gauge* both you and your subordinate will use to judge how well that subordinate is performing.

Strategy. Plan along with your staff rather than plead with or threaten them.

1. Ask each employee to develop his or her own performance goals to get them involved in the decisions that affect them.

2. Explain how to develop an objective, including dates by which specific tasks will be completed. "By June 1st, I will have produced 75 widgets."

3. Follow up in writing so that both boss and worker have the same written document to refer to if questions arise.

LuAnn was faced with a ten percent increase as part of her company's goal for the coming year. She called her workers into her office, one at a time, to talk about goals and objectives.

SEPARATE THE PERSON FROM THE PROBLEM

There's an entire field of study called "conflict resolution." Maybe you've heard of it. While much of the field examines politics or labor negotiations, there are a number of techniques that are particularly useful to managers. One such technique is the ability to separate the person from the problem. For example, say you have two employees who are constantly at loggerheads. No amount of effort seems to work. Listen closely to *what they say* (i.e.: how they communicate with each other). If the debate gets personal, such as, "You can never trust people like Bob, he lies constantly. No one like him, either." Or, "Look at her, she's always strutting around like that. She's always so incredibly arrogant!"

As a manager, you should see the problem right away. Neither side is really dealing with the problem at hand. They're merely throwing mud at the other person and not even remotely getting close to a solution. Your task is to get the two parties to move beyond the name-calling (or "ad hominem attacks") and really address the core issues. "I'm not interested in getting into personalities, or what you personally think of each other, I'm interested in solving problems," should be your response. "As I see it, what is at issue here is. . . ." and get them to address the core of the dispute. Not until you separate the personalities from the problem will you even come close to resolving the core problem. Even though the combatants may act somewhat irrationally, remember, you gain nothing by playing by their rules. Always stay above the fray. Always keep your cool.

What to say. When Stuart objected to putting his goals in writing, LuAnn explained how to go about setting an objective.

LuAnn: "Don't panic, Stuart. Instead of saying *generally* that you'll improve coverage, be specific. You already know how many contacts you are now making and what percent results in stories. Just figure how many more contacts you'd have to make a month to reach your goal of a ten percent increase. For example, if you now make 50, increase your contacts by ten percent to 55. Then we'll negotiate a reasonable workload."

Stuart begrudgingly complied, but later told LuAnn he really liked having measurable objectives because he always knew where he stood. Stated objectives increase subordinate loyalty.

How to reject poor work by matching it with written goals. You can enforce excellent standards and still be well liked. Besides giving precise directions and helping your subordinates state well-defined objectives, you also have to be direct and sensitive when accepting and rejecting work turned in to you.

> **TIP:** Openly discuss your expectations and return anything that's sub-standard. If you accept sloppy workmanship, you will continue to be given sloppy work.

Strategy. Your objective is to help your employees reach and maintain a high level of performance. Be consistent in your expectation and tactfully refuse to accept any work that is not up to *your* standards.

Jimmy is a boss who wants everyone to like him. Therefore, when work isn't up to par, Jimmy always asks his assistant to correct it instead of sending the work back to the individual. As a result, some of his staff take advantage of his vulnerability. Jimmy also has a habit of apologizing for giving difficult assignments and then finds it hard to order that the work be redone.

What to say. To avoid resentment, Jimmy practiced stating ways to say that he knows the worker wants to do better. For example:

Jimmy: "Ira, I've marked the sections that aren't clear or that need documentation. I'm sure you'll want to correct them."

By being consistent about the quality he deemed acceptable, Jimmy gained new respect from his team. The more you expect, the more you get, especially if what you expect was mutually agreed upon in advance and you remain firm.

GIVE MOTIVATING FEEDBACK

Good feedback is specific, given as soon as possible, and presented in a professional, non-threatening manner. Your *objective* in giving feedback is to assist your subordinates and encourage them to talk about their assignments.

> **TIP:** Tell your subordinates you know you can depend on them to come through. When they feel you're counting on them, they try harder.

Strategy

1. Reassure them you have confidence in their skills.

2. Make it appear easy for them to accomplish the desired improvements.

Russ thought he understood what Mac had told him to do until midway, when he checked his progress. Mac managed to demoralize Russ without giving him a single clue as to how to improve his original effort.

Mac: "Oh, this is bad, Russ. You're going to have to do it again. I thought when I gave you this job, I could count on you to come through for me. I certainly didn't anticipate this kind of mumbo jumbo. I expect a good draft this time next week."

What to say.   Mac had to spell out what he wanted from Russ. I suggested that he offer constructive, specific suggestions.

Mac: "Russ, you've got some good information here, but the purpose of this piece is to motivate. I think it's too heavy. I've marked some paragraphs for us to discuss. How do you feel about switching . . .?"

It's not only important to be specific, it's also vital to have a good *tone* when giving feedback. More than what you say, it's how you say it, if you are going to inspire loyalty.

Correcting mistakes on delegated work.   Mistakes provide the opportunity to grow. The freedom to handle responsibility isn't worth a hoot without the freedom to make mistakes. If you let your subordinates experiment with a better way, as long as it is within the framework of your rules, even if they make mistakes, they'll learn from them. You can't be certain the work you delegate will be error-free, but that's the price of progress.

The art of delegating balances requirements of the task with capabilities of the person chosen to do it, and then backing off. As Teddy Roosevelt advised executives, have enough sense to pick good men to do the job and enough self restraint not to meddle with them while they do it.

TIP: Examine your own delegating pattern if you're feeling overworked. Make sure you aren't hanging on to a task you know you should give up. Sometimes we simply enjoy doing something and refuse to let it go.

Once you delegate, you have to deal with subordinates who make errors that have to be rectified. The *objective* is to resolve the trouble with criticism that instills, not kills, the spirit to try harder. Yell and threaten enough and anyone will tune you out.

Strategy

1. Stress the need for results that have to be achieved instead of emphasizing each detailed step to achieve them.

2. Install controls, such as periodic progress reports, that let you catch major blunders before they occur. Be reasonable—don't hamper your staff, requiring them to get signature approvals at seven different levels of management.

Vince, reluctant to delegate, failed to show confidence in his subordinates. He checked up on their every act and decision and his unasked-for advice was having an adverse "why should I try?" effect. It was only after he recognized their disinterest and half-hearted efforts that he accepted the need to be tactfully helpful.

What to say. Enable your staff to figure some things out for themselves.

Vince: "Hank, I know you can handle this. Here's a folder with the information you'll need. If you run into trouble, let me know. I'll be anxious to read your weekly reports."

By supplying the guidelines, telling when and how to report and then backing off, Vince allowed Hank to learn to anticipate difficulties. Let your subordinates resolve some problems and grow in the process.

How to correct the new worker. Another supervisory headache occurs with new people who come with great rave notices. Although you review procedures with them, nothing turned in is the way you want it or need it. This type of new worker has his or her own system and doesn't bother to check with anyone.

TIP: Observe newcomers closely. Having experience elsewhere won't necessarily produce what you want. They may be experienced—in doing it wrong.

In areas where conforming to your procedures is essential, your *objective* is to make the new worker understand that nothing less is acceptable.

Strategy

1. Be firm, but tactful. Wait until your anger cools before speaking.

2. Emphasize the importance of following rules, and the consequences if they're not followed. Document this talk for possible future action.

3. End on a note of encouragement.

Marcus was happy to welcome Jackie whose good reputation preceded her and carefully explained that they had to have certain appraisal estimates on Tuesday. When Tuesday came, all Jackie gave him was an excuse. Marcus could only take his lumps and apologize to his boss for the embarrassing delay.

What to say.   Marcus was seething but delayed the confrontation until he composed himself.

Marcus: "Jackie, I realize we do things a little differently here. But you knew we were committed to have those estimates this morning. Not being ready puts all our jobs in jeopardy. Study your manual. I'm depending on you not to let this mistake happen again. Show me the excellent work I know you are capable of doing."

While new workers need special understanding and support, they also need a firm hand to learn to do things your way.

How to coach without encroaching.   Ideally, a supervisor/coach gives precise directions, then lets the worker figure out how to accomplish the task. If the worker is stuck, instead of telling, ask questions (How long would you estimate? What would you need in order to . . .?) And then if you have to tell, suggest (Wouldn't it be better if we . . .?)

TIP: Give your subordinates the chance to solve their own problems. Qualified workers who sit on a thorny problem usually rise to the challenge. Your aim is to have your staff work independently. They're not learning if they're leaning on you.

Strategy.   Manage by exception. Give your staff breathing room by telling them:

1. To come to you only with something unusual or a problem they can't solve.

2. To feel free to come to you because resolving a difficult situation is a mutual learning experience.

SET A DATE

If you think that giving deadlines with assignments is being too strict, think again. Employees actually desire this kind of structure. Make sure they understand exactly what is expected of them, and when it is due. Knowing that a project must be handed-in on a specific date helps the employee better structure his or her time, and allows you to plan better. More important, it gives a subordinate the sense of direction he or she needs from the top, a key management attribute.

For some employees, you merely have to brief them orally, and you know the assignment will be done. Others may require more coaching, or written reminders of what is expected. If necessary, draft a memo. Spell out what is needed and when. If the employee doesn't come through, you have solid evidence of what was expected and when it was due.

Remember to keep a careful record of when projects are due. If you don't honor your side of the deal by following up and asking for results, employees may be under the impression that deadlines don't really matter. This sets a bad precedent. Don't let this occur.

Norm admitted he'd lost faith in his department. He revealed to me that his staff members know what's expected, yet he makes calls they were to make and prepares reports they were to write. One day he overheard his assistant Larry comment to the others:

Larry: "The boss believes he's the only one who can do it. Norm can do it better. Norm can do it faster. Norm is so anxious to have something to crow about, he insists on pecking at each job himself."

Norm was hurt, but he saw himself then as his crew saw him. A few had already transferred to another department.

What to say.   Norm agreed to stop intruding on this subordinates' space, but he also had to discourage them from hiding errors.

Norm: "We all make mistakes. When you goof up, we'll review it so we can both do a better job."

Compulsive doing or checking makes a boss a flop at the top. Once Norm stopped henpecking, he had happier workers plus more free time to think about the total operation.

Expressing support instead of going over a worker's head.   Even though you allow your subordinates to tend their own trees, with hands off unless they get stumped, you still must obey the chain of command.

TIP: Aid, don't invade.

Strategy.   Do your job and let your assistants to theirs. Express respect for their competence. They need and deserve your support. Your objective is to assist, not belittle, your assistants.

Marsha is a new division director trying hard to have everything run smoothly. One of her unit heads, Terry, was upset because a project director under Terry's domain had a problem, called Marsha, and Marsha immediately suggested how it should be handled. Terry complained that Marsha wasn't being supportive and loyal to her officers.

Marsha: "But Terry, how can I refuse to help anyone who comes to me?"

Terry: "By referring her back to me. Helping project directors is my job."

What to say.   Even though Terry works under Marsha, Marsha went over Terry's head. The department director saw her error. The next time a project coordinator came to her, she handled the situation differently.

Marsha: "I appreciate your concern, but I think you should start by calling Terry. If there's still a problem, your boss Terry will tell me about it."

Marsha reinforced respect for Terry by placing responsibility where it belonged. And in doing so, she strengthened the loyalty ties.

ADD FUN, FLAIR, AND STYLE TO YOUR DIRECTIVES

Show your showmanship. It's no sin to enjoy work and put life into the daily routine. An exhilarated leader is magnetic. If management doesn't understand the importance of having fun, they may be making everyone lackadaisical.

Set your unit's mood and pace.   Send the message that your baliwick is a pleasant place. As the manager, your style and tone permeate the air.

> **TIP:**   What you say to subordinates speeds up or slows down the pace. Your *objective* is to find a comfortable, but challenging rate that keeps the atmosphere calm and free of constant anxiety.

Strategy.   Guide those who go over or under that rate. Ease up when the group is tired ("Why don't we call it a day?") and let them catch their collective breaths. Control anyone exerting undue pressure.

Cloe is a classic workhorse who's always last to leave and often takes work home. Jill, who supervises her, was concerned that (1) she'll burn out, and (2) she makes everyone tense. To harness Cloe's energy, Jill agreed to enforce her rules.

Jill: "Cloe, everybody leaves by 5:30—no exceptions without my personal authorization."

When Cloe, as usual, was the first to offer help, Jill began gently and politely to turn her down.

Jill: "Thanks a million, Cloe, but I already have the help I need."

Once Cloe was subdued, the office calmed down. It takes only one person pushing too hard to get everyone else on edge, so if you direct a workhorse, tighten the reins. Maintain a challenging, but genial, mood and pace.

Use verbal showmanship to gain involvement.   Showmanship is developing an effective style or flair that generates interest and excitement. It's not so much what you say, but how you say it. It's your way of involving everyone at every level in what's going on.

> **TIP:**   Make it possible for each one to say what he or she thinks by creating a friendly environment. Your objective is to make your subordinates feel that it's "their" company or department, or organization.

Strategy

1. Know when to substitute a human instead of an academic approach or a display for a discourse.

2. Dare to be different by using games or gimmicks to point up problems or help workers identify and pull together.

Carla was contemplating how to assemble her team to perform the boring task of stuffing and sealing envelopes for a special mailing that *had* to get out on time.

What to say. Make it sound enjoyable.

> **Carla:** "You are expected to attend a coffee at 3:00 P.M. that will appeal to your love for loquacity. While sealing envelopes, there's many a quip 'twixt the lick and the lip."

Set up contests to inject enthusiasm, divide work and conquer apathy. When you ask for help, is it always the same few who always volunteer? You can spread extra assignments more evenly with a little system to divide the work and conquer the apathy.

TIP: Try friendly rivalry. It's fun and catching. The task isn't a grind if you make it a game.

Strategy. Use a competitive approach. Define ground rules, prizes, and other incentives promoting extra work as a contest. For the prize to be an incentive, it has to be something the worker doesn't have or isn't likely to get.

What to say. Get them excited.

> "Ok, gang, we're going to divide the unit into three teams. Ed, Gini, and Whitley will be captains. Members of the team that logs the most hours will be given extra leave time, and the person with the highest amount gets a weekend trip . . ."

People often work harder for a small group with which they identify than they will for themselves. When they're working as part of a team, they are often inspired more by loyalty to their group and desire for group success than they are by the prize being offered.

There's no match for enthusiasm to light a fire under your workers, but you're fingered as phony if you don't feel it yourself. Above all, it is your own sincerity and concern for your staff, both as individuals and as members of your team, that ignites the feelings of loyalty you hope they feel for you.

Summary Points

- Make yourself accessible to hear staff complaints.
- Always offer motivating feedback. When they know you're counting on them, they'll try harder.
- Set clear goals and expectations.
- Don't depend on people catching facial expressions or other nonverbal clues for really important directives. Spell it out when you really want to be understood.
- Add a bit of flair, fun, and style to you directives.
- Remember: "Aid, Don't Invade."

CHAPTER 10

WORKING WITH PEERS: PRACTICAL TIPS

There is one more important group within the work world with whom you must often communicate: your co-workers. Co-workers can be like a double-edged sword: they can both help advance your career and they can be your most direct competition. While in previous chapters we spoke about the need to impress your boss, and the need to run a tight, responsive shop for employees, communications with co-workers is by far the trickiest of them all.

One attribute, above all, will help you go very far: be a team player and always appear as one. If there's one lesson you'll learn from the corporate world of today, business is less about individuals and more about teams. Just take a look at some of the major industrial awards being given out these days. They're usually awarded to teams, not individuals. Most software these days is made by teams, integrated, and working together for a common purpose. More and more Nobel Prizes are awarded to teams rather than individuals, for example.

By showing you can work with others, you address several audiences simultaneously: those above you see you have excellent potential and can be trusted, those below you know you take into account the opinions of others, and those on your level will find you a pleasure to work for. Now, how do you do it? There are several techniques that are sure to help you in this area. Andrew Dubrin's *Winning Office Politics* offers a blueprint for how you can make the most of your relationship with co-workers, how you can put out fires fast, use compliments properly, how to avoid being disliked or misunderstood. He also offers some practical advice on how to achieve these goals using real-life examples. To get ahead in today's competitive business world you simply can't afford to alienate or isolate yourself from your co-workers. As the British poet John Dunn said, "No man is an island unto himself." If you want to climb the ladder fast, you better learn how to work with the people around you on your way to the top.

GAINING THE SUPPORT OF CO-WORKERS

Gaining the power edge is best played in a step-by-step, logical sequence. To eventually become powerful and influential in the organization, it is important to first gain favor with peers. Solo artists who neglect to cultivate their peers on the way to power may never get to exercise that power. A study of power in corporate life showed that individual performers received rewards for their immediate accomplishments, but did not always achieve the level of career success they sought. A frequent problem was that they had not developed the kinds of connections necessary to succeed in higher-level jobs. Keep in mind also, that when a company downsizes, co-workers are sometimes asked their opinion about who are the most valuable employees.

What if you want to live a comfortable and secure life, free from the competitive pressures of a higher-level job? Cultivating peers is still important. You may need their support to help you get your job accomplished or you may need them to come to your defense when you are attacked from above. Developing friendships on the job is also important for mundane reasons such as having an office friend take care of your job properly while you are sick at home.

What about the office curmudgeon who wants to be left alone to complete tasks without having to bother others in the office? Such a person still needs to cultivate— or, at least, not totally alienate—co-workers. It is self-defeating to be bad-mouthed by co-workers or recommended as the first person to be axed in cutback times.

Be a Team Player

An essential strategy for cultivating your peers is to function as a team player within your group. Two studies recently conducted indicated that approximately 45 percent of men and women endorsed team play as important for getting work accomplished through others. Although men were perceived as using team play more frequently than women, 43 percent of our respondents thought that both sexes make equal use of teamwork. To become a better team player, certain basic principles should be kept in mind.

BE SUPPORTIVE

A potent way of behaving like a team player is to support other group members: Support can take any form of showing that you believe in and are willing to help others. You can give verbal encouragement for the ideas expressed by others, listen to another person's problems, or help someone with a knotty technical problem. Karen noticed that Frank, one of her office mates, was perched in front of his personal computer. He was rubbing the back of his neck with his left hand, and had a worried frown. Although on her way out to lunch, Karen stopped to say: "Your body language tells me your stuck. I'm not an expert, but I've made about every common mistake possible on a computer. What can I do help?"

Karen's co-worker explained that he was doing something wrong in attempting to rename a file, and that he couldn't concentrate on his work until he figured out what he was doing wrong. Karen calmly showed him that he was using the right command, but he did not specify the right computer drive. Larry's problem was solved, and Karen had developed an ally. The next time she and Larry were in a joint meeting, Larry vociferously endorsed her suggestion for the department expanding its services.

SHARE CREDIT FOR VICTORIES

"We won team, we won," said Frank excitedly to his four lunchmates. The world's largest manufacturer of air conditioners is going to use our new electronic switch in every one of their units. I just got the good news today. Thanks to all of you for giving me so many good suggestions to explain the merits of our switch. I know that the vice-president of marketing will be pleased with our sales department."

It seems as though Frank is reliving the past glory of his basketball-playing days at college. One interpretation is that as he closes a sale he fantasizes that he has thrown the ball through the hoop in the final second of a basketball game. Possibly, but a more parsimonious explanation is in order. Frank is astute enough to recognize the importance of sharing his accomplishments with other people on the team.

When and if Frank should become the boss, the people who shared credit for his success will probably accept him as a manager who cares about the welfare of his subordinates. Equally important, the next time Frank needs help in taking care of a customer, his teammates will offer their cooperation.

MAKE USE OF HUMOR

In order to be seen as a team player, it is sometimes important to overcome the envy of co-workers when you receive a promotion. Humor can help you defuse some of the envy and resentment. Business owner I. C. (Ishwer Chhabildas) Shah did it this way when he worked for a large company and was promoted to product manager. Shah told his potentially envious co-workers that the vice-president for marketing chose him because the product had too many chiefs and not enough Indians. As a kicker, Shah told them that the initials to his name, I. C., meant "Indian Chief."

SHARE INFORMATION AND GIVE OPINIONS

At most of the staff meetings she attends, public relations specialist Tamara makes comments such as "Let me share with you some important information I've picked up on that topic," "I have some scuttlebutt that might be worth something," or "Let me give you my candid, but very personal reaction, to your proposal." Statements and actions like this have helped Tamara to develop her reputation as a good team player in her department. She is also seen as a person to count on when help is needed. Tamara explains why she is so open with and helpful to her co-workers:

> Before entering the public relations field, I was an account representative selling stocks, bonds, and other investments. There were about 15 of us in one large office during a period when most of the individual investors had lost interest in the market. Gradually, we began to guard our potential clients jealously. Management placed a lot of importance on generating new business.
>
> One incident proved to me that I no longer wanted to work in an office where people are only looking out for themselves. A woman walked into our office without a prior appointment, asking to make some investment. Something like that happens very rarely. She was referred to Milt, whose turn it was to get the next "over the transom" inquiry. I thought the woman looked familiar.
>
> As the woman was leaving the office, she stopped by my desk and reminded me that we had been classmates in college. She told me that she had recently inherited some money and decided to invest about $20,000 in blue-chip stocks. I jokingly asked her why she hadn't come over to my desk when she recognized me. She claimed that Milt had told her it's not a good idea to purchase stocks from friends because a friend can't be objective.
>
> I felt pity for Milt, but I guess he needed the commission badly. Milt helped me learn something about myself. I could enjoy working in an atmosphere only where people cooperated with each other.

Touch Base with Co-workers

Brett, an information systems specialist, had an idea that could conceivably reduce the operating cost of his department by about $45,000 per year. According to his logic, his division really didn't need its own computer because the parent company—some 200 miles away—recently had installed a computer powerful enough to handle more work than the parent company needed computerized.

Brett planned to propose that his division sell its own computer and have a hookup installed to the parent company's computer. He realized that if this idea were presented in a department meeting with no prior warning it could create a furor in the department. Perhaps other people in the department (including the boss) would think that such a move would shrink their power as an information systems department.

Brett decided to presell the idea by holding private discussions with every-one above entry-level positions in the department, including the boss. It took Brett six rest-break conversations, ten luncheon conferences, and four after-hours drink sessions to gain acceptance for his idea.

When Brett presented his idea, replete with flip charts and cost figures, everybody at the meeting smiled. They agreed that, in the long run, if Brett's ideas were accepted by top management, the department would be remembered for its contribution to the corporate welfare. If Brett had surprised his co-workers and boss by presenting his ideas in a meeting without forewarning, he might not have received the support he needed. His proposal might have been shot down with a series of distortions and rationalizations. People don't like big surprises in meet-ings when the surprise might affect *them*.

Ask Advice

Asking co-workers their advice about both work and nonwork problems can help you strengthen your relationships with them if done with finesse. However, asking for too much advice result in your being perceived as a pest or an overly dependent person. If you do ask for advice, it is important to share credit for the success of your ideas with your advisors. Seeking advice is an effective relation-ship builder because asking for another person's advice is a compliment. It implies implicitly that you think the other person has good judgment or possesses valid information. Here are several examples of the type of advice seeking that will tend to enhance relationships with co-workers:

- I've noticed that you're a very creative person. What do you think I should do to enhance my creativity?
- What do you think I could do to help me get my work done during normal working hours? I'm tired of bringing home work at night.
- The company has finally agreed to repaint my office. I get a choice of off-white or beige. Which color do you think best fits my personality?

Notice that the first question could be interpreted as a competitive threat to a co-worker. If you become more creative, you might outshine the person whose advice is being asked. The second two questions, however, can be answered hon-estly without giving someone a competitive edge. Below are a few examples of the type of advice-asking to avoid because valid answers to them could place you in an advantageous position, thus worsening your co-worker relationships. (The purpose of office politics, of course, is to obtain an advantageous position. However, co-workers do not want to think that you are gaining advantage directly at their expense.)

- I have never won a suggestion award. In what areas do you think the company is looking for good suggestions?
- What do you think I could do to be regarded as a top performer by the boss?
- What do you think I should do to become more promotable in the eyes of management?

Exchange Favors

Quid pro quo arrangements with others in the workplace are a standard way of getting things accomplished. Our research suggests that one-third of managerial, professional, and sales workers believe that exchanging favors is an effective way of getting work accomplished. At the same time, reciprocity is a good way of cultivating a network of peers. The approach is particularly effective if you do a favor for someone today without asking for something in return. Although your intent may be to cash in your I.O.U. in the future, your act of generosity will not be forgotten.

Jack, a mortgage processing manager in a bank, provides us a healthy and sensible way of exchanging favors. Patti, a sales manager in the mortgage department, and he were chatting in the company cafeteria about Patti's upcoming presentation to management. She explained that she would be trying to sell the executive group on a new program that would pay a commission to mortgage representatives for mortgages they secured for the bank. Commissions were to be paid to representatives as an incentive for encouraging realtors to place home mortgages with the bank.

Patti said that although her plan was straightforward and sensible, she needed to add some pizzazz to her presentation. "Somehow, I've got to convince the executive group that my plan is financially sound. A simple flip-chart presentation with an arrow pointing toward the northeast probably won't do the trick. It's too much of a cliché."

Jack came to Patti's rescue. He volunteered to prepare a computerized spreadsheet analysis what would show management how much additional profit would be generated from different levels of commission. The facts and figures for the analysis could be derived from existing bank records, combined with a little speculation. Jack told Patti he could do the entire spreadsheet analysis at home in one evening, working with his personal computer.

Jack followed through as promised, and the results were indeed impressive. Top management was convinced that Patti had done her homework, and the new commission plan was implemented within six months (a rapid move within a bank). Jack now had bonded his relationship with co-worker, and would certainly receive her support if needed in the future.

Express an Interest in Colleagues' Work, Family, and Hobbies

Almost everyone is self-centered to some extent. This basic fact about human behavior makes expressing an interest in the job activities and personal life of co-workers an effective tactic for building relationships with them. Sales representatives rely heavily on this fact in cultivating relationships with established customers. They routinely ask the customer about his or her hobbies, family members, and work activities. Index files and computer disks of the astute salesperson contain job and personal facts about customers such as major job responsibilities and hobbies.

Here is a sampling of the type of questions to ask co-workers for the purposes of getting them on your side:

- How is your work going? (highly recommended in almost all situations)
- How are things going for you? (works with everyone excluding a completely paranoid personality)
- How did you gain the knowledge necessary for your job?
- How does the company use the output from your department?
- How's your career going?
- How is your newborn doing? (works well even if the infant has a medical problem, providing you ask the question compassionately)
- How well did Crystal do in the county cat show?

A danger in asking questions about other people's work is that some questions may not be perceived as well-intentioned. There is a fine line between honest curiosity and snooping. You must stay alert to this subtle distinction. A payroll specialist once asked an administrative assistant in her department, "What did you do today?" The administrative assistant interpreted the question as intimating that administrative assistants may not have a full day's work to perform.

Store Up a Reservoir of Good Feelings

Writer Jane Michaels correctly observes that people who are courteous, kind, cooperative and cheerful develop allies and friends in the workplace. Storing up a reservoir of good feelings involves practicing basic good manners such as being pleasant and friendly. By the simple act of being nice, you obtain some co-worker support. Every reader of this book probably is aware of this observation, just as they are aware that the oil level in a car should be checked before every trip. Nevertheless, not remembering to use such basic facts can be hazardous to your work relationships and automobile trips.

Storing up a reservoir of good feelings also involves not snooping, spreading malicious gossip, or weaseling out of group presents such as shower or retirement gifts. In addition, it is important to be available to co-workers who want your advice as well as your help in times of crisis.

A solid tactic for storing up a reservoir of good feelings is to be a good listener. It is also the simplest technique of gaining the support of co-workers. One of the biggest impediments to good listening among impatient, success-oriented people, is that they are too eager to react to comments. Have you noticed how Type A people tend to interject comments before the person they are supposed to be listening to has finished his or her sentence?

Becoming an effective listener takes practice. A good way to practice becoming an effective listener is to communicate nothing except for a few nods of approval while your co-workers respond to the questions you ask them about their work and personal life.

Share Gossip

Gossip is now being taken seriously be management scholars. In the past gossip was thought to be province of the small-minded people in the office who had nothing more constructive to do with their idle moments. Careful scrutiny of the subject, however, reveals that gossip serves several important work purposes. Gossip improves morale by adding spice and variety to the job. It may even make some highly repetitive jobs bearable. Gossip is seen as a humanizing factor in an otherwise technological and depersonalized workplace. At the same time it is a deep-well source of team spirit.

Another important purpose of gossip fits directly into its use as a vehicle for building peer relationships. Gossip is considered to be a socializing force because it is a mode of intimate relationship for many workers. It also serves as the lifeblood of personal relationships on the job. If you are able to pass on juicy tidbits of information to co-workers, your stature with them will increase. Nevertheless, if you overdo your role as a course of gossip you will not be trusted; others will fear that you will soon be passing along rumors about them. You also obviously run the danger of being perceived as a "gossip."

DON'T BRAG!

Braggarts almost never fit into successful group environments. Most people really hate to hear people who drone on and on about their accomplishments. This kind of behavior is a one-way ticket to isolation, not to mention reducing your chances of career advancement.

While it's true that people prefer no better topic to speak about than themselves, there are creative ways to let people know what you've done or accomplished without coming across as an attention-craver. For example, say you got a letter-to-the-editor published in a major newspaper, or you won an important sporting event over the weekend. Instead of ceremoniously making a grand announcement, you might come in and say to one colleague, "You're not going to believe this, but they actually published my letter . . ." and be self-effacing. Wait awhile. Don't worry. If your office is like most, word will circulate on its own. Or, "Well, I don't know how it happened, but I got first place in the 10K marathon this Saturday. No one was more surprised than I was." Let them then ask questions about your accomplishment. Odds are, if you approach the subject the right way, they will be truly interested and eager to hear the details. Also, this offers you an excellent opportunity for others to toot their horn a bit. This kind of give-and-take is vital for establishing the right level of rapport with your fellow co-workers.

An important consideration in passing along gossip is not to spread negative information about people unless you know it to be true, and that it will soon be public information. Suppose you heard from a very reliable source that a company executive was soon to be indicted for insider trading. A scandal of this nature always becomes public knowledge, so it would not be a discredit to you to pass along such a rumor. (A common misinterpretation is that rumors deal only with false information.)

In order to impress co-workers with your fund of gossip, you need to cultivate information sources. Usually this means trading information with other people in order to bring about an equitable exchange between passing along versus receiving gossip. If you only collect information, your sources of information will dry up quickly. Such was the case with Arnold.

Arnold, the manager of a planning department, had a staff of three planners working for him. The department was involved with collecting information that had a bearing on the future of the company—activity that did not keep them continuously busy. Periodically, Arnold would ask his staff members questions such as "Okay, what's hot today?" or "What's the scuttlebutt?" Almost never did Arnold reciprocate by furnishing his staff with tidbits that he had collected. One day, Tom, a planner in the department, confronted Arnold. "Arnold why don't you tell *us* something for a change?" said Tom. "You're in a position to receive a lot more inside information that we are."

Arnold persisted in his predilection for one-way communication. Soon, his own department was no longer a source of morsels of information. He then had to cultivate other sources of information in order to gather gossip that he could in turn pass along to co-workers.

In gathering raw material for passing gossip along to co-workers, it is useful to keep in mind what type of gossip is perceived to be the juiciest. Information about job changes, including resignations, firings, demotions, transfers, and special assignments is always in demand. Information about office romances, extramarital affairs, and separations is in even more demands. New areas of high-intensity gossip include rumors about cross-dressing, sex-change operations, sexual threesomes or foursomes, and the contraction of a serious sexually transmitted disease.

Information about mergers and acquisitions, hostile takeovers, and layoffs is also of topical interest, but strictly speaking this information is classified as rumor rather than gossip. Gossip refers more specifically to tidbits about people.

Be Diplomatic

Despite all that has been said about the importance of openness and honesty in building relationships, most people fail to be convinced. Their egos are too tender to accept the raw truth when faced with disapproval of their thoughts or actions. To foster smooth working relationships with peers it is therefore necessary to gloss over disagreement. Diplomacy is still an essential part of governmental and office politics. Translated into action, diplomacy often means finding the right phrase to convey disapproval, disagreement, or discontent. Here are some delicate situations and the diplomatic phrases to handle them.

A co-worker asks, "Did you hear about the affair the boss is having with Jason?"

(You want to say, "Why are you so small minded? The two of them are adults and can do what they want.")

The diplomatic answer: "No, I don't pay attention to details about people's personal lives. But I would certainly be interested in any news you might have about work."

Another worker in the department gets a new hairstyle that makes her look like an adolescent male. She questions, "How do you like my new hairstyle? My hairstylist claims it works wonders for me."

(You want to say, "I hate it. You look just like a nephew of mine whom I detest.")

The diplomatic answer: "I like the clean lines of your new style. But your previous hairstyle did a much better job of emphasizing your femininity."

During a staff meeting, a co-worker suggests that the entire group schedule a weekend retreat to formulate a five-year plan for the department. The boss looks around the room to gauge the reactions of others to the proposal.

(You want to say, "What a stupid idea. Who needs to ruin an entire weekend to do something we could easily accomplish within a workday afternoon?")

The diplomatic response: "I've heard that retreats sometimes work. But would spending that much time on the five-year plan be cost effective? Maybe we could work on the plan during one long meeting. If we don't get the planning accomplished in that time frame, we could then reconsider the retreat."

Put Out Fires Instead of Fighting Them with Fire

Diplomacy is a form of smoothing over potential conflict in order to preserve relationships with another person. Another form of resolving conflict is to find a solution to a conflict with a co-worker rather than retaliating for an unsavory deed. Nancy, a registered nurse, resented Cathy's carelessness about checking supplies. She repeatedly asked Cathy to be more careful, but without success.

Nancy decided to retaliate by not checking the supplies when it was her responsibility. Unfortunately this time the supervisor found out about the checking errors. Both nurses came close to receiving official reprimands on their records. A better approach for Nancy would have been to offer to check supplies for Cathy. In return Cathy might perform a task that Nancy disliked. In this way, Nancy could establish a good working relationship with Cathy. Constantly nagging Cathy to do a better job of checking supplies could only injure their relationship.

Use Appropriate Compliments

An effective way of cultivating your co-workers (or 99 percent of other human beings) is to compliment their work or something with which they are closely identified such as their children or hobbies. Compliments to co-workers are less fraught with misinterpretations of your intent that are compliments to your boss or higher-ups. People of higher-rank may interpret your compliments as politically motivated, so extra sincerity and finesse are required. Three important points about compliments should be kept in mind, as they could make the difference between getting the results you want with compliments versus wasting time with misdirected flattery.

COMPLIMENT CONCRETE ACCOMPLISHMENT

Cora, a real estate broker in a large office learned in a human relations course that it is more effective to compliment a person's actions than a person's traits and characteristics. People generally find it more meaningful for you to point out what a good job they have done than to state what fine people they are. Besides, complimenting a person's characteristics may sometimes make that person feel self-conscious.

Cora found a number of ways to implement this technique in her real estate office. The payoff to Cora is that the other realtors in the office gave her a helping hand when it was needed. One such instance took place when an out-of-town client wanted to be shown a few homes in the $300,000 range. Unfortunately, the day he chose was the very day Cora's daughter was graduating from high school. Despite his envy, a co-worker of Cora's gave the man a tour of the more expensive neighborhoods in town. Here are two of Cora's most effective compliments:

Jack received a handwritten message from Cora stating:

> Congrats, Jack on giving us a lesson on the art of overcoming difficult odds. We all thought it would be impossible to sell a retired couple a home in a suburban neighborhood densely populated with children. Your sales pitch that the young children would give the couple a new interest in life was certainly an ideal display of sales acumen—particularly because it proved to be true.

> Henry, the office handyperson and "gopher," was told in front of the president of the firm, "Hooray for Henry. We're the only real estate firm in the area whose FOR SALE signs didn't blow down during the last storm. And because ours was the only FOR SALE sign standing in the Chestnut Street neighborhood, I received calls from three prospective buyers."

INDIVIDUALIZE YOUR COMPLIMENTS

A powerful way of using compliments is to individualize them rather than using the same compliment for everybody. Your co-workers will perceive you to be insincere if they all hear the same compliment from you. Tony, a high-school teacher, kept a written record of the compliments he had paid to other teachers. He wanted to ensure that he would not be seen as the type of person who dispenses insincere flattery. During a high-school open house, he heard complimentary comments about two other faculty members made by parents.

Rather than accept these compliments at face value, Tony asked the parents for clarification. He asked both parents specifically how the teacher in question was helpful to their children. Armed with specifics, Tony was able to pass on two penetrating compliments. To Fred, he said, "I heard something very positive about you last night at the open house. Mrs. Gonzalez said that because of you her oldest son is no longer afraid of math." To Doris, he said, "I heard something at the open house last night that might be of interest to you. Mrs. Austin said that you are one of the few teachers who has been able to understand the eccentricities of her son. I know her son, and he surely is difficult to understand."

FIND SOMETHING TO COMPLIMENT

Another important point to consider when complimenting co-workers is that some people have few praiseworthy actions. Nevertheless, it is still worthwhile to find *something* to praise about every one of your co-workers. People remember compliments for a long time, and even your least competent co-worker occasionally does something that warrants attention. Marsha, a social worker in a community agency, found a way of complimenting each one of her peers although she had to stretch her imagination at times. Two examples:

> Clyde, a cynical and hostile old-timer, in recent years processed more cases than any other counselor in the unit. He was able to process so many because of the abrupt treatment he gave to most of his clients. His opening statement to most people seeking his help was, "Okay, what are you trying to get from me?" To compliment Clyde, Marsha said, "You certainly seem to do a good job of chasing away the people who have no legitimate need for our help."

> Priscilla, a marriage counselor in the agency, was the opposite of Clyde. She tended to cling on to clients, which resulted in her seeing less than her share of clients. In thinking up an authentic compliment for Priscilla, Marsha said, "Priscilla, could you help me develop skill in making clients depend on me for advice and support? I notice that your clients take their relationship with you very seriously."

Become a Center for Provisions

Political players for small stakes sometimes cultivate peers by providing them with emergency supplies, snacks, and physical remedies. They become distributors of legal substances to co-workers who want to be taken care of by others.

KEEP A LIST

People love it when they remember certain things that are important to them. Birthdays are the most obvious example. If your office manager doesn't already do so, you may want to keep a record of whose birthday falls when and organize an event, or at least a communal birthday card. Although most people would rather forget the fact they're a year older, everyone really appreciates the fact people remembered and went to the trouble.

Keep mental notes of people's interests. If you have trouble remembering small details, write it done somewhere for easy reference. You never know when it will pay-off. Maybe you overheard that a colleague likes professional basketball. Just yesterday at a party, a friend offered you tickets to the play-offs but you couldn't make it. You can make a real ally by hooking the two of them together. Maybe a colleague is looking for someone to do the printing for his division. It just so happens you contract out to the best printer in town who can offer him a discount. Again, you've made an ally who can be useful sometime down the line.

Picture your relationship with co-workers as an ever expanding circle of allies and friends. The larger the circle, the greater the chances advancing. The smaller the circle, the harder you'll find it to get anywhere.

MANIPULATE OFFICE SERVICES AND SUPPLIES

Some people systematically cultivate peers by the very nature of their formal authority to hand out supplies—particularly when funds are limited. To capitalize on such a position, you have to treat people *un*equally. In a system where everybody gets a share of supplies based strictly on need, there is no particular advantage to playing the role of the office supplier. Good-natured Monica, describes how her job as the office supplier has improved her lot:

> I have two jobs in my office. I'm in charge of the word-processing center; I'm also in charge of handing out office supplies. When I want a special favor from a person, I can be very generous with word-processing services and office supplies. If somebody is nice to me, or if I figure I may need help from that person later on, I make sure the word processing gets done promptly.

Manipulating office supplies works even better. The company has a series of requisition forms people have to fill out to obtain supplies such as yellow pads, paper clips, rubber bands, and staples. If I'm trying to be nice to somebody, I might throw in an extra lined pad or whatever. It's not stealing because the supplies are used on company premises. If somebody gives me a hard time, or I'm not interested in that person doing me a favor later on, I pull the strict company policy routine. I might even make a comment that the person is using too many of a particular item in comparison to others in the office. If I want to be mean, I make sure that there is a written justification for every supply request.

Maintain a Goodie Drawer or Desk-Top Dish

Another way to gain favor from co-workers is to supply them with an assortment of candies or other treats. A goodie drawer or desk-top dish might contain items such as gum drops, chocolate candy, sticks of gum, or raisins and nuts. The people you cultivate with this approach tend to be office moochers, but even a moocher may someday be of help to you. Charlie, the keeper of the goodie drawer in his office, illustrates the potential value of such an arrangement:

> Accuse me of going out of my way to please people if you will, but friendships are important to me. I keep fresh candies on my desk and in my drawer. Because of it, people often pay me a visit. It is a small token to pay for making friends. Your friendship may be returned when you need it the most. Like the time my mother phoned me one morning at work to tell me that my cat had just died.

> I was just too upset to work, yet I felt foolish asking the boss I could go home to make funeral arrangements for my cat. I brought my problem to Jane, a woman who had made many a trip to my desk for an afternoon sweet. I explained my problem. Jane was so sympathetic that she offered to have my calls transferred to her desk and to explain to callers that I was tied up on some important project. By the next day, I felt better able to cope with my job despite the loss of my cat. It also made me feel good to know that Jane cared enough about me to help out in a pinch.

Serve as the Office Paramedic

"Rachel, I have a terrible headache. I don't have time now to make a trip to the drug store for some aspirin. Could you help me out?"

"Say, Rachel, I burned my left hand this morning. Like a fool, I tried to catch the coffee percolator when it slipped from my hand. Do you have any soothing ointment in your kit?"

Rachel is neither a physician, nurse, physician's assistant, nor a nurse's aide. She is a friendly billing specialist who keeps one drawer in her desk loaded with first-aid supplies. It is said that the only emergency she cannot properly handle is a snakebite. Rachel is genuine in her desire to serve other people. She glories in the role of office paramedic. But Rachel also has an ulterior motive. She explains it unashamedly:

"Helping other people in the office with their ailments has endeared me to them. I think I have more friends in the office than anyone else. Work would be a lonely place if I didn't have any friends. People have come to count on me, and that's pretty good for a billing specialist. If it weren't for my first-aid station, I think I would be just another clerk in the office."

Being the office paramedic can also pay dividends beyond those sought by Rachel. The paramedic can be a communications hub. He or she can pick up valuable tidbits about new developments in the office. A paramedic in one office learned of a new opening while handing out a headache tablet. She was the first to apply for the position and was selected. The new job represented a $3000 per-year salary increase for the friendly paramedic who could now upgrade the location of her office first-aid station.

Make a Good Showing at the Office Party or Picnic

We have all heard about the importance of acting sober, refined, and professional. The guidelines, however, are slightly different when you are trying to cultivate co-workers. Your emphasis should be on doing and saying things that will help form a bond between you and others at your level.

A starting point is to set political goals. Think in advance about which people you want to cultivate. Don't neglect the opportunity to compliment a co-worker's home or possessions, or comment on his or her charming spouse or "significant other." Complimenting a person's spouse or a special friend, however, must be done softly to avoid arousing threats of envy. Roxanne, for example, alienated a co-worker by mentioning at a picnic, "Your boyfriend is so cute. Let me know when you grow tired of each other."

Avoid talking shop excessively. Because work is a shared experience for those at the party or picnic, there is a natural tendency for many people to talk about happenings in the office, factory, or store. Talking shop at office parties and picnics may make you appear shallow and narrowminded. Instead, build your image by discussing sports, hobbies, current events, or other areas of shared interest. Prior to leaving for the party or picnic, invest twenty minutes reading the newspaper or receiving news from television or radio. You can then bring up tidbits of news that are relevant to the situation, thus appearing well-informed.

One of the most important informal rules for conducting yourself at the office party or picnic is to look like you're having fun. Move about the party or picnic area rather than standing or sitting in one place. Chat with many people and smile frequently. Being the "life of the party" is a tired cliché, but appearing relaxed and happy is a good way of building relationships with your office mates. If you dread parties and picnics, practice smiling in the mirror before attending. Also, use relaxation techniques such as consciously inhaling or exhaling periodically, and relaxing your muscles.

At the office picnic, engage in sports in a noncompetitive, friendly way. Even if you are an advanced player in volleyball, softball, or pitching horseshoes, don't offer advice unless asked. Avoid spiking a ball into a co-worker's face just to impress. If you win at an individual sport, win by a very close margin. If you are a neophyte at whatever sport is being played, join in anyway and laugh heartily at your own ineptitude.

Finally, if you are unattached and can arrange it, invite a sexy, charming person to accompany you to the picnic or office party. Even if you have to rent one, bring a beauty queen or hunk to the party and have that person flaunt his or her good looks. Encourage the person to flirt with your co-workers. At a picnic ask the person to wear a tank top or similar shirt that reveals the outline of his or her contours. Such garb is particularly titillating and is not really outrageous enough to suggest promiscuousness.

The downside to the charming-companion technique is that you may engender the envy of co-workers and superiors. Nevertheless, the net effect is likely to be positive. John, a financial analyst, puts it this way: "I had only been with the firm for a few months, when a big holiday bash was scheduled. I had met this truly gorgeous administrative assistant when I was taking my company physical. I phoned Meg (the administrative assistant) and explained who I was, and asked her if she would be willing to be my escort to the company party. She told me that she liked the idea of attending as my escort rather than as a date. Since she already had a regular boyfriend, being my date was out of the question.

"Meg turned in a beautiful performance. She wore a black strapless gown, three-inch heels, and a string of pearls. Co-workers were coming over to talk to us like crazy. During the next week in the office, four people, including one of the gals, complimented me on my good taste.

"And the story has a very happy ending. Meg and her boyfriend broke up in early February. She called me to tell me she was now available. We have been seeing each other regularly ever since."

Improve Their Social Life

Under the right circumstances, improving the social life of one of your office mates is an effective way of cultivating that person. The "right circumstances" means that the person you are trying to fix up wants to be fixed up. Otherwise, you probably will create an enemy rather than an ally. A recommended initial gambit is, "I think a friend of mine would be interested in meeting you. Would you be interested in meeting this person?" Doug is a case history of a successful application of this approach to cultivating your co-workers. He describes his winning tactic:

> I'm an attorney in a large law office. A new attorney named Gary joined us as a corporate tax specialist. He was also new to town, and had been divorced for a number of years. The guy seemed so lonely that I befriended him. I realized from my own bachelor days that the last think a single man wants is to spend his evenings having dinner with a married couple. So I got right to the heart of the matter.
>
> I asked Gary if he were interested in meeting unattached women. He said definitely, yes. I then made up a list of all the unattached women I knew—those I would like to date if I had the opportunity. My list contained six names. I turned over this list along with their phone numbers to *him*. Gary was appreciative of my friendly gesture. He became doubly appreciative when the third lead developed into a solid relationship. One payoff was that I felt wonderful having helped out a newcomer to town. Another was that Gary came to my rescue at a meeting of the professional staff. I proposed that the partners give us more options on selecting a retirement plan. Gary was the first to second the motion, concurring with my proposal. After Gary spoke, several others also expressed their agreement.

Being a matchmaker for co-workers may not always be the best way to help them with their social life. Instead, help them develop skill in meeting people for themselves. A widespread method of developing leads for social life is to place an ad in the personal section of the local newspaper. Many unattached people are hesitant to place an ad, so you may have to encourage your lonely co-worker to place an ad. Taking your generosity one step further, you might help your friend compose an appealing ad.

You can develop skill in writing ads yourself by studying the personal ads and looking for good models, including key phrases. For example, a person 50 percent overweight is described as "full bodied," and a "professional" is any employed person who is not an entry-level worker. Study a book about personal ads to gain additional insight into and skill in preparing such an ad.

Sue, a licensed practical nurse, took an aggressive approach to helping a co-worker rebuild her social life through a personal ad. She learned that Becky, another nurse on the floor, was in the process of breaking up with her boyfriend. Without asking Becky's permission, she placed an ad describing Becky (the ads are anonymous). Sue had the responses mailed to her, and brought the most promising ones to Becky as a surprise. Reluctantly, Becky did telephone one of the men who answered the ad. An immediate romance developed, and Sue had created a permanent ally in Becky. Beware, however, that many people would become upset if somebody else placed a personal ad on their behalf.

Avoid Being Despised and Hated

Niccolo Machiavelli noted approximately 490 years ago that a prince should take steps to ensure that he is not despised and hated. Machiavelli believed that so long as you did not deprive other men of their property and women, you would not be despised and hated. In today's work environment, you can be despised and hated for much less. To avoid encouraging their wrath, be careful not to:

1. Use their desk when they are out of the office, and leave the desk strewn with your belongings.
2. Sit on their desks.
3. Try to sell them life insurance, mutual funds, or tax shelters.
4. Win a $2000 suggestion award using an idea you obtained in conversation with one of them.
5. Correct their mistakes in public.
6. Sneeze over their lunches.
7. Ask to borrow money.
8. Borrow money and then do not pay it back.
9. Always have your work completed on time.
10. Smugly mention that you forgot it was payday, so you will pick up your paycheck next week.

Act Like an Innocent Lamb

Being nonpolitical can be a winning political strategy. If you develop the reputation among your co-workers of being an Innocent Lamb, they will trust you and support you when you need support. To develop such a reputation, you will need to avoid all devious political tactics and, in general, appear more interested in the welfare of the firm than in your personal welfare. Steve, an industrial engineer, pulled one of the most clever ploys my research has uncovered. His tactic made an immediate and lasting impression on his boss and co-workers. Steve describes his coup:

> As an industrial engineer, my job is to save the company money. The cost savings I suggest should far exceed my salary and benefits. If I don't provide a good return on investment for my services, I am a liability to the company, not an asset. One assignment I had two years ago was to design a system for decreasing the cost of paperwork in the company. I spent about three months studying the forms we used for internal purposes.

> After completing the study, I made my recommendations to our boss and his boss. They were both impressed by the annualized cost savings of $25,000. It looked as though my proposal had a good chance of being implemented.

> In the meantime, I had shown my report to Sybil, one of the less experienced engineers in the department. She had a particular interest in the flow of paperwork. She told me she liked my report very much. So much so that I sparked her thinking to piggyback on to some of my ideas. Her calculations revealed that her method would save the company about $50,000 per year. Her analysis looked accurate to me.

> I requested an appointment for us to meet with my boss. I said my plan for the redesign of the paperwork flow in our company should be discarded. In its place, I proposed that we use Sybil's ideas which would save the company an *additional* $25,000 per year. My boss said, "Sounds great to me. But don't you realize that Sybil will now get the primary credit for this important system?"

> I told my boss, it isn't important who gets the credit. The important issue is that our department does its very best for the good of the company. He looked at me as a father does when he has just learned that the son has received an outstanding citizenship award. Sybil, too, was smiling. I knew I had set a good relationship for myself with two people whom I thought were well worth cultivating.

Summary Points

- Your primary goal: be a team player.
- Be supportive of colleagues. Show interest in their work and their concerns.
- Always give credit where credit is due. *Never* steal credit unduly.
- Ask advice from colleagues. People value the fact that their opinions count.
- Give out personalized compliments when appropriate.
- Become a center for provisions.

CHAPTER 11

COMMUNICATING SILENTLY: BODY LANGUAGE IS A POWERFUL TOOL

If a picture is worth a thousand words, then a gesture can speak volumes. Have you ever had a conversation with someone who couldn't look you in the eye? It doesn't matter what he *said,* you're not likely to find that person believable. Or what about the person who bites her nails in interviews and starts to shift aimlessly. Is this the kind of person you want on your sales staff? They may have the right credentials, and perhaps even say the right words, but do they have the right stuff? Communications is a lot more than the written or spoken word. *How* we say it, what facial expressions we use, what tone of voice is used, and what gestures accompany our words play a key role in interpreting the visual signals we constantly send.

While you already know it's important to choose your words carefully, it's equally important you understand gestures, how to read them and how to interpret them from others as well. For example, all people have a natural sense of personal space. Various studies have been done showing different cultures have different tolerances for personal space. People today even talk about "ATM space" the polite, socially acceptable distance people should maintain at automated teller machines. If this doesn't sound important, see what happens when you move in too close for someone's comfort. No one likes to feel their personal space has been "violated." You may not have said a word, but gestures alone say a great deal.

In James van Fleet's *Conversational Power: The Key to Success with People,* he offers some excellent tips on how you can establish your own personal "space," project the power of your personality through simple gestures, avoid basic mistakes that place you in a weakened position, and project an image of calm and control that employers want, and employees expect. These are the subtle—and sometimes not-so-subtle—signals you should be sending everyday in the business world.

How to Use Body Language to Project the Power of Your Personality

The Immense Benefits You'll Gain from This Chapter

1. You can project the power of your personality to others by your physical appearance and demeanor. For instance, an erect posture with your head up and chest out shows you have supreme confidence in yourself by your self-assured manner and bearing. As a result, others will have full confidence in you, too.

2. The way you look at person can control a bad situation and get things back to normal quickly without your having to say a single word. I'll give you an example of how to use that power later on in this chapter.

3. You can use body language to discipline your employees and get them to do a better job for you. Your physical presence alone is enough to stimulate people to get to work. To see and be seen is a cliché, but it never fails to get results for the boss.

4. You'll gain the reputation of being a "born leader," when you use body language to project the power of your personality. People will automatically turn to you for assistance and advice.

5. When you know how to read another person's body language, you'll easily learn his secrets. He won't have to tell you what he's thinking; you'll know. This knowledge will give you a distinct advantage over him.

The Powerful Techniques You Can Use to Gain These Benefits

Why Nonverbal Communication Is So Important to Understand

Nonverbal communication is freer from deception than verbal language. We find it easier to lie with words than with our bodies. For instance, have you ever tried to keep your hands still, or keep from biting your lips, or not sighing when you were extremely nervous or worried about something? Impossible, wasn't it? No matter what you said, your body told others what you were really feeling.

When someone is talking to you, you usually look at his face first to see if his expression goes with what is being said. Then you listen to the tone of his voice to see if there is a hidden meaning somewhere. Finally, you actually listen to the spoken words. Even if the spoken words are cynical or sarcastic, you will accept them as a joke if the speaker's face is jovial and happy.

For instance, my children always knew that if I said Robert instead of Bob, Lawrence instead of Larry, Teresa Lynne instead of Teresa in a louder than normal voice, they had done something wrong and a serious conversation was about to take place. You are communicating nonverbally not only when you use gestures, but also when you change the volume or tone of your voice.

If you feel that nonverbal communication is not important to understand, then please consider this: University studies indicate that over 90 percent of the meaning of any message is transmitted nonverbally. That being so, it becomes extremely important to you not only to know how to use body language yourself, but also to be able to read another person's body signals.

How to Look the Part of a Commanding and Powerful Personality

To have the look of power and command so that people will always give way to you on sight, you need not be six feet tall or built like a professional athlete. The way you carry yourself is the key. I have seen tall physically strong men turn and run in battle, while small short ones stayed and fought the enemy with courage. Power comes from within, and is primarily a matter of attitude.

Of course, there are certain physical characteristics you can develop that will help you project the power of your personality: a steady unflinching gaze, a tone of voice that implies complete self-confidence and commands immediate obedience, and above all, a solid presence that lets people know you are exactly where you ought to be.

If you show confidence in yourself and always act as if it were impossible to fail, people will gain strength from your example. Your physical appearance and manner must depict a confidence sometimes even beyond what you might actually feel. By controlling your voice and gestures, you will be able to exert a firm and steadying influence on your colleagues as well as your own employees.

People always have the greatest respect for the leader who remains cool in the midst of trouble. But they have no use whatever for the one who panics at the first sight of something gone wrong.

You can increase people's confidence in you when you view a tough situation with a calm and cool presence of mind. By assuming such a positive attitude, you appear to take the entire burden on your own shoulders. You give your employees the feeling that there is no need to worry and that the problem can be solved.

Your people will have confidence in your strength, courage, and ability to set matters straight. You will be able to project the power of your personality so that they will quickly obey every one of your commands without fail.

How to Use the Steepling Technique to Project Your Power

Smart people who know how to project the power of their personalities often make a steeple with their hands. Watch a group of people during a business meeting. As the boss listens to a subordinate's suggestion, he will often steeple. This shows he is seriously thinking about what the other person is saying. As his thoughts become deeper and more profound, he may steeple in a higher and higher position until the steeple nearly hides his face.

Medical doctors, psychiatrists, and psychologists are all avid steeplers. The implication is that they are deep thinkers and extremely intelligent and important people. Use the steepling technique and people will draw the same conclusions about you. This technique is a powerful adjunct you can use, not only to project your own power, but also to turn off another person's play for power.

How to Create Your Own Space Bubble to Establish Your Turf

In companies and corporations, the general rule of thumb is that the more powerful you become, the larger the area you can call your own. Low-ranked employees may work together in groups in one large room. Their supervisor might have only a glassed-in cubicle from which he can both see and be seen by his subordinates.

A young executive can be blessed with a private, although small, office. As a member of the power elite, even if you're a junior one, you will be entitled to that.

No matter how small your office is, you can expand your own space bubble of power by placing visitors' chairs against the farthest wall as far away as possible from your desk. Another person should never be made to *invade* or *encroach* upon your territory by putting his arms on your desk.

If you have the authority to select the furniture for your office, always pick soft easy chairs or a low sofa for your visitors. When you are sitting in the power position behind your desk, and your visitor is slumped down or sprawled out in an easy chair or low sofa, he is immediately at a disadvantage. It's much easier for you to retain the upper hand psychologically when your visitor is sitting in a weaker position.

How You Can Use Body Gestures to Your Advantage

You already know how to use the steepling technique to project the power of your personality. Another way you can project power is to appear completely relaxed and at ease.

For example, in an interview, the power person is relaxed and at ease in his posture and manner. He can choose to sit, stand, even stroll around while talking to the other person. If a man, he might even straddle a chair or put his feet up on the desk. If a woman, she can place her hands on her hips and spread her feet slightly to project her power.

But the person being interviewed is powerless to do any of these things. He is limited to sitting up straight, usually on the edge of the chair, in a completely motionless position.

You can also project the power of your personality by maintaining a neutral facial expression. At a high-level meeting of business executives, the ranking individual rarely smiles, even when greeted cordially by others. Less powerful people will usually smile throughout the entire meeting.

How to Use Your Eyes to Invade Another Person's Territory

A powerful person is accustomed to staring down another individual as a way of invading his territory. Usually, if the boss stares at an employee, the employee will lower his eyes and only glance up now and then to sneak a quick look at his supervisor.

There's a trick to this staring technique. *Never, never look directly into the other person's eyes.* You can't win if you do that. Instead, pick a spot in the middle of his forehead just above the level of his eyebrows. Keep your eyes glued to that one spot and no one will ever be able to stare you down. Eventually, the other person will have no choice but to lower his gaze.

How Body Language Can Clearly Reveal a Person's Inner Thoughts and Feelings

A person doesn't have to say a word to let you know what he's thinking or how he feels. His hands, eyes, mouth, and body can give away how he really feels inside.

Hands can indicate fear and anxiety in a number of ways: fingers twitching or drumming the knees, clinging hands, palms wet and clammy, hands visibly nervous when holding a cigarette, clenched fists, hands gripping the arms of the chair until the knuckles turn white.

Eyes can reveal fear by shifting back and forth, refusing to meet the other person's gaze, or by excessive blinking. The mouth shows fear when one bites his lips or licks them or has a tightly clenched jaw. The body held stiff and rigid indicates a deep-seated anxiety; so does excessive perspiration or constant deep breathing with heavy sighs.

THE CAMERA DOESN'T LIE

Many top schools have gone hi-tech in terms of helping their students find jobs. Some even offer video training for interviews. While this may sound silly, it's not. When the competition is as fierce as it is today every little bit counts—including nonverbal gestures. If you have been told, or you suspect that non-verbal gestures may be a problem on the job, there is one creative solution available: make a videotape, and study it carefully.

For example, if a concerned colleague politely tells you could improve your presentation skills, it might be a good idea to videotape yourself just to see what nonverbal clues you pick up. (You can do this at home for privacy, by the way). What you see might surprise you. After all that time polishing your speech, only now do you see in full color that you put your hand in front of your mouth when you speak— a strong verbal clue that you aren't confident in what you're saying. Or perhaps you shift from side to side when you stand, sending the audience the false signal of boredom or nervousness. Have a spouse or trusted friend watch the tape as well they may be even better at spotting rough spots. Most important, learn from your mistakes; most non-verbal clues are fairly easy to correct. While it may take years to learn proper "Oxbridge" English, it certainly shouldn't take too long to get the proper gestures down correctly.

The male abdomen is also used in body language. In courtship, a man will tighten his abdominal muscles and pull in his belly to display his strength and virility. When he is depressed, he will often over-relax these muscles and let his stomach sag visibly downward. The degree of tension of the abdominal muscles will tell a great deal about the emotional and mental status of a man.

One way to tell if a person is really listening to you or not is to watch the position of his head while you are speaking to him. If he is your employee and is really attentive to what you're saying, he'll usually tilt his head to one side. Less powerful people often do this when they are listening to instructions from their superiors.

The less powerful person, as your employee is, for instance, will also mirror exactly the body posture of the more powerful person. If you lean forward and cross your arms, he will soon do the same. If you cross your legs, so will he. If you look anxious while speaking to him, he will soon show body language signs of anxiety, too.

How a Schoolteacher Can Stop Trouble Without Saying a Word

Eugene B. Lynch, a university psychologist and educator, not only knows how to stop trouble in a classroom without saying a single word, but he also passes along this information to other potential teachers in his courses.

"Maintaining order and discipline in the classroom is often the biggest job the teacher has," Dr. Lynch says. "If the instructor will use my system, he can eliminate between 70 and 90 percent of classroom disruptions. When used properly, discipline is almost invisible. Let me give you an example of that:

"A teacher tells her class to begin working on arithmetic problems. But in a few moments, Johnny decides he'd rather do something more pleasurable.

"Seeing this, the teacher walks over, leans over Johnny with her hands planted squarely on his desk, looks him straight in the eye, tells him quietly to get back to work, stares at him for a full count of three, and then leaves. Johnny suddenly develops a deep interest in arithmetic.

"Close physical proximity is one of the most important elements in maintaining discipline," Dr. Lynch goes on to say. "So is a quick response to disruption. A lot of teachers think that if you ignore the problem, it will go away. But that is simply not true. Immediate corrective action is necessary to retain control of the class.

"So respond quickly. From then on it's mostly body language, facing the child directly, having a tone of voice and a facial expression that shows you mean business. Eyeball-to-eyeball contact is also extremely important. The use of body language also helps the teacher keep his mouth shut. When he doesn't talk, he can't end up with his foot in his mouth or make a fool out of himself in front of all the other students."

If you will note, the close physical proximity that Dr. Lynch mentions is an invasion of the student's space bubble. This serves to deflate his ego, and makes him more susceptible to direction by the teacher.

How to Project the Power of Your Personality on the Phone

Although you cannot use the body language of your hands or eyes over the phone, how you use your voice and the words you use can still vividly project the power of your personality. For instance, you should never refer to yourself by your given name. If you call someone on the phone, don't say, "This is Joe." Don't even say, "This is Joe Davis." Instead, say, "This is Davis." The use of first names encourages unwanted familiarity. In power circles, familiarity is an invasion of privacy. It punctures your space bubble. Be courteous and polite, of course, but keep people at arm's length from you.

When answering the phone, don't use your title. To do so implies that you can't get by without it. Don't say, "This is *Mr.* Davis, or *Superintendent* Davis, or *Doctor, Professor, Major,* or whatever. Just say, "Davis," or "Davis speaking." When introducing yourself to someone, simply say, "I'm Davis," or "My name is Davis." That's enough.

If you are a woman, follow exactly the same procedure. This places you on the same level as your male colleagues. Never refer to yourself as *Miss, Ms.,* or *Mrs*. This invites too many chauvinistic remarks, especially about the title, *Ms*.

Telephone selling, or telemarketing as it is also called, has increased greatly since the early seventies when the cost of driving a car went up drastically. Many companies and corporations today use the phone instead of the traveling salesman to get orders and to do business; and so do retail firms.

I usually get anywhere from two to four calls a day from local stores wanting to sell me something. Most of these calls are made when I'm eating supper, watching television, reading the newspaper, whatever, and I don't want to be disturbed by anyone. It takes a powerful personality with a terrific message on the other end to get my attention. He has to offer me a great big benefit of some sort right away to get my interest.

Many of the calls I receive sound like this: "I'm going to be in your neighborhood tomorrow checking on (water purity, roofing, sidewalks, siding, whatever). Could I drop by and see you so I can show you what I have to offer?"

My answer to this is that I'll not be home. That kind of call offers me no benefit whatever. The only benefit appears to be to the caller. In other words, it will be convenient for him to call on me since he's going to be in my neighborhood anyway.

As Elmer Wheeler, one of America's greatest salesmen, once said, "Your first ten words are more important than the next ten thousand." His statement is especially applicable to telephone selling.

So if you want to be successful in telemarketing, you must grab the person in the first few seconds by offering him a benefit he can't possibly refuse. There is simply no other way to get him.

IT'S NEVER TOO LATE TO CHANGE

Pay attention to successful role models around you. While there is always the occasional "screamer" or nervous eccentric who make his or her way to the top, odds are, most successful people you will encounter almost always project an outward appearance of calm collectedness. It's almost a feeling of inner serenity. There is a reason for this. They are projecting the image of control and of responsibility; no wonder they were promoted to where they are today.

What these people are like behind the scenes or in private is virtually irrelevant. To the outside world, it appears nothing can shake them. They are calm, they are in control, they know it and now the outside world knows it too. If you are already like this, congratulations, you possess a tremendous asset in the business world. If you're not, you know what you should be aiming for. Remember, no one is saying you should change your personality completely. Rather, making a conscious effort to both walk, talk, and act the part can help project the power image you need to get where you want to go in business. By the way, it shouldn't surprise you to know that more than a few top businessmen have taken acting lessons at one point in their careers. If all the world's a stage, then know your role inside out.

WHY YOU SHOULD ELIMINATE THESE WORDS FROM YOUR VOCABULARY

Certain words and phrases automatically place other people above you when you use them. You can bring yourself up to their level immediately by eliminating these words completely from your vocabulary.

I refer specifically to the use of the words "Sir" and "Ma'am." Never use these words either alone or in the phrases so often heard: "Yes, Sir . . . No, Sir . . . Yes, Ma'am . . . No, Ma'am."

The use of *Sir* and *Ma'am* immediately places you on a lower level than the other person whether you realize that or not. These two small words simply *submissiveness* rather than courtesy and respect. You can still be courteous and show respect for the other person without being submissive. For example, if your boss asks if you've completed a certain task, don't answer with "Yes, Sir!" Say instead, "Yes, Mr. Jones. I have."

Don't reply with only *Yes* or *No* when answering a question. It sounds too curt and brief and borders on being insolent or discourteous. Answer *Yes* or *No* in a short sentence just as I showed you in the above paragraph. If the person to whom you are speaking has a title, use that, too, in the place of *Sir* or *Ma'am*. For instance, you can say, "Yes, Doctor, I have . . . No, Professor, I have not."

HOW TO INTERPRET BODY LANGUAGE IN SOCIAL ACTIVITIES

It is very important for you to be able to interpret body language at social activities, especially in business or at office parties to keep yourself from making the wrong move or stepping on the wrong person's toes.

For instance, if your boss and some of the top brass have formed a little circle that excludes all others, don't try to invade their area uninvited. You can easily recognize when they don't want others to be included in their conversation if they are sitting on a couch and the two at each end are "bookended," that is, turned inward to enclose the person in the center and with their backs to the outside. This serves to lock out intruders, for the implication of this kind of grouping is, "This is a closed discussion . . . keep out . . . you are not invited."

If they are standing in a group, elbow to elbow in a "circle the wagons" posture, it also means they want to be left alone. Sometimes one man will put his foot up on a coffee table to prevent any outside intrusion into the group. Men will also tend to protect a woman by placing her in the middle of the circle or by placing themselves between male visitors and the female.

If men and women are forced to sit very close together, face to face, and they are not on close intimate terms, they may cross their arms and legs protectively and lean away from each other while talking, almost as if they had bad breath.

SIX FINAL TIPS ON HOW TO PROJECT THE POWER OF YOUR PERSONALITY WITH BODY LANGUAGE

When you want to communicate equality with your associates (this is especially important to a woman), you can use these simple but powerful body language signals. These are also valuable to project the power of your personality to your subordinates or to your boss as well, or to assert your status as an executive or a manager.

1. *Don't smile unless you are genuinely happy.* This does not mean you have to walk around with a frown on your face as if you were carrying the

weight of the whole world on your shoulders. It means exactly what it says. Don't smile unless you are really happy. A neutral facial expression best conceals your inner feelings and emotions.

2. *Don't allow other people to interrupt you.* If someone does interrupt you, even if it's your superior, simply say, "I'm sorry, but I wasn't finished," and then resume speaking at once where you were cut off. This is usually enough to stop the other person dead in his tracks unless he is abnormally obtuse.

3. *Don't restrain your body gestures.* If you need to use your hands or arms to make a point, do so. The only thing to avoid here is pointing your finger at someone as if you were accusing him of some wrong. This turns everyone off completely.

4. *Look people straight in the eye.* I've already told you that the trick to this is staring at a spot in the middle of the forehead just above the eyebrows. This is one of the most effective techniques you can use to make the other person back off. If he's trying to argue with you, saying nothing but staring at him this way will cause him to become nervous and flustered. You can make your point without ever saying a single word.

5. *Use your space bubble effectively.* Many young executives fail to do this and then wonder why their personal private space is always being invaded. The proper placement of office furniture is often the key here.

6. *Be completely relaxed.* I don't mean that you should be sloppy about your dress or careless about your appearance. The key to being relaxed is self-confidence. If you know your job, you don't have to be nervous and filled with tension. You can relax and really enjoy your work.

Summary Points

- Making your hands into an inverted-V "steeple-like structure" is a non-verbal sign of seriously listening to the other party.
- Avoid nervous behavior like darting eyes, excessive blinking, rubbing your hands, shifting back and forth.
- One way of maintaining a power position is maintaining a neutral facial expression throughout a meeting. Higher ranking individuals will do this throughout. Low-ranking individuals will likely smile and be more animated.

- Never stare directly at a person's eyes. Maintain eye contact, but don't stare.

- Attentiveness to another person is often indicated when the head is tilted one side.

- To maintain an upper hand, even if you are nervous inside, always appear relaxed and at ease. Like the ad says: "Never let them see you sweat."

CHAPTER 12

DEALING WITH DIFFICULT PEOPLE: A PRACTICAL HOW-TO

Ingrates. Buffoons. Tyrants. Back-stabbers. Chameleons. Lugabouts. We've all worked with our share. The bosses who demand much and give precious little in return, the colleagues who pretend they're your friend but stab you in the back. These are the people who take another terrific job and make it difficult to go to work in the morning. In a perfect world, there wouldn't be such people. And while it would be great to daydream about a perfect world, as a businessperson, you have better things to do.

How to deal with such people?

One way to start is by acknowledging that there is a problem and trying to solve it rationally, even if the other person isn't terribly rational. Remember, your mission in life is not to make this person into the perfect employee, boss, or co-worker. Your job is to accomplish certain tasks at work, and to do them well. This means working with a variety of people who sometimes bring a lot of baggage to their work, and who sometimes rub you raw. You don't have to be best friends, you just have to know how to cooperate. Now, where to begin?

Muriel Solomon's *Working with Difficult People* offers an excellent set of strategies and tactics that can be used in almost any situation: with bullies, hot-heads, perfectionists, worriers, showoffs—whatever or whomever the problem is. The sections excerpted below include an overall summary of major points in deal-ing with virtually any situation, as well as some typical situations you are likely to find in any working environment. Throughout, Solomon offers strategic advice: what are you trying to accomplish with this particular type of person, as well as tactical examples of how to handle difficult people. If you're currently working with a problem person, you're not alone and this chapter may help you tremen-dously to solve your dilemma and make your work environment a productive one.

WHEN YOUR BOSS IS UNBENDING

At times your boss is like a race horse wearing blinders to hide his peripheral vision. Other times he's just plain stubborn as a mule.

Some bosses are so rigid about enforcing the fine print, they can't see the handwriting on the wall. Others are obstinate about making modifications even when current conditions cause hardship. Some won't change their minds because pride doesn't permit them to admit their position spells t-r-o-u-b-l-e.

In any event, you'll never reach the winner's circle telling bosses they're wrong. They'll just get defensive and become even more intractable. Especially if you embarrass them in front of others "with the facts that prove" your case. Even if they agree, they'll get back at you, consciously or subconsciously, at a later time.

Instead, start cultivating a polite, sincere, and relaxed manner. Bosses are more apt to listen when you try to show them how to get what they want while you get what you want.

Comma Counters

Comma Counters are stubbornly pedantic, demanding perfection on the insignificant.

These bosses have a petty outlook. They see the microscopic parts without also backing up to get a telescopic look at the larger picture. With overemphasis on minor details, they deify preciseness and undeviating conformity.

The problem for you is that they won't risk trying for a better way. Frequently, they not only lack imagination, but also have no *practical* understanding of what's involved in getting your job done.

WHAT YOU'RE THINKING

My boss has tunnel vision, He's uncompromising when it comes to adhering to our procedures, clinging rigidly to our scheduling practices. Recent reports of data from other organizations show they are getting more mileage out of their facilities by slightly extending the hours and doubling the shifts. He won't listen. He just stresses the importance of keeping records and filling out forms.

A COMMA COUNTER'S THOUGHTS

Al is rocking the boat, but I am sticking with something I know I can depend on. The scheduling plan we've been following for years works perfectly fine. I'd better not catch him bending my rules or not completing every last one of the forms on time.

Strategy

Your goal is to help your boss get a broader view, a more comprehensive understanding of what's involved. Be straightforward. In a confident, calm yet enthusiastic tone, convey your sincerity.

1. *Learn the history.* Maybe your boss has been burned before on that issue and, if so, let him know that *you* know he's had some experience with this. Express empathy for his needs and concern for how your boss, personally, would be affected if the current practice is continued.

2. *Present authoritative evidence whenever possible.* This is especially important if the boss believes you're asking him to put his reputation on the line. Stress the benefits that will be important to him and your organization, showing why the risk is minimal and how the changes also benefit the boss emotionally.

3. *Scale down your request.* Keep the changes and costs to a minimum. Talk about taking smaller steps over shorter periods of time.

Tactical Talk

"BOSS, MY CONCERN IS THAT OUR CURRENT SETUP IS NO LONGER A SAFE WAY TO GO. THE DRAIN ON OUR RESOURCES IS CAUSING . . ."

"HERE'S A RECENT STUDY THAT SHOWS HOW WELL THIS APPROACH WORKED IN SEVERAL RESPECTED ORGANIZATIONS."

"WHAT IF WE THINK ABOUT A TRIAL RUN LIMITED TO THREE MONTHS? IF THERE'S NO MARKED IMPROVEMENT OR NEW PROBLEMS ERUPT, WE CAN ALWAYS GO BACK . . ."

TIP: When bosses ignore larger trends, while stubbornly enforcing minor details, contrast the danger of being swept aside with the benefit of going with the flow. Reassure those who bury their heads in the sand, afraid to take risks. Talk about trail testing instead of permanent changes.

Inflexibles

Inflexibles are iron-willed bosses who won't listen and stick tenaciously to their ideas.

They are in charge and don't you dare forget it. Their way is the only way because they say so. They rigorously and intolerantly impose unreasonable strictness.

Don't complain to these bosses if this causes you any difficulty. They don't want to hear why it would help you if, just this once, they'd make an exception. Their rigidity is unshakable, their resolve seemingly can't be curved, bent, or diverted. Your problems won't influence them to modify their views. They suddenly can't hear what you're saying, no matter how pointed your comment. They're too busy worrying about keeping control.

WHAT YOU'RE THINKING

I want the boss to see that I'm smart and I can come up with good ideas. But I'm getting cold feet about making more suggestions. It's so hard to get her even to consider doing something another way or trying something new. She just wants to indoctrinate us with her ways, to follow exactly in her footsteps. The old ideas are so well insulated, new ideas can't penetrate the stone wall she's built up.

AN INFLEXIBLE'S THOUGHTS

I've got to watch Patricia a little more closely. I think she's questioning my authority. I can't have any upstart trying to diminish my power by coming up with plans for more participatory management. I'd be a fool to go along with that and lose my control over my workers.

STRATEGY

Your goal is to get your obstinate boss to let a friendly, fresh but critical air flow over your policies and precedents. To achieve more open discussions, try these tactics:

1. *Understand where the boss is coming from.* In presenting your ideas, focus on management's concerns. Explain how your proposal meets the objectives the boss is always talking about. Point up probable consequences if the idea is not accepted.

2. *Explain the mutual benefits.* Explain the benefits not only for the boss and the company, but also to you. Let the boss see how eager you are for this plan to work. Show your willingness to knock yourself out to make it succeed.

3. *Acknowledge costs and obstacles.* If applicable, prepare a budget and list staffing suggestions. Explain how you'll overcome anticipated road-blocks.

4. *Go in the back door by creating the market.* Begin by documenting demand, asking opinions from those who'll be using your product or service. When users become caught up with your idea, suggest how they can help you persuade your boss to bring it about.

TACTICAL TALK

"BOSS, I'VE HEARD YOU SAY HOW IMPORTANT IT IS FOR THE COMPANY TO INCREASE OUR NET . . . I SUPPOSE YOU'VE CON-SIDERED CONSOLIDATING, BUT HOW WOULD IT BE IF WE WERE TO COMBINE . . . ?"

"I KNOW IT WOULD TAKE QUITE A BIT OF TIME TO FIGURE OUT THE LOGISTICS, BUT I'D BE HAPPY TO DO THIS ALONG WITH MY REGULAR ASSIGNMENTS . . ."

"I'M GLAD YOU LIKE THE IDEA. I WONDER, WOULD YOU BE WILLING TO HELP GET IT OFF THE GROUND? WOULD YOU FILL IN THIS BRIEF QUESTIONNAIRE SO I COULD TAKE YOUR THOUGHTS BACK TO MY BOSS?"

TIP: If your boss won't bend, reshape your request and repeat it. People refuse for one reason and agree for another. When bosses are determined to maintain the status quo by practicing thought control, help change their minds by pulling with them instead of against them. Tap into the potential of product/service users by getting them to change the boss's mind for you. Although you've violated no rule, should your boss accuse you of being aggressive, apologize. It's easier to say you're sorry afterwards than to get permission from an iron-willed autocrat beforehand.

Pig Heads

Pig Heads hold to a course of action blindly, stupidly, and stubbornly. They are obstinate, poorly informed, balky bosses who stupidly and persistently adhere to some course of action. They won't listen to your assignments. You can't persuade, plead or reason with them because to get them to change their course, they'd have to admit they made a mistake. Pig Heads are prejudiced by some pre-conceived, unreasonable judgment they made before they had the facts and now, although the facts contradict their initial opinion, they won't budge. You feel trapped because your boss's bull-headed directives don't mesh with the tasks you're supposed to perform.

WHAT YOU'RE THINKING

The boss doesn't know what he's talking about. He's too stubborn to listen and learn what's going on here. I'm going to be held responsible for his stupid idea that I know is going to fail. If I follow though, I get the blame. If I don't do it, the boss will dump all the lousy assignments on me.

A PIG HEAD'S THOUGHTS

I may not have had actual experience in contacting new clients, but I studied the subject and I resent Sharon's arguing with me over the procedure to use. I've told all my people that I insist on everyone doing this according to my plan. If I let Sharon change the orders I gave her, that would be admitting her way is better than mine. I can't do that. It would be too embarrassing.

STRATEGY

Your goal is to refuse a direct order without causing resentment or being insubordinate. You want restrictions eased so that you can do your job with minimum interference and, hopefully, gain the boss's approval.

1. *Present a substitute to the boss's plan.* Get new ideas from mentors, networks, seminars, or libraries, then ask the boss again. If you don't have time to prepare a full counterplan, you can still better the odds for success. Slip some sound suggestions into the obnoxious order.

2. *Attempt to solve the boss's problems.* Before you present your idea, ask yourself how it would help cope with cutting costs, increasing sales, minimizing mistakes, or whatever other organizational matter is making the boss apoplectic.

3. *Add an emotional appeal.* Link your idea to a personal longing. Do you think your boss wants to feel more secure, get more recognition, have more free time, find a stage to show off some skill?

4. *Act as though you expect acceptance.* Your boss is more apt to agree if you anticipate agreement rather than hostility. Positive expectations encourage positive responses. Attribute to the boss traits he'd like others to think he has.

5. *If the boss won't budge, obey the order precisely.* Don't criticize, but do get the order in writing to protect yourself. Document all your actions to show you were following the boss's orders. If you're lucky, your bull-headed boss could eventually get kicked out or transferred. If not, you've continued to do good work, armed against unfair accusations.

TACTICAL TALK

"FOLLOWING YOUR LINE OF THINKING, IT SEEMS THAT YOU'RE SAYING . . ." *(Insert your improvement. It's worth a try.)*

"I KNOW YOU AREN'T AWARE OF THE SITUATION BECAUSE IF YOU WERE YOU WOULDN'T ALLOW THIS DECLINE TO PERSIST. WHAT DO YOU SUGGEST WE DO? WHAT WOULD YOU THINK ABOUT . . .?"

"BOSS, I KNOW YOU'RE A REASONABLE PERSON AND THE OTHER DIRECTORS OUGHT TO RECOGNIZE YOUR EFFORTS TO MAKE THE COMPANY MORE . . ."

"I'VE SUMMARIZED OUR DISCUSSION IN THIS MEMO TO MAKE SURE WE PROCEED THE WAY YOU WANT."

(You slipped in some changes and the boss balks.) "OK, I'LL PREPARE ANOTHER MEMO FOR YOUR SIGNATURE CORRECTING THE ITEMS YOU POINTED OUT." *(Once he signs, the boss—not you—will be held responsible.)*

TIP: Do all you can to let your boss save face. Bolster him instead of saying he's wrong. Ask if doing something else might help. When a pig-headed boss refuses to budge and your experience and instincts tell you that you're in jeopardy, survival requires you protect yourself. Written records and signed instructions become a bullet-proof vest. Arm yourself.

Concentrate on the wants of rigid and obstinate bosses. If you hit the right button, they themselves will find justification for doing what you suggest. If your boss believes that you are really sincere in wanting to help, that you've somehow tied your future with the boss's, then he'll begin to trust you. The stubborn walls will start tumbling down.

DON'T BE OBSESSED

In a previous chapter, we talked about separating people from the problem. Well, what do you do if the person *is* the problem? One of the best bits of advice is to not let these problems overwhelm you. If you're like most people, you take your job seriously, you have a lot invested in your career. Therefore, these problems tend to magnify. But in doing so, they are robbing you of valuable time and energy you otherwise would have spent working at your job.

How do you get such thoughts into proper perspective? There's no one answer for everyone, but there are a few techniques you can apply. First, try talking about the matter with someone who is more experienced than you, yet has no connection to your place of work. Just talking the problem out—getting it off your chest—can be a tremendous relief. Do you spend your free time and weekends obsessing about others? Do you regale friends and loved ones with horror stories from work? Stop right there! Instead, use that time constructively to clear your head. Take a walk, go to a movie, or a museum. Visit some friends. Sometimes a change of scenery helps clear your mind and put things into better perspective. Remember, the goal is to separate yourself from the problem, and find the most *constructive* way to deal with the situation without resorting to their tactics. Don't let problems swallow you whole.

WHEN YOUR COLLEAGUES ARE DECEPTIVE

Your boss has a certain amount of power over you as you do over your subordinates, but it's supposed to be different with your peers. You're supposed to be on the same level. You're supposed to pull together as a team and help each other. In the real world, some colleagues just pretend to do this.

These cohorts are so concerned with getting ahead and looking good, they don't want to admit that some of their acts can make you look bad. Sometimes they misinterpret your actions, believing that you're looking down at them, and move to get back at you. Others, knowingly and unknowingly, use your brainpower to generate their copycat proposals.

For the time being, you're stuck with the daily headache of dealing with deceitful colleagues. Your concern is keeping their underhanded behavior from interfering with your career.

Brainpickers

Brainpickers exploit your ideas, stealing credit for and profiting from them.

Brainpickers are phony office friends who pretend to care about you, but only care about information they can extract from you. Instead of suggesting that you team up and brainstorm some idea or activity to which you both contribute and claim credit, they probe your mind with delicately worded questions. Then they take your brainchild and adopt it or adapt it as their own.

You thought once you left the street and entered the office you were safe from thieves? Just as pickpockets steal your wallet, Brainpickers steal your ideas. Because these con artists don't use guns, you didn't even know you were being robbed.

WHAT YOU'RE THINKING

It wasn't just my imagination. Larry pumped me for information about the best way to organize the program so that we'd have the cooperation of all the agencies under the umbrella. Now I find my ideas in this memo from the boss, lauding Larry for coming up with the plan that can help the department achieve better coordination. I can't decide whether to quietly punch Larry or loudly expose him for the thief that he is. But how can I prove that the ideas were really mine and not Larry's?

A BRAINPICKER'S THOUGHTS

Boy that was a great memo that the boss sent out praising me for my coordinating ideas. I'll add this to my list when it's time to hit the boss for a raise.

STRATEGY

Obviously, you won't gain anything from a confrontation. The Brainpicker has already convinced himself that your ideas came to him as divine inspiration. Learn from your mistake. Your objective now is to separate your concepts into those you want to present as your own proposals and those that need the collective wisdom of a group to be properly developed. Then direct the flow of your ideas.

1. *Plug the leak*. Once you've fingered the folks who want to drain your brain, be polite but tight-lipped. Just stop supplying the information.

2. *Welcome discussion when concepts affect other units*. You don't want to work in a vacuum, not when you need the cooperation of your cohorts.

But don't limit yourself to a one-brainpicker audience. Enlarge the group. Call over other colleagues or bring up these matters at lunch or at staff meetings.

TACTICAL TALK

(tight-lipped) "YES, LARRY, THAT REALLY WILL BE A PROBLEM, BUT I HAVEN'T THOUGHT IT THROUGH YET. WHY DON'T YOU BRING IT UP AT THE NEXT MEETING?"

(group discussion) "YOU KNOW, GUYS, THE BOSS HAS REQUESTED THAT WE MEASURE THE CHANGE IN . . . I WONDER IF THIS APPROACH COULD WORK IN EACH OF OUR UNITS. WHAT IF WE WERE TO . . ."

TIP: OK, you were snookered by the Brainpicker. Be glad this happened to you now. You'll be wiser in the future when you come up with a really brilliant gem. Then you'll know how to nourish, protect, and present your prize-winning idea.

Back-Stabbers

Back-Stabbers are nice to your face, but very critical of you behind your back.

These colleagues stab you in absentia. They are bad-mouthers, telling lies or being critical about you when you're not there. When you're with them, they act like they're your friends. But out of sight, the phonies betray your trust, revealing some disclosure you confided about your personal life or opposing some action you've taken.

They keep trying to outwit you or get some measure of control over you. Maybe they misinterpreted your action. Maybe you did something that angered them, but you can't imagine what it was. You're scratching your head while you're pulling the blade out of your back.

WHAT YOU'RE THINKING

I still find it hard to accept that Kate would say anything bad about me behind my back. But three people heard the same thing, so it must have really happened. I guess in an office you can't have any really close friends because the competition is too keen. From now on I'll keep details about my private life to myself. But how do I stop Kate from bad-mouthing me again? And what made her do it in the first place?

A BACK-STABBER'S THOUGHTS

Diane was bragging so much about the progress her staff had made. She's making the rest of us look like a bunch of loafers. I'm really sick and tired of everyone thinking she's perfect and using her work as the standard we should all follow.

STRATEGY

Your objective is to stop the back-stabbing. If criticism made about your work is legitimate, that has to be aired and resolved.

1. *Confront Back-Stabbers*. But simply report what you heard. Don't start swinging. Ask them to spell out specifically whatever accusations they allegedly made. Speak up firmly, without showing any anger or voicing any blame.

2. *If the mistake was yours, apologize immediately*. Sometimes you become a victim of Back-Stabbers if they perceive you were insensitive to their feelings. If, for example, they believe that you meant to put them down by elevating yourself, you could have made them feel insecure and want to strike back to you.

3. *Provide a graceful way out*. If Back-Stabbers accuse you unjustly and then deny having made the reported statements, let them off the hook. Once they know that you know they've attacked your reputation and you won't sit still for such immature behavior, Back-Stabbers will back off. But if you create an emotional scene, a tip-off that they got a rise out of you, they may keep it up.

TACTICAL TALK

"KATE, I'D APPRECIATE YOUR CLEARING UP SOME CONFUSION. I'VE BEEN TOLD THAT YOU SAID I DID . . . DID YOU MAKE THAT STATEMENT, AND, IF SO, I'D REALLY LIKE YOU TO EXPLAIN TO ME . . ."

"WELL, I'M GLAD TO HEAR WHAT WAS REPORTED TO ME WAS AN EXAGGERATION AND THAT YOU DIDN'T INTEND IT AS CRITICISM."

"KATE, I HAD NO IDEA YOU FELT THAT WAY. IF I HURT YOUR FEELINGS, I'M SORRY. I CERTAINLY DIDN'T MEAN TO IMPLY . . ."

TIP: If you allow the back-stabbing to persist, it can eventually harm your reputation. Such actions are childish and it takes your calm, no-nonsense demeanor to make the culprits behave as adults.

Underminers

Underminers undercut your efforts and set you up to fail.

Undermining colleagues take back-stabbing a step further. They weaken your position by clever, crafty means. They lie in wait to make a sneak attack. When the ambush occurs you are completely surprised. Their maneuver is more serious then the Back-Stabbers' because it can result in sapping support and enthusiasm and reducing the impact of your efforts.

Sometimes Underminers hurt your work by subtle means such as purposely being late with needed information or supplying you with flawed data. Or, agreeing to go along with a proposal until they sense no support, and then backing out to leave you holding the bag.

They often level a charge when there's no opportunity for you to defend yourself. When you do, the damage is already done. Maybe they didn't mean to make you fall flat on your face, but they certainly are grandstanding at your expense.

WHAT YOU'RE THINKING

Why is Danny doing this to me? He sends a memo to the manager stating that my program is not hiring minorities in accordance with company policy. First of all, he has distorted the facts by giving an inaccurate account. Secondly, he never bothered to check with me before writing that attack. What is the game? Why is he undermining my program? And what can I do to counteract this?

AN UNDERMINER'S THOUGHTS

I'll send copies of this memo to all the minority groups. That will show them that I'm really in there fighting for them and I may be able to milk some publicity from it. Then the manager will see how hard I'm working, that I'm right on top of things, actually visiting the sites of our programs to observe for myself conformance to policy.

STRATEGY

Your Underminer is playing politics and, unfortunately, you are the butt of dirty tricks. You were probably selected as the target because you appeared weak and vulnerable. If you stay still, you're dead, and can go no where but down or out of the organization. You must launch a counteroffensive.

1. *Prepare a crisp outline of the real facts.* Go over it again and again to strike all the inflammatory, emotional words describing the despicable, treacherous act. What you do with this depends on the situation. If the damage wasn't too serious, sending the correction to your boss, and copies to the Underminer and everyone else involved, may be sufficient to clear your good name.

2. *When it's serious, pay a visit to all the people you know with clout.* If you have mentors, this is the time to get help. Hand each one copies of both the offensive evidence and the rebuttal you prepared. Ask their advice and get their help. Powerful people who work well behind the scenes generally know the diplomatic language to use that results in correcting misinformation. Whether or not you have other mentors, go in to see your boss.

TACTICAL TALK

Don't add fuel to the flames:

Not this: "IF HE HAD BOTHERED TO CHECK, HE WOULD HAVE KNOWN THAT . . ."

But this: "WHEN THE FACTS ARE CHECKED, IT WILL BECOME APPARENT THAT . . ."

A sneak has trouble handling a face to face encounter:

You: "DANNY, I DON'T KNOW WHY YOU SENT THIS MEMO, BUT THE INFORMATION IS INACCURATE. THIS PAPER WILL GIVE YOU THE FACTS THAT YOU NEED. I KNOW I CAN DEPEND ON YOU TO CORRECT A FALSE IMPRESSION."

Your boss is responsible for your work. He must be kept informed:

"BOSS, THERE HAS BEEN SOME MISLEADING, DAMAGING, AND INACCURATE INFORMATION CIRCULATED ABOUT MY PRO-

GRAM. I'VE COME TO ASK YOUR HELP IN SETTING THE RECORD STRAIGHT. HERE ARE BOTH THE TROUBLESOME MEMO AND MY RESPONSE . . ."

TIP: When you have been sandbagged by a colleague, it knocks the wind out of you. Take a few deep breaths, then realize the Underminer's intention wasn't to squash you but to inflate himself. Regardless of motive, you still have to clear the muddied record and prevent future sneak attacks.

Deceptive colleagues use various means to step on you in order to make themselves appear taller. You have to protect yourself because their pouncing weakens your prospects of career advancement. Responses you can choose to use range from zipping your lips, settling legitimate criticism, confronting your accuser, to launching a counteroffensive.

WHEN YOUR SUBORDINATES CAUSE DELAYS

Subordinates who seem bored, scared, or resentful and who dilly dally instead of doing what they know has to be done create conflict among other workers. Untreated, the tension can grow into a serious loss in productivity. But before looking at the common types who cause delays—those who can't do, and those seeking revenge—you should carefully examine the atmosphere in your office. If the air engulfing procrastinating subordinates is too stressful, rigid, or frigid, some part of the problem is not with the people but with the system.

Checklist for Managers Dealing with Procrastinators

DO YOU CREATE GOOD RAPPORT?

( ) Do you establish a good emotional climate in which workers are free to learn, produce, and try innovative approaches?

( ) Do you put procrastinators at ease so that they're comfortable talking to you, sensing that you identify with their needs?

( ) Is it pleasant and sometimes fun to work in your office?

( ) Do you avoid humiliating workers publicly with shouts and threats, or clobbering them privately after each mistake, or bribing them to do more?

( ) Do you reinforce the procrastinators' identity with their group through informal office get-togethers, events, and friendly competition?

Do You Eliminate Contributory Factors?

( ) Do you check that disturbing noises, poor lighting and ventilation, wrong tools, malfunctioning equipment, and insufficient training don't contribute to delays?

( ) Do you have enough staff, not expecting one person to supervise too many workers?

( ) Are you certain your rules don't overlap or require endless steps to get permission to carry out tasks?

( ) Do you make the objectives, directions, and time frames absolutely clear?

( ) Do you firmly enforce the deadlines you've set and make clear the consequences of nonperformance?

Do You Take the Time to Motivate?

( ) Do you explain to subordinates how their jobs contribute to the total effort?

( ) Do you reassure them of your confidence that they can perform well and deliver honest praise when they do?

( ) Do you discover your workers' ego needs and help them feel important?

( ) Do you link what you want done with the personal goals they've set for themselves?

Have You Instituted Helpful Mechanisms and Systems?

( ) Do you have a plan in place that allows subordinates' ideas to bubble up to the top?

( ) Do you show workers how to break up their jobs into logical parts?

( ) Have you designed a system to reward completion of major stages?

( ) Do you use display charts to graphically show status, improvement, and comparison of results among units?

( ) Have you a system for rewarding workers with recognition events, additional training, raises, and promotions?

Clockwatchers

Clockwatchers try to get away without working and have a "it's not my job" indifference.

These subordinates look lazy and unconcerned. They resemble dead wood, shirking work and playing hooky from meetings and projects. Clockwatchers are capable, but refuse to put forth a drop more effort than they have to.

Frequently their indifference stems from a lack of pride in the company's product/service or in their particular part in producing it. Nobody ever told them what they do is important or appreciated. Sometimes, when you scratch below their apathetic surface, you find subordinates who are frustrated by red tape or a specialty rut. If they're bored, unchallenged and underutilized, they may deliberately delay turning in their work just to get a little excitement going. They may use procrastination to create problems so that they can be recognized for solving them.

WHAT YOU'RE THINKING

I don't know what happened to Cheryl. When she first came here, she was so full of promise and excited about working in this company. Now I can't seem to penetrate her what's-the-use attitude. The more I talk, the slower she works. Because we have to process so much data on a daily basis, when Cheryl doesn't finish, I have to give the remainder of her work to the faster workers who, of course, resent the overload. They feel they're being punished for working faster. All this has given me one big morale problem.

A CLOCKWATCHER'S THOUGHTS

When I first came to this office, the boss said they were looking for people able to implement the projects that would move us ahead. I wish I had taped that conversation to play back to him! I am so bored that it's torture to turn out my assigned work. My talent is untapped. I have no chance to contribute even though I'm sure many times I know a better method than the one they're using. The only way to get any notice around here is to be late with an assignment.

STRATEGY

Your goal is to get Clockwatchers to assume responsibility for performing their assignments on time, enabling you to treat all your workers fairly with an equitable workload.

1. *Look first at your instructions.* What's crystal clear to you can be blurred confusion to your subordinates. Be sure you've spelled out specific objectives and deadlines.

2. *Ask what's wrong instead of accusing.* Give Clockwatchers the chance to talk. Ask their opinions and suggestions and say you'll consider them—which doesn't mean you'll use their ideas, but will *think* about using them.

3. *Begin a pride in the company/department/job program.* Implement a comprehensive approach including individual involvement such as discussion groups or quality circles, team competition, recognition system, and better channeling of internal and external communications. Seek subordinates' ideas and allow subordinates to make some of the decisions affecting the outcome of their tasks.

4. *Create challenge, excitement, fun.* To make room for the spontaneous, eliminate extraneous regulations that tie workers down. Utilize their untapped potential. Not using their potential wastes a valuable resource and can be a root cause of worker dissatisfaction. Let subordinates learn something new by attending workshops, seminars, conferences, and training programs.

Tactical Talk

"FRANKLY, CHERYL, I WAS ANNOYED THAT YOU DIDN'T FINISH THIS ON TIME UNTIL IT OCCURRED TO ME THAT I MAY NOT HAVE MADE CLEAR TO YOU THE IMPORTANCE OF THIS DEADLINE . . ."

"WHY DO YOU THINK YOU'RE HAVING TROUBLE COMPLETING YOUR ASSIGNMENTS? ARE THERE SOME OBSTACLES YOU WANT TO TALK ABOUT? WHAT WOULD YOU SAY WILL HAPPEN IF YOU CONTINUE . . .? CAN YOU SUGGEST SOMETHING WE CAN DO TO GET YOU BACK ON TRACK?"

"I SENSE THAT SOME OF YOU ARE GETTING A LITTLE BORED, SO I'D LIKE ALL OF YOU TO DISCUSS AND RECOMMEND NEW WAYS TO MAKE YOUR EFFORTS MORE SATISFYING. AN EXAMPLE: ROTATING JOBS SO THAT EACH OF YOU COULD LEARN THE MAJOR ASPECTS OF THE OPERATION."

> **TIP:** Don't nag. Learn why Procrastinators drag behind. Many Clockwatchers aspire to go higher. They're competent enough, but are frustrated because they are hog-tied or unchallenged. They feel stuck in a job that doesn't fit their ambitions and needs. If you're considering a development program for them, be sure other workers don't perceive this as a reward (as in "I work fast and get loaded down with his unfinished work. He works slowly and gets more training!"). Plan learning opportunities and job rotation as part of the broad picture, colored by input from the entire staff.

Duds

Duds put off asking for the help they need and delay everyone else.

Clockwatchers know how to proceed. Duds don't. Although they are paralyzed by the fear of making mistakes, Duds are ashamed to admit they don't understand some concept or don't know how to accomplish an assignment. Complex procedures perplex them, but they don't want their bosses or their peers to judge them as incompetent.

Easily frustrated, fearing failure and plagued with anxiety, they procrastinate rather than risk doing something wrong or poorly. It's the only way they can see to cope with the potential blow to their self-worth.

What You're Thinking

George keeps promising me that survey I asked for, but he doesn't deliver. This isn't the first time that I've depended on him and he didn't follow through. I need that survey for the planning session with the staff next week. I wonder why he's stalling. I never thought of George as lazy, but maybe I've been wrong. Could I have overburdened him with other assignments? I have to do something about this situation immediately.

A Dud's Thoughts

I keep telling the boss I need a little more time to finish the survey. I didn't want to upset him by saying I couldn't get it done on time for the planning meeting, but I had to have the extra time to plow through the books in order to check my work. I'm still not sure I've done it right. I wish I could hide until this problem goes away. It's not going to go away and I'm going to be fired!

Strategy

Your goal is to strengthen procrastinators you suspect are fear-ridden so that they are able to finish their work on time.

1. *Free them to seek help when needed.* Let them know you expect to be asked when something isn't clear or if they need more information or other resources in order to proceed. Don't spoon-feed them, but nourish and support them to increase their self-confidence.

2. *Get them to agree their procrastination is a problem.* Don't assume that they know the trouble their behavior is creating. Be clear about your priorities. Get them to identify the root cause of the delays and the probable consequences if they continue acting that way. Be calm, nonthreatening and a good listener.

3. *Decide together how the problem will be solved.* Consider if they've been mismatched in their jobs or overloaded and if you have to do some shifting of responsibilities. Agree to interim, smaller, measurable objectives and reasonable deadlines. Plan with them, not for them. Schedule times for future meetings.

4. *Follow up with feedback and recognition.* Reward them with honest praise when they finish each stage to help them feel a sense of accomplishment. If the work isn't done on time, express your disappointment and encourage them to do better. Reinforce good completed work with other incentives.

TACTICAL TALK

"GEORGE, I WANT YOU TO KNOW THAT I'M AVAILABLE EVERY AFTERNOON AT 3 IF YOU HAVE ANY PROBLEMS. YOU'RE GETTING A LITTLE BEHIND SCHEDULE, WHY DON'T YOU COME IN AND WE'LL SEE WHAT WE CAN DO ABOUT IT?"

"DO YOU UNDERSTAND WHAT HAPPENS IN THE REST OF THE OFFICE WHEN YOU ARE LATE WITH YOUR PART OF THE WORK? I NEED PEOPLE I CAN DEPEND ON TO SUPPLY DATA FROM WHICH WE CAN MAKE GOOD DECISIONS. I WANT TO BE ABLE TO DEPEND ON YOU. WHY DO YOU THINK YOU'VE DELAYED TURNING IN YOUR SURVEY? THINK ABOUT THAT AND WE'LL TALK AGAIN TOMORROW, SAME TIME."

"I WISH YOU HAD COME TO ME SOONER WITH THIS, GEORGE. HERE ARE SIMILAR TYPES OF SURVEYS THAT YOU CAN USE AS A GUIDE TO CHECK YOURSELF. IF YOU NEED MORE HELP, GO SEE HARV. WE ALL NEED A HAND AT TIMES. IT'S NO SIN TO ASK FOR ASSISTANCE. THE SIN IS IN NOT ASKING FOR IT. FROM NOW ON I KNOW YOU'LL SPEAK UP."

> **TIP:**   Make sure your procrastinating subordinates feel comfortable about asking for help just as soon as they get stuck. Impress upon them why your priorities must be met.

Coach the Duds, reassuring them that you know they're trying. After you've done your best to relieve their fear and anxiety, and given them any additional training that's called for, a few may continue to procrastinate. Try to find a better match of worker and job or help them transfer to more suitable work.

Rebels

Rebels use delaying tactics to get even with you. Because they're afraid to tell you why they're angry, these spiteful Rebels want to get back at you without taking any risks. The tactic they choose is procrastination, using neglect, carelessness, or deliberate misbehavior to result in late and bungled projects.

Their actions may have been triggered by the way you said something or a company policy or procedure they regard as offensive. Whatever it was, it bruised their ego or made them feel inadequate, and they think the safest way to get even is to cause a slow-down in office operations. Interfering with whatever you want done gives them the satisfaction of gaining a measure of control over you.

WHAT YOU'RE THINKING

Theo does a pretty good job of hiding his hostility, but I still sense it. I suspect that it was he who intentionally messed up the quarterly report so that it would have to be redone. Also, Theo gave me some lame excuse when he held off placing those important orders. Whenever I want to talk to him he's taking an extended lunch or out on sick leave. He must know that his delaying tactics are wrong. He's got a good job, good pay, good benefits. Why is he being a troublemaker? I have to straighten him out.

A REBEL'S THOUGHTS

I was told during my interview that this job would give me a chance to make a difference. Instead, I find they settle for substandard results. My boss doesn't seem to care because she has her favorites to take care of. Why do we have to adhere to her stupid time schedules when there are so many other factors to be considered? There's no room here for imaginative and creative thinkers who can see more potential for the organization. We're so entrenched in procedures, we don't even know why we're working. The last time I made a suggestion, I got slapped down. I won't risk any more rejection. I'm not a part of what's going on. Well, they can just wait for this darn report while I take my time and do it over the right way. I'll show her I won't settle for her criteria.

STRATEGY

Your goal is to regain control by getting the Rebels to stop hiding their hostility. Until you can get them to speak to you honestly about what's troubling them, instead of resorting to procrastination as tactical revenge, you can't get them back on track.

1. *Blame the system for the problem.* Shifting the blame away from them lets Rebels save face and gives them an opening to express themselves. Explain the situation as it appeared to you and why you consider it a problem. Listen to the response without interrupting.

2. *Ask questions.* Put aside threats and attacks. Successful probing requires a light, friendly tone. Clear the air by making it easy for them to be open and candid with you in a private discussion. In effect, give them permission to unleash their hostility toward you.

3. *Express agreement whenever possible.* Without getting defensive, you can be firm in that you won't allow the operation to be jeopardized. Help them understand why they procrastinate. Together, identify potential ways to handle the situation.

TACTICAL TALK

"THEO, THE QUARTERLY REPORT IS QUITE LATE. THAT PRESENTS A PROBLEM FOR OUR DEPARTMENT. HOW DO YOU SUGGEST I EXPLAIN THE DELAY TO THE BIG BOSS?"

"WHY DO YOU THINK WE HAD THIS TROUBLE? THEO, PLEASE FEEL FREE TO BE FRANK. REALLY, IT WON'T BOTHER ME AND I WON'T HOLD IT AGAINST YOU IF YOU CRITICIZE SOMETHING I'VE DONE."

"YOU MAKE A GOOD POINT, THEO. BUT AS YOU KNOW WE HAVE TO TURN IN THOSE REPORTS ON TIME. WHAT WOULD YOU RECOMMEND TO CORRECT THIS SITUATION?"

> **TIP:** Don't assume that workers who don't criticize openly aren't critical. However if you give Rebels a chance to clear the air and let them have a say in decisions affecting their responsibilities, most of them will be glad to get back to work.

When your subordinates are procrastinating, don't just sit there and smolder until it's time for their annual evaluation. First determine why they are causing delays. If they're bored, often the ennui will flee if they're given a challenge and a voice in suggesting solutions. If they're paralyzed by fear of failure, make it easier and more acceptable for them to ask for help immediately. If they're stalling to seek revenge, get them to articulate the hostility they've been hiding. To maintain your control, you may have to (a) enable your subordinates to feel more freedom on the job and (b) explain how they benefit from your goals.

WHEN YOUR BOSS IS EXPLOITATIVE

Sometimes you may wonder how certain bosses are able to advance as far as they have within the organization. You know that you're swifter with the facts and figures. Maybe so, but they are probably head of the class in office politics. Perhaps they're slick about avoiding blame and quick about grabbing applause, especially for work done by peers or subordinates. They may spend most of their time making friends and making deals, promising anything and everything. They can be charming in the way they pump you up in preparation for dumping on you projects no one else wants. Or, they may be insensitive when they ask you to put in an unreasonable amount of time or effort.

Whatever the particular manner may be, you're convinced that these exploitive bosses are using you. Because of their position and power, you feel that they've got you over a barrel and it's no barrel of fun to accept this kind of treatment.

Connivers

Connivers imply consent and blame you when the wrongful act backfires.

The bottom line is that conniving bosses won't gamble on their own ability. Taking a risk means accepting a situation as beyond your control and manipulators *have* to feel in control. Therefore, Connivers maintain command by hiding behind a powerful position.

They want everyone to believe they had no knowledge of what went wrong. They're usually careful not to leave telltale fingerprints on clues that could point back to them. Although you and the boss discussed the proposed action before proceeding, rather than share any responsibility for the fiasco, he leaves you out on a limb. If it's necessary to save their own hides, Connivers even saw off the branch. Either way, you become a victim.

What You're Thinking

A few months ago the boss said we had to seek additional funding. I checked the crucial points with the boss while preparing one of the proposals to a potential source. Unfortunately, the proposal was rejected. All of a sudden it became "Keith's proposal," as though the boss had nothing whatsoever to do with it. He played a big part in calling the shots and, of course, he had to sign off on the application. I may have picked up a reputation as a loser and I sure hate being the gall guy, but how can I buck the boss?

A Conniver's Thoughts

It's a shame that proposal Keith prepared didn't get funded. I thought it had a pretty good chance. But at least the one Carole wrote did come through. So, as far as the big boss is concerned, my department and I are still looking good.

Strategy

Your goal is not to buck the boss, but to stop feeling victimized. Keep in mind that if the boss acts the same with the rest of the staff, his troublesome behavior is not directed at you exclusively. Your aim is to secure his support instead of being his shield.

1. *Appeal to his sense of fairness.* Your boss hasn't been losing any sleep thinking about you or how you are affected. He's worried about protecting himself. Utilize questions to reveal to him the true situation. Ask questions that penetrate to the core of the problem. If the discussion is not going the way you want, change the direction by asking more questions.

2. *Make suggestions that will strengthen his position.* It's obviously very important to him that he be well regarded by his peers and superiors. Try harder to dig up information and refine it for his immediate use and offer it tactfully. Help the boss become what he'd like everyone to believe he already is.

TACTICAL TALK

"BOSS, I'VE ALWAYS REGARDED YOU AS A FAIR-MINDED PER-SON, SO I DON'T THINK YOU REALIZE THE POSITION I'M IN. DID YOU MEAN TO IMPLY THAT I ALONE WAS RESPONSIBLE FOR THE REJECTED PROPOSAL? I FEEL LIKE I WAS LEFT TWISTING IN THE WIND. THAT WASN'T WHAT YOU INTENDED, WAS IT?"

"BOSS, ANALYZING THESE REPORTED EVENTS, THERE'S A DEFI-NITE PATTERN EMERGING THAT YOU MIGHT WANT TO ACT ON BEFORE EVERYONE ELSE JUMPS ON THE BANDWAGON. EVEN IF WE DON'T REACH THE PROJECTED AMOUNTS, YOUR APPROACH WILL BE RECOGNIZED AS INNOVATIVE AND WILL HELP MOVE THE ORGANIZATION IN A GOOD DIRECTION."

TIP: While driving you up the wall, Conniver bosses are similar to backseat drivers who refuse to take the wheel. Because they can't tolerate being regarded as inept, they protect their self-image, probably unaware that they habitually blame others for making a wrong turn. Point out the benefits as you gently steer them toward accepting a challenge.

ONE, TWO, THREE . . .

This is a little bit of advice I wished I followed more. If you're like most people, you wish you had a dime for every time you exploded in anger over some stupid remark or incident with an impossible person. I know they're would be a lot of rich people walking around if that were the case. I was always taught in situations like that—where I'm just about to lose it—to count to ten. "But I tried that and I still was angry!" I'd answer sometimes. "Well, then count to twenty!" was the answer. Good advice. While you may feel a little foolish counting out numbers to yourself, the principle is not just homespun advice, it's sound psychology. A little distance from the problem helps put things into perspective. You've heard the phrase: "Time heals all wounds?" You'd be surprised what even *ten seconds* can do! Believe me, if counting out a few seconds can prevent you from saying or doing the wrong things in front of your boss, it's worth it.

Camouflagers

Camouflagers have hidden agendas, telling half-truths and omitting necessary facts.

Whereas Connivers hide so that no one will think they're ineffective, Camouflagers hide so that no one will learn their true personal goals. These bosses won't level with you, always masking the real reason for their request. They are pleasant, nonthreatening, pretending they are as concerned about you as they are about getting the job done. They make deals: "If you do this for me, I'll do that for you."

Camouflagers constantly maneuver and manipulate. They're so busy trading favors they're barely able to make their deadlines. And they really believe they can outthink you. How could you learn that what they're suggesting wasn't meant to help you but to bail themselves out of some self-inflicted difficulty? You do as they ask, and find yourself repeatedly disappointed and frustrated.

WHAT YOU'RE THINKING

I don't understand the boss. Why did he have to wait until the last minute to worry about that report that is due tomorrow? He said if I burn the midnight oil and finish it by 10 A.M., he'll remember my cooperation next time raises are being considered. He forgot, that's what he promised me six months ago. Budget time came and went along with another broken promise. Then when I tried to ask him about it, he was suddenly too busy to talk to me. I wonder how I can ever trust him again.

A CAMOUFLAGER'S THOUGHTS

Boy, I really slipped up on that Liberty Bell report and it's due at tomorrow's 11 A.M. meeting. I've got to talk Reena into doing it for me and getting it done tonight. I could tell her that I'll mention her name to the board and then I'll dangle a possible raise. That should do it.

STRATEGY

To the guideline of doing whatever the boss asks as long as it's not illegal, immoral, or unethical, add another qualification—unreasonable. When you can't do what is requested, your goal is to escape without incurring the boss's wrath or vengeance.

1. *Forget long-range deals and broken promises.* The leopard won't change his spots. Any agreement on advancement that you reach with the Camouflager has to be in writing and preferably witnessed. Don't do what he asks because you expect the promised prize. Do it if you can because you want to be regarded as a reasonable, cooperative, and dependable worker.

2. *Suggest an alternative to your doing the task.* Maybe a rush job can be divided among a few of you or perhaps there's a way to get an extension. Maybe by teaching someone else to do a technical task, you could be unchained from your desk.

3. *Sound like a team player even though you're not playing his game.* Don't get angry, or threaten or remind the boss that you've heard that song before. Play it cool, cheerful, and helpful. A pro pitches in without making deals whether acting as doer, mobilizer, or encourager.

TACTICAL TALK

(accepting) "BOSS, I'D BE GLAD TO WORK ALL NIGHT ON THE REPORT BECAUSE I KNOW HOW IMPORTANT IT IS TO YOUR DIVISION. WE CAN DISCUSS RECOGNITION AND RAISES LATER. THAT'S NOT WHY I'M DOING THIS. BUT I WILL NEED A LITTLE HELP WITH MY ROUTINE TASKS TOMORROW. DO YOU THINK CLARK COULD TAKE OVER A FEW OF THEM FOR ME?"

(rejecting or hedging)"BOSS, I'D BE GLAD TO WORK ALL NIGHT ON THE REPORT BECAUSE I KNOW HOW IMPORTANT IT IS TO OUR DIVISION. BUT WE'RE RUNNING TOO GREAT A RISK THAT I MAY NOT BE ABLE TO FINISH IT ON TIME FOR YOUR MEETING. HOW ABOUT DIVIDING THE FOUR SEGMENTS AMONG CLARK, DAN, MARLENE, AND ME?"

TIP: Act professionally even when your boss seems to have forgotten how. If your boss is a wheeler-dealer, that's his problem, not yours. You can be above the shenanigans by changing the scenario. Also, it would help you to find a mentor other than your boss.

Flatterers

Flatterers insincerely give you excessive praise in order to use you.

These bosses believe if they constantly say things designed to please you, greatly exaggerating reality, they are pouring on personal charm and charisma.

("This project would have been an absolute flop without you.") They want you to like them on a personal level in order to win your support and loyalty. They're afraid their plan, procedure, policy, or assignment can't stand on its own merit. So they employ unwarranted praise to gain your acceptance of them and their request *as one package*. Inflating your ego and promising rewards of success to make you want to join in does work for awhile. There's nothing we enjoy more than hearing the boss give praise we honestly believe we earned. And, conversely, nothing makes us more suspicious than a boss heaping elaborate compliments we regard as undeserved and phony. This method of motivating their workers can boomerang for Flatterers when their plans can't stand up and you begin to lose faith in the leader you're following.

WHAT YOU'RE THINKING

What's going on? The boss tells me everything I do is great. The results of the last meeting were great, but the previous ones were nothing to brag about because I didn't have time to make them better. Does she know the difference between mediocre and quality, and would she know how to give excellent work widespread distribution? Or, does she have some ulterior motive, buttering me up with lavish praise to get me to do something I might ordinarily object to?

A FLATTERER'S THOUGHTS

You can't show too much attention too often to win over your employees. Nothing gets them to strive for excellence every time like compliments. Besides, after you compliment them, it's easier to tell them something they won't want to hear. They're going to have to put in a lot of extra hours to get our department the extra support we need. I must make all of them team players, totally loyal to me.

STRATEGY

Your goal is to get ahead, preferably with your boss's help, but without buying into a phony plan. The harm caused by Flatterer bosses is that they leave you disillusioned because you sense a leadership vacuum. However, this may be your opportunity. You may be able to fill at least some of the void.

1. *Maintain your objectivity.* Take the saccharine remarks with a grain of salt. If you're being praised for a task that fell short, be gracious and appreciative, and then speak up on what is needed for improvement. If your relationship is cordial enough, make a joke out of the flattery and tease the Flatterer.

2. *Get clear statements of desired results and individual roles.* Research useful data the boss can employ in deciding policy. Encourage group discussions from which better strategies and clear blueprints can emerge. A team that has a part in the planning is automatically more interested in the outcome. You can raise the spirits of your group without being the boss.

TACTICAL TALK

"I APPRECIATE THE KIND REMARKS, BOSS, BUT I KNOW YOU'D LIKE IT TO BE EVEN BETTER. IT SEEMS TO ME THAT IF WE COULD ALLOT A LITTLE MORE STAFF TIME AND EQUIPMENT, WE COULD MORE THAN DOUBLE . . ."

"OK, BOSS, THIS FLATTERY WILL GET YOU WHATEVER YOU WANT."

"DON'T YOU THINK WE NEED A TIGHTER PLAN TO MAKE THIS SUCCEED? IT SEEMS TO ME WE HAVE TO BREAK DOWN THE STAGES INTO . . ."

TIP: A Flatterer boss gives you the chance to enhance your own leadership skills. Help your boss plan to stand on firmer ground so that he won't have to rely on phony compliments to motivate the team.

Slave Drivers

Slave Drivers are overly ambitious and demand unreasonable pace or overtime.

You may indeed be working for cruel Simon Legree but, before we get into that, consider two other possibilities:

One, the boss keeps piling on work without a peep of protest out of you. He hasn't the foggiest notion how you feel and assumes you are prioritizing your assignments and putting off the less important until you have time to catch up. You're afraid to speak up lest you jeopardize your job. So you keep being overburdened because you never say no. The pain is self-induced and the remedy is self-help.

Two, the boss keeps piling on work because of pressure imposed on him from top management. You're in a relay race without the fun and prizes. The system is poorly coordinated or the signals are crossed. Again, if you remain mute, you remain on the whirling merry-go-round.

On the other hand, a genuine Slave Driver boss, afraid to make decisions, may habitually slide these matters from his desk to yours. He may abdicate his responsibility because he feels inadequate, lacking some necessary skill for his present post. He could resent your potential and keep you overloaded to maintain his control, or maybe he demands excellence without allotting the time it takes to hone your product. It's time to negotiate the preposterous workload your boss is demanding.

WHAT YOU'RE THINKING

Why is the boss so mean to me? What a hassle getting stuck with that lousy tri-county committee one more time. It means traveling an extra 25 miles back and forth twice a week to attend late evening meetings and dragging myself in exhausted the next morning. But I don't dare complain. If I do, the boss will get back at me and give that promised appointment to someone else. I'm trapped.

A SLAVE DRIVER'S THOUGHTS

That was a good move delegating Ron again as my representative on the tri-county committee. He's a very skillful debater. He'll argue our position well and I won't have to make any quick decisions. He didn't seem too pleased to be going, but he's really the only one I can depend on. He's a good sport. He'll get over it.

STRATEGY

Your goal is to be treated fairly and to be compensated appropriately when you're asked to put in additional hours.

1. *Determine if you are really being overworked.* Were you asked to work extra hours or are you being a compulsive performer who can't let go of the work until it's "perfect"?

2. *Determine if the burdensome assignment could be divided among your colleagues or done by one of them.* If it's a one-person job, consider that what you think of as a drag, your peer may envision as an opportunity to become more visible. That person may be delighted to learn the procedure from you.

3. *Negotiate better terms with your boss.* Query your boss on why you're being drowned in extra work. Decide what the boss needs most and how you can help him get it. And just as important, decide what you need most

(e.g., more time for the job or more time off, more money, more staff, modified objectives) so that you can articulate this after expressing your concerns about being overburdened. Don't reveal your anger and don't attack the boss's motives. Appear calm and cooperative as you suggest ways to change the situation.

4. *Gang up on the boss with very gentle pressure*. Sometimes if all the staff join in some good natured teasing, it can slow down a dynamo.

Tactical Talk

"BOSS, DON'T YOU THINK IT'D BE A GOOD IDEA FOR US TO HAVE A BACKUP PERSON FOR THE COMMITTEE? MAYBE IF ALLISON CAME ALONG AS AN OBSERVER, WE COULD BE TRAINING HER . . ."

"BOSS, I REALIZE THE SIGNIFICANCE OF OUR FORMING AN ALLIANCE, BUT I NEED YOUR HELP IN FIGURING OUT HOW TO HANDLE MY OTHER FOUR MAJOR ASSIGNMENTS . . . SPECIFICALLY, I HAVE TO UNDERSTAND YOUR PRIORITIES SO THAT WE AGREE ON A TIME SCHEDULE . . ."

"BOSS, I KNOW HOW IMPORTANT THE NEW SYSTEM IS, BUT FOR THE PAST MONTH SINCE WE PUT IT IN, I'VE BEEN ASKED TO WORK SEVERAL EXTRA HOURS A WEEK WITHOUT BEING COMPENSATED. IF THAT'S GOING TO CONTINUE, IT DOESN'T SEEM FAIR TO ME. HOW DO YOU FEEL ABOUT IT?"

TIP: You can't assume the boss knows what you're feeling if you keep still. Without groping or griping or putting the boss on the defensive, you can learn to refuse or reshuffle assignments. Focus the discussion on the Slave Driver's desire to get the work accomplished when and how he wants.

Some bosses deliberately drain every last ounce of work out of you, or cover up their real reasons for their requests, or blame you in order to protect themselves. More often, exploitative bosses act like that because they are preoccupied or insensitive, unaware that they appear to be tricky. You're only ensnared when you're too scared to speak up. There are always other options to suggest. You can be cooperative without becoming the fly who steps into the spider's parlor.

SUMMING IT UP

How you deal with a specific boss, colleague, or subordinate who's currently making your life miserable depends on the outcome you want to accomplish. However, several general guidelines also can help you.

1. *Put Problem People in Proper Perspective*. You're nothing but an afterthought to them, so don't take their antics personally. They're not concerned about you because they're too busy worrying about themselves. You just happen to be either an obstacle or an essential ingredient to their getting what they want. You have to figure out how to break free of their control.

2. *Take Your Pick—Positive or Negative*. You can't concentrate on constructive, creative alternatives while you cling to negative feelings. Go somewhere to vent your emotions and cool off. Think about the result you really want, the consequence or outcome that most benefits you. That will help you let go of the hurt.

3. *Don't Expect Difficult People to Change*. They won't. And in one way that's good. Because their behavior is often predictable, this enables you to plan ahead, plotting the tactics you'll use next time. Troublemakers may not change, but by choosing a better approach *you* can change the outcome.

4. *Learn to Respond as Well as to Listen*. Come forward and state that you feel annoyed, upset, enraged. No one can read your mind. Sometimes the offense was totally unintentional and can be easily resolved if allowed to surface. Ask questions instead of making accusations. If you let others save face, you give them room to change their minds.

5. *Give and Request Frequent Feedback*. Regardless of your position in the organization, you need to know the perceptions of your boss, peers, and workers. Don't stew about what someone else may be thinking—ask! Use open-ended questions to let emotional people vent their feelings before you try to reason with them and explore options. When you link your objectives with another's wants, not only do you have his attention, but also you both win something.

6. *Look First at Policies and Procedures*. That starts the disagreement on a high professional level and prevents blaming a person's distasteful attitude or sinister motive. Don't place blame unless *you* made a mis-

take for which you apologize quickly and move on. If you both pay attention to each other's needs when identifying options—your stand may depend on which side of the desk you sit—each of you can feel you are exercising some control. At times all that's needed is a simple change in the system.

7. *Deal Directly and Discreetly.* Choose face-to-face talks over memos that can be misconstrued, phone calls that can conceal facial reactions, or ambassadors who do the talking for you. You don't want an audience for personal disagreements. Confront your accusers, tactfully putting your foot down when others are walking over you. Get right to the point because a preamble of excuses or warm-ups robs your effectiveness.

8. *Document for Self-Protection.* Get potentially troublesome verbal agreements in writing to prevent the other party from reneging. For assignments you fear may be hazardous to the health of your career, keep your boss informed with periodic progress reports. Send copies to anyone affected, as evidence, in case a misunderstanding should occur.

9. *Be Straightforward and Unemotional.* The more you remain calm and matter-of-fact, the sooner you gain another's confidence. People want to feel you're leveling with them, that they can trust you. Remember that respect from others begins with self-respect. Don't continue a conversation with anyone, even your boss, who refuses to give you the courtesy and deserve. You have options, such as asking for politeness or leaving the room.

10. *Be Gracious.* Someone else's rudeness doesn't give you the right to be rude. Turn a bad situation to your advantage by disarming the offenders, treating them with the kindness you'd like to be shown, sharing credit, and allowing others to feel important. Make friends with your enemies— you never know when you'll need them. Others won't have to run you down to build themselves up if you're gracious in showing appreciation and giving recognition. When your own ego is healthy, you are rich. You can afford to be generous.

Summary Points

- *Never* take it personally. While the problem may seem to overwhelm you, you're probably no more than afterthought to the offender.

- The bad news is you're not going to change most people. Nor should you try. The good news is most difficult people are predictable. This gives you a leg up.
- Two wrongs don't make a right. Just because they're rude, don't demean yourself by playing by their rules.
- The best communication is face-to-face. There's no ambiguity.
- For real problem makers, it is best to keep a documented record of their deeds.
- Familiarize yourself with your company's rules and procedures on such matters.

SECTION FOUR

LETTERS

INTRODUCTION—LETTER WRITING: PENNED-PERFECT

It may not be a part of your job now, but chances are, somewhere down the line, you will be called on to draft a variety of letters for any number of circumstances. Whether it's an irate customer who needs to be turned-around into a lifelong customer, a personal letter to an employee, or a sales letter that will get results, you will need to commit yourself to writing over your signature.

As a businessperson, you've probably heard it a million times. We live in a service economy. Industries no longer mass produce exactly the same item to everyone, and to heck whether the customer likes it. The old attitude expressed by one car maker for example, "you can have any color you want, as long as it's black," is about as outdated as the models they once described. Companies that fail to understand that competition is so fierce today because customers know that if they don't receive satisfaction with one firm they can easily take their business somewhere else. And they often do. One of the more effective tools you have as a businessperson both in keeping employees and customers happy is letter writing—one of the most personal forms of communications available next to a face-to-face meeting. There is something about the personal nature of letter writing that makes it very different from memo writing. Not too many people frame memorable memos they've received. More than a few will have letters on their walls, though. These are the communications that most represent the writer as a person.

It's therefore imperative that your writing accurately reflect what you want to say, the proper tone you want to use, and the style and flourish you want to use and the message you wish to convey. If you are hesitant about business writing in general, this section will help make the task of business letter writing a breeze. Most of the following chapters include sample texts you can use or adopt to your particular needs, as well as important tips on how to write your letters.

Chapter 13

Personal Letters

Dear Bob,

Congratulations, I just got the news. They couldn't have picked a better V.P. for the West Coast office.

Best wishes,

Tim

Personal business correspondence may sound like a contradiction in terms. Business? Personal? If you've ever run a small business or worked for a firm where you oversaw employees, you know it's not. Letters of this nature are often expressions of what you would have said to the individual if you have spoken to them in person. They often express something more than the run-of-the-mill letters many business people churn out that keep the wheels of business turning. Yet like any business person, often you don't have the time, and a letter can be more cherished or remembered sometimes better than a conversation.

Whether it's congratulating an employee on winning an award, expressing sympathy on the passing of a business friend, or declining an invitation, putting it in writing means putting it on the record, and phrasing it in a way that will have lasting impact. These are the types of letters that sometimes end up being framed and placed on the wall by the grateful recipient.

Wilbur Cross' *Small Business Model Letter Book* outlines several ready-made personal business letters that cover everything from expressing condolences, congratulations, thanks, and regret for a variety of situations. They are readily useable for whatever your own individual writing needs may be.

Personal Business Correspondence

This chapter is anything but a catch-all for letters and other correspondence that do not fit neatly into previous categories. Rather, it covers those subjects of a personal nature that commonly require letters from small-business owners and managers and professional people who deal with the public. These include condolences, congratulations, appreciations, apologies, invitations, presentations, requests for favors, maintaining social relations, and recognitions of achievements, among other topics. As the sample letters demonstrate, very often personal correspondence of this kind, though perhaps triggered by a sense of duty or responsibility, can reflect positively on the writers and the organizations they represent.

Writing a personal letter is frequently a substitute for a face-to-face visit. It helps to continue or cement a better relationship. It can mean that extra little dialog that shows you care or have a special concern for the recipient. Or it can nudge a person to take some form of action that is desired but not yet a reality. Since some of these letters are casual in style and content, why not use the telephone instead? The answer is that you most certainly can, time after time. Yet there is something about a letter, about expressing yourself on paper that is both more substantial and more permanent in its quality than a phone call. The person who takes the time and makes the effort to sit down and write has something of an edge over the phone caller. And, as studies have documented, the visual message is more likely to be remembered than the aural message. Even a brief note is frequently a reminder that can be placed in a conspicuous spot on the desk or tacked to a bulletin board.

Should you use a company letterhead or your personal stationery when writing a letter that is part business? Should it be typed or written by hand? There is no well-defined formula or protocol, and in the end you have to make that judgment yourself, based on your familiarity with the recipient. Generally, the less well you know the recipient, the more formal the format should be.

Some Questions to Ask Yourself

1. Who is the proper recipient for the message I am composing?

2. Is this the proper time for the letter to be sent?

3. How important is my own personality in writing and signing this letter?

4. What is the objective of the letter?

5. Am I making it clear what action or opinion is expected of the recipient?

6. If I were the recipient, how would I react to this particular letter and what would I think of the sender?

If the letter is social in its nature and content, but prompted for business reasons, its visual appearance should be more like that of a letter you might write at home, rather than one written in the office. People tend to react negatively to a personal letter they feel has been delegated to a secretary to write and type. "If a correspondent doesn't have time, or the interest, to write in person," is a typical comment, "then the letter shouldn't be sent at all."

How to Do It

1. Open with a personal comment, to set the tone.
2. Use conversational language instead of formal business terminology.
3. Relate your company to the subject and the recipient in a pleasant, low-key manner.
4. End on an upbeat note.

Even when a personal letter makes critical comments or includes some kind of rebuke, it should get across the fact that you are sympathetic to a problem and are convinced that the writing of the message is for your mutual benefit. In most cases, even a direct reprimand to an acquaintance or associate can conclude with a positive air of assurance and result in action for your common good.

Writing Letters of Condolence

The most difficult letter of all to write is one of sympathy on the occasion of a death, life-threatening illness, serious accident, or other tragedy. It is particularly tough to compose when—as is often the case in business situations—neither the victims nor their loved ones are well known to the writer. One way to lessen the burden is to send an appropriate card and include a handwritten note. But the most acceptable, and usually the most comforting, way to communicate is with a personal letter that evidences the time and sympathetic thought you have given to this tragic occasion.

You will find a number of model letters in this chapter, that will help you face this letter-writing challenge.

Some Tips for Writing Letters of Condolence

1. Never start with "I want to express. . . ." Few people ever *want* to write such a letter. In any case, just say what you have in mind.
2. Leave the bereaved with a fond memory of the deceased, especially if you knew him or her well.
3. Don't try to emulate your minister or explain how "time will heal all wounds . . ." and the like.

4. If you feel you *must* do something "inspirational," enclose a clipping rather than trying to compose immortal words.

5. Offer personal assistance only if you knew the deceased very well and if close relatives are likely to be really in need of help.

6. Be yourself and try to put yourself in the position of the recipient.

7. Don't try to make the deceased out to be something better than he or she really was. The deception always shows through.

8. Remember, the worst consolation letter of all is the one that never gets written!

CONGRATULATIONS

To Daughter of Employee—Fashion League Award

Dear Annette:

We are all so proud of you for winning the Fashion League Design Award and the scholarship that goes with it. Your mother had been so concerned that your shoulder injury and the costs of rehabilitation would prevent you from completing your work and your entry presentation. But you did it and that shows that you have another skill besides your artistic talents: the determination and will to achieve. That will serve you well in your future career.

As your mother has probably told you, we can always provide a part-time job here in our design department when you are looking for work during the summer or whenever else the Fashion School gives you a vacation.

Congratulations and good luck.

With our best wishes,

To Employee—Outstanding Volunteer Award

Dear Ms. Salgado:

Congratulations on winning the "Outstanding Volunteer" award from the Maybank Industrial Association. Our company is proud to have you in its ranks. And our industry has the good sense to recognize real talent and dedication on occasions like this. We wish you great success in your work here and hope that you will continue to look upon community volunteer work as a worthy complement to a fine career.

Sincerely,

To Business Associate—Outstanding Community Service

Dear Jason:

We were pleased and proud to see your accomplishments mentioned in the enclosed clipping from *Today's Globe*—pleased because we have enjoyed such a fine business relationship with you and your colleagues and proud because your skills and interests have enhanced the image of this neighborly community which we mutually call our hometown.

My first reaction was to wish that there were more people like you in Springfield. And my second reaction was to realize that there actually are because of your leadership and guidance. And there will continue to be more because of your influence on the young people who are growing up here.

We thought you'd like an extra clipping for Jason, Jr., to put in his scrapbook. And tell him that the Old Man has a lot of friends who are cheering him on.

Cordially,

ADVICE

To a Young Person Deciding on a Career

Dear Les:

"I wish I'd become a lawyer instead of an engineer—they're the guys making all the dough."

"I've had a good life at the bank, but I would have sure contributed more to mankind if I'd become a conservationist."

"Wouldn't you know, I could have been a successful artist and had a lot more colorful life than if I hadn't been scared about starving and ended up as a teacher."

When you get to be my age, you hear comments like these all the time, usually prefaced by the wish, "If I had it to do all over again, I'd. . . ." But you have to make your mind up and be decisive when you are young and have just gotten your degree and then go striding along the road you picked. It doesn't do any good to limp along and keep looking back and wondering whether you have made the right choice.

Since you asked for my advice it is this: evaluate your career options. Select the one that looks best. Then plunge in and tackle the job with enthusiasm and the conviction that it's the best one in the world for you. Don't look back and don't start comparing, at least not until you reach my age and need something to gab about with your old friends.

I'm sure you'll choose well and I wish you the very, very best.

Sincerely,

To a Widow—Franchise Plans

Dear Sally:

You are right to make plans, now that you are widowed, to occupy yourself with some form of meaningful employment. However, I do not think a franchise like ours is the answer because you expressed the idea that you want to be independent, and that is not always as easy as it sounds in our kind of small business. If you do have a franchise in mind, though, be sure to determine in advance how much control the franchiser can legally exert over the way you run the enterprise. Consider these limitations, for instance:

- You would have to pay the franchiser an upfront fee and then continue to pay royalties, based on gross income.
- You would not really own the business but only the right to handle the products or services being offered.
- A franchiser can legally limit any changes you want to make in business functions or physical designs.
- If the business goes sour through fault of the franchiser, you can sue him, but are likely to get hung up with substantial legal fees and headaches.

Whatever you decide to do, please let me know. I'd be happy to have our attorney look over any contract you are considering and red flag any points that could cause problems.

Affectionately,

THANK YOU

In the hustle and bustle of business and trying to keep abreast of more critical kinds of communications, we tend to ignore courtesy letters or postpone writing them. Yet thank you letters are important and can go a long way toward building a company's image or enhancing personal relationships. Here are a few appropriate examples.

Professional Award

Dear Dr. Schrontz:

On behalf of myself and my partners at Jacobsen, Fox, and Lindner, I am delighted to relay to you our acceptance of the Fairlawn Civic Improvement

---
GREAT JOB!

Survey after survey show that aside from adequate compensation, employees crave recognition for their accomplishments. You would be surprised what even a short personal note from the boss can mean to an employee yearning for some form of acknowledgment.

Keep an eye out for people under your wings who have won awards or have other major events in their lives like weddings, births, promotions, business awards, and so on. Many business people do this routinely to create a greater sense of familiarity and closeness with their employees. When heartfelt, well-written, and timed just right, it can project your image as a caring boss who respects and looks out for your most important business asset: your people.

Award for this year. As you so kindly requested, we will all be present at the Architectural Society Host Breakfast on November 3.

We feel honored that you singled out JF&L for this annual citation. But we are even more gratified that the award is associated with the design of the Lake Wilmington Municipal Boathouse because of the environmental and ecological features incorporated in its construction and maintenance plans. We have focused much of our professional time and energy on preserving and enhancing natural beauty in all our basic renderings and artistic concepts.

Sincerely,

Small-Business Award

Dear Gus:

One of my friends is a noted artist. He has a studio that is lined with award plaques, honor scrolls, medals, and other testimonials to his talents and finesse.

I have only a single award: the one your committee so graciously bestowed on me last week at the media presentation dinner. Yet I am more proud of what it means than my artist friend is of his whole roomful of honors. I say that from the heart. So thank you again for your recognition, and please pass along my appreciation to the others on your committee.

Sincerely,

Professional Favor

Dear Mr. and Mrs. Larue:

You were most thoughtful to recommend our line of fall fashions to your new neighbor, Mrs. Darnley. She seemed to be very pleased, both with our wares and the courtesy of our sales staff. So I just wanted you to know that everything went well, and we appreciate your support of our establishment.

Sincerely,

Gift

Dear Trevor:

You were most thoughtful to send me a battery-operated thesaurus and spelling corrector after you visited our offices last week. It is a most remarkable device and I have placed it in a prominent position on my desk, where I assure you it will get plenty of use. I write at least a dozen letters a day to friends and business associates. Since I am not the world's best speller, I frequently have to look up words in my old, dog-eared dictionary, a time-consuming process. Now, thanks to you, I can eliminate the step with a mere push of the buttons and write more letters in less time.

We enjoyed our discussion, which should prove to be most fruitful for all of us, and we look forward to your next visit.

With best regards,

Professional Club Membership

Dear Dr. Roemer:

Your invitation to join the Executive Affiliate of the Engineering Guild is accepted with appreciation. Until you mentioned it in your letter, I did not realize that I was the first nonengineer in the Guild's history to be admitted to membership. I am deeply honored. I should confess to you, however, that this statistic may soon be a relic of the past. Because of the intensification of my assignments in the field of mechanical engineering, I have been studying at night for a professional degree. If all goes well, I shall hold my B.E. degree within three months.

Sincerely,

Declining an Invitation

Dear Ms. Hugel:

Thank you for inviting me to attend the award luncheon in honor of Denise McConomy. I must regret your kind invitation since it conflicts with a program to which I have long been committed, and which cannot be passed over. Please extend my regrets to the honoree as well.

Cordially,

Declining Appeal to Run for State Office

Dear Barry:

It is flattering that you envision me as an aggressive and fiery legislator in Hartford, fighting for the rights of the people and the conservation of our ancestral lands. I have always admired the statesmanship of legislators in our Nutmeg State and considered them many cuts above the norm. However, I have to be realistic and honest and see myself as what I am. Personable? Yes, and good at my job, running a manufacturing business. Bright? To an extent, since I was usually on the dean's list at Trinity. Dedicated? Quite, in my career, but perhaps more so on the home front, where I like to putter around and be with family. A politician? No way. I can't wheel and deal, and I'm a sitting duck for those that can.

Thank you kindly for even thinking of me in the Connecticut Senate. But, for the good of the people, I have to decline to run at this time.

Sincerely,

APOLOGY

Unseemly Conduct

Dear Mr. Messinger:

My emotional outburst during Dr. Praeger's seminar, "The Limits of Liability," was uncalled for and rude. For that I apologize, to you, to our instructor, and to the assembled participants. I have no excuse for such behavior, particularly as an attorney whose professional demeanor calls for retaining control of oneself and remaining calm, even in the most heated clashes of defendants and prosecutors.

Upon reflection, I realize that I should have ignored the naive viewpoint of the participant who made a verbal attack on our firm's integrity. Others in the room did so, while my blowup seemed only to confirm the charge made by the accuser that we were culpable.

Please give my apologies to Dr. Praeger.

Sincerely,

Missed Appointment

Dear Natalie:

It is dismal to think that I could be losing my memory at such a young age. But how else could I forget that we had an appointment for a luncheon that would have been truly delightful tasty, and bubbling with good cheer? I keep reaching for excuses, but have absolutely none.

Please forgive me and let's reschedule our plans—perhaps for next week. I'll give you a ring.

Sincerely,

ANNOUNCEMENTS

Retirement Plans

Dear Gene:

As it happened to all of us, to use *Time* magazine phraseology, the moment to retire is on my horizon. I see the date as a year from now, give or take a few months, depending largely upon the wishes of a successor. I urge you, therefore, to initiate an early search for likely candidates for the directorship of the school. I have two persons in mind, but would prefer holding their names in abeyance until the Board has submitted its own preliminary list.

If I may make one suggestion, I see the director as one with less of my business background and more with educational qualifications. I have long realized that, while I was adept at stimulating the preparation of sound business courses, I was less successful in instituting the best teaching procedures. A professional educator would, in my opinion, be superior to an executive as the director. But l leave it in your hands.

Sincerely,

Separation from Spouse

Dear Charles:

It may come as a surprise to you, but my wife of 30 years and I have agreed to a separation, effective by the time you receive this letter. One of the problems has been that our two careers have kept us constantly separated during the last five years as our respective businesses have required regular flights to many different parts of the country, and often over long periods of time.

Martha and I are separating in a friendly manner and have both agreed that it is only fair to write all of you who have done business with one, or both, of us over the years. Martha will remain in the condominium at our old address. And I can reached at the office or, during nonbusiness hours, at the address and phone number on this letterhead.

Thanks in advance for your understanding.

Sincerely,

Postponing a Social Event

Dear Renee:

The anniversary party is off.

I bit off more than I could chew. I wanted it to be the biggest, best, and most congenial event of the season—just for people like you. So I planned it accordingly.

Then the stock market fell. And with it my hopes. Good sense compels me to rethink the immediate future.

But I promise you, as soon as we affect a turnaround, *then* I'll throw a double party: one for this anniversary and one for the next.

In the meantime, my . . .

Sincere regrets,

SYMPATHY AND CONDOLENCE LETTERS

The following letters are characteristic of those sent by businesspersons to individuals and families, some of whom are known personally to the writer and others known only through their relationship with the deceased.

THE PERSONAL TOUCH

Where do you draw the line between business and personal? When it comes to letter writing, it is impossible for this book—or any other book—to say. It all depends on how well you know the person, what the circumstances are, and what exactly you want to say. In certain cases, it's a good idea to dispense with your word processor and scribble a personal handwritten note.

There is no better way to express a personalized note than taking the time to write it in your own handwriting. It's best to use a smaller sized paper that looks like it came from personal stationery—not the standard 8-1/2″ × 11″ sheets used in most business writing. You don't necessarily have to go the expense of buying paper with your name attached, but it should look nice.

Make sure your handwriting is neat and legible. If you're like most people these days, you write virtually everything on computer, and your handwriting skills may leave a lot to be desired. Take the time and do it right. The person receiving your note will definitely appreciate the effort.

Death of a Longtime Business Friend

Dear Louise:

It was such a long, long battle, and I don't know anyone who showed more grit and determination than Warren or courage on your part. We all had tremendous admiration and respect for Warren during his illness, right from the time he first wrote us to explain what was happening.

It is comforting to you, I'm sure, to have such great support from family and friends, near and far. And there is little I can say to provide any greater degree of comfort. But it might be of value to you to know that Warren has been a great inspiration. At times—fortunately not too many—when we have had setbacks or I have felt depressed about one thing or another, I have often thought about Warren. How would *he* have handled such problems? Certainly with more fortitude and faith and optimism that I have been displaying. And it will always be thus, as long as I have the mental capacity to think clearly. And for that, I am eternally grateful to Warren—and to all of you who have lived with your problems so graciously and devotedly over the years.

For these things I am thankful, and I feel that Warren's memory keeps him alive in many thoughts besides mine.

Sincerely,

Death of an Immediate Business Associate

Dear Ms. Templeton:

The thoughts of all of us here at your father's office are with you at this time, and particularly so since we knew your late mother as well and remember her when she used to bring you by for a visit with some of us. You can well be proud, as we are, of what your father accomplished during his illustrious career, first at the University and then with our firm. "Doc," as we affectionately called him, was one of those rare people who could lead people into full cooperation on some very difficult and complex projects without ever seeming to pressure them or establish impossible deadlines. He will be missed here more than I can tell you. But our loss can never compare with that of you and your brothers and the grandchildren.

We count our blessings for having known and worked with him as long as we did.

Affectionately,

Death of a Colleague

Dear Mathilda:

The other night, I was working late, actually almost until midnight, when I heard our elevator door click. I jumped because I was alone in the third-floor newsroom and for an instant I thought of but óne person. Regularly, for many years when I was meeting our weekly deadline, I would be startled at one or two o'clock in the morning by that familiar click and there would stand Dave. He couldn't sleep, so he would come down to the office to talk.

Often, he would be wearing his overcoat right over his pajamas and I knew it would be a long night because he loved to talk, and I loved to talk to him. We gabbed of many things, fools and kings, sometimes until daylight when the janitor would run us out. He'd tell me how what he really wanted to do was to run a special kind of garage in a little town somewhere in Ohio and talk to people and tinker with cars. What a guy!

I owe so much to him, not alone in warm memories of friendship but in tangible things. I recall, as a newly married, moving into a crackerbox of a house that had no air conditioning. "What you need is a nice screened porch," Dave said to me during a visit one sultry afternoon. My wife agreed.

Dave returned the next night to take measurements. He ordered the lumber, the cement blocks, and the following weekend he and I began building a screened porch. He was extremely handy. I was his flunky. But we built that porch together. You truly get to know someone after you've both bashed your thumbs a few times while nailing sheeting for the roof.

In later years, he advised me about a lot of things, particularly about some investments that helped to pay for my son's college education. I was grateful for that, and I'm thankful that my son also showed his gratitude to Dave long before he passed on.

Well, Mathilda, it all came home so forcefully the other night when I heard the elevator click at midnight and thought of Dave. It's funny how the little things like that in life remind you of the truly big things—like Dave.

Affectionately,

Death of a Colleague's Spouse

Dear Sarah:

It does not take a letter from me to tell you how sad we all are at Arthur's passing. Although I never worked with him personally, I knew him as one of the most forthright and reliable people on the business scene, who could always be counted on to live up to his commitments and carry his share of responsibilities, no matter how heavy. Beyond that, of course, we extend deep sympathy to you for your loss and pray that you are comforted by family and loved ones nearby.

Four of us from the office will be attending the memorial service next week, representing just a few of the many businesspeople in the community who would like to pay our last respects to your husband.

With sympathy,

Death of an Employee's Child

Dear Norma:

My two partners and I join in extending sympathy to you on behalf of the entire firm for the passing of your young son. I only wish I had the gift of expression to be able to comfort you better in this time of great sorrow. But you can be sure that you are in the thoughts and prayers of all of us at this time. May God be with you and grant you a measure of peace in the memory of one who was so loved and loving.

Sincerely,

Death of an Employee's Father

Dear Sheldon:

My wife and I were saddened to read in the *Daily Argus* this morning about the death of your father in Boston. We knew he had been ill for a long time, but that in no way lessens the loss you must be feeling at this time. We hope that you are close to family and friends who will give you fond support and love. Flora joins me in sending our heartfelt condolences to you and your loved ones.

Sincerely,

Belated Condolence

Dear Andrew:

I was grieved to hear that your partner had been killed in an automobile accident two weeks ago. I was in Chicago on business and did not receive the news until yesterday, upon my return. You have my deep sympathy, and even more so since I lost a close associate last year under similar circumstances and still feel a sense of shock when I think back on it. I did not know Alan anywhere nearly as well as I know you, but I'll always recall him as one of the brightest young men in our field and one with a keen sense of humor under fire.

Although I missed the memorial service, I have asked our treasurer to send a company donation to the Heart Association, as mentioned in the newspaper clipping that my wife showed me.

Cordially,

Announcing Death of a Business Partner

Dear Mrs. Proctor:

The death yesterday of our senior partner, Otto Julius Leftwich, was so sudden and unexpected that neither our firm nor our professional association has yet made any plans to commemorate his name and achievements. It would be fitting to answer any inquiries you receive in your capacity as secretary with something like this. "The members of the Association are saddened by the departure of the man who was recognized as a pioneer in accounting procedures and who gave unstintingly of himself in developing programs to attract young people to the profession. Plans are now underway for a memorial scholarship in Dr. Leftwich's name, which will be announced by the Association during its next monthly meeting on October 19."

You might also want to send out a brief profile, which can be copied from the Association's directory. I'll be in touch with further information and suggestions shortly.

Cordially,

Get Well—Serious Illness

Hi, Trevor,

When I was in the hospital two years ago, you paid me almost daily visits and it was great for my morale. Now that I want to return the favor and visit you, I am told that I have to wait a few days. It's just like in the office—one delay after another. In the meantime, I can at least send you this silly card and my hope that you'll be up and about in no time. You'll end up better than ever. Remember, I did. And at one time they didn't think I'd make it through until the next breakfast. See you soon. Mindy sends her love.

Regards,

Get Well—Accident

Dear Stephanie:

Your husband left a message while I was away, telling me about your automobile accident. While I am distressed to hear of your misfortune, I am relieved to know you'll be out of the hospital by the time you get this note. As I think I told you earlier this week, I am going out of town for the financial seminar, so will not have a chance to visit you in person. But I did want you to know that there is no urgency about your returning to the office. The most important matter is to get yourself back in shape. Take all the time you need. And don't worry about the bills—our new accident and health plan will cover you for most of the hospital costs.

I hope to see you back in your usual good health by the time I return.

With best wishes from all of us,

To Father After Accident to His Daughter

Dear Mr. Manninghouse:

As the father of three daughters, I can well understand your apprehension that the accident suffered by your daughter, Melissa, might leave her with a facial disfigurement. Please rest assured that such is not the case. I have conferred with two specialists at the hospital and studied the x-rays. I am told that the healing process itself will eliminate what now looks like a nasty cut. Following that, minor plastic surgery will remove remaining scar tissue and Melissa's skin will show no signs of the injury.

Medical miracles are many, but they cannot erase the memory of the traumatic moments your daughter experienced when her stamping machine malfunctioned or the days of pain that followed. However, you can be certain that the company will accept full responsibility for the accident and do all in its power to ameliorate the distress caused to both patient and family. Everyone here is most sympathetic, and I believe you can judge that yourself, in light of the number of visitors Melissa has had and the way her fellow employees have reacted.

Sincerely,

To Spouse of Accident Victim

Dear Marlene:

My secretary phoned me to report having heard that Chester was seriously injured in a boating accident while deep-sea fishing near your Florida home. While it is a relief for me to know that he is off the critical list and resting more comfortably in the hospital, I wanted you to know that all of us—the ones he calls "the Old Gang"—are rooting for him. We have some cards and little remembrances we'd like to send him as soon as he gets home again. So please keep me apprised of his condition and whereabouts, so I can pass the information around.

In the meantime, my very best to you and your daughters.

Affectionately,

Summary Points

- Personal business letters can greatly help cement business relationships.
- The less well you know the recipient, the more formal your writing should be.
- Use conversation language. Avoid business jargon.
- Open with a personal comment.
- Always close on an upbeat note.

CHAPTER 14

SALES LETTERS: MAKING THE PITCH

When you think about it, almost everything you do in business would be irrelevant if it weren't for sales at some point. Whether you're in a service industry or a goods-producing industry, if profits aren't being made, you'll likely not have too much to write about in the long run. For some businesses, the sales letter is the classic method of prospecting for clients or customers. You've probably received hundreds at home and work. Think about the ones that really stood out, that really made you want to buy whatever it was they were selling. A good sales pitch can go a long way. What was it that made it stand out?

Was it the punchy opening line? The testimonial from a well-known figure? The way the writer seemed to know exactly what you were looking for? The fact that it was short and sweet and didn't waste your time?

Whatever form it took, there are right ways and wrong ways to do it. For example, studies have shown you can lose your reader well before the end of the first paragraph. Therefore, you've got to have a great opener—and a great closer for that matter—to make the letter work for you.

Rosalie Maggio's best-selling book, *How to Say It: Choice Words, Phrases, Sentences and Paragraphs for Every Situation,* excerpted below, offers excellent tips on writing sales letters, including tips on inserting "power words" that grab your reader's attention and keep it. It also includes model openers, model closers, and sample letters for a variety of situations. Feel free to borrow, adapt, or change as your needs fit. The texts should give you an excellent starting point for getting your mailing ready.

SALES LETTERS

"The advertisement is one of the most interesting and difficult of modern literary forms." (Aldous Huxley)

Almost every letter that's sent out by a company, business, or organization is essentially a sales letter. Even "nonbusiness" letters like sympathy notes, congratulations, thank you letters, or apologies carry a second-level message that asks the recipient to think well of the firm.

In 1988, nearly 62 billion pieces of direct mail advertising weighing 7.6 billion pounds were delivered by the Postal Service—that's 250 pieces and nearly 31 pounds for every woman, man, and child in the United States.

In 1988 revenues from direct mailing advertising amounted to $270 billion; they are expected to have nearly doubled by 1992 to $500 billion. This is big business, and sales letters may be the most financially important ones you write.

Although computerized mailing lists have considerably reduced direct mail marketing costs, only about five out of every one hundred mailings are even opened by the recipient. This has two implications: you may want to use the envelope itself in such a way as to entice the person to open it; you will want to make those five opened letters so appealing that you get more than the average three out of five responses.

Sales letters aren't appropriate for all products and services, but they can usually get the reader to make the call or visit the store where the real selling can be done. Because they are productive and economical (compared to print and video advertising, for example), they are an integral part of most firms' marketing strategies. For many small businesses, they are the only practical and affordable advertising tool available.

Whether you're selling a product, a service, an idea, space, credit, or good-will, the sales letter requires more work before you begin to write than it does to actually write it. Henry Ford said, "Before everything else, getting ready is the secret of success." You need to know everything about your product or service. You need to know your reader, assembling as much data as possible. Then you must pinpoint and develop a strong central selling point. A number of other factors may be considered as well (timing, developing a coupon or sample). Only when a great deal of preparatory work has been done can a successful letter be written. Do not begin to write too soon.

Because they are so essential to a company's success, sales letters have become sophisticated and professional to the point that many corporations and businesses no longer generate their own. The buzzword today is "integration," and many large companies use full-service agencies to handle every aspect of their advertising needs, including sales letters. You can locate such firms in the Yellow Pages under Direct Marketing, Advertising Agencies, or Public Relations Counselors.

Kinds of Sales Letters

- announcements: changes/new products
- congratulations: purchase/new account/payment

- direct mail advertising
- follow-up: inquiries/sales letters/sales
- form letters
- goodwill
- introducing new products/services
- invitation: open house/sale/membership/new account
- questionnaires/surveys
- responding to inquiries
- special promotions/sales/free gifts and services
- thank you: sale/new/account/revived account
- trial offers: products/programs/services/subscriptions

How to Say It

- Get the reader's attention.
- Establish contact.
- Create an interest in what you're selling with a strong central sales message.
- Arouse the reader's desire for your product by using specific, vivid words and images to describe it.
- Convince the reader that responding to your offer is a smart move, offering "proofs" (samples, testimonials, statistics) of your assertions.
- Tell the reader how to obtain your product or service.
- Stimulate and encourage the reader to take immediate action.

What Not to Say

- Do not say, "We never hold a sale! Our everyday prices are so low that we don't need to." Human nature likes a sale. Even customers who regularly use your products or services and think they are reasonably priced like a bargain. By offering occasional discounts, sales, clearances, and special purchase promotions, you'll create a sense of excitement and willingness to buy in both old and new customers.
- Avoid the first-name, palsy-walsy approach. Business columnist Louis Rukeyser received an impressive amount of reader response after a col-

umn on form sales letters. According to him, "The artificially intimate stuff appears particularly irritating."

- Avoid subtle (and unsubtle) threats such as "You'll be sorry if you don't order now," "Yours while they last," "Don't miss this opportunity," "Don't pass this up." While a few readers may allow themselves to be stampeded by the hurry-hurry line, many more will call your bluff. Weigh this sort of approach carefully. A similar approach tells prospective customers that since they have not ordered anything during a certain period, their names will have to be removed from the mailing list if they don't order soon. This is actually effective in many cases as people fear missing out on something later on. While it doesn't work all the time and is a type of sales threat, it can be effective with judicious use.

- Do not scold customers, correct them, condescend to them ("you probably don't know this, but . . ."), tell them they're going about things the wrong way but not buying/using your product, laying down too many rules, regulations, requirements.

- Avoid jargon or concepts that make it difficult for the reader to quickly grasp your message. In pitching an engineering book to engineers, you will use some technical language, but the letter should still be intelligible at some level to laypeople.

- Although warnings could be issued against badmouthing competitors and making unwarranted claims for products, both these tactics have been used (although not often) and used successfully (again, not often). Your use of such approaches will depend on your perception of your firm and product as being "above" this or not.

- Do not make too many points in one letter. Concentrate on your strongest one or two sales points, add one in the postscript of you like, and save the others for follow-up letters.

- In general, don't ask questions. It is poor psychology to get your reader into a "dialogue" in which they might not answer your question "correctly." Questions also derail your reader from the one-way train of thought that leads to a sale. Once you start building toward a certain conclusion, don't interrupt your sequence with questions. In particular avoid negative questions like "How can you afford to turn down this offer?" or "Why would anyone not want to own one?" Questions like these bring the idea of refusal to full consciousness.

- In most cases, you are better off without such hyperbolic claims for your product as astounding, revolutionary, incredible, sensational, extraordinary, spectacular. Use instead concrete features, benefits, details, and product claims. Understatement is often very effective.

Tips on Writing

- There is complete agreement on how to begin a sales letter: with a bang! There is no agreement, however, on what sort of a "bang" will work for you. Possibilities include: a surprising fact or statistic; a touching or dramatic anecdote; the offer of a gift, coupon, or booklet; a thought-provoking question or quotation; a joke or riddle; a celebrity endorsement, quote, or tie-in; a who-what-when-where-why paragraph; your strongest selling factor; nostalgia; addressing the reader by name (although this is not always agreeable to the reader) or as "someone special" singled out for the letter; perhaps even a negative or unexpected statement.

- There are a few more concrete guidelines for ending the sales letter. Because your main goal is to incite the person to immediate action, you tell them what you want them to do (order, call, mail a card, come to the store) and tell them how easy it is to do this ("enclosed is a postage-paid reply envelope"); echo your letter opening in some way—if you started off quoting a celebrity, finish by saying something like, "And that's why so-and-so won't drive anything but a . . ."

- Keep your paragraphs short.

- Beginning, middle, and end, the focus must remain on the prospective customer. Describe the product in terms of benefits to the customer, how it relates to their needs, problems, and interests, how it can improve their lives, save them money, make them feel more confident. The customer has only one question: "What is this going to do for me?" It's up to you to develop a strong client-centered message and persuade potential buyers that they need your product not so much because it's a great product, but because it is great for *them*. You will be using the words "you" and "your" frequently in such letters.

- It is rare that a sales message does not include somewhere the cost of the item or service. There is good reason for it; customers tend to ignore the message otherwise on the assumption that they can't afford it. Cost is a determinant in most purchases; if the customer has to call to find out, the extra trouble is often not worth it when a competitor's cost is available in its sales message.

- Make it convenient and desirable for the reader to respond. Convenience means order blanks accompanied by postage-paid reply envelopes, prepaid form postcards asking for a sales rep to call or for additional information, a toll-free number to call for local distributors or to place orders, order now-pay later, a listing of store hours and locations. To increase the desirability of responding, offer discounts, bargain prices, delayed no-interest payments, gifts, in-store certificates, coupons, brochures, samples, or a free trial period.

- Although both are necessary, emotional appeals tend to be more effective than intellectual appeals. Your letter should be underpinned with an appeal to some basic human emotion: love ("your child will have hours of fun!"); the need for love ("heads will turn when you wear this"); prestige ("your home will be a stand-out with this . . ."); ambition ("learn new management techniques overnight"); security ("smoke-alarm with built-in battery tester").

- Repetition is helpful in emphasizing a main point, in clarifying complicated material, and in lending an attractive rhythm to your letter.

- State very clearly what you want your reader to do: send for this, buy that, call this number, send in the coupon, order from this catalog.

- How long should a sales letter be? Most advice would probably come down in favor of the one-page letter. On the other hand, some well-written four-page letters have enjoyed a high response rate. And of course a poorly written letter is in no way redeemed by being short. It is perhaps more logical to concentrate on what absolutely needs to be said—whether that takes one page, two, or four.

- You can create and foster credibility by means of testimonials, case histories, research studies, statistics, company reputation, product usage test results, comparison with similar products, free samples or trial periods, guaranties/warranties, celebrity endorsements, photographs of actual use, user pools.

- Sales letters aimed at former customers emphasize your appreciation for past business, your desire to serve the customer again, products or services introduced since your last contact with them, your confidence that you can satisfy their needs. You could ask if there is a reason that they no longer bring their business to you. This may provide you with useful information. Or it may remind the customer that there *is* no particular reason.

- Give the person a good reason for acting right now: limited supplies, expiration date of sale offer, prices going up later, early-response discount, etc.

- When possible, quote satisfied customers (particularly well-known ones) who can testify to the product's or service's usefulness.

- Whenever possible, guarantee the buyer's satisfaction in some way.

- Some sales messages can make effective use of such attention-getting devices as colored ink or paper, graphics, boxed information, unusual type faces or paper finishes, or such design elements as heads, subheads, white space, indented material, and bulleted lists. Important parts of your message can be handwritten, underlined, capped, italicized, or set in some combination of these. This attention-getting approach is not for every sales letter. If you are selling bank cards, life insurance, healthcare services, or other "serious" products and services, you would do better to adopt a more traditional format.

- The postscript has become extremely popular in sales letters—probably because of its effectiveness. Repeat your most powerful selling point here, or feature a new and strong sales point such as money-back guarantee, a time limit for the offer, an additional bonus for buying now.

- Keep your letter exciting, pithy, and active. Use colorful descriptive words (words that are too general leave no trace in the reader's mind), strong verbs, appealing images. Sometimes a sales letter writer is so intent on either educating the prospective customer or building up a case via statistics, background information, and reports, that they forget how boring and how un-client-centered such a message is.

- There is a fine line between the clever gimmick, hook, ploy, or attention-getter and the too-cute-for-its-own-good approach. When taking a risk with a novel overture, have a number of people from different backgrounds read and evaluate your letter. If it is clever, the rewards are great. If you stray on the side of coy or insensitive, the results can be fatal.

- Convey to your reader that responding positively to your offer is the only sensitive course of action to take.

- Consumers love free gifts, samples, and coupons!

- Dale Carnegie once said, "I deal with the obvious. I present, reiterate and glorify the obvious—because the obvious is what people need to be told." Never assume anything on the reader's part, and do not be afraid to state the obvious.

- For a select audience, you may want to use good quality stationery, first class postage, and an individually typed address to ensure that your recipient opens it.

- Choose a specific tone for your letter and maintain it throughout. Is your product one that can be described well in a friendly, neighbor-to-neighbor tone? Or will readers respond better to a serious, intellectual tone? Other tones include: humorous, brisk and businesslike, urgent and hard-hitting, sophisticated, lively and fast-moving, technical, soothing and reassuring, mysterious, informational, emotional.

- Sometimes a series of letters is effective. When you have good reason to believe a segment of the market is susceptible to your product (because of previous purchases, for example), you may want to contact them several times—but not with the same letter each time. The letters can differ from each other either by focus (highlight a different benefit of your product or service in each letter), by intensity (time is growing short, our offer will expire soon), or by offer (two-for-one price in one letter, a discount in another).

Special Situations

- A sales message is often combined with another message. For example, a letter congratulating someone on their new business mentions how the sender's products might be useful. A cover letter accompanying the new spring catalog points out new products or an improved ordering system. Thank you letters, announcements, letters of welcome, and seasonal greetings have all been used to carry a sales message.

- When you send samples, product literature, or information in response to a customer's request, the cover letter must be a sales letter of the best type. Although the enclosure should sell itself (or the product it describes), the cover letter can carry a strong sales message and additional incentives to become a regular customer (describe other benefits, enclose a cents-off or discount coupon, include a catalog and order form).

- With a versatile product or service (or a number of different products in your line), you will want to match up certain features or certain products with a particular segment of the market and target them with a letter tailored to their needs. For the same product, you might send out six different letters to six different types of customers. A greenhouse manufacturer might write different sales letters to farmers, suburban homeowners, businesses, apartment dwellers, and even college students (the desktop miniature greenhouse).

• When you are already selling a certain group of customers one product or service, you may want to target them with a sales letter promoting another product or service that, out of long habit, they don't "see" anymore. For example, customers who regularly use a hair salon may forget that they can also buy an extensive line of hair-care products, use tanning booths, or schedule manicures.

Format

• Most sales letters are computer-generated form letters—either standard form letters or letters in which individual names, addresses, and salutations are filled in using a mass mailing merge feature. The latter gives form letters a more personal look (unless you are also inserting the person's name here and there throughout the letter, which actually gives the opposite impression).

• Some form letters are printed on good-quality paper, signed individually, and mailed first class.

WORDS

absolute	electronic	nostalgic
acquaint	exclusive	optional
adaptable	expert	portable
advantages	exquisite	powerful
affordable	extensive	practical
all-new	feature-packed	precision
attractive	flair	privilege
authentic	flexible	productive
available	free	professional

bargain

benefit

brand-new

breakthrough

brilliant

classic

clever

comfortable

compact

convenient

dazzling

delightful

dependable

discount

durable

economical

effective

efficient

genuine

guaranteed

half-price

handy

helpful

high-quality

indulge

inexpensive

informative

ingenious

innovative

invaluable

low-cost

low-priced

luxurious

money-making

natural

new

profitable

rapid-action

rebate

revolutionary

state-of-the-art

stunning

successful

super

thrifty

tremendous

unbreakable

useful

valuable

versatile

warranted

waterproof

wholesale

worth

PHRASES

absolutely free

acquaint you with

add a new dimension to

advanced design

a great gift idea

all for one low price

all in one easy operation

all-in-one portable convenience

all of this at your fingertips

an impressive collection

an incredibly low introductory rate/price of

appreciate your business

a price you'll appreciate

a revolutionary approach

as an added bonus

at a discount

at a fraction of the cost of

at Culver, it's been our commitment since 1921 to

at great savings/no expense to you

at your discretion

benefits and privileges include

blends in beautifully with any

both practical and beautiful

budget-pleasing prices

build upon the excellence that

built-in features

can choose from over 20 styles/cards/models/varieties

can make a dramatic difference to you

carefree upkeep

come in and try

compact design

complimentary copy

contemporary/gracious design

custom personalization

did you know that

direct-to-you low prices

direct your attention to

discover how you can

does three jobs at once

easier and more enjoyable

easier to use than ever before

easy and comfortable to wear and use

easy/carefree maintenance

easy-to-follow instructions

elegant styling

engineered for dependability

enjoy it year round

every item is offered at a discount

exciting details/offer

experience the pleasure of

extremely pleased to be able to offer you

fast, efficient way to

fast, safe, easy-to-use

finely crafted

fit-any-budget price

for just pennies each

friendly and helpful

full refund

fully automated/warranted

get full details

gives you your choice of/the opportunity to

greater safety, convenience, and pleasure

guaranteed for two full years

have the satisfaction of knowing

hundreds of daily uses

if not completely satisfied

if you accept this invitation, you will be joining the select company of those who

if you respond right away

if you send payment now, you'll receive

I'll think you'll discover that

I'm writing to tell you about

in these fast-moving times

invite you to

it can pay for itself in

join millions of others who

just a reminder that

lasting beauty

lets you enjoy more of your favorite

low, low prices

loyal customers like you

mail the enclosed card today

makes any day special

may I send you this

money-back guarantee/offer

money's worth

more advanced features

more powerful and sensitive

more than fifty years of service

no matter which set you choose

no more mess/lost sales/typing
errors/fuss/worry

no-risk examination

no strings attached

not at all as costly as you might
expect

now, for the first time,

now is the time to learn more about

of particular importance to you

one of the largest and most
respected daycare centers

one size fits all

on the enclosed Charter Invitation

our top-seller

outstanding features

over 50,000 satisfied customers

please take this opportunity

practical and decorative

preferred customer/rates

previously sold for

professional quality

prompt, courteous service

proven reliability

provides the finest home hair care
at the least cost

puncture-resistant

ready to spoil you with its powerful
features

reasonably priced

reduced price

reward yourself with

risk nothing

rugged and dependable

satisfaction guaranteed

simple to operate

so unusual and striking that they
will be enjoyed again and again

special introductory offer/value

step in the right direction

stop those costly losses with

surprise that special someone with

take advantage of this opportunity

take a giant step forward now,
today, towards

take a moment right now to look
over this

takes the gamble out of choosing
between

the intelligent way to

the many advantages of

the most versatile, powerful, and exciting study aid available

the perfect gift for yourself or a loved one

there's a world of enjoyment waiting for you with

the whole family can enjoy

this is one reason among many to order

time is growing short, so do send today for your

timeless elegance

to fit all your gardening needs

to suit your individual taste

unconditional money-back guarantee

under no obligation to

under our simple plan

unequaled savings and convenience

unique and invaluable

unique limited edition creations

urge you to

use it anywhere, anytime

user friendly

we expect a tremendous response to this offer, so

we look forward to sending you

we're making this generous offer because

we urge you to send today for

what better way to

why not order today/take advantage

with all this, you might expect these casseroles to cost as much as $25 apiece, but

with no obligation on your part

with our compliments

won't cost you a thing to

won't find better quality anywhere

won't you take a few moments right now to

worldwide provider of quality

you have been selected to receive

you'll be amazed to discover

you're a winner with your favorite

your key to peace of mind

your money back

your name has been proposed as someone who might like to own

you will appreciate the outstanding quality of these

SENTENCES

And don't forget—your fee includes a free gift!

And there's more I haven't mentioned—its dependability, for example.

At this low price, every home should have one.

Be the first in your community to have one!

But act now—we expect a sizable response and we want to be certain that your order is processed.

But that's not all.

Call today to arrange a demonstration.

Compare the savings, protection, and service you are currently paying for with what you could be getting with American Auto Insurance.

Discover savings of up to 50%.

Discover the elegance of a genuine leather briefcase with discreet gold initials.

Don't miss out!

Do your holiday shopping the easy way.

Enjoy it for a 15-day home trial.

Final notice!

Give us a call at 1-800-555-2110.

If you are not completely satisfied, simply return it for a full credit.

In order to make this offer, we must have your check by September 1.

It's a first!

It's a no-strings offer.

It's simple to get your free, no-obligation information on rates, available discounts, special services, and easy claims filing.

It's time for a change/for a new approach!

Join us today.

Just bring this letter with you when you come in to sign up.

Just what makes the Blount Filing System so great?

Mail the coupon now.

May I make an appointment with you next week to explain/show/demonstrate our latest line of products?

No other car can offer you this degree of prestige and affordability.

Now there's a new magazine just for you.

Offers like these don't come along very often.

Order one for every family member.

Orders are subject to credit approval.

Please do it promptly.

Please do not send any money now!

Please don't delay your decision—we except a heavy demand for the Ellesmere filet knife.

Please don't hesitate to call for a free demonstration.

Please look over this offer very carefully.

P.S. To lock in these great rates, we must receive your deposit by October 15.

Returning the postage-paid reply card does not obligate you in any way.

Send for your free copy of the Bemerton planning guide.

Send in the card now, before you forget.

Send no money now—we'll bill you later.

Take a look at the enclosed brochure for a sneak preview.

Telephone now for an appointment.

Telephone Sarah Lash, your personal representative, for an interview.

Thank you so much for reading my letter, and I look forward to hearing from you.

The Art Deco look fits almost any decorating scheme.

There is absolutely no risk on your part when you order.

There's no cost or obligation of course.

There's plenty more!

These low prices are effective only until June 1.

This is just one more reason why our products have won such overwhelming acceptance.

This is why I'm writing you today.

To get your full-color booklet, just complete and return the enclosed postage-paid reply card.

Try a sample . . . free!

Use the order form and postpaid reply envelope enclosed to receive your first Holiday Bell absolutely free.

We cannot extend this unusual offer beyond May 25, 1993.

We invite you to complete the enclosed reservation request form and return it now to confirm your choice of dates.

We'll bill you later, after you've made up your mind.

We'll start you off with your first issue/book/figurine free.

We note that you have not used your charge account recently.

We're determined to win you over to Dalgarno office furniture.

We're making this unprecedented offer to a select group of homeowners.

We take all the risks.

We've missed you.

We want to make it as easy as possible for you to order.

What could be simpler?

Why not do it now, while the form is handy?

Why not say "yes" today?

Won't you join us by being among the very first to become a Charter Subscriber?

Won't you please let us hear from you right away so we can include your order with the many others we expect?

You can choose from over 150 different programs.

You can now acquire a snowblower for far less than you ever thought possible.

You'll appreciate these fine features.

You'll like our convenient evening and weekend hours; you'll love our brand-new equipment and experienced teachers!

You'll see that Rockminister China isn't like other china.

You'll wonder how you ever did without it.

You may not have ever bought/invested/tried, which is why we are making you this no-risk trial offer.

You must see the complete series for yourself to appreciate fully how it can enrich your life.

PARAGRAPHS

- Are you still paying premiums for the same homeowner's policy you signed up for ten years ago? Have you thought about comparing what's available today with what you bought ten years ago?

- If for any reason, at any time, you are not satisfied with your Haverley Air Cleaner, you can return it to us for a complete and prompt refund. No questions asked.

- P.S. The cookbook of your choice and lucite book stand are both yours free—without obligation. All you need to do is send in the enclosed form.

- Send no money now. You will be billed at the time of shipment for any items ordered, plus shipping and sales tax (if applicable). But you do not have to pay until you are totally convinced of the high quality and value of our lithographs and prints. If you are not delighted in every way, just return your purchases within 10 days, and you'll owe nothing!

- The enclosed Special Introductory Invitation can be guaranteed for a limited time only. We urge you to reply within the next 21 days.

- There's only one sure way to convince you that Bryerley Bath Beads are the last word in luxurious skin-softeners. We're enclosing sample packets of two of our most popular Bryerley scents, Gardenia and Lily of the Valley. Try them and see if you don't notice a big difference!

- Congratulations on your election to membership in the Society for Historic Preservation! If you accept this membership offer—and I certainly hope you will—you will become part of a unique and influential group. As a member you will enjoy such important benefits as voting privileges on matters of national importance, a subscription to the monthly magazine, *Preservation,* and many more. Please mail the enclosed Confirmation of Election by May 31.

- P.S. This is your last chance to buy the kits at these low prices. Rising material costs require a moderate price increase effective later this year.

- You want to give that special child in your life the finest reading—his or her very own books—but you don't have the time to look at thousands of children's books to find the best. That's where we come in.

- Is a housecleaning service for you? We think so because you want the best for yourself and your family . . . and that takes time. Time you don't always have after working all week and meeting important family needs after hours. We can offer you thorough, reasonably priced once-a-week housecleaning that will make all the difference in your life. Think about what you could do with the hours you now have to spend on housework. Think about walking into a clean house at night. And then think about giving us a call to schedule an estimate interview.

SMALL LETTERS

Dear Executive:

   According to several management studies, the single most important characteristic of an effective executive is the ability to manage time.

   Are you meeting all your deadlines? Can you list your current projects in
order of importance? Do you have a good idea of where you are headed over the
next week, month, year? Can you find things when you need them? Do you assign
work in the most time-effective ways?

   If you answered no to any of these questions, you're sure to benefit from our
popular, effective Time Management Workshop.

   In just two days you will learn how to set priorities, how to use special tools that
will help you organize your time, and how to develop interpersonal skills that will
help you deal with unnecessary interruptions, inefficient staff, and group projects.

   In fact, we don't want to be one of those interruptions, so we suggest that you
save time by making time for the next Time Management Workshop in your area.
You can do this in under a minute by checking off a convenient date and signing
the enclosed postage-paid reply card or by calling 1-800-555-1707 to register.

   This is one workshop that won't be a waste of time!

                                             Sincerely,

                              . . . .

Dear Marietta Lyddon,

   You were a member of the Atlas Fitness Club from March 15, 1990, to
November 18, 1990, and according to our records you worked out regularly.

   Whatever your reasons for not being with us the past several years, you may
want to know about some changes that have taken place since you were last here:

   New this year: Olympic-size pool with extended hours, 5:30 a.m. to midnight. A lifeguard is on duty at all times.

   New this year: Membership packages designed to fit your use patterns. You
may now choose between an all-use pass or a pass that specifies morning hours,
early morning hours, after-five hours, evening hours, late evening hours.

   New this year: Peripheral services that our members—most of whom are
busy working people like yourself—have requested: a personal check-cashing service; yogurt, soup, and mineral water machines in the lobby; a telephone for the
use of members making local calls; all-new padlocks for the lockers.

   New last year: We now have 50% more equipment in the weight lifting
room, and three new Nautilus units.

If you liked us before, you'll love us now. I think it's worth a look, and I'm so convinced of this that I'm going to offer you a two-week membership for FREE.

All you have to do is bring this letter with you when you come to give us another look!

Sincerely yours,

. . . .

Dear MasterGold Cardmember,

A revolutionary new service is now available to valued MasterGold card-members—and you're among the first invited to enroll.

CreditReport service is a valuable new credit tool that will allow you to guard your privileged credit status. Membership in CreditReport entitles you to:

- Unlimited access to copies of your CreditReport record. This is the one many credit managers and loan officers see. Now you can know what's in your credit report before you apply for credit or financing and avoid potentially embarrassing situations.

- Automatic notification when anyone receives a copy of your CreditReport files. This way you know exactly who is receiving your credit report, and when.

- Your financial profile—this valuable tool lets you organize your personal finances in one convenient document. Once completed, you may place your all-purpose credit/loan application on our computers—ready to be electronically transmitted to any participating credit grantor—in an instant.

- Convenient application for loans or financing at participating credit grantors. A membership card is recognized at thousands of credit grantor locations—where shopping for the best credit terms can mean big savings on interest payments.

- Credit card protection: At no extra charge we'll register all your credit, charge, and ATM cards in case of loss or theft. And we'll also provide for change of address for all your cards should you move.

Best of all, your membership includes an unconditional money-back guarantee, so you can enjoy all the privileges of membership without risk.

This is a valuable service for MasterGold cardmembers. I urge you to look over the enclosed materials and consider this special offer now.

Sincerely,

SALES

A sales letter is only one of many factors in the sale of a product or service. A need must exist—or be imagined; the customer's interest must be aroused and a choice must be made among competing salespersons and products. A sales letter probably won't accomplish all these things, but it can persuade the reader that he or she will be helped by buying the product or service.

One technique for persuasion is to use POWER words. Using words to make people DO things is the key to business success. Listed here is a sampling of power words, effective in pepping up a sales letter:

able	free	powerful
absolute	great	professional
advantage	guarantee	proved
brilliant	hard-sell	quality
confidence	help	quickly
controlled	immediate	results
delighted	impelling	satisfaction
detail	insight	scientific
different	instant	solved
economical	know	stunning
effective	largest	successful
electronic	latest	super
emphasis	lowest cost	today
expert	money-making	tremendous
extensive	new	value
fact	now	volume
fair	oldest	you
flare	persuasive	yours

As will be observed in the models, sales letters also take advantage of visual aids. These include such devices as CAPITAL LETTERS, "quotation marks," underlined words, dashes—, dots . . ., short paragraphs, phrases punctuated as sentences, indented paragraphs, exclamation points, and postscripts.

The purpose is to hold the attention of the reader, who, thus becomes eager to read on to find out what is interesting enough to deserve this special presentation.

Insurance sales letters and advertisements often emphasize fear—fear of what *could* happen—so you had better be prepared with *our* insurance coverage. Fear is one basic appeal. Other basic appeals, which are general themes or topics running through the letter, include love, pride, greed, ambition, sex, hate, and loyalty. An emotional appeal is usually more effective than an intellectual presentation.

A word of caution when appealing to these various emotional feelings; don't belittle the reader, exaggerate, trick the reader, be flippant, or abuse competitors. A little puffing of your item or service is good, but respect the intelligence of your reader.

However intelligent the reader, he or she has a limited attention span. Cover only a few selling points in each letter (or preferably only one). Trying to tell everything only confuses the reader.

What you say should be directed toward the audience you have chosen. Sell an elitist magazine to college educated people, sell farming equipment to ranchers, sell wrenches to mechanics. Your audience can be targeted geographically down to specific postal Zip Code numbers.

The reader will want to know *why* he or she should buy; not what the product or service can do, but what it will do *for the reader*. This statement can be strengthened by a guarantee. Present a testimonial from a well-known person, offer a free trial period or a money-back guarantee. Let the reader know you are interested in his or her welfare.

The proper length of a sales letter is debatable. One theory is that no one reads past the first page, so don't make it any longer. Another theory is that if the first page gets the reader's attention, the fourth page will clinch the sale. One standard suggestion is to tell the story and then stop, regardless of length. Another standard is to tell only enough to make the reader ask for more information. The proper length, in the final analysis, will be determined by the writer's best judgment of the presentation to which the majority of the selected readers will respond.

Selling the reader must begin with a strong statement of interest to your particular audience, be he or she a druggist, accountant, housewife, business executive, dog lover, or doctor. Also, the first sentence must relate to the statements that follow.

There are many types of attention-getting opening sentences:

- Reference to a previous personal contact
- A sentence encompassing who, what, when, where, why
- A question
- An unusual remark
- A story
- Invoking a well-known personality
- A well-known quotation
- Using the reader's name (if not obviously inserted into a blank space that doesn't fit the name)
- Use of gimmicks, such as enclosing a stamp, pencil, or address labels; or a question on the envelope that is answered inside

Endings are also important. Having presented your sales story and gotten readers interested, he or she must be moved to action. Tell the reader exactly what to do and when: "Mail the enclosed card today"; "This offer ends June 30"; or "Phone us right now at 888-888-888." Of most importance, make the action easy: "Phone us toll-free at 800-000-000"; "Use the enclosed postage-paid envelope"; or "We are open 7 days a week."

When reviewing your written letter, a few checkpoints may be helpful:

- Are sales points presented clearly and simply?
- Are enough *facts* presented to make the letter convincing?
- Are the strong points emphasized in short, two-or-three-line paragraphs?
- Is the appeal enthusiastic? A great salesperson is one who sets into motion the contagious emotion of enthusism.

How to Do It

1. Use an effective attention-getting opening.
2. Develop a central selling point.
3. Be vivid and specific in talking up the product.
4. Present proofs of your statements.
5. Close by moving the reader to specific action.

Model Openers.   The following are ideas and suggestions for sales letter openers:

It's your money that's involved, and the stakes are HIGH!

Here's an indispensable invention for anyone who . . .

Strength in numbers may be good for the military, but not for the fashion-conscious woman. Barbara's Exclusive Fashions promises what the name implies.

This letter is unlike any we have written before.

Select any three books from the list below. I'll send you two of them *free*.

If you're not sure you want _____, I can understand.

If we have selected our prospects as carefully as we think, you qualify on two accounts.

Have you looked at mountain property and failed to buy because . . .?

We would like you to select any three important professional books—value to $93—for only 99¢ each.

We nurses can never know enough about IV therapy, can we?

I wonder if you have ever had an experience like this one—

Here are nine hard-sell secrets to triple your advertising results.

This may be your last chance to . . .

You're hard to find. Mr. Anderson.

Levitz has opened a great new store in . . .

Just a little note to say HELLO, and to let you know what's happening at Todd Valley.

A mortgage is a wonderful thing.

You don't know me from Eve.

Today I feel like a salty sailor.

I feel like the flinty old mule skinner.

Has your eye ever been caught by a picture so beautiful you couldn't look away?

Mark Twain once remarked, "Always do right. This will gratify some people and astonish the rest."

The two most abused words in manufacturing sales are *quality* and *service*.

This letter will keep you from being fined . . . severely penalized . . . or deprived of your livelihood under the 19__ Tax Reform Law.

You can well imagine the kind of quandary we are in.

Would you like an estimate of the present value of your home?

The average home is now for sale every three or four years.

You couldn't have chosen a better time to request the enclosed booklet.

I am most grateful to loyal customers like you who have made 19__ the greatest year in our history.

We live in an age where there seems to be a club for just about every purpose you might imagine.

The San Francisco area has long been known for its cosmopolitan tastes.

You probably get a lot of mail like this—and it goes in the round file—but don't be too hasty!

Do you know Socrates' chief attribute? Pertinacious curiosity—and with it he came to represent the highest achievement of Greek civilization. This quest for answers has drawn Zellwell Chemicals into the search for relief from the common cold.

You can buy a Stone's lifetime battery today, next month, or probably ten years from now. But not at our special price of $55.20. That price ends February 28.

Have you ever looked in the mirror in the early morning and said, "There has to be a better way"? We have said that too. And we can help you. Jones Correspondence Courses can prepare you . . .

Did you know that the average person uses a mere 10% of his or her brain power? Why not double that, or even triple it? You can. Our new book tells you how.

So many of us are tired on the day-to-day dull routine of a salaried job. Now you can do something about it! Chicken Little Franchises offers . . .

Too many expenses have doubled in recent months. Why not double your income? Our training course has doubled the salaries of a great many men and women. It can do the same for you.

As chairman of the Board of Trustees, I'd like to personally invite you to . . .

When General Electric calls on us for information, that is something to be proud of.

Wilcox and Associates has changed its name. We thought you might be interested in the story.

Model Closings. Here is a list of suggestions to spark the reader into action:

So do the right thing for yourself—mail the card today.

Your credit is good. Just tell us what you want.

Won't you take advantage of it *now*—to put a quick stop to costly losses?

Save yourself some time. Just initial this letter and return it in the business reply envelope enclosed.

Allen Albright, a fellow you are going to like, will be around Tuesday morning to show you samples and to write your order.

Your copy of this interesting publication is ready for you. Just initial and mail the enclosed card.

Send no money. Simply mail the card.

We take all the risk. You enjoy the food.

This letter is your guarantee. Keep it but send us the card—today.

The enclosed order blank should be mailed immediately.

Do not delay—send the order blank now.

Simply check the card and put it in the mail today.

Remove the coupon below and mail it with your order at once.

Mail your check today in the convenient envelope enclosed.

We've cut all the red tape—simply mail the card.

Break out of the summer slump. Return the order blank right away.

Don't write a letter. The enclosed check-off card is for your convenience.

Before you put it aside, sign and return the card.

Just sign the card and have your secretary mail it promptly.

Our supply is limited. Act now!

Send no money. If not satisfied, don't pay.

There are no strings attached to this offer. It is simple. Just mail the enclosed, postpaid card.

Put the card in the mail to start the ball rolling.

It's your move. Telegraph orders are filled overnight.

If for any reason you're dissatisfied, simply return . . . and owe absolutely nothing.

When it comes to service, ABC Corporation produces results.

We will be happy to assist you. Please give us a call.

Investment—Real Estate

Dear Friend:

Although their incomes have climbed during the passing years, many people today are living beyond their means. Some try to help themselves by taking on extra work, but there is a limit to what a person can earn in an eight- or even twelve-hour day.

An excellent solution is to make a sound investment that will provide enough READY CASH for increasing future needs. Listed below are a few of the more popular types of investments:

STOCK MARKET	Considered somewhat unstable, a speculation on the general economy
SAVINGS BANKS	Yields up to __% annually: the bank then often takes YOUR money and invests it in Real Estate
REAL ESTATE	One of the safest, surest investments that can offer substantial profits if the following rules are observed!
1. LOCATION	As close to a MAJOR CITY as possible
2. POPULATION	City requires a past and present history of growth
3. HIGH GRADE PROPERTY	Not desert or swamp, but good, usable land
4. UTILITIES	Water, roads, electricity, gas, phones
5. PRICED RIGHT	Buy UNDER comparable land prices, if possible

We would like the opportunity to prove to you that even as little as $__ monthly may bring substantial returns over the years. Billions have been made with land located in the path of progress. In these days of high taxes, the opportunity to keep big profits is due to the many favorable tax concessions allowable in Real Estate.

Mailing the enclosed card may open your eyes to a new path leading to attractive long-range profit opportunities for you and your family in years to come.

Sincerely,

Business Magazine

Dear Executive:

How does your business compare with similar ones? What are you doing right? What are you doing wrong?

Read the monthly *Business Journal* and know where you stand—and why.

This magazine contains a wealth of information to help you operate more efficiently.

We feature interviews and profiles of business people, your peers—and also your competitors. Are they doing better than you? Why?

Articles about individual businesses reveal successful as well as not so successful policies and strategies. Are you placing too much emphasis on one aspect of your operation and neglecting others to the detriment of the company?

Business Journal keeps you abreast of governmental activities that affect your business, international business opportunities, financial markets, business statistics with special emphasis on trends, political changes and investment strategies.

Business Journal is a monthly magazine with complete economic and business coverage. The competitive advantages of reading this publication are yours for only $30 a year. We have enclosed a copy for you to examine. Do you want to continue in business without being this well informed? Please mail the enclosed card now.

Sincerely,

Magazine—Elitist

Dear Mr. Deskins:

World Journal reveals the influence of the world's best minds on our politics, science, environment, cities, and the couple next door.

Become a part of this intriguing world by learning what the great thinkers are accomplishing.

True, ideas from the world's greatest minds will conflict, but that stimulates other minds—including yours—when you read this exceptional magazine. Even with its sophistication, it is well written and easy to read.

What subjects does *World Journal* embrace? They vary from written portraits of great people and their ideas to what you as an individual can do to improve our environment. The articles and departments cover Books, Art, Poetry, Short Stories, Essays, Commentary, Medicine, Environment, Politics, Humor and the great dissenters who write letters to the editor.

This entertaining and stimulating magazine is yours for only $24 a year. Please mail the enclosed card today. We will bill you later.

Sincerely,

Mortgage Insurance

Dear Mr. Hodges:

A mortgage is a remarkable obligation.

Do you have a mortgage? Most families do. Few families could afford to live in their comfortable homes without a mortgage and its monthly payments spread out for twenty to thirty years.

You are making regular payments from your salary and your family is secure. But what would happen if suddenly you were no longer there? Who would continue the payments? Would the family continue to feel secure?

We have the answers. We can provide you with a simple insurance plan that in the event of your death will pay off the mortgage. Your family can continue living in their home. They can retain their feeling of security.

All this is available for only about one percent of your mortgage annually.

Surprising? Yes.

Simple? Yes.

Your neighborhood representative, Mr. Al Hoerner, will phone you soon to arrange a time to allow you to see how this plan works—how simple it is—and how inexpensive—especially when you consider the potential benefits.

Sincerely,

Homeowner's Insurance

Dear Neighbor:

Your homeowner's insurance is due to be renewed next month. Before you renew, please ask yourself these questions:

IS MY AGENT A NEIGHBOR AND FRIEND?

AM I UNDER INSURED—OR OVER INSURED?

DOES MY COVERAGE MEET MY PARTICULAR NEEDS?

AM I PAYING MORE THAN NECESSARY?

If you are unsure of any of your answers, please call me at 000-0000. You can become better informed with absolutely no obligation.

Sincerely,

GETTING STARTED

How to begin? Starting a sales letter is never easy. And the pressure is on because it can be the most critical part of the letter. If you already know the person, the best way to begin is to make reference to a previous personal contact, or something you have in common. This always grabs the reader's attention. Some people like to begin with a question: "Would you throw your money down the drain? Of course not!" Others prefer beginning with a story, perhaps a personal anecdote that sets the scene: "Last summer I was traveling cross country with my family, when it hit me . . . Why not build a better . . ." Using quotations is always a good idea, especially when they are well-known figures who are directly addressing what your selling. Endorsements are always excellent selling vehicles. If you're really stuck, try this. Write the rest of the letter first. Write about the product or service, why it's unique, and why they should buy it. When you're comfortable with that, go back to beginning and start anew. Sometimes writing out the basics first helps inspire you to come up with that dream opener after all.

Health Insurance

Dear Mrs. Ashland:

Perfect health and never an accident! A wonderful dream, but unreal for most of us.

That is why Total Health Plan was started. If you have no hospitalization insurance or a policy that pays less than $1000 a day, Total Health can help you. Current hospital stays cost closer to $2000 a day, and intensive care can be many times that.

TOTAL HEALTH PLAN PAYS FULL COVERAGE

We do not limit you to 80% of the cost, as many health plans do. When costs go up our payments go up to cover those increases.

Your entire family can receive full coverage, maternity benefits are included, and we cannot refuse your application or cancel your policy—only you can do that. You can count on our being here when you need us because our service has continued uninterrupted since 1931. In support of our financial stability, we are rated A+ (Superior) by A. M. Best Company, an independent insurance analyst.

To introduce you to our plan, just mail the enclosed enrollment form with a check for only $7. When we receive your check, you will be enrolled and covered for 30 days.

Our guarantee: you have those 30 days to read your policy in detail and decide if you wish to continue at our normal rates. If you wish to cancel after 30 days, your $7 will be refunded.

It is your health. We are here to help you keep it. Please mail the enrollment form today—for your peace of mind.

Sincerely,

Dentistry

Dear Mr. French:

Professional dental care is the first step to a lifetime of healthy teeth, overall health, and an appearance you can be proud of.

Doctor Samoto, D.D.S. and I, Doctor Hardwich, D.M.D. are established dental practitioners in this area, having worked as a team in one location for 14 years.

We can do cosmetic dentistry to repair chipped or broken or darkened teeth or to repair unsightly gaps. Small but significant changes in appearance can often be made without anesthesia. We will be happy to discuss in detail how these techniques can be used in your particular case.

Of course we are professionally trained to help you with general dental care including cleaning, cavities, gum care, crowns and the old fashioned toothache.

As part of our service for you, we will obtain your dental records and request from your previous dentist any medical problems or special care you require. This eliminates unnecessary examinations and X-rays.

We have a pleasant office with soft music in the background, a relaxing decor, and tropical fish aquariums for your viewing interest. You will find our staff helpful and friendly.

Sincerely,

Book Club

Dear Reader:

Book club selections still on best-seller lists?

Many of them are when you enroll in the PRIMUS BOOK CLUB. Keep up with what is going on in the world and what your friends are talking about. And the price is right.

For only $10 you can choose three books currently or recently on best-seller lists. If not completely satisfied, return the books and we will refund your $10—OR—you may select another three and retain your membership. You will be pleased to find that PRIMUS BOOK CLUB gives you about 40 percent off the normal retail price.

Every month you will receive a newsletter describing the First Selection and up to 40 other books of current interest. Do nothing to receive the First Selection. If you prefer another title, indicate your preference on the accompanying card and mail it to us. You will have 14 days to make your selection or to notify us that you do not want the monthly First Selection. If the newsletter is delayed, you may return unwanted books. To retain your membership you are required to purchase only one book in each six-month period.

Be informed. Don't let the world pass you by. Read the latest of fiction, humor, biography, economics, politics, science and more. Enroll now in the PRIMUS BOOK CLUB.

Another cost savings: if you send your payments in advance, we will pay shipping and handling charges.

Please fill in and mail the enclosed enrollment card. Start right now to become entertained and enlightened.

Sincerely,

Real Estate—Homes

Dear Mr. and Mrs. Henshaw:

Another home SOLD . . . at 0000 Windmill Way, Saratoga. Please stop by and welcome your neighbors.

SOLD by Nolan Associates, your neighborhood realtor.

We offer top $$$ for our SELLERS—Speedy sales for our SELLERS—Personalized, professional service for our SELLERS—98% of homes listed are SOLD!!—We don't just collect listing . . . We service what we list!

We offer speedy sales—courteous service—and a free evaluation of your home.

Please use the enclosed GOLD MARKET ANALYSIS CERTIFICATE for a market evaluation of your home.

Please phone today: NOLAN ASSOCIATES, 000 Hamilton Ave., Saratoga, FL 00000. Phone 000-000-0000.

Sincerely,

Dear Mr. and Mrs. Sutherland:

Once in a lifetime there is a special place.

Just beyond the gentle rise overlooking a flowering meadow you come upon a secluded setting of prestigious homes. The tree-covered slopes are fenced and guarded, ensuring protection and peace of mind.

The custom-built homes are designed by A. I. A. architects and are priced from $695,000. Homesites of from two to five acres are also available from $250,000.

These are the Wallingford Estates of Saratoga—telephone 000-000-0000.

Sincerely,

Dear Property Owner:

Within the next year over two million people in the United States will sell their houses, some successfully, some at a sacrifice.

Backed by Pacific Real Estate's 22 years of success in selling real estate in this area, you can depend on a most satisfactory sale. We know that home buyers compare and look for charm, comfort, convenience, location and "the best deal." We will help you prepare your house for these "fussy" buyers. We have learned much during the past 22 years.

We were the first realtors to establish a training school offering state-accredited courses in real estate in this community. All our sales people attend this school.

We initiated the local board of realtors which started the community multiple listing service, which vastly expands the visibility of our sales efforts.

A free appraisal of your home's value and marketability is available just by phoning us at 000-0000.

Pacific Real Estate is here to help you whether you are buying or selling or both. Give us a call.

Sincerely,

Dear Mr. Sommers:

All fired up.

Desk piled high. Morning gone. Energy too.

Day pushes on. One last call and out the door.

Goodbye traffic. Goodbye smog. Honking horns turn to silence.

Quiet mountains, Skittering quail. Quiet time.

Scampering rabbits. Time to think. Time to breathe.

Relax, Unwind.

Regroup.

Recharge.

At Tatum Ranch, Phoenix

A master-planned community.

(signature)

(Reprinted from a magazine advertisement, with permission from SunCor Development Company.)

Real Estate—Mountain Property

Hi Folks,

Just a friendly note to let you know that we aren't really in the high mountains. More like nestled in the foothills. But you can see the mountains from your back porch and the wildflowers, and hear the birds chirping, and the afternoon breeze whispering through the trees.

Property values are rising monthly, so don't wait too long. The number of homes Rancho Verde has built now exceeds 600, and our qualified, local sales staff has increased to meet the growing demand. We know you want to talk to sales people who own cabins and houses here and who know this area. John was born only ten miles to the north. Tim has owned a cabin here for seven years. Sarah has lived for twenty years adjacent to our estates, and just can't bear to move next door. I tramped through these woods as a child and live in the third house to the left down there. You are not dealing with strangers when you drop in to visit us.

If you are interested in buying a lot for future development, a comfortable cabin or a completed home, any of our sales people will be glad to help.

Write your name and address on the enclosed card and we will mail you a few pictures of these foothill estates. Or just call us at 000-000-0000.

Your friends at Rancho Verde,

Wrist Watch

Dear Mr. Farnsworth:

Your watch: elegant yet rugged, on exciting possession with proven Swiss quartz accuracy and dependability—for discriminating men and women.

The Aargo watches in either classic or contemporary designs, including slimline and water resistant, are not ordinary. They have hand crafted, precision movements. The crystals and hands are scratch proof, and so well made you may never see an indication of wear.

Prices range from $1,500 to $14,500.

From our vast collection in gold or stainless steel or the combination of both, you will find the exceptional masterpiece you are proud to wear—an Aargo. Impressive.

A color brochure will be mailed when you return the enclosed card.

Sincerely,

Camera

Dear Ms. Won:

Accept no limitations.

A horse and jockey breaking from the pack, stopped at full speed by the autofocusing Minolta Maxxum 8000i. Because both rider and camera rose to the challenge.

Here, Maxxum's Predictive Autofocus anticipates the horse's charge for exact focus in a split second. While our Sports Action Card, one of 14 unique, computer-like Creative Expansion Cards, automatically pre-programs Maxxum to take advantage of its unsurpassed shutter speed. Freezing every detail, even at the pace of a wire-to-wire winner.

Maxxum, the world's most comprehensive autofocus system, offers more than 30 lenses to help you unleash your creativity as never before.

The possibilities are as limitless as your imagination.

For details or product information, see your Minolta dealer or write: Minolta Corporation, 101 Williams Dr., Ramsey, NJ 07446. In Canada: Minolta Canada, Inc., Ontario.

Sincerely,

Dear Mrs. Vaught:

Action Pictures! Beautiful color!

If you can see it, you can capture it with your Auto-10 camera—simply. Why simply?

Because your Auto-10 sets the exposure *and* the focus. The results rival those of the professionals: rich colors and clear details, even as the amount of light changes.

The Auto-10 is a precision instrument for beautiful photography, compact, light weight and easy to handle.

You can enhance the range of your creativity with any of Auto-10's 30 precision ground lenses from telephoto to wide angle, a motor drive for quick action sequences, automatic flash, and other accessories to make your photography more precise and more convenient for you.

See your local dealer today. Dealers are listed in the accompanying brochure.

Action photos make lasting memories and are fun with your Auto-10.

Sincerely,

Computer System

Dear Mr. Graham:

Quick letters; instant revisions and updates while on the road; no wasted time. That is the Mercator Laptop computer.

Take a look at it: small enough to fit in your briefcase, only 9″×11″×1.5″ and weighs only 5 pounds. The Mercator is a high performance instrument with a hard disk and a 40-column, non-glare screen—all for an easily affordable price.

The Mercator gives you instant access to files and programs, offers desktop publishing capability and easy transferability between your laptop and your office computer.

A Mercator portable printer is available. It is lightweight, compact and provides quality output on plain paper.

For further details and technical data, please call 1-800-000-0000.

Sincerely,

Dear Mr. Bowers:

No longer need haste make waste.

The Xerox 0000 electronic printing system is both amazingly fast and precise.

That is why the Xerox 0000 is used by such companies as Fast-Tax, a computer firm that processes hundreds of thousands of income tax returns each year. Up to a million pages of returns are processed in one day. The Xerox 0000 converts the input data and uses laser beams to precisely print the tax forms—and even collates the forms automatically.

That is managing information the way it should be managed: accurately, with a minimum of waste and a maximum of haste. It is all done with the Xerox 0000 electronic printing system.

Call your local representative, Mr. Alvin Goodman, today at 000-000-0000. He can explain this and other Xerox systems—one of which will meet your needs and do a better job of managing your information.

Sincerely,

Specific Customer—Roofing Tile

Dear John:

This confirms our conversation concerning real estate developer Allen Company's plan to close down their roofing tile operation in Oakland, California and go to the open market for their tile requirements.

The Johnson Corporation is in a very good position in the Bay Area to be a dependable long-range source of supply for roofing tile. Johnson has two tile plants in the immediate area of the Allen Company's housing developments. One plant is in Dublin, which is 30 miles east of your development, and the other is in San Jose, which is 35 miles south of your current operation. These two tile plants are under one Resident Manager who correlates the two operations to give the best possible service to our customers.

At your convenience I would like to arrange a tour of our Bay Area operations for you and for anyone else from your company who would be interested in seeing what Johnson has to offer as a source of supply.

You stated that your National Director of Purchases will visit Oakland the week of December 6 to discuss with you the procedures and guidelines for acquiring quotations on your tile requirements. You also asked me to contact you the following Monday, December 13 to further discuss what our next steps should be.

If, during your Director of Purchases' visit, he would like to see some of Johnson's operations, we would be more than happy to make any arrangements that would be convenient. If not, John, I look forward to talking to you on December 13.

Best regards,

Sales Promotion Book

Dear Mr. Elender:

Would you like to make big money using the incredible power of the hard-sell approach that gets ACTION from your prospects? . . . actually doubling or tripling the effectiveness of your ads, sales talks or merchandising techniques?

You will quickly learn from *The Ten Keys to Money* the clues to advertising—and selling—and be ahead of your competitors whether in retailing, wholesaling, manufacturing or servicing. You will learn the hard-sell approach that it takes to get ahead these days. Immediately, you will write powerful and absolutely persuasive ads and promotional materials.

You will be able to look at the ad you or your associate—or your competitor—wrote and know that, "this is a selling ad," or that, "this needs reworking, and I know *exactly* how to change it."

You want to be skeptical? The *10 Keys* are time-tested, scientifically sound and success-proved techniques used for over twenty years by the country's few most highly successful—and rich—sales people.

The *10 Keys* are explained in simple language by Tom Morlick, a successful salesman himself, in his book *The Ten Keys to Money.*

The book is yours for only $14.95. Money back if not absolutely delighted beyond your wildest expectations.

Rush the enclosed postpaid card today!

Sincerely,

Dear Mr. Capel:

You can Boost Sales . . . Slash Selling Costs . . . Perk up Profits . . . with this rich storehouse of tested and proven sales promotion ideas!

Modern marketing places more and more emphasis on effective sales promotion as a sure way to boost sales volume and reduce the cost of selling. And, one of the best sources of good promotion ideas is a close working knowledge of what others in creative sales promotion are actually doing. This handbook brings that goal within your reach.

The *Sales Promotion Handbook* is virtually brimming over with hundreds of practical techniques for getting ideas, training dealer personnel, measuring results, exploiting every possible sales outlet for your products and services. For example, if you are looking for ways to build up stronger selling effort on the part of your salesmen—your own or dealer representatives—you will have at hand some of the best motivational programs ever developed.

If your daily problems involve old sales territories, allocating budgets, or writing effective promotion copy, this handbook will provide you with many examples to stimulate your own thinking and imagination.

Without cost or obligation, see how the new Dartnell *Sales Promotion Handbook* can help you boost sales and profits.

Read the *Sales Promotion Handbook* for 15 days with no obligation. The all new 6th edition contains 1206 pages of stimulating sales promotion ideas. It is fully illustrated and indexed. The cost is $45.50.

Just fill in and mail the enclosed card today.

Sincerely,

Gift of Food

Every year 'bout this time . . . we start feeling downright sentimental . . . start taking time to think of the special ladies in our lives. Lots of other folks do, too—and that's why we put together this special booklet of gifts for Moms of all kinds, on their day.

Harry and I picked these gifts especially for Mother's Day. We think there's something special here to please every Mom you want to remember at this special time of year. You'll find truly original gifts of the finest quality—such as our tangy Royal Gala Apples, imported fresh from New Zealand . . . flowers and exotic foliage plants she can grow in her home . . . our new Sweets and Sentiments, a delicate hand-crocheted pouch filled with a box of our luscious Mint Truffles . . . and our famous homemade food gifts from the kitchens here at Bear Creek!

Best of all, our prices include everything . . . all the extras you usually pay for at stores. Harry and I will gift pack and deliver in the nicest way . . . and every gift will be sent with your own personal greeting.

Mother's Day is May 11 this year . . . and that's just around the corner. Harry and I need your instructions just as soon as you can get them to us. So please fill out your order right away . . . and return it in the special postage-paid envelope enclosed. We guarantee *you'll* be pleased . . . and so will *she*!

David

(Reprinted by permission of Harry and David, Medford, Oregon.)

Bakery

Greetings:

San Francisco has long been known for its fine foods. Barocchio's Bakery will become a part of this tradition. We recently moved into a most modern bakery with a team of exceptional baking specialists whose two concerns are quality and taste.

Our bread line is complete with varieties from bleached to black, from white enriched to 12-grain, from extra sour to honey bran.

Each day we bake a selection of cookies, pies and sweet rolls. Choose cakes from white angel food to German chocolate fudge.

The enclosed sheet of coupons will enable you to sample a wide range of our products at a 50% discount.

We value our customers and are certain that once you have tasted our bakery goods you will know they are a part of San Francisco's tradition of fine foods.

Sincerely,

Income Tax Consulting

Dear Mr. Tiffany:

You're probably going to pay too much in personal income taxes this year.

You are, if you're the kind of totally involved executive we think you are.

With everything else on your mind, there's a good chance you may fail to take some perfectly appropriate steps to minimize your taxes.

This makes it all the more important that you get the advice and counsel of the professionals at Deloitte, Haskins & Sells.

To start with, we'll systematically review your current financial picture and your returns for previous years (Who knows? We may very well find refunds you've overlooked.)

Then we'll go further, and help you devise financial strategies to meet your long-term business and family needs—your needs for trust arrangements, perhaps, or the sale of a family business, or exercising some stock options.

At Deloitte, Haskins & Sells, we think income tax and estate planning is a very personal matter.

When we say we don't stop at the bottom line in serving clients, we include thousands of businessmen and professionals among them.

They're individuals who look to us for planning for the years to come—just as much as for our help in filling this year's return.

Of course, not everybody requires our kind of help. But if you do, perhaps we should talk.

The sooner, the better.

Call our local office at 212-790-0500, or write 1114 Avenue of the Americas, New York, New York 10036.

Sincerely,

(Adapted, with permission, from a magazine advertisement.)

Service Contract

Dear Mr. and Mrs. Cody:

Just a reminder that your Service Contract will expire soon.
Don't let it!
Actually, your service contract is more valuable to you as your set gets older. That is when repairs get more complicated and are therefore more costly. One service call may cost as much as the annual contract.

Renew your contract now. You will save time and money and be assured of fast, efficient service from Terry's Appliances.

We are enclosing a renewal contract for one year. You can sign and return it in the enclosed, postpaid envelope. You pay only $__ for our low cost renewal policy.

Don't worry any longer about uncertain appliance repairs—that are always needed at an inconvenient time. You may use your Master Card or VISA card for easy payment.

Why not sign and return the contract today?

Sincerely,

Inactive Customer

Dear Andy,

The loss of a business friend may not seem as tragic as the loss of a personal friend, but still a part of one's self fades away when a friend is gone.

We seem to have lost you as a business friend, and we feel the loss. Is there something we have done, or something we have *not* done? As a personal favor, could you give us, briefly, the reason for apparently leaving us. Just a short sentence or two on the back of this letter is all we ask. You can mail it in the postpaid envelope enclosed.

We have recently expanded our warehouse capacity and increased the variety of paper and stationery items to serve you better. A request for a quote or an order for a carton of Scotch tape would be most welcome. We will do everything possible to become a business friend of yours again. Please let us hear from you.

Sincerely,

Collection Service

Dear Mr. Caplan:

Tylenol may be replacing aspirin as a headache remedy—but headaches remain. Especially collection headaches. Perhaps your collection remedy should be changed.

If you are plagued with "headache" accounts, let us help you. We have many years of experience and an outstanding track record of clearing up old accounts.

Our method is as simple as it is effective. First, we send out a letter that is both imaginative and skillful. It commands respect. And it gets results. Most collection problems are solved at this point.

For more reluctant debtors, we send a trained expert who is tactful and persuasive and can hold your goodwill.

Give us a try. Send us a list of your past due accounts. If the first letter succeeds, you pay us nothing. We must, however, charge a modest fee for sending our personal service representative. If we collect nothing, you pay nothing.

With nothing to lose but your "headache" accounts, and the probable recovery of your inactive assets, give us a call today at 000-000-0000.

Cordially yours,

Public Official

Dear Mr. and Mrs. Baker:

I would appreciate your serious consideration of my candidacy for City Council when you vote on April 8 this year. You have been among the few who take the time and interest to vote in Municipal elections, which indicates your concern about local government.

Forecasts show that I have an excellent chance of winning a seat in this forthcoming election, as my years of volunteer involvement in community affairs and present position of Planning Commissioner have provided the name recognition and background that is necessary to be a viable candidate in _____.

As it is physically impossible to contact every voter personally, and as the press gives only equal and therefore minimum coverage to any candidate, I have to communicate by using signs and mailed campaign literature. To reach every voter with just one message requires over $7,500.

I hope to be able to provide each voter with sufficient facts upon which to base his or her selections on April 8. If I miss your house, it's because I did not have the funds to supply all the literature and postage necessary to mail it to you. If this happens, please understand. I cannot spend any campaign funds unless they are donated by supporters who want to see me on the City Council.

If you really want to help me and yourself for the next four years, $1 or more now and your vote on April 8 will do it.

I have always said that the way to keep an elected public official honest is to have his campaign financed by $1 each from 7,500 people rather than $7,500 from 1 person. I am sure you share that opinion.

Sincerely,

Executive Recruiter

Dear Mr. Butler

Is your valuable time wasted in interviews and background checks of potential executives who later prove unqualified for the job? Has questionable information by a candidate slipped through the hiring procedure only to surface when the performance record of an executive is called into question weeks or even months later? Do you find too few qualified individuals from which to choose?

ZEROING-IN

How do you target your readers? This is really a marketing question beyond the scope of this book. However, unless you have a large budget for a big mailing, you should really do your homework when it comes to developing a list. The average rate of return on many mailing is often less than 5 percent, sometimes a lot less. To increase your odds these days, many marketing people are finding as many "niche markets" as possible—avoiding huge mailings and going directly to where the potential buyers are. No matter how you do this, either through a marketing firm, or your own internal research, one element you can control is the style of language. It is very important to make sure your letter matches the style of writing the recipient is expecting. Someone who is identified as a city-dweller and a lover of classical music is not likely going to be swayed by an appeal to buy tickets to a tractor-pull event. Every good author must ask the same question: Who is my audience? Know them inside and out.

James and Jordan can assist you in recruiting qualified candidates for your available positions—and often with less cost to you in both time and money.

Here is why:

- James and Jordan's executive search service covers the nation.
- We have referral agreements with other recruiting agencies.
- We are on top of the current salary market: what is being asked and what is being offered.
- We know the latest labor and fair employment laws, ruling and court decisions.
- We refer to you only qualified and motivated candidates.
- We practice complete confidentiality.
- We approach our work from our client's viewpoint.
- We have a large number of satisfied clients to whom you may refer.

In taking over the search for executives, James and Jordan completely eliminates one of your business problems.

Further information is available by returning the enclosed postpaid card. We look forward to working with you.

Sincerely,

Personal Credit

Dear Mr. Nordstrom:

Very likely you have heard about Individual Financing. This is our bank's special finance service created for people with an above average income and credit standing. It occurred to me that you might be interested in hearing a bit more about it.

With Individual Financing you enjoy the remarkable independence of administering your own long-term credit needs. If your annual net income is $25,000 or better and you also qualify in other respects, you'll have a credit line of somewhere between $5,000 and $25,000. Use it whenever you want to for personal, family, or household purposes simply by writing a special check of $500 or more.

Individual Financing can give you the flexibility you want through these valuable benefits:

1. There is no charge until you use it.
2. You can pay more than the minimum monthly payment, if you wish, thereby reducing the amount of future financial charges.

3. No collateral is required.

4. There are no prepayment penalties.

5. No bank visits are necessary each time you need a loan.

6. Credit life insurance of up to $25,000 is available.

Please take this opportunity to complete and sign the enclosed application and financial statement. You can be sure this information will be handled in confidence. By signing this application, you are under no obligation. Mail it in the prepaid return envelope provided. Soon after we receive your application, either a loan officer or I will call you.

Cordially,

Furniture, Retail

Dear Mr. Mosland:

Parsons has opened a great new store in Phoenix at 00000 Camelback Road. Although we're new to this area, Parsons has been satisfying home furnishing needs since 1919. These years of experience have shown us that when you shop, you want selection, availability, and value. Parsons can offer you all that, and more!

We have expanded our selection of 200 room groupings to include our new Formal Gallery. This collection features American of Martinsville, Hibriten, the Burlinghouse Globe Collection, Thomasville, and the many other famous name brands that complete our three million dollar inventory.

As an introduction to our new Phoenix store, we're offering you at 20% discount on ALL regularly priced merchandise. In addition, we have a get-acquainted gift for you. It's a beautiful piece of native Indian pottery, absolutely FREE with any purchase of $200 or more.

To make shopping at Parsons even more convenient, we're inviting you to open a charge account today. With this card you can charge your purchases and never have to worry about a down payment, or tying up your credit lines on other charge cards. And your card will be welcome at any of our ninety-eight locations nation wide.

All you have to do is complete the coupon below and return it in the enclosed postpaid envelope. It's so easy, why not do it today?

Sincerely,

Art Object

Dear Alumnus:

We are pleased to announce that the University of Washington Alumni Association has commissioned world-renowned Reed & Barton Silversmiths to create in rich and precious metals a Limited Edition Damascene Insculpture (metal etching) of our famous landmark—the Rainier Vista.

This uniquely beautiful metal etching, handcrafted in pure silver, 24kt. gold electroplate, burnished copper and bronze is being produced exclusively for Washington alumni—and for no one else. It is being offered at this time only, through this single announcement, and will never be issued again.

Each richly detailed Damascene etching of the Rainier Vista will be faithfully recreated by skilled artisans in Reed & Barton's famous patented process. The rare art medium of Damascene involves more than 20 separate hand operations in the creation of each metal etching through the painstaking blending of silver, gold, copper, and bronze.

Mounted to produce a handsome three-dimensional effect, each insculpture will be in an antiqued gold and silver leaf frame, dramatically displayed against a rich velveteen background, as depicted in the attractive brochure enclosed.

A Certificate of Registration will be affixed to the reverse side of the Rainier Vista frame, and will bear your name, your class year, and your limited edition number.

Since this is the only time that the Rainier Vista Damascene Insculpture will ever be offered—and since only Washington alumni will receive this information—these exquisite works of art are almost certain to become collector's pieces.

Reed & Barton will honor all orders postmarked on or before March 31. They cannot guarantee to honor orders postmarked after that date.

The original issue price of this framed etching is just $125, including delivery. We have made arrangements to have all orders entered directly with Reed & Barton Silversmiths. You may pay for your University of Washington Insculpture with a $25 deposit, if you prefer. After you have received your insculpture, the unpaid balance of $100 will be billed at the rate of $25 a month for four months. All of these details are described on the enclosed postage-paid Reservation Form.

Please mail it before March 31.

Sincerely,

Life Insurance

Dear Wells Fargo Master Card Customer:

As you know, Wells Fargo Bank, known for its service to Californians since 1852, makes available to you many financial services including your convenient Master Card account. We are pleased that Wells Fargo has selected us to add to these services by making available to you a product design for the protection of your estate and the future security of those dependent on you.

You are undoubtedly aware that what you can buy with one dollar today is hardly more than half of what you could buy with that same dollar ten years ago. The other half has been lost to inflation.

With this in mind, we offer you a unique Term Life Insurance Plan that is competitively priced, has a special anti-inflation Benefit Protection Option, and features convenient premium payment through your Wells Fargo Master Card account.

Let me tell you about the highlights of this special plan:

Adults under 60 can select up to $50,000 of Term Life Insurance benefits.

You and your spouse, if under age 60, can protect your insurance benefits against inflation by including the Benefit Increase Option in your coverages. This option will automatically increase your insurance benefit until the total benefit doubles.

You can cover the balance in your Master Card account with your insurance benefit.

You have the convenience of having the monthly premiums billed to your Wells Fargo Master Card account.

Medical examinations are not required to apply for this insurance.

You will own your policy—it is your personal property.

You can have lifetime protection, regardless of any change in your health, because at any time prior to age 60, while your coverage is in force, you can convert this policy to a whole life or endowment policy without evidence of insurability and without a medical examination.

We are proud to offer this Term Life Insurance Plan to you and to support it with the strength of our company, a member of AMEX Life Assurance Company group which, for 127 years, has provided Californians with quality insurance plans at competitive rates.

I urge you to read the enclosed material which further explains the Plan, then evaluate your insurance needs, complete the enclosed application, and mail it to us today.

Sincerely,

Cost Savings

Dear Customer:

Valley Truck Supply is now in a position to reduce the cost of your truck replacement parts. This is due to our growing number of satisfied customers over the past few years.

Volume discounts are available to customers buying as few as XXXX of an item with, however, a dollar minimum per order.

Please refer to the enclosed sheet for a list of commonly purchased parts and the discount rates.

We hope this program will help you provide faster service to your customers. We look forward to continuing to serve you in the future.

Sincerely,

Store Sale

Dear Mr. and Mrs. Letterman:

Just a note to let you know that we at Staples' Family Store are already having our After Christmas Sale—before Christmas—so you may enjoy your savings before the holidays.

These will include shoes, shirts, blouses, slacks, and everything in the Children's Department.

This is Staples' way of wishing you the best Christmas ever.

We look forward to meeting you during this season of good cheer.

Sincerely,

Follow-Up Sales Letters

A successful salesperson is likely to be one who uses follow-up letters. They are effective because they generate orders from current customers and new prospects, build goodwill, iron out misunderstandings and provide written records that may forestall future disagreements.

Additional purposes of follow-up letters are to thank buyers, to remind customers that it is time to reorder, and to introduce new products.

Because the ending of a letter is the most emphatic position to close your letter in a pleasant manner.

How to Do It

1. State the reason for the letter.

2. Explain the subject of the letter.

3. Indicate the steps you are taking to assist the reader.

Dear Policy Holder:

As you know, it's almost time to renew your Comair Service Policy. It has been a pleasure serving you this past year. Enclosed you'll find a new contract form with simple instructions. Please read it carefully, then sign and return it with your check to ensure uninterrupted service coverage.

We are enclosing one of our current brochures with all of the options and prices listed. If you have any questions please feel free to call, and one of our representatives will be glad to stop by your home and assist you.

Again, it has been a pleasure serving you this past year, and we look forward to doing so for many years to come.

Sincerely,

(Reprinted with permission from Bob Unruh of Comair Service Systems, Peoria, Arizona.)

Dear Mr. Tucker:

It is with genuine pleasure that I thank you for your purchase of our Model VII tractor. Choosing Normans as your dealer represents your faith and trust in us, and I, personally, would like you to know that that is a matter of great importance to us.

Please be assured that we shall endeavor to deserve your confidence and friendship. It is our company policy to conduct our business in a manner that gives full attention to providing the best service to our customers. Our personnel are chosen for their enthusiastic and pleasant attitudes and are trained to give courteous and efficient service on which you can depend.

I hope it never happens, but should Normans ever fall short of your expectations, I would consider it a personal favor if you would let me know about it.

Sincerely,

Dear Mrs. Spencer:

It has been some time since we have been in touch with you. I hope this note finds you well and ready to enjoy the holiday season.

We have been busy at Sun Ridge. You may have noticed our dramatic landscaping and seen ads locally for our many special events. Rio Salado College is now located on our campus, and Sun Ridge is bustling with activities.

We would be delighted to have you stop by for a new look at our community. I look forward to hearing from you. In the meantime, I wish you the happiest of holidays!

Cordially,

Summary Points

- Get the reader's attention fast.
- Create an interest in what you're selling.
- Show them they're making a smart move: offer testimonials.
- Don't clutter. Focus on your one or two top selling points.
- Avoid being too "familiar" or sounding condescending.
- Keep letters short, to the point, and in active voice.
- Always state what you want the reader to do.

SECTION FIVE

SELLING

INTRODUCTION—SELLING

Whether you are a salesperson by profession or not, business today requires a lot of salesmanship. You might need to sell your services to potential clients, or "sell" an existing client on an idea, or "sell" your boss a new proposal.

People who have the ability to "sell" products, services, even ideas, are the ones who will get farthest in business. Think about it. Maybe you know people in your profession who perhaps didn't go to the most elite schools, or didn't exactly bother to learn every last detail about your product line, but when they go out there and sell, there's nothing the client won't buy. How do they do it? How is it that they can go out there everyday, face the prospect of rejection, and still come back with a better than average batting average?

It's not just luck. A lot of it is developing poise, self-confidence, and a positive attitude. It's communicating all of this plus a wealth of knowledge about what it is you're trying to sell. Some of us are born salesmen, others have to learn the skill. If you're in the latter group, there are skills you can learn, practice, and internalize to help turn you from wallflower to star performer.

This section includes practical tips on both verbal, nonverbal, and written aspects of selling: how to write a winning sales presentation; how to recognize nonverbal cues that can be danger signs during a presentation; how to stroke your prospect's ego; how to come up with that killer opening line.

These are skills you can use to help both sell your product or services, but also to stay ahead within your company. You want to be the one who "sells" the winning idea at the next staff meeting, right? You want to be the one who "sells" the client on the idea of expanded services. You achieve these goals not by being passive and hoping for the best, but by actively marketing and selling yourself. These can be critical skills for company, and for you personally.

CHAPTER 15

GETTING A POTENTIAL CLIENT'S ATTENTION: SOME HINTS

You've been asked to meet with Jim Smith at Ad-Key industries. The person who would ordinarily meet with him is sick, and the account could be riding on your shoulders. Without that account, your firm might have a lousy quarter, maybe even a lousy year. You know the product line inside-out, you can anticipate virtually any question, but are you ready to take your act on the road?

The most obvious situation in which you will need salesmanship skills is when pitching to a prospective client or customer. You're on stage. You're performing. You're the center of attention for the next half-hour. You better be ready. But how to prepare?

There are various techniques you can use to help increase the impact of your "performance" before a prospect. Andrew Dubrin's *Stand Out!* excerpted below, offers a variety of techniques you can easily learn to help develop and polish your sales capabilities. Everything from winning opening lines, using buzz words, referencing prestigious customers, to what manner and etiquette never fail to impress. If you ever have to "take your show on the road" and present the company's public face, can you afford not to have these techniques down pat?

COMMANDING THE ATTENTION OF PROSPECTIVE CUSTOMERS

Impressing a prospective external customer is critically important any time he or she has a choice between you and another supplier. Your prospect also has the alternative of not making a purchase. You must find some way to make the prospect see the merit in you or your product and service. If you are an outside sales representative the importance of creating a positive impression is obvious. It is less obvious, however, that many of your internal customers must also be impressed. A trainer, for example, often has to impress a line manager (the prospective customer). Frequently, the manager has the choice of using the trainer's program or bringing in a trainer from the outside.

The tactics and strategies described in this chapter focus on impressing prospective customers. Many of them also will help you gain the edge with others in the work place. For example, proper use of "stroke your prospect's ego" will impress all but the most callous and self-effacing people you encounter on the job.

Quickly Learn Your Prospective Customer's Name

Back to human relations 101: Learn and remember the full name of your customer prospect. The challenge is more difficult today because of work-place diversity. Many prospective customers have names of different cultural origins from your own. Furthermore, many women and some men have hyphenated names. It therefore requires extra concentration on your part to learn the person's name. A Jim Smith raised in the midwestern United States may have problems learning immediately the name of his prospect, Afsaneh Nahavandi-Malekzadeh. To assist in learning the prospect's name, Jim should take Afsaneh's business card and say the name silently to himself. Jim should then say, "I'm pleased to meet you, Mr. Nahavandi-Malekzadeh." Jim's prospect may let him off easily by responding, "Just call me 'Navi,' it's easier."

The importance of learning a prospect's name is illustrated by the situation of Bob Delaney, a manager in a photochemical company. Bob had attempted to sell a production manager, Harold Fatima, on a system for improving one of the company's most important photochemicals. The system involved purchasing an expensive computer system. Due to high capital investment, Harold was reluctant to explore the proposal.

Six weeks later, Bob came across Harold while shopping at a mall. Immediately, Bob addressed Harold by name. Harold was impressed that Bob remembered his name and therefore willingly entered into conversation. After a ten-minute chat, Harold asked Bob to call him during the week to discuss how the proposed system would improve quality. Eventually, Bob's group got the assignment, and he now had a major internal customer. Remembering a customer prospect's name created a positive enough impression to facilitate Bob's gaining the edge.

Another critical part of learning your prospect's name is to be hesitant to use a first name unless invited to. Also avoid nicknames unless the prospect states a preference for the shortened name. Nicknames have decreased in popularity, and many people find it annoying when a stranger uses another form of their name. Even if the prospect prefers a nickname, you may not know the shortened form he or she prefers. For example, nicknames for Richard include, "Rick," "Rich," and "Dick" (mostly for people over fifty).

Many women named Deborah detest being called "Debbie," or "Deb"; some men named James cringe when called "Jim"; many men named Andrew or André recoil when called "Andy"; and many men named Robert preferred to be addressed as "Rob" not "Bob." On the other hand, many people believe that only their parents or spouses should use their full first name. To create a good impression simply ask your prospect, "Which is your preferred first name?" Your good sense of etiquette will help you gain the edge.

After you have learned your prospect's name, use it several times during your conversation. Using your prospect's name helps hold his or her interest in the conversation. Yet avoid overusing the name. You could appear to be an in-person replica of a computerized sweepstakes contest letter that inserts a person's name every other line. ("Yes, JACQUELINE DUMBROWSKI, you are one of 3,000 finalists in our contest. You, JACQUELINE DUMBROWSKI, might be holding the ticket that will make you an instant millionaire. Think, of it, JACQUELINE DUMBROWSKI, from CLEVELAND, OHIO, your dreams could come true.")

Listen and Engage in Customer Problem Solving

There are two basic approaches to person-to-person selling. One is the sales-oriented approach in which the sales representative uses high-pressure selling techniques to persuade the customer. Quite often this approach makes sense because you have one product or service to offer, and the prospective customer has expressed no interest in talking to you. House siding and encyclopedias are often sold in this manner.

Marketing experts more highly recommend the customer-oriented approach to selling. To use the customer-oriented approach, you have to identify customer needs and then propose solutions. This approach often impresses prospective customers because they perceive you to be a professional problem solver rather than a high-pressure sales representative.

The customer-oriented approach to selling begins with careful listening on your part. You have to encourage the person to talk about problems that your service or product could possibly help solve. Rita O'Malley uses a listening approach to enlarge the client base for her collection agency. She observes, "It's largely a waste of time in my business to use the hard sell. What does work for me is to have prospects talk about their cash-flow problems. Most companies have some deadbeats as customers. The trick is to get them to admit it. Then I have a chance for a sale.

"First, I have to get an appointment to see a business owner or the credit manager in a larger firm. We have not found this to be a major problem since most companies are at least curious about our services. Once I'm in the interview, I simply mention that we collect delinquent accounts and charge nothing if we fail. Next, I usually make a low-key request such as, 'Tell me about some of your delinquent accounts.'

"The answer to my first request usually consumes at least five minutes. Then I ask a few specific questions like, 'How quickly would you like to get your money from these customers?' and 'Do you have a large enough staff to track down all people who are hurting your cash flow?'

"After my prospect has opened his books to me, I explain that our firm is designed to help with precisely the problems he or she describes. The prospect is then usually ready for a full description of my services. If I do a good job of listening, I get a new client from at least one third of my client prospect meetings. I am there to show how I can help resolve some important business problems."

Rita makes the right impression partly because she does not think of her meetings with client prospects as sales presentations. Instead, Rita sees them as problem-solving meetings in which she helps companies improve their collections.

At times you may be discouraged because the general picture suggests there is not a good fit between the prospect's needs and what you have to offer. Before giving up and moving on to the next prospect, listen even more carefully for a small potential niche for yourself. Back to Rita. One credit manager she spoke to recently said that he was *almost totally* satisfied with his firm's collection procedures.

Rita's sales instincts bubbled to the surface. "Why not *totally* satisfied?" asked Rita. The credit manager explained that there were a few uncollectible accounts lying around that the company had written off. "Would you be willing to give me a shot at getting back some money from those hopeless accounts? It won't cost you anything unless we bring you back some cash," she asked. Rita did salvage some money for the prospect. Since then she has continued to receive a steady dribble of business from that account. Rita made a good impression by listening enough to help the client prospect realize there was some small room for improvement in his company's collections.

Use an Attention-Grabbing Opening Line

To impress customers, as in many other worthwhile endeavors in life, you need a good opening line. For maximum effectiveness, the opening line should appeal to an important need of your prospect. If your opener is attention grabbing, but is not related to a client need, it will be forgotten quickly and so will you. The

---

DON'T FLY BLIND

You've probably heard the phrase "familiarity breeds contempt" more than a few times. Well, it's not true when it comes to knowing your prospective client or customer. If you were going on a job interview at this firm, you would want to know as many details about the company before the interview, correct? Then why should it be any different if you want to sell them something?

The key to good salesmanship is understanding where the other person's needs lie. If you understand exactly how it is they do business, where they could use your product or service, then you will send the signal to the prospect that not only have you done your homework, but you are already familiar with how they work. This is critical!

People don't want to waste their time tutoring you from the ground up. They want people—suppliers, subcontractors, whoever—to fit in right away. Long before you even call for that appointment, make sure you and your marketing people gather as much data as possible.

---

attention-grabbing opening line is important for internal as well as external customers. Internal customers will usually grant you more time to make a good impression, however, because you are both on the same payroll.

One reason an attention-grabbing opening line impresses is because it reflects a quick insight into an important customer requirement or need. When the opening line addresses a fear, it can be very impressive. Steve Berkowitz is a sales representative for a firm that sells software to combat computer viruses. One of his opening lines to information systems managers is, "I've got software that will virtually eliminate any fear you have of viruses wiping out valuable company data." Steve's pitch has enabled him to get into many companies to make detailed sales presentations. Once inside the company, he uses a variation of the same line again quite successfully.

Here are some attention-grabbing opening lines for impressing prospective customers. You might be able to adapt the key idea contained in these lines to your circumstances. The general theme is to target in on a problem facing the firm, rather than to focus on your product or service.

- "How would you like to convert some of that solid waste you are recycling into low-cost fuel for your company?"

- "How would you like to reduce inventory shrinkage in your store to less than one percent?"
- "What would be your interest in introducing a program in your company that would increase productivity by 7 percent and decrease turnover by 15 percent?"
- "How would your impotent patients like to have a clinically tested device that will enable them to attain an erection whenever they want? Think of how grateful they would be to you, their doctor."
- "Do you ever worry about your home being broken into while you are at work or on vacation?"
- "How would you like a guarantee that you will have enough money to send your newborn child to an exclusive private college?"

All of these attention-getting lines are designed to satisfy an important customer need. We cannot guarantee that lines of this nature will win over every customer prospect. However, they represent yet another sensible tactic for gaining an edge by creating a favorable impression.

Display Product Knowledge

Establishing good relationships with customers and customer prospects remains an important part of selling. People still prefer to buy from people they like, assuming these people are satisfying an important need. In order to satisfy consumer needs, a sales representative must have intensive knowledge about the product or service he or she offers.

The problem of limited product knowledge is more likely to plague retailers than companies who sell through sales representatives. Retail salespeople often handle so many different products that extensive product knowledge is difficult to develop. The high turnover in the retail field also limits the opportunity to acquire intensive product knowledge. Another problem is motivation. The financial incentives offered sale associates are typically not high enough to motivate them to study carefully the products they sell. Because of these factors, the retail store that makes product knowledge part of its marketing strategy can be at an advantage. A good example is the Stereo Shop.

The Stereo Shop is a small chain of consumer electronics stores with an emphasis on stereo sets. All the sales associates are electronics buffs. Within the last year, I visited my local Stereo Shop to purchase a camcorder. (A very satisfied customer had recommended that I visit the Stereo Shop first.) Not wanting to bother learning a new gadget, I asked the sales associate to show me the simplest camcorder to operate. I insisted that I wanted a model that I could operate much like an old-fashioned movie camera. After recording an event, I wanted to insert the VHS film directly into a VCR for replay.

I found just the model I wanted for $1,200. It even had a light on the top, much like a miner's hat. I said to the sales associate, "Fine, this is just what I want." He challenged my thinking, asking me why I wanted a camcorder and what I hoped to achieve by using one. I mentioned that I would be shooting films of students, training seminars, street scenes, sporting events, and family members. I also explained that I wanted to have copies made of my tapes so I could give them to family members and friends.

The sales associate explained that the model I had in mind would be inadequate for my purposes. If I would be willing to spend an extra ten minutes in learning how to use an 8mm camcorder, I would benefit greatly. The image and sound quality would be much higher than achievable with the VHS (large film size) model. Furthermore, he explained, I could play the output from the camcorder through a television without having to record on a VCR. All I had to do was connect two wires between the VCR and a compatible television set.

The sales associate also pointed out that the best model to fit my purposes was smaller than the one I looked at first, and it cost $400 less. Convinced by his expertise and his ability to understand my true requirements, I bought the camcorder he suggested. The equipment has proved to be ideal, and I have since returned to the same Stereo Shop to purchase a VCR, videotapes, and camcorder tapes.

Twice when I had a problem coordinating my camcorder with the VCR, I called the Stereo Shop. A sales associate solved the problem for me over the telephone. From my standpoint, the intensive and extensive product knowledge of their sales associates has given the Stereo Shop the edge.

Sprinkle Your Presentation with Buzz Words

The choice of the right buzz words will influence many prospects. The setting is especially right for using buzz words when your prospect uses them. Buzz words are effective because they appeal to people's need to conform and belong to a group. If you use the jargon and the popular phrases of the day you will help your prospect feel more comfortable during your presentation.

Buzz words are also useful because they point to problems that affect many organizations. Two buzz words that should remain in vogue for the rest of the century are "cash flow" and "Total Customer Satisfaction." Weave both of them into your presentations to arouse the attention of most prospective customers.

Cash flow refers to the actual cash on hand of any organization or business. A company may have booked $3 million in new business, but until some of that money is collected there is no cash on hand. While waiting for its money, the company still has to pay salaries, real estate taxes, insurance, and scads of other overhead expenses. An effective way of impressing your prospect is therefore to describe how your product or service improves cash flow (his or hers, not yours).

Bart Vanderstyne, a sales representative for a company that distributes vending machines, made cash flow the center of his presentation. He explains why: "I found out that the places I called on weren't too excited about vending machines. The only reason they would let them into the building was to placate employees. Many employers believe that employees spend too much time at the vending machines.

"For a while I emphasized employee satisfaction in my presentation. The people I called on either didn't care about employee satisfaction, or they weren't convinced vending machines made a difference. My placements of vending machines surged when I started explaining how our machines improved cash flow.

"I promised my prospects that they would receive monthly checks from us as a guaranteed commission on sales. We stock the machines, repair them, collect the cash, and pay commissions promptly. Although we couldn't promise large sums of money, it would still be cash in their hands. I found out that even companies you would think are wealthy still want some extra cash each month."

By using the buzz word "cash flow," Bart was thus able to get prospects to listen to him seriously. The term "cash flow" served as a reminder that any legitimate activity that brought in cash would make an important contribution to the company.

Also look for opportunities to incorporate the term Total Customer Satisfaction into your pitch to prospects. Total Customer Satisfaction means that pleasing customers is the primary justification for being in business. It also means that quality is measured in terms of how well the customer is satisfied. Another important consideration is that a company gets very little repeat business, and no referrals, unless customers are satisfied.

During your sales presentation explain how your product or service will enhance your prospect's ability to improve customer satisfaction. For example, a person who operated a delivery service would point out how satisfied a prospect's customers would be to receive their shipments promptly.

Angelo Carpenter runs a tiny subcontracting firm called Quality Components. He was finally able to generate enough cash to make a living after he pitched his presentation in terms of quality delivered to the customer's customer. During his sales presentation Angelo uses the term Total Customer Satisfaction frequently.

Angelo explains to prospects what he would do should anything go wrong with one of his components. He stands ready personally to visit the customer's customer to rectify the problem. Angelo also emphasizes that he works closely with his own customers at every step of the manufacturing process. This close arrangement ensures that his components will satisfy the people who buy equipment from his customers.

A twist on the buzz-word tactic is to use different buzz words to appeal to different prospects. Few salespeople make enough use of this effective technique. Automobile dealer Sam Perkins exemplifies someone who uses buzz words effectively. Sam is one of the leading sales representatives at a large dealership that sells six different makes of autos. After inquiring about a prospect's occupation, Sam skillfully uses a few buzz words related to that occupation.

In talking to engineers, for example, Sam will make this comment: "The reason this car isn't so well known is that the company doesn't invest much in advertising. They would rather put the money into engineering refinements. A lot of people who own this brand are more concerned about engineering standard than trade puffery."

The dealership Sam works for is located near a large hospital. He has therefore also collected a few buzz words appropriate for the health-care profession. When talking to a physician or nurse, he alludes to safety facets of the car. He uses buzz words he picks up in health magazines and in conversation to emphasize the safety features. One of his favorite lines is, "This auto has an air bag designed to reduce head trauma, hematoma, and spinal-cord injuries in case of collision." Sam claims his sales to medical personnel have increased by one third since he began to sprinkle medical buzz words into his sales presentation.

Sam's buzz words are not mere gimmickry. His use of terms of interest to his prospects is a legitimate way of establishing rapport. Using buzz words to better relate to your prospect is yet another variation on the most basic sales principle of all: Appeal to your potential customer's interests.

YOU'RE SPEAKING MY LANGUAGE

It sounds like a foreign language to people who don't know your business. But to you, it's a welcomed tongue. Every profession has its own buzz phrases that are unique and stand out. The legal profession is the best and most obvious example. So much of what they say seems so foreign to the uninitiated. Engineers are no different, so are software programmers and medical researchers. Each has its own set of buzz phrases, acronyms, jargon, and vocabulary that says "I belong to this group."

If you are meeting with a prospect who speaks your same "language," it is strongly recommended you use those buzz phrases to your advantage. It helps build closeness. It's the equivalent of being stranded in a foreign country where you understand no one and they don't understand you, then suddenly a stranger approaches and addresses you in your mother tongue. Finally, a kindred soul!

If you feel that the other person understands these phrases, by all means use them. It says "we understand each other perfectly." If you are meeting someone from a profession whose terms you may not understand, it may be a good idea to do a little research on what their buzz phrases are so you can mention a few to make an impression. It shows you made an effort to reach.

Overestimate the Difficulty of the Prospect's Problem

Assume you are in the enviable position of having found a prospect with a pressing problem. Perhaps you made a cold call and uncovered the problem by encouraging the prospect to talk. Even better, assume that the prospect called you in to help satisfy the problem. A tactic to use to gain the edge in these circumstances is to at first overestimate how difficult—and therefore expensive—it will be to solve the problem. The scenario we describe is akin to the drama that occurs when your car breaks down on the highway and you are towed into an auto-repair center.

After listening to a description of your problem, the estimator says: "It sounds like your motor has seized. If you do need a new one, that would run about $3,500. However, would you like me to begin work and see if I can salvage your engine? If I could do it, the repairs would run about $850." Realizing that you have a cash flow problem, you say with a prayerful tone, "Go ahead. That would be great if you could fix my engine for $850."

By making a worst-case prediction about the extent of your engine damage, the estimator has placed you in a position whereby you grab the opportunity to spend $850 at his or her shop. Here is how overestimating (or exaggerating) the difficulty of the problem can impress an internal customer. Martha Bardot, a training director, was called in by the vice president of manufacturing to discuss a potential training program. The vice president represented an important internal customer prospect for Martha.

The vice president explained to Martha that because the company was shifting the manufacturing of one product line to a plant in Mexico, 250 production workers would be declared surplus. However, the company had about 50 clerical and customer service positions to fill at other places in the company. The vice president wanted to know how large a training program would be required to prepare about 50 production employees for clerical and customer-service work.

Martha was quite enthused but explained that she would have to carefully study personnel records to estimate the scope of the training required. She commented, "Many of our production workers have a literacy problem. They read at a very low level, their grammar is weak, and some of them have never operated a computer. This would indeed be a giant retooling effort."

Martha returned a week later with her analysis of the gravity of the problem. She explained to the vice president that her personnel records indicated that many of the production workers had a higher literacy rate than she had thought. If the right workers volunteered for retraining, the budget for the program would be $150,000 less than she had originally thought. The vice president was impressed, and Martha then prepared a serious proposal to undertake the training program.

Underestimating the difficulty of the problem works because your prospect believes he or she is getting a bargain. This illustrates how the negotiating skills described in Chapter 17 can be applied to diverse situations in which you are trying to gain the edge.

Show That You Have the Authority to Cut a Deal

Small-business owners frequently call on customer prospects. Top corporate executives also invest some time in personal selling. One reason these high-ranking people call on prospects is that they know it is impressive. Prospects enjoy the flattery of being called on by an owner or a top-ranking official. Also, the prospects are impressed by dealing with someone who has the authority to cut a deal. A sales representative who must first check back with the office to approve a price is less impressive.

To impress prospects, it is helpful to make it clear that you have the authority to strike a deal. Sean Anderson, an industrial sales representative, explains how this tactic worked for him: "We were attending a pre-award bid meeting for a major contract. This type of meeting is used to define major points of a contract. The customer let us know that company management had appropriated the funds, that the project was a go.

"Our marketing manager then asked the customer where we stood as far as getting the contract. The customer said that we were approved for the contract. The customer said that we were approved for the contract. We were among four finalists for the project. Our marketing manager then told the customer prospect that our company would give their company an extra aisle in their system for the same price. However, they had to sign the contract now to get this concession. [The "aisle" in the system was worth about $1 million.]

"The customer held an emergency meeting, and we were awarded the contract the next day. We returned home with the contract in hand. The ability to cut a deal impressed the buyer enough to award us the contract and close out the other companies. The fact that the marketing manager was the son of the owner gave him extra clout when it came to making a deal."

Sean's analysis was right on target. The authority of the marketing manager to grant a $1 million concession was impressive and gave Sean's company the competitive edge it needed.

Stroke Your Prospect's Ego

A universally effective tactic for influencing people is to flatter them sensibly. The technique is well suited to impressing prospects because the buyer in a buyer-seller relationship feels that he or she deserves special treatment. The only time buyers do not feel they deserve special treatment is when opportunities are limited for receiving the product or service they want. For example, a cosmetic surgeon who has an excellent track record for making his patients look ten years younger does not have to flatter customer prospects. The surgeon has a long line of potential customers clamoring for his or her services.

Use subtlety in stroking the ego of your prospect. Blatant ego strokes may sometimes appear too obsequious. Following are some examples of subtle, refined, and indirect appeals to the ego of customer prospects. Tailor them to your individual requirements.

- Careful research shows you that your prospect hit a hole in one on the golf course last year. After a brief introduction you say: "I was looking forward to shaking your hand. I've never shaken hands before with anybody who has hit a hole in one. Despite how much I practice, I doubt I'll ever match your achievement."

- "I like the way your office is decorated. The furnishings are impressive yet a visitor like myself feels comfortable here."

- "I brought with me a copy of an article you wrote for *Cement Industry News*. I was very impressed. After our business discussion is concluded I would like to ask you a few questions about the article."

- "I understand you were the product manager on the new generation of laser printers made by your firm. I want to compliment you. Our firm purchased two of those printers, and they are of the highest quality."

- "I've been told you have tremendous technical knowledge. I was therefore looking forward to discussing some of the advanced features of our equipment with you."

Observe that the ego strokes just presented emphasize work accomplishments. The one exception is the comment about the golf score. It is safer to deliver work-related compliments in the first several meetings with prospects or customers. Some people feel that comments about their physical makeup are presumptuous. If a male compliments a woman's appearance she might interpret it as a mild form of sexual harassment. Instead of creating a positive impression, the man has probably disqualified himself as a potential vendor.

Listen Patiently to Objections

Objections are almost in inevitable in selling face-to-face. Not every external customer will say yes immediately to buying your product or service. Not every internal customer will accept immediately the output or service you have to offer. You will impress your prospect if you listen patiently and carefully to objections. A classic example comes from a marketing handbook published many years ago.

An experienced stockbroker listened to a prospect complain that the security he was offering was flawed because it had been steadily dropping in value. The stockbroker nodded sympathetically. When it became apparent that his prospect had finished expressing his objections, he said: "You are right, Dr. Williams. The price of this stock has dropped 50 percent in the last six months. That is exactly why I am recommending it to you. At this low price, it is now underpriced and is an excellent buy in the opinion of our analysts."

The physician was impressed that his objections received careful attention and were acknowledged. The broker agreed with the physicians' observations that the stock had dropped in value. With his observations validated by the sales representative, the prospect was now in a receptive mood to buy. A different approach would have been for the stockbroker to say, "Yes, the stock has declined lately. Yet the decline has been smaller than for many other stocks in the industry." A rebuttal that challenges the prospect's observations may make the prospect defensive and unwilling to buy.

Listening to a prospect's objections is also valuable because it gives you a chance to clarify his or her confusion. Nicholas Barsan, a real estate agent who often earns more than $1 million per year, works hard at dealing with his prospects' confusion. A buyer had agreed to purchase a $250,000 house in Jackson Heights, New York. The buyer later telephones the home office and finally decided to cancel the deal. The less experienced real estate agent who had set up the deal turned to Barsan for help. Would Nicholas mind talking to the client (who now must be accurately classified as a prospect)?

Nicholas paid a personal visit to the prospect, a meat packer. The man was despondent because his accountant had just informed him that he would be taxed heavily if he sold his current home. Purchasing a new house would therefore be out of the question. The meat packer reaffirmed his intention to call off the deal.

After listening to the prospect's concern and worry, Nicholas explained that the accountant misinterpreted the tax laws. In reality, the tax law favors sellers who buy a more expensive house. The meat packer was still vacillating. Nicholas reminded him that his new home would be bigger and in a nicer neighborhood. Also, it had an apartment that could be rented to help pay the mortgage. After a tense pause the prospect gave a firm nod. Nicholas and the prospect then shook hands on the deal.

Nicholas explained to the younger real estate agent, "He will buy. He was just confused. You have to get to the heart of the problem, what bothers someone." The point here is that Nicholas could never have gotten to the heart of the problem without carefully listening the prospect's confusion. A basic fact about human behavior is that people want their objections heard. Listening to these objections and concerns creates a positive impression.

Overcome Objections with Humor

Poking fun gently at your prospect's objections will often create a good enough impression for you to overcome the objection and consummate the sale. The humor has to be good natured and must not hint that the prospect is foolish. Also, the humor should provide insight into the value of your product or service.

A story has circulated about a successful sales representative who sold commercial time for a radio station. The rep called on a foodstore-chain executive who had never advertised on radio. According to the executive, radio advertising did not sell because no one paid attention.

The sales representatives said, "Would you please give radio advertising a try if I could convince you that people really did pay attention?" The executive responded with a skeptical yes. The sales representative then suggested that the station could run ten spots a day announcing that the stores were all infected with roaches! After the executive stopped laughing, he placed an order.

An impressive form of humor is a comment that agrees with the objection yet exaggerates its veracity. Your humorous comment thus corroborates your prospect's logic but pushes it to its extreme consequences. Two examples will help illustrate this point:

- A sales representative at an automobile dealer is attempting to sell an expensive sports car to a middle-age, single man. The prospect places his chin in his left hand and gently strokes his chin with his thumb suggesting interest. He verbalizes an objection: "Isn't this really the type of car for a man who wants to lead a wild life?" "Absolutely right" responds the sales representative. "If you buy this car you'll attract more young women than you can handle."

  The car dealer's humorous comment impresses the prospect because it confirms his hunch that the sports car is associated with a wild lifestyle. The comment about the young women also appeals to one of the man's fantasies.

- A sales representative from a health-club equipment company is trying to sell an executive on installing a fully equipped athletic room on company premises. The executive muses, "This would be quite an investment, but I guess we would have a lot more healthy employees." "I agree with you wholeheartedly," retorts the representative. "You would have so few employees becoming disabled from heart attacks, you could just about shut down your employee recruitment program."

The sales representative's exaggerated comment helps the executive appreciate more fully the implications of improving employee physical fitness. The executive is impressed because his thinking is corroborated and expanded. As a consequence, the sales representative has moved one step further toward converting the prospect into a customer.

Make Reference to Prestigious Customers

A straightforward way to impress prospects is to drop names about prestigious companies who currently use your product or service. The technique is effective because most executives have positive attitudes toward well-known companies. Assume that three of an executive's relatives were laid off by General Motors, and a GM car he bought was a lemon. Despite these problems, the same executive will be highly impressed that a sales representative from an office-cleaning service has GM as an account.

Business consultants routinely attempt to impress client prospects by name dropping. Although ethics often prevents them from mentioning the specifics of what they do for a client, many consultants will freely mention the names of clients.

Jeff Triad was desperately trying to convince a small but high-volume supplier of computer equipment to carry his company's line of peripheral equipment. The supplier was located in New York City. Despite sending marketing literature, technical specifications, and making several phone calls, the supplier's director of marketing was not impressed with Jeff. He would not even agree to an in-person sales presentation.

Jeff then decided to use a little name dropping to give him the edge. He had been working for a long time on a big sale to the United Nations. Jeff telephoned the small supplier's marketing director once more. In the midst of the conversation, Jeff casually mentioned that he would be in town Thursday for a meeting at the United Nations.

At that point the customer became impressed because Jeff was in command of such a large, prestigious account. (Jeff did not actually say that the deal was completed with the UN.) The clincher was Jeff's suggestion of shifting the UN meeting to a later or earlier part of the day to accommodate the marketing director's schedule. The director finally agreed to meet with Jeff. The sales meeting went well. As a result, the computer-equipment supplier now sells peripheral equipment manufactured by Jeff's firm.

The marketing director of the computer supply firm was impressed because the UN appeared to be using the peripheral equipment manufactured by Jeff's firm. The tacit assumption is that the UN, or any other prestigious organization, is staffed by intelligent, discerning people. In reality, a delicatessen two blocks down from the UN might be a more impressive account. A small business often makes more intensive use of equipment than does a large organization that can afford loads of back-up equipment.

Make Cost-Cutting Suggestions

Cost-cutting seems to be permanently in style. Consequently if you show a prospect how to shave costs, you may make a positive impression. Too many sales presentations do just the opposite; they suggest ways for the prospect to increase expenses. Although the expenses may be for laudable purposes, they still decrease cash flow. The standard approach to making cost-cutting suggestions is to show how your product or service will actually decrease costs. Julie Flavin, a human resources manager, used such an approach.

Julie called on her internal customer and boss, the vice president of human resources. Julie explained that she had a new program she thought would benefit the company. Because a lid had been placed on new expenditures, Julie's request for an appointment met with a cool reception. Nevertheless, she was granted the chance to present her proposed program.

Julie explained how she wanted to formalize a program that would reduce expenses by about 25 percent on the hiring of temporary workers. Her plan was to develop a cadre of in-house temporaries who would become a supplementary work force. Instead of the company using the services of temporary worker agencies, Julie's department would keep track of reliable part-time workers. As these workers successfully completed one assignment for the company, they would become part of a pool of office temporaries. Some administrative costs would be involved, but agency fees would be drastically reduced.

Julie's cost-saving—and good-will-building—plan impressed her boss. She was given the authority to proceed with her plan on a limited budget. The program of in-house temporaries proved to be an effective cost saver, and Julie had gained the edge.

A nonstandard approach to impressing customer prospects with cost savings is to point to ways to save money not directly related to your product or service. This tactic must be implemented with considerable tact and sensitivity, however, to avoid appearing presumptuous. Few potential buyers expect a sales representative to tell them how to run their operations. The tactic works best if the cost-saving suggestion is dropped casually into the sales conversation.

Milt Brodsky is a successful office furniture sales representative. He is well liked by his established accounts because of his friendly manner, his sensible recommendations, and his honest deals. Milt also likes to help his established accounts and prospects in any other way he can. One of his helpful methods is to make cost-saving suggestions. Milt was calling on a customer prospect whose business was expanding. He hoped to sell the company the office furniture they would need for expansion.

"Congratulations on your growth," said Milt. "It's nice to know that a local company is doing so well when so many other companies are cutting back. I suspect you may be moving a lot of stuff from one location to another. We moved ourselves a few months ago. We saved thousands of dollars by using a local mover, Byrne Brothers. Have you thought of using a local instead of a national mover?"

In reality, the prospect had not thought of using a local mover and made a mental note of Milt's good suggestion. The prospect was impressed enough to listen more attentively to the balance of Milt's presentation.

Making cost-cutting suggestions helps create a favorable climate because it communicates a genuine interest in the client's welfare. The cost-saving pitch is more impressive when there is no business link between you and the source of your money-saving idea.

Know Your Competition

A customer prospect is likely to be impressed if you know your competition. A balanced viewpoint of your competitor's strengths and weaknesses is part of knowing the competition. To acquire competitive knowledge, many successful sales professionals keep careful files. Your file should not be so thorough, however, that it appears like snooping. For example, knowing the specific price offered by your competitor might appear to be spying.

Phil Hopkins, the owner of a commercial landscaping service, provides a healthy example of knowing the competition. Phil was attempting to land an account to landscape a newly developed suburban office park. He knew that his firm would be a serious competitor because it had the capacity to handle a project of this magnitude, and its reputation was solid. Phil had kept careful notes on the capabilities of other commercial landscaping firms in his area. He believed that this would be another factor in his favor in obtaining a contract.

Phil met for the third time with the managers responsible for awarding the landscaping contract. Believing that this was his last chance, Phil offered his final rationale for hiring his firm: "I'm glad to know our firm is still being considered to landscape your office park. I think that we can do a beautiful job for you. Our two best competitors also do an artistic job. In fact, Beechmere Landscaping might have one of the best landscaping artists in the business. But we're ahead of the competition in one important respect. If any of our plantings do not take hold, we'll be back right away to redo the job. That's one part of the job that most landscapers hate. Please check our references, and check the references of our competitors."

The principals of the development company did follow up with a reference check of previous customers. Phil's knowledge of the competition proved to be right on target, creating a very good impression. His firm received the contract, and Phil delivered as promised when two pine trees turned brown the first year.

Downplay Commercialism

A high-level impression tactic is to appear that making money for your firm is not your major motive. Some firms place sales representatives on salary to downplay commercialism. The rationale is that if the sales representative is not desperate to make a commission, he or she will serve the prospect better. Paul Walworth, the head of an architectural firm, purposely downplays commercialism to impress prospects. After discussing a project with a client prospect, Paul patiently explains that his firm *might* be interested in working with him or her.

A typical sales pitch for Paul is: "We are a very busy, small firm. We are limited in how many clients we can handle. We therefore work only with people who want some exciting architecture performed. We also insist on strong creative control. Our firm simply will not be associated with a design we think has aesthetic pitfalls." A few client prospects reject Paul as being too arrogant, yet most are very impressed. Paul gains the edge by downplaying commercialism. (He is also playing hard to get.)

Be a Walking Advertisement for Your Product or Service

Some prospective customers are impressed if you use yourself for an advertisement. Even if they are not highly impressed, at least you will attract their attention. Ed Falcon, a young sales representative for a home appliance store in Toronto, uses this tactic. He carries with him a red vinyl case with a gold imprint, "Kerwin Home Appliances."

Ed finds his best results with this technique while waiting on line at restaurants and at the bank. Many people react in the same way to his vinyl case: "Oh, you are with Kerwin Home Appliances." Ed smiles graciously and says, "Yes, I am. I suspect you would have not asked me unless you might be interested in a new appliance. Here is my card." Ed and his sales manager both agree that the walking advertisement is a money maker for the store. Ed has gained the edge by self-advertising his products in a novel way.

Being a walking advertisement for yourself is a positive tactic. Similarly, it is important to avoid being a walking advertisement for not using your product or service. Jeff Deckman, a manufacturing engineer, recalls receiving a telephone call from a sales representative for a financial investment firm. The sales rep was pitching corporate bonds that promised a high yield. Jeff inquisitively asked the sales representative how many of these bonds were in his personal portfolio. The representative replied, "I don't buy bonds." Jeff replied, "Neither do I," thus ending the conversation. One of the oldest clichés in sales should not be forgotten when attempting to impress prospects: "Have faith in your own product."

Display Good Manners and Etiquette

Good manners and etiquette have made a strong comeback in recent years as an important tactic for impressing people in business. Conversely, poor manners and etiquette can disqualify you from consideration. Little touches such as addressing people by their last name upon introduction, letting them through a door ahead of you, and sending a follow-up thank-you note can be very impressive.

Michelle Pelouse, a sales representative for an office supply company, provides this affirmative statement about etiquette. "I have found that just by being polite and courteous, I get a lot of new business. I do the basic things I learned at the Bryant and Stratton business program. These include offering prospects my business card and writing them notes of appreciation for having listened to my presentation.

"Before I call on a prospect I make sure I know how to pronounce his or her name correctly. I also ask people when would be the best time to telephone them again.

"Politeness is extra important in my business, because office supplies have become a commodity. Customers simply buy from whomever they like the best, assuming your costs are in line."

One of the reasons good manners and etiquette give Michelle the edge is because too many other people gloss over their importance. Assertiveness may be important in attracting a prospect's attention. Yet combining assertiveness with practicing good etiquette give you a distinct advantage.

Dress Like Your Prospective Customer

The stereotyped Dress for Success look is gradually being replaced by Dress Like Your Prospect as a way of impressing potential customers. If you are calling on prospects in Silicon Valley, wear the casual, loose fitting, unisex style of clothing sold at Gap stores. If you are attempting to sell a prospect in an area where protective gear is required, wear a hard hat. If you don't have enough sense to wear the hard hat, you will appear too unfamiliar with the situation to solve a client's problem.

Dressing like your internal customer can also be important. If you are a financial analyst who is analyzing manufacturing costs, take off your jacket when you visit the manufacturing area. If you are a manufacturing representative working with marketing on product design, wear a suit when you visit the marketing department.

Dressing in a manner similar to your customer works because it helps you establish rapport. An important aspect of feeling comfortable with others is the feeling that the other person has similar tastes and preferences.

Appeal to the Olfactory Sense

It's worth a try to impress customer prospects by giving off the right scent. Experiment with different colognes, toilet waters, powders, and perfumes until you find the scent that works best for you. People vary as to which scent is the most impressive for them. Researchers at a Japanese cosmetics company have found that sage and cypress can produce a calming effect, and jasmine can relieve anxiety and cure drowsiness. These scents would therefore put a person in a receptive mood for a sale.

Giving off the right scent can be impressive because the prospect might think it is your presentation, or your presence, that is so relaxing and uplifting. At a minimum, a pleasant scent adds to your impact. Sydney Woods, a seller of Infiniti automobiles, claims he would not show up on the salesroom floor without cologne. "It makes me appear distinctive and affluent," he claims.

Relate Warmly to Voice Mail

A frustration facing many sales representatives is that they are more likely to hear a voice-mail message than speak to a person when telephoning prospects. The challenge of voice mail is that you have to leave a message so compelling that your prospect will return the call. Ted Garland, a sales representative for a computer components firm, explains how he handles the situation: "My biggest problem these days is that I hardly ever get the chance to talk to a person. Even with established customers, the best I can do is leave a message and hope that he or she returns the call.

"I noticed that the messages I was leaving were beginning to show signs of irritation and frustration. One of my established accounts told me so. I may have been turning off some prospects by leaving messages that sounded angry. So I purposely tried to sound as warm and friendly as possible when I spoke to a voice mail system. The tactic has worked okay. My percentage of return calls has increased, leading to a larger number of sales."

Ted thus gained the edge by having the insight to cope with an important work-place change. You are more likely to speak to a voice-mail system than you are to a person unless you are calling people in the executive suite.

Help the Customer Make a Purchase

A final tactic here for impressing customer prospects is to help them make a purchase. Customers are often irritated by salespeople who focus on making a sale rather than on helping them make the best choice. Often the pivotal factor is that the customer needs to be hand-held in making up his or her mind. Omar Khan, a successful seller of upscale beds, is especially adept at convincing customers that he is looking out for their needs and interests.

Omar's tactic is to first help prospects define their budget and also to talk about any special requirements, such as back problems. Omar then shows them the bed that best fits their price range, while candidly point out the bed's advantages and disadvantages. He also points out the total costs under several different financing plans.

One could readily dismiss Omar's tactic as simply using low-pressure tactics. He goes beyond that, however, because he offers so much helpful advice and presents so many relevant facts. Omar's professionalism impresses customers and gives him the edge.

Quickly tying all the information in this chapter together, following is a checklist of some important tactics for impressing prospective customers. Many of these tactics apply to both external and internal customers.

1. Quickly learn your prospective customer's name.

2. Listen and engage in customer problem solving.

3. Use an attention-grabbing opening line.

4. Display product knowledge.

5. Sprinkle your presentation with buzz words.

6. Overestimate the difficulty of the prospect's problem.

7. Show that you have the authority to cut a deal.

8. Stroke your prospect's ego.

9. Listen patiently to objections.

10. Overcome objections with humor.

11. Make reference to prestigious customers.

12. Make cost-cutting suggestions.

13. Know your competition.

14. Downplay commercialism.

15. Be a walking advertisement for your product or service.

16. Display good manners and etiquette.

17. Dress like your prospective customer.

18. Relate warmly to voice mail.

19. Help the customer make a purchase.

Summary Points

• Quickly learn the prospect's name.

• Use appropriate buzz words and industry jargon to show familiarity.

• Always stroke the client's ego.

• Know your product and know what the competition has to offer too.

• Listen patiently to objections; Don't lose your cool.

• Overcome objections with humor.

• Help the customer make the purchase.

CHAPTER 16

ON-THE-LINE: MASTERING PHONE SALES

It's 6:30 P.M. You're starting to relax from a hard day's work and are just about to sit down to dinner with your family when it happens. As if on cue, the phone rings and rings. Finally, you pick it up. "Hello my name is Jack Smith, I'm calling from PDQ Products and would like you to know about our exciting new line of high-tech widgets." Just about now you wish you had let the answering machine pick it up.

Not everyone likes getting these calls, but if they didn't work why would companies continue to use this method? The fact is, this is the most direct way of reaching potential clients short of sending a huge sales force out in person. Obviously, you know that's not practical, nor feasible, when it's easier to pick up the phone and "touch someone."

If your business is large enough to require some solicitations, you are already working in volume. With so many prospective clients or customers just a phone call away, you certainly wouldn't want to have any of your associates ad-lib or deviate from your central message. Therefore it's extremely important that you create a "leak-proof" script that keeps the person on the other line long enough to get their attention and make him or her a customer.

Jack Griffin's *The Do-It-Yourself Business Promotions Book,* excerpted below, details how you can write scripts for these calls and how to make these presentations work to your advantage. If done right, this can be a highly effective selling technique for your firm. But like most good business communications, the key is planning.

NO HANGUPS: FULLY SCRIPTED TELEPHONE SOLICITATIONS

How to Do It

Telemarketing expert Robert J. McHaton observes: "The shortest distance between a salesperson and a prospect is the telephone line." The telephone is a powerful communications tool. Old-time, door-to-door salesmen (and they were invariably men) had to work to get a "foot in the door." The telephone is virtually an *automatic* foot in the door: few people can resist picking it up when it rings (though, increasingly, voice mail and answering machines are used to "screen" incoming calls). The telephone is also a great leveler of the competitive playing field. It is available to the smallest, most modestly capitalized of businesses as well as to the *Fortune* 500 giants, and, increasingly, it is those blue-chip firms that are making most extensive use of telemarketing. If you wish to consider telemarketing as a business in itself rather than as a business technique, then, surely, telemarketing is one of today's fastest-growing industries.

"Spontaneous" sales (which, incidentally, should never *really* be all that spontaneous), are most effective when used in "lukewarm" or "hot" selling situations: situations in which you have already established some form of contact or relationship with the target customer. This chapter covers strategies for making "cold" calls; that is, calls to prospects who are total strangers to you and with whom you have no relationship.

STRATEGIES FOR MAKING "COLD" CALLS

You have four basic choices for making such calls:

1. Winging it
2. Following an outline
3. Following a full script
4. Using an ADRMP

WINGING IT

There are people in the world who certainly seem to be "natural born salespeople." And there are people who just love to talk on the phone. Put these two personality types together in a single human being, and, chances are, you have a telemarketer who can make sales without a script or outline of any kind. If you're convinced that you are such a person, then all that need be said is, *Well, bless your heart,* and you need not read on.

Most of the world, however, lacks this kind of talent—just as most of the world can't play basketball like Michael Jordan or play the fiddle like Isaac Stern. For those folks, winging cold calls (as distinct from lukewarm and/or hot calls) is

Exhausting
Demoralizing
Time-wasting
Ineffective

So why do it?

FOLLOWING AN OUTLINE

Creating and following an outline, which you keep before you as you make your calls, allows you or your *experienced* and *knowledgeable* sales staff to cover the bases with a prospect without, however, sounding "canned." It allows a good salesperson to imprint each sale with his or her own personality, yet it helps to ensure that:

1. All relevant product/service benefits are covered.
2. All terms and conditions are covered.
3. No promises are made that cannot be kept.
4. The product/service is not misrepresented.

Outlines also tend to increase the volume of calls over the number that can be achieved through spontaneous calls. Less time is wasted. Having that outline in front of you makes calling less of an emotionally demanding experience and, therefore, keeps your energy level higher, which results in more calls and more effective calls.

The outline should consist of selling steps and product/service benefits. You will need to include at least nine steps in the outline and as many key selling elements (especially product/service benefits, terms, conditions, and so on) as required.

1. *Verify the prospect's name.* Why? Who cares, if it's a cold call? Getting a name at the very beginning of the call gives the call a purpose. It tells the caller that you are calling him or her—not just anybody. It also allows you to use your prospect's name, an act that, in and of itself, breaks some of the ice of a cold call by establishing a rudimentary relationship between you and the callee.

2. *Identify yourself and your firm.* You can't "trick" your prospect into listening to what you have to say by withholding the fact that you are calling from a company that is trying to interest him in buying something. It doesn't work that way. In fact, failure to be upfront about who you are and where you are calling from will trigger instant suspicion, resistance, impatience, and a desire to hang up. Give your name and the name of your firm: "This is John Doe, calling from XYZ, Incorporated."

3. *Then tell the callee why you are calling.* Don't delay on this point, either. But be aware that certain words are *poison* in most selling situations and in a cold call situation particularly. These lethal words include:

buy	contract	deal
cheap	cost	decide
		sell

Announce the purpose of your call, but use *positive* words to do so. For example:

alternative	gain	taste
benefit	inform	test
breakthrough	information	touch
choice	money	trustworthy
choose	new	value
desirable	opportunity	wanted
distinctive	option	win
easy	prove	wise
family	see	
free	smart	

In short, combine telling your prospect why you are calling with a good reason for the prospect to take your call and to listen to you.

4. *Ask a "test" question.* Many sales professionals have a prejudice against questions. They want to do the talking and let the customer do the listening to reduce the risk of being shut out. Cold callers actually experience relatively few out-and-out hangups. Most people find it difficult to hang up—even on an unwanted sales call. Instead, often, they will listen to your pitch (at least for a while), even if they are not remotely interested in what you are selling. True, you haven't been shut out. But you have wasted time you could have devoted to a more promising prospect. It is, therefore better to launch out with a test question. But, like a good-hearted teacher, give your callee every opportunity to "pass" the test. Ask an appealing, inviting, intriguing question. Frame it to highlight benefits. Don't start out by poisoning the well with something like "Would you be interested in buying . . ." This is like asking, "Would you please reach into your pocket and give me some money?" Begin by testing your customer. Just make sure you ask a question that invites a yes. Often, it helps to make a statement, then simply ask for confirmation. "I have reason to believe that you would be interested in hearing about a new (*product*)

we've developed, which (*briefly describe benefit*). Is that the case?" A test question structured in this way not only launches your sales pitch, it also invites a yes—yet it allows the customer to say no, if he really and truly is not interested. The negative response will allow you to say, "Thanks for your time and have a nice day," hang up, and go on to the next prospect.

5. *Make the presentation.* We will cover this in detail using examples. In an outline, this section should clearly list all selling points, always emphasizing product benefits rather than product features. The features of a product or service are what it does. The benefits are the good things the product or service will do for the customer. Usually, benefits are intimately linked to emotion and feeling. "Acme detergent will clean your dishes better than any other detergent" describes a product feature. "Acme detergent enhances your dining experience because you and your guests feel as if you are dining with brand-new, pristine china" describes a product benefit.

6. *Overcome objections.* Your outline should anticipate customers' objections to buying your product or service, and it should provide quick-reference strategies for overcoming those objections. Experienced telemarketers put their outline (or their script) on a clipboard, using a short sheet of paper. Beneath the outline or script sheet or sheets is a longer sheet, labeled at the bottom (so that the label is clearly visible) with a type of objection: "TOO EXPENSIVE." When you turn to this sheet, you find an outline strategy for countering this particular objection. Clipped beneath this sheet is an even longer one, labeled at the bottom with another usual objection: "TOO DIFFICULT TO INSTALL." Beneath this is yet a longer sheet of paper labeled "TOO DIFFICULT TO USE," and so on. In this way, responses to objections are "tabbed" and immediately accessible. You might consider using computer software to create the electronic equivalent of the tabbed clipboard, with responses to objections that can be "popped up" readily on your monitor screen.

7. *Ask for the order.* When you counter an objection, don't ask your prospect if you answered his question. Former New York City mayor Ed Koch was famous for his familiar tag line, "How'm I doin'?" Well, that worked for Ed, but it's not the right message to send to your prospect. Instead, immediately follow your counter to his objection by asking for the order. "Asking" does *not* mean "Would you like to order one?" This asks for a

yes *or* no. Instead, ask for the order by giving your customer a choice that invites only a positive response. "Would you like to charge your order on a major credit card or would you prefer C.O.D.?" Or "Would you like the upright or horizontal model?"

8. *Verify information*. Make sure your outline includes a checklist that asks for verification of the customer's name, billing address, shipping address, and credit information. Make sure the outline prompts the salesperson to read back the order to the customer.

9. *Thank the customer*. Don't leave this to chance. The outline should remind the salesperson to thank the customer for the order.

FOLLOWING A FULL SCRIPT

If you want to exercise maximum control over how your product or service is telemarketed, you must create a fully scripted presentation. This simply takes the outline to the next level, making the same points, achieving the same goals, but fleshing out the skeleton. Use the nine outline steps just listed to guide you in creating a script. Keep it within 300 to 500 words in length—a maximum of about ninety seconds of telephone time without rushing.

The verbatim script has the following advantages over the spontaneous approach and the outline approach:

1. It can be used effectively by the experienced as well as the novice "tele-marketing communicator." This means that you can hire low-cost tele-

---

THE DINNER-TIME CALL

Many people are turned off by telephone sales people. They've heard about three-quarters of a million pitches and have become jaded. Are these people impossible to reach? Some perhaps, but many are still potential customers for you. Working from good information is a way to greatly reduce potential rejections. Make sure the lists you are using include people who are really potentially interested. If you're selling lawn care products and the phone numbers you have been given are for apartment dwellers in the city, you are clearly wasting your time. There is no substitute for solid market research long before you ever dial the first number.

---

phone help (retirees wanting to earn extra money, students, aspiring actors, and so on). With low-cost help, your time is freed up for other tasks, and you can put more people on more phones to increase call volume.

2. Verbatim scripts ensure adherence to your selling goals and policies.

3. Verbatim scripts reduce misunderstanding and the possibility of misrepresentation by well-meaning (or, for that matter, ill-meaning) overzealous sales personnel. In this way, the scripts can increase customer satisfaction.

4. Verbatim scripts reduce training time and expense.

Are there disadvantages to verbatim scripts? Yes, there are:

1. A poor, inexpressive, lackluster telecommunicator will make the customer feel that he is being read to, that he is being subjected to a canned spiel.

2. Working from a script may reduce the individual initiative of the telecommunicator.

3. If an inexperienced telecommunicator attempts to depart from the script—to answer a question, for example—he may falter and become confused.

4. If adherence to the script is rigidly required, it may be difficult or impossible to meet customer objections and counter resistance.

BULLETPROOFING YOUR SCRIPTS

Most of the potential disadvantages of telemarketing scripts can be anticipated and overcome by taking four steps:

1. Prepare an effective script.

2. Include tabbed responses to objections.

3. Get through to the right person.

4. Work on your delivery and voice.

An effective script should follow the same steps as an effective outline, with these additions:

Use language that talks *to*—not *at*—your customer.

Wherever possible, use *you* rather than *we, I,* or the *company.*

Formulate a strong opening statement that gets your prospect's interest.

Incorporate questions into the script that are designed to get and keep your prospect involved.

Use questions that can be answered either with a "yes" or that prompt a positive choice among positive alternatives.

Sell benefits, not features.

Use descriptive language.

Use testimonials and examples, especially examples of success.

End with an "action closer"—prompting the customer to act now.

Address objections.

As in preparing an outline presentation, anticipate potential customer objections and provide responses to them. Using a clipboard with labeled and tabbed objection responses is a good way to handle this in a fumble-free manner. If you are equipped with personal computers and appropriate software, you can create responses to objections that can be "popped up" on your screen. As you gain experience selling your product or service over the telephone, compile a list of objections you actually encounter. Formulate responses to each of these objections and incorporate them into your script material.

In general, it is ineffective to attempt to counter an objection with an argument. Disputes generate hostility, and hostility does not produce sales. If your customer protests that the merchandise is "too expensive," your saying "No, it is not" won't help. A better strategy for countering objections and resistance is to put the issue back on the customer, by asking a question or by obtaining more information from him to get him to tell you just what would allow you to make the sale. If you do want to present what is, in effect, a counter*argument,* do so by supplying genuine, useful information rather than simply telling the customer that he is wrong.

Let's return to the "too expensive" objection. You might respond with: "What do you pay now?" Then work with the answer—"Does that price *include* freight?" Or "What quantities do you have to buy to get that price?" Or "Are you really satisfied with the quality (the warranty, the color, the variety, the service . . . whatever)?" Or "When you say 'too expensive,' what are you comparing our product with?" You might also present an *informative* counterargument, turning the objection into an opportunity to amplify your pitch: "'Too expensive'? Not when you consider the quality—we used eighteen-gauge steel throughout, 30 percent heavier than the competition—and the service. We're on call 24 hours a day, seven days a week."

What if your prospect hits you with a flat "I don't want it"? How can a scripted presentation handle *that*?

Don't agree. Don't surrender. Don't hang up. Respond: "Please tell me why you don't want it?" Notice that the question is framed as a polite request, not a demand ("Why don't you want it?"). Many objections can be met similarly:

I don't like it. "Please tell me why you don't like it."

I don't need it. "Please tell me why you don't need it."

And so on.

Two very common objections are the put-off—"I'm not interested now. Maybe later"—and the assertion of policy: "I never buy on the phone." You should have responses prepared for these. If the customer says "not now," respond that the offer is limited and may not be available later. Alternatively, ask the customer when you should call back: "Okay. May I call you back this afternoon, or would tomorrow morning be better for you?"

If the customer asserts that she never buys on the phone, ask her why:

"Please tell me why you don't do business on the phone."

"I understand your hesitance. Have you been burned in the past?"

"Please tell me why you don't trust me."

"A large number of *Fortune* 500 companies now do most of their purchasing over the phone."

"Do you get a better guarantee from another supplier?"

Get through to the right person. One objection you might encounter is that the callee needs permission to make a purchase or is not the person responsible for purchasing. Don't respond with frustration. Use this objection as an opportunity to identify the right person to call: "I see. Can you, please, tell me who makes the decisions regarding purchases?" Better yet, ensure that you call the right person to begin with. Before dialing the phone, take the time and effort to identify the person who makes the purchasing decisions, and start with her.

Work on delivery and voice. Telemarketing does not require the highly trained voice of a television or radio announcer, but it does call for a person who can deliver the scripted presentation clearly, smoothly, with clear pronunciation, with conviction, at an even pace, and with enthusiasm. Pace—don't rush, *ever*— and enthusiasm are the two most important qualities. Pace is a matter of practice, of training yourself or your staff to read the script at a moderate tempo. Enthusiasm is best developed from a genuine understanding of and enthusiasm for whatever it is you are selling. Silly as it may at first sound, you should also make the presentation with a smile. True, the callee cannot see you, but if you smile, chances are that all the positive inflections of voice and verbal delivery that go with a smile will be transmitted over the telephone wire.

The script itself does much to foster enthusiasm. Keep it simple, and keep it positive. Write in a way that encourages a positive, enthusiastic, smiling approach. This is not as difficult as it may at first seem. Simply take a potential negative—

"I must secure credit approval before I can ship."
and turn it into a positive—

"I'll ship that right out as soon as your credit approval arrives."

One surefire way to convert a potential negative into a real positive is to shift from "I" to "you":

Not
I think that

But
You will discover that

Not
I need to point out that

But
You will be interested to know that

USING AN ADRMP

There is an alternative vehicle for the delivery of the fully scripted telephone sales presentation. The automated dialing-recording message player (ADRMP) automatically dials preprogrammed telephone numbers and plays a recorded message to whomever answers the phone. The advantages of the ADRMP?

1. A machine is a tireless caller that, like the mechanical bunny used to promote a certain brand of batteries, keeps going, and going, and going, and . . .

2. A machine presentation ensures absolutely unvarying presentation of your prescribed sales presentation.

3. A machine will never lose its temper.

4. A machine permits you to record a professional voice, perhaps even the recognizable voice of a well-known celebrity.

TO BE OR NOT TO . . . UH . . . BE

One of the things that annoys me most about telemarketers are those who deliver their lines without clearly knowing the script, the product or showing any enthusiasm whatsoever. When was the last time you bought anything from someone who mumbled their lines, didn't know how many sizes it came in, or acted like they'd really rather be doing something else? Not likely any time recently.

People want to hear enthusiasm, they want to hear that this is a product worth investing in. They don't want to hear bored college kids making a few extra bucks by droning on about some product they've never even seen before. If you are making the pitches, be extremely cognizant about how you sound, how you moderate your tone, and how you project yourself positively.

If others are doing the calling for you, make sure everyone on your staff is trained properly. If you've ever called a 1-800 service line and heard the announcement "this call may be recorded for training purposes," now you know why. It is both to remind the worker that they are accountable for how they treat customers and to serve as an educational means for showing others what to avoid as well as how to do it right on the phone. Remember, the person delivering the script may be the only contact the buyer has with your company; never blow a first impression. You're unlikely to have a second chance.

Disadvantages? You bet there are:

1. Many people resent a "computer" intruding on their privacy and will slam down the receiver without listening to *any* of the actual sales presentation.

2. Even those customers who do listen to the recorded message may resent being treated like a target for an electronic dart.

3. Using an automated means of reaching customers may suggest that you intent to treat your customers like machines.

4. A machine cannot respond to customer questions or counter customer resistance.

5. ADRMPs are under attack in some states and jurisdictions and are subject to restrictive legislations or may even be illegal.

In general, an ADRMP is a poor choice for small-business promotion, mainly because it works against the greatest asset a small business has: a size and scale of operation that promote personal service and one-on-one contact with customers. ADRMPs do have a future, but they will probably prove most consistently useful for follow-up. For example, a mail-order fulfillment operation might program the phone numbers of customers who have placed catalog orders, and the ADRMP may call them to confirm that the order arrived—asking the customer to call only if the order has failed to arrive. For such follow-up tasks, the ADRMP is actually perceived as a positive customer service asset, an extra service. An ADRMP is also a good choice for initial collection "reminder" calls. Customers who have neglected to make a payment will be less embarrassed by a machine reminder than by a human caller and, therefore, less likely to resent the reminder.

Generating Leads

SCRIPT 1

Good morning/afternoon. This is *(Name)* from *(Name of company)*. Could you please give me the name of the *(owner, manager, etc.)*?

Thanks.

Would you connect me, please, with *(Name of owner, manager, etc.)*?

Thank you.

(Name of owner, manager, etc.), this is *(Name)* from *(Name of company)*. I am calling you today to give you some information you will want to have: *(Name of company)* has just developed a *(product)* that will *(identify key benefit)*.

Do you currently use *(type of product)*?

Are you aware of the full benefits of *(type of product)*?

Let me ask you, if I may: Do you currently *(describe activity)*?

Then you will definitely benefit from *(product)*. And I would like to tell you exactly how:

(list benefits in detail)

May I suggest that we have one of our representatives call on you to demonstrate for you the competitive edge *(product)* will give you? Who should our rep contact?

What would be a good time for our rep to visit?

In the meantime, would you like to see our literature?

Thank you very much for your time, *(Name)*, and have a good day.

SCRIPT 2

Is this *(Name of callee)*? Good morning/afternoon. My name is *(Name)*, and I'm calling from *(Name of company)* because I would like to know a few things about your *(type of product/service)* needs. Can you take just a moment or two to help me?

Great. Thanks.

Do you currently use *(type of product)*?

No? Would you tell me, please, why you don't?

Are you aware that using *(type of product)* can increase your revenue from *(type of operation)* by *(% amount)* percent or more?

Let me tell you how. *(Explain key points.)*

Would you like to learn more about *(type of product)*, what it costs, and what it can do for you?

Great.

I would like to set up a visit by one of our account representatives. Does *(time period)* look good for you?

Okay. What day during that week? We'll need no more than *(number)* minutes of your time. Is morning or afternoon best?

It's been a pleasure talking with you, and *(Name of representative)* will see you on *(repeat day and time)*. Thanks very much for your time, and have a good day.

Setting Up a Sales Call

Hello. May I speak with the *(manager, owner, etc.)*, please? Thank you.

Hello, *(Name of manager, owner, and so on)*, this is *(Name)*. I'm calling from *(Name of company)* this morning to introduce you to our new line of innovative *(products)*.

To introduce our new line, I can offer you a very special price on *(product)*.

Can you tell me, please, what brand do you use now?

How much do you pay?

Well, here's what you get with any of our *(products)*:

(list benefits)

Now ordinarily you would pay from *($ amount)* to *($ amount)* for quality like this, and, based on your long-term satisfaction, you would find these prices quite reasonable. But, for a limited time, I can offer you discounts of *(% amount)* to *(% amount)* percent off these prices.

One of my field reps will be in your area during *(time period)*. I can arrange or him to call on you, if you would like, to take advantage of this offer.

Terrific!

Let's set it up now. *(Secure details of time, place, etc.)*

(Name of rep) will see you, then, at *(time)* on *(day)*. It's been great talking with you, and have a good day.

Making the Sale

SCRIPT 1

Good morning/afternoon, My name is *(Name)*. May I please ask the name of the person who handles purchasing for *(department)*? Thank you very much.

(Name of right person), this is *(Name)*, with *(Name of company)*. We manufacture *(products)* for a wide variety of companies like yours, including *(list three big-name customers)*.

Do you currently use *(type of product)*? What brands? What are you accustomed to paying?

Well, then, you will be interested to hear what I have to offer.

Our *(product)* is unique and highly cost effective. It provides *(list benefits)*, and every firm that has used it, including *(list three big-name customers)*, has voiced great enthusiasm for it. For example, *(Name)* at *(Name of customer company)* has reported that *(brief quotation relevant to product benefit)*. At *(Name of another customer company)* revenues have increased by *(% amount)* percent because of *(product)*.

(Name of callee), *(product)* is fully guaranteed for *(period)*. What kind of guarantee do you have at present?

I'm sure you will agree that our guarantee offers quite an advantage. And, remember, service is available—on-site—daily.

We ship in quantities of *(quantity)*, and the price for each unit is *($ amount)*. With your approval, I will send *(quantity)* to you. Would you like express delivery—ship date *(date)* for a charge of *($ amount)*—or standard at *($ amount)*?

Do you require a purchase order?

[Customer responds: *(Yes)*.]

Do you have a fax number? Great. Go right ahead and fax the P.O. to *(company name, fax number, etc.)*

[Customer responds: *(No)*.]

Fine. Then let me make sure I'm spelling your name correctly. And your title is? And now, *(Name)*, let me just confirm *(quantity, price, shipping mode, and date)*.

Thank you, and have a great day!

SCRIPT 2

Hello. Is this *(Name of callee)*? Hello, *(Name of callee)*. I'm *(Name)*, calling from *(Name of company)*. I am calling to let you in on an opportunity to improve your bottom line on *(type of business)*.

Am I correct in assuming that you would like to increase your share of this market?

Great. Then I'm speaking with the right person.

(Name), do you currently use *(type of service)* or do you handle this in-house?

It has been our experience that few business professionals can find the time to do a cost-accounting study to determine just how much in-house *(type of service)* costs. So let me offer you the results of our survey of *(number)* of businesses that are similar to yours. We find that in-house *(type of service)* operations consume *(number)* hours per week and cost a minimum of *($ amount)*, but can run as high as *($ amount)* in some cases.

You agree that such costs are unacceptable?

So why accept them? We can fulfill all your *(type of service)* needs for *($ amount)*.

You heard right, *(Name)*. For *($ amount)* per *(time period)* you get: *(list services)*. And that means you save *($ amount)* each and every *(time period)*, and you also get *(additional benefits)*.

Now it will take us *(time period)* to set up your account, so it will be to your advantage to place a service order with me today. I can expedite processing and get you on the system no later than *(date)*. All I need is some basic information: *(list)*.

You will be booked into the system *(number)* days after we receive your first payment of *($ amount)*.

Let me just make sure I'm spelling your name correctly. The title of your position?

If you sent *($ amount)* to *(Name of company and department, address, etc.)* today, our field representative will call on you by *(date)*, and you will be on the system no later than *(date)*, which means that, this month alone, you will save about *($ amount)* in *(type of service)* costs.

I am very happy that I spoke with you today, *(Name)*, and we look forward to serving your *(type of service)* needs. Have a great day!

Summary Points

- Stick to the script, but never sound wooden or insincere.
- Verify the person's name and always identify yourself and your firm.
- Launch a test question that will lead the person to be interested in more information.
- Anticipate objections ahead of time.
- Sell benefits, not features.
- Use testimonial and examples.
- Close with a pitch asking them to act *now*.

SECTION SIX

NEGOTIATIONS

CHAPTER 17

WHAT TO ASK DURING NEGOTIATIONS

You're negotiating a deal for your company. It's getting close to the dreaded 11th hour and the other side throws a zinger at you that you simply never expected. Not just left field, but far left field. *"Where did that come from?"* you say to yourself. How do you recover? The other side is making demands that seem way out of line. How do you put an end to it? Do you respond angrily? Do you call their bluff? Do you hurl the same thing at them?

After much practice, you'll realize it's sometimes better to ask the right question than to say the wrong thing and regret it later. Is it buying for time? Perhaps, but it's an intelligent strategy that has worked time and time again.

Asking well-phrased questions, politely, can help relieve pressure on both sides and gives you the means of getting information from the other side they might not ever have volunteered. At an impasse: "What else can either of us bring to the table to close the gap between our positions?" Feeling manipulated: "Are you experiencing outside pressures to conclude these negotiations?" Negotiations don't have to stop dead because the other seems to want it to, keep the talks alive and moving in a positive direction.

Sam Deep's and Lyle Sussman's *What to Ask When You Don't Know What to Say,* excerpted below, offers all types of "escape hatches" for those situations when you're at a loss for what to say, but want to keep the momentum going, maybe even find out some key information that was never volunteered.

NEGOTIATING

You negotiate when you meet to resolve conflict with someone whose goals are incompatible with yours. Examples of the negotiation situations you may confront include resolving a vacation dispute with a coworker, working out a supply agreement with a vendor, creating with your employee the conditions of a new responsibility, and establishing your salary in a job you have just been offered.

In these encounters we are searching for a win-win outcome. In other words, you want both you and the other party to walk away winners. This result is much preferable to one where what one person wins the other must lose.

Unfortunately, the goal of win-win resolution is easier said than done. Through lack of training, lack of experience, or lack of self-confidence, too many potentially constructive outcomes are sacrificed at the altar of unilateral demands and self-interest.

In this chapter you will see how the correctly phrased question can turn destructive disagreement into constructive consensus.

Someone Poses a Take It or Leave It Ultimatum

You're starting to feel pressured into accepting a proposal you would rather not accept. You also sense that the other party is as frustrated with the negotiation as you are. Even though you're upset, you continue the discussion to get more issues on the table. Unfortunately, the other party makes a final offer and says, "Take it or leave it."

> If We Can Come Up with an Alternative, More Attractive to
> You than the One Just Proposed,
> Would You Still Want Me to Take It or Leave It?

With this question you raise the prospect that further discussion can lead to increased benefits for both of you. You're also telling him that the current offer may be less attractive than the one that has yet to be discussed.

The other party may find your question intriguing and respond with a door opener ("What do you mean?"). Your task then is to focus on mutual equity and to generate creative solutions to your common needs. Focus your energy and thoughts on *why* you want what you want, not *what* you want.

If he refuses to open the door and merely repeats his either-or proposition, do a quick cost-benefit analysis to determine whether the proposal fills your needs and allows you to walk away with dignity. If so, accept; if not, reject.

> Do You Want Me to Take It or Leave It *Now,*
> or May I Have Time to Think More About Taking It?

This question enables you to stall for time. You don't want to feel pressured to make a decision you might later regret. You also want to make sure that you and the other party have exhausted all options. You want to create the impression that any gains in bringing the negotiations to an early close are not as great as the costs of overlooking an option that is currently not on the table.

ARE YOU FEELING PRESSURED TO BRING THE DISCUSSION TO A CLOSE?

This alternative is designed to stall for time without labeling the motives of the other party. He may or may not be using the take it or leave it gambit as a pressuring tactic. You don't know. What you do know is that you're feeling pressure and you don't like it. Don't alienate the other party by attributing motives to his ultimatum. Find out what pressure he is under and help alleviate it if you can.

You're Pressed to Respond to an Unreasonable Deadline

"You've got until five tonight to make your decision." This statement sends shivers up your spine and causes a knot in your stomach. You need much more time to think about the options, and you hate being pressured.

WHY CAN'T WE NEGOTIATE THE DEADLINE?

His statement is an assertion, a statement of what he wants. Since you're in the process of negotiating, any statement of wants is subject to revision. Your question labels his deadline as negotiable.

If he gives you a reason for the stated deadline that seems rational and is acceptable to you, then work within it. If you don't accept the reason, tell him why.

If he refuses to give you a reason, tell him that his refusal creates unnecessary pressure in the negotiation. Add that this pressure will only serve to produce an outcome less satisfactory than would have been created without the pressure. Tell him that deadlines should be mutually agreeable unless there are external constraints.

IF YOU'RE UNDER PRESSURE TO MEET THIS DEADLINE, WHAT CAN I DO TO HELP REMOVE SOME OF THE PRESSURE?

Negotiators often represent the interest of others rather than themselves (for example, purchasing agents representing the manufacturing department or a recruiter representing the human resource department). In these situations, deadlines are imposed by others and simply communicated by the negotiator. Find out if this is the case. Tell the person that you'll be happy to ease the pressure on both of you by developing reasons why the deadline should be set back and by communicating those reasons directly to the parties who imposed the deadline.

If the other party set the deadline, ask him to consider alternative times. Get him to see how selecting an alternative time will bring about a more favorable outcome for both of you.

WHAT'S MAGICAL ABOUT FIVE TONIGHT?
WHY NOT EIGHT TOMORROW MORNING?

With this alternative question you're asking for a rationale. The qualifying adjective "magical" is a tongue in cheek suggestion that you see the deadline as arbitrary. But if not, you're willing to hear why.

The Other Party Plays "High Ball" (Unreasonably High Demands) or "Low Ball" (Unreasonably Low Offers)

You know that negotiations typically involve some form of game playing, but you honestly believe the other party has broken the rules. You've just been insulted; you've been made an offer far below what you think is reasonable and fair. You control your anger long enough to ask a question.

WHAT'S YOUR REASONING BEHIND THIS OFFER?

The natural and expected response to a ridiculously high demand or a ridiculously low offer is to get angry and accuse the other party of deceit and dishonesty. With this question you give the party the benefit of the doubt and move from the what to the why.

If you can't elicit a reason other than "Because that's what I'm offering," follow with a genuine counteroffer and the reasons behind it. Let him know that there are valid and justifiable reasons why you believe your counteroffer is reasonable. Don't label the initial offer as insulting. Rather, stress the fairness of your offer, based on the reasons you provide.

If he is able to provide support for this position, listen very carefully. When he's finished talking, respond to each of his reasons in turn. Question the assumptions and premises of his reasons. Where you find fault, indicate why.

WHAT DO YOU THINK I SEE AS A FAIR OFFER?

With this question, you're getting the other party to engage in empathy and to focus on mutually equitable solutions. High ball/low ball, whether motivated by chicanery or not, puts pressure on you and unless challenged produces a solution that will ultimately return to haunt you both.

If the other party can't engage in empathy or seems to stick with his initial offer, tell him why it's in his interest to have you walk away a winner, too. If he looks dumbfounded at your suggestion, tell him why he wins when you win. Tell him:

- You'll walk away thinking better of him.
- You'll look forward to helping him out in the future.
- You'll realize that he also had your interests at heart and because of that you will look out for his interests in the future.
- Others who may hear about this equitable outcome will think more of him and thereby make relationships with him more beneficial in the future.

WHAT CRITERIA DO YOU THINK THE FINAL RESOLUTION SHOULD MEET?

This question forces the other party to move from *what* he wants to *why* he wants it. It's possible that when you hear his reasons you may no longer see his position as a high ball or low ball. In any event, this alternative question gives you another opportunity to focus on mutual equity. Stress that the lack of mutual equity hurts both of you in the long run.

THE PERFECT COMEBACK

"Darn! I wish I had thought of that line beforehand." Sound familiar? Virtually everyone has said it after missing their golden opportunity for a comeback line. This chapter has the perfect comeback lines—or more correctly—comeback questions already made. The trick is to know when to use them. You will have to recognize when the right situation crops up.

But to be effective, it must appear spontaneous. Therefore, you will need to read the text closely, making mental notes along the way. You may want to even write down the questions somewhere, so you'll know what to say when. Again, the trick is making it look as effortless and spontaneous as possible. If it looks rehearsed or forced, it will not have the same impact on the other side.

You Reach an Impasse

You've been at it for almost six straight hours. Your team is exhausted, their team is exhausted. You've haggled over the major issues and the minor issues. But you're still at odds regarding the final solution, and neither side appears ready to budge. Just as frustration is about to turn into despair you get an idea.

WHAT ELSE CAN EITHER OF US BRING TO THE TABLE
TO CLOSE THE GAP BETWEEN OUR POSITIONS?

Again, you are looking for strategies to create win-win outcomes. Even though you may both believe you're deadlocked, always view deadlocks as only temporary, never permanent. This question may bring the one bargaining chip to the table that you have both overlooked and that could break the deadlock.

Welcome anything the other party brings. Ask the other party for the same receptivity to your suggestions.

If you're willing to concede one point, do so. Don't let your pride and ego get the best of you. Right now all you have is impasse and frustration. If you make a concession or split the difference, you may have a win-win outcome.

WHAT CONCESSION DO YOU NEED TO CLOSE THE DEAL RIGHT NOW?

An impasse may be nothing more than a natural state of exhaustion and frustration. When this occurs you need a zinger, a question that smashes through the mental blocks. This question is designed to end the stalemate and get the mental juices flowing once again.

It's quite possible that a final concession will close the negotiation and remove the frustration for both of you. If you can grant one that will cost you less than the value of the final agreement, you'll be glad you did.

IF IT WERE NOW SIX WEEKS INTO THE FUTURE AND
WE WERE LOOKING BACK AT THIS NEGOTIATION,
WHAT MIGHT WE WISH WE HAD BROUGHT TO THE TABLE?

With this question you're forcing a change in perspective. You're saying let's look at it in retrospect, as if it were completed and we're now in the future. Let's take off your mental blinders and look at our problems in a new and fresh way. If you're looking for creative problem solving, set the example yourself. Take off your perceptual blinders and start generating as many fresh alternatives as you can.

Anything that will change perspective will serve as the catalyst. Sometimes simply calling for a break will work. If you opt for this strategy, your break should last longer than one hour but less than twenty-four hours.

The Other Party Is Torn Between Accepting or Rejecting Your Proposal

You've offered everything you can possibly offer. You sense that the other party is receptive to your proposal but is still reluctant to make a final decision. You're worried that she may decide to seek a better offer elsewhere. Rather than pressure her with a take it or leave it ultimatum, you take a different approach.

WHAT'S YOUR BEST ALTERNATIVE TO ACCEPTING THIS PROPOSAL NOW?

This question is designed to crystallize the pivotal choices: accepting what is currently on the table, hoping to get a better offer from someone else, or maintaining the status quo.

After you've posed the question, listen intently to the answer. Help the person articulate the consequences of not accepting your proposal. If she has trouble answering your question use follow-up probes: What other current offers do you have? Are they better than mine? If you accept the best offer, will you come out better than you would if you accepted mine?

The answer may create either of two scenarios. The first is an opportunity to make a final offer equal to or better than the alternative offer currently considered, and the second is to move the person off dead center, thereby bringing closure to the negotiation, even if that decision is to reject your offer. Once you realize that a decision based on remorse will ultimately prove unwise, you can still define a rejection of your offer as winning.

IF YOU REJECT MY OFFER, WHAT WILL TAKE ITS PLACE THAT'S ANY BETTER THAN WHAT YOU ARE ASSURED OF RECEIVING FROM ME?

This person is torn because of indecision. This question is designed to provide a nudge.

Get her to do a quick cost-benefit analysis. She knows exactly what you're presenting. What is available from another party who might be competing with you in the negotiation? Comparing the two offers might highlight the attractiveness of your offer. If not, find ways of outshining the competing offer or find selling points in your current offer that she may have overlooked.

If there is no other offer, the decision is between the status quo and what you propose. Sometimes the security of knowing what you have is strong enough to compensate for the insecurity of not knowing the future even if the future promises increased benefits. That's why many people reject attractive job offers or fail to switch to new vendors: They are simply comfortable and secure with the old. Your questions should force the other party to challenge the security of the status quo and to recognize the benefits of your offer.

How Can You Be Sure That You Will Get a Better Deal Elsewhere?

Sometimes the other party might be playing you against another bidder. If this is the case, probe to determine if the other bidder really will deliver what is promised. This question also provides you an opportunity to match an offer if you believe it's in your best interest to do so.

You're Asked if Your Offer Is the Same as That Quoted to Others

You're trying to recruit a college graduate to fill a vacancy in your department. At the conclusion of two days of on-site interviews you make him an offer. He thinks about it for a few minutes. After what you feel is a deafening silence he asks, "Has any applicant for this job been offered more money?" You respond to his question with your own.

What Do You See as a Fair Offer, and Do You Think We're Making One to You?

The purpose of the question is to get the other party to focus on the merits of this offer independent of negotiations into which you may have entered with other parties. If the person says that it's not a fair offer, find out what he would need to make it so and negotiate from there. If he says it is fair, he then must simply make his final decision.

If he says that he can only judge what's fair once he knows what others have received, tell him that individual offers are made on the basis of individual applicants. If someone has received more or less, it's because you saw that person as more or less qualified. But the real issue is whether or not he believes your offer is fair based on what he needs and what he thinks he's worth, not what someone else is receiving.

Stress that it's in both of your interests to treat him fairly, regardless of what anyone else gets. Make it clear that you don't want to bring anyone on board who will ultimately be unhappy with his or her salary.

Do You Think I Believe It's in My Long-term Best Interest to Treat You Unfairly Now?

There is a natural tendency for negotiators to question the fairness of your offer relative to offers they think others may have received. This questioning will increase as the other party's paranoia or distrust of you increases.

With this question you minimize the paranoia and distrust. Your strategy is to get the other party to recognize that your intent is not to win at all costs but to create a win-win solution. You're emphasizing that you have not won if the other party feels as if he or she has lost. This question is a powerful cue to discuss your long-term relationship. Often this discussion is the push needed to decide.

Do You Believe That People Can Be Treated Differently and Still Be Treated Fairly?

Get the other party to accept the reality that no two people are exactly alike, no two situations are exactly alike, and hence no two negotiations will be exactly alike. Different people can be treated differently and still be treated equally. Expand upon this important point.

Stress the criteria you are using to make your offer. Get him to focus on the criteria, not the offer itself. If he thinks the criteria are unfair, ask how he would make the decision. Remember, you want to focus on why he wants what he wants. Reasons are more supporting of win-win than demands.

You're Feeling Pressured, Controlled, or Manipulated

You feel like you just walked onto a used-car lot. What started out as a relaxed negotiation between two parties interested in securing a mutually agreeable solution has turned into a situation where you're feeling pressured and manipulated, and you don't like the feeling.

Isn't It in Our Mutual Interest for Both of Us to Walk Away from This Negotiation Feeling Satisfied?

This is a pointed question that solicits a specific answer. And the answer you're likely to get is yes.

Follow that answer with a statement indicating that you feel extremely frustrated and anxious and don't see how you can walk away from the negotiation with the goal the other party has already agreed to, that, mutual satisfaction.

Don't ascribe motive or intent. Simply describe what the other party is doing—or, better yet, what is happening—and how that makes you feel.

How Would You Feel if the Roles Were Reversed and You Had to Respond to the Pressures I'm Currently Experiencing?

This question focuses on the pressure you're experiencing without attributing motive or intent. You're not exactly sure why the other party is pressuring you, but you are willing to give her the benefit of the doubt. Be certain to emphasize the word "feel" and not the word "you" in either of its two locations in the sentence.

One of the most powerful techniques for diffusing the pressure is empathy. Get the other party to look at the situation through your eyes. This technique is sometimes enough to encourage her to remove any pressure she may have exerted on the negotiations.

Tell her in specific terms what you mean by pressure. Say what you're feeling and experiencing. Describe *what* she's doing to make you feel this way, but do *not* ascribe intent to her behavior.

Are You Experiencing Outside Pressures to Conclude These Negotiations?

Put yourself in her shoes. By asking if there are outside pressures you're acknowledging the difficulties she may be facing. This thoughtfulness may make her more thoughtful of you. If you sense that there might be pressure she is reluctant to disclose, follow with probing questions.

A Peer Is Fighting Turf Battles with You or Is Trying to Get a Bigger Piece of the Pie at Your Expense

It's been a tough year and your boss has asked all department heads to pare their budgets as much as possible. Because of this you're knocking heads with the manager of another department. When the two of you sat down to negotiate your budgets, you weren't prepared for outright war. This person won't budge an inch and is making you fight for everything. You look him straight in the eye.

How Do You See Our Department Helping Your Department to Achieve Its Goals?

The surprise element embedded in this question may succeed in side-tracking an empire builder. Its ultimate purpose is to move him from viewing the negotiation as win-lose to win-win. You want him to realize that helping your department is ultimately in his best interest. And if you're both working for the same employer, it is.

If the other person is hedging and can't seem to think of how you help him, take out a sheet of paper and list all the ways your department helps his department. Get him to focus on the bridges that exist between the two departments, not on the moats.

You might feel like you're pulling teeth to get him to acknowledge the bridges and interdependence, but pull anyway. Once you've established that your department helps his department and vice versa, you're in a better position to develop a mutually equitable budget.

IF OUR DEPARTMENT DIDN'T PROVIDE THE SERVICES WE DO, WHERE WOULD YOU GET THEM AND HOW MUCH DO YOU THINK THEY'D COST?

The first question is designed to reinforce the value of your department. One reality of organizational and family life is that we tend to take one another for granted. We usually don't realize how much a person or thing means to us until we no longer have it or until we have to replace it. Encourage your colleague to think about how much he would have to pay for your department's services if he had to purchase them on the open market.

It's also in your best interest to consider the value of your colleague's department. If you expect him to consider your value, you should engage in the same empathy. In so doing, you may realize that his share of the corporate pie should be increased and that you both win when it is.

HOW DO YOU WANT OUR NEGOTIATIONS TODAY TO SET THE STAGE FOR NEGOTIATIONS A YEAR FROM NOW?

Here you're moving the focus from the present to the future. Colleagues who try to secure organizational resources at your expense often fail to consider that the acrimony and bitterness created today will show up in future negotiations.

Summary Points

- Respond to "Take-It-or-Leave-It" tactics by asking if there are any alternative offers that could be more attractive on your part.
- Respond to unilaterally set deadlines by asking "Why can't we negotiate the deadline?"
- Don't pressure people into a take-it-or-leave-it stance. Ask "What's your best alternative to accepting this proposal right now?"

- If you're feeling needlessly pressured or manipulated, ask them to see what it's like in your shoes: "How would you feel if the role were reversed and you had to respond to the pressures I'm currently experiencing?"
- When fighting an internal turf battle, you can clip the wings of an empire builder in another department by moving the negotiations away from a zero-sum game: How do you see our department helping your department achieve its goals?"

CHAPTER 18

How to Do It Like a Pro: Negotiating Secrets

Salesmen have opening lines that knock 'em dead. Managers have methods they use to fire up the troops. Call them tricks of the trade. Every profession has them. As a businessperson, you will need to know how to negotiate successfully. And negotiating has its own set of tricks too. If you've never done it before, or if you have, and you're still not confident, then this chapter is for you.

Burton Kaplan's *Everything You Need to Know to Talk Your Way to Success,* excerpted below, details twenty-two concrete steps you can follow, anytime, anywhere, to become a successful negotiator in virtually any situation. All negotiations, Kaplan says, start from the same premise: What do I want? What does the other side want? Where is there common ground? Although simply stated, this is the basis from which almost all negotiations, big and small, begin.

Following the twenty-two secrets outlined in this chapter will help prepare you for virtually any negotiation and give you a critical guidepost from beginning to end. Internalize them so you'll have a leg-up the next time you sit down to negotiate.

Negotiating: Twenty-Two Secrets of Professional Negotiators That Inform, Inspire, and Persuade Others

Every human contact involves a negotiation—for time, for space, for money, for something! That's because it is only human to always want something from others—anything from a raise in pay from your boss to a better reputation among your neighbors.

Love, sex, marriage, relationships, community life, buying and selling, business, power—no matter what the focus happens to be, our job is the same: To somehow convince others it is in their interest to allow us to have what we wish for and want from them:

- If you are single, it might be a first-date with someone special.
- If you are in the market for a car or a place to live, it might be the price you pay or the terms.
- If you are a party to divorce, it might be fair visitation rights.
- If you are in sales, it might be the business of your customers.
- If you are in management, it might be keeping your work group focused on your most immediate concerns.
- If you are in the clergy, it might be more parishioners.

Let me illustrate that last point since it sounds pretty extreme to think that negotiations are so much a part of our daily doings they figure even in our spiritual lives.

Have you ever watched a top-notch TV preacher work the audience?

To tell you the truth, I don't approve of their pleas for funds, but I have to admit they know a thing or two about how to manage successful negotiations.

Late one night, I got caught up in one ministry's program. A man and a woman were team preaching. Back and forth they took the sermon. First, him to her, quoting Gospel. Then, her to him, retelling parables.

As they developed long and vivid descriptions of the tortures of the unredeemed, I saw agony grow on the faces in the audience. It was suffering I imagined to come out of feeling like your legs straddle a spreading chasm: your back foot on the side marked yesterday, the front one on tomorrow.

The more the preachers talked, the more resolve I saw on the faces of those who seemed inclined to come forward.

In the end, hundreds of people, perhaps a thousand, rose in the audience and made their way to the stage!

The Misunderstood Majority: Why Seven Out of Every Eight People Cannot Negotiate

Unlike the TVangelists who, broadcast after broadcast, successfully negotiate for souls, most folks don't always get what they want out of their business and personal negotiations. Obviously, the preachers know something about negotiating it might do the rest of us some good to learn.

The preachers know that failures of negotiation come not out of what we might want (after all, what could be more hopeless than a desire to save the unredeemable?) but about what we *do* about what we want. And what we do most of all is talk. Therein lies the problem. Let me explain.

According to a reliable national poll of Americans, roughly eighty percent of us think we belong in the top ten percent of how well we get along with others. Which means, of course, that seven out of every eight people who think they negotiate well with others, simply don't.

Are you among these? Well, if people stop listening before you stop talking, count yourself one of the misunderstood majority.

HOW TO MAKE YOUR DREAMS COME TRUE

In this chapter, I want to show you the secrets of professional negotiators that turn indifference into attention, conflict into cooperation, rejection into acceptance, distance into warmth, dreams into reality.

Here you will find the proven methods that empower you to negotiate for anything and get it, and a step-by-step process to make it part of your life.

Using practical methods and surefire techniques, you will express yourself freely and fully, get results, and strengthen relationships—and at the same time—no matter what the issues, no matter what the circumstances, business, personal, or otherwise.

Eight Ways Negotiation Makes Everyone a Winner

Whatever your role in life, applying the skills of negotiating is winning proposition all around. At the same time successful negotiations give you what you want, they

- Encourage the people who work for you to perform in the face of overwhelming odds.
- Inspire them to become more than they are.
- Correct them when they are in error.
- Stimulate them when action is called for.
- Give people in your personal life ideas they can build on.
- Direct them when they are confused.
- Enrich their lives.
- Help them sort out problems and find solutions.

With daily practice, the secrets of professional negotiators I am about to give you are certain to become part of your second nature in no time at all.

Whether you are a minister, marketer, or mason, a butcher, baker, or candlestick maker, a health worker, or homemaker, in commerce, private, or public life, they cannot fail to improve your business and personal relationships with people at every level. And when they do,

THESE TWO SPECTACULAR BENEFITS ARE YOURS FOR A LIFETIME

For perhaps the first time in life you will experience rock-solid self-confidence and an automatic can-do response to the business challenges you face daily. Whether you are detached or emotionally involved, dealing with your CEO or your co-workers, prepared or ad lib, you make an on-the-spot difference. This is certain to give your career the growing influence and visibility higher-management recognizes.

"I got an e-mail note from the head honcho of the division the other day," reports Freddie Croft, 32, who works in pharmaceutical research in Triangle Park, North Carolina. "She asked me to tell her how we've been able to keep department payroll in line without losing key players. I said it took a whole lot of trust on everybody's part but we kept at it because we knew what we wanted, we knew what they wanted, and within our little group we worked out a fair shake all around."

Freddie's experience tells me plenty. Mainly, it says that negotiating to find common ground is a winning situation all around: Your career gets the attention it needs and deserves.

And, because you make others feel like they belong in your thinking, they give you the willing support and loyal cooperation that earns job security.

The agreements you foster in your social, personal, and private life have the power to last, and grow even stronger over time because you work to ensure that everybody's needs, including your own, are taken care of.

"I've been married 25 years and my colleagues kid around that if I had killed him the first time I felt like it, I'd be a free woman by now—the most I would have gotten would have been 10-to-15 years," reports Miami trial lawyer Isabel Bacardi, 54. "We were both adults when we married, we knew what we were up against, and give or take, we've made it last."

Here's the moral of Isabel's story: Each of us holds a permanent seat at the negotiating table we call life. The rules are simple. Perform skillfully and you get what you want, don't and you get dumped on.

Are You Able to Negotiate Win-Win Outcomes?

To give you a personal portrait of your negotiating strengths and weaknesses, I've prepared several questions.

There are no right and wrong answers, nor is there any time limit.

After you read each question, simply choose the response that you feel is most appropriate most of the time.

1. Can you express in a sentence or two what you want out of this chapter?
   - ❏ Yes
   - ❏ No

2. When you negotiate, do you ask others what they want?
   - ❏ Yes
   - ❏ No

3. Some people discover what they want by putting their own interests first. Do you?
   - ❏ Yes
   - ❏ No

4. When you are dealing with what you want, are you one of those specificity nuts—people who dot all the "i's" and cross all the "t's"?
   - ❏ Yes
   - ❏ No

5. When you want to find out what others may think of as confidential information, do you begin with a general question? For instance, when you want to learn how much they make, do you begin, "Your field sounds like a rewarding one. Can you tell me something about it?"
   - ❏ Yes
   - ❏ No

6. If a person tells you what he or she wants, do you think it is good idea to tell it right back to them?
   - ❏ Yes
   - ❏ No

7. Do you think a good understanding of where the other fellow is coming from is as important as a good understanding of what he wants?

❏ Yes

❏ No

8. Can you name the three powerful body signals that tell you a meeting of the minds is imminent?

❏ Yes

❏ No

9. In the heat of negotiations, when tempers are up, do you think it is a good idea to find something to admire about the other person's point of view?

❏ Yes

❏ No

10. When negotiations are showing signs of breaking down, do you think it is better to hang in than to reschedule?

❏ Yes

❏ No

Now that you have completed the exercise, simply add up the number of "yes" answers.

Most people will score between four and seven "yes" answers.

Each question you answered with a "no" indicates an area of opportunity. As you read ahead, you will find practical, workable techniques to develop your skills in these areas.

How to Stop an Argument Dead in Its Tracks

In a moment, I am going to give you 22 secrets of professional negotiators. But first, to be certain we're on the same wavelength, let's agree that a negotiation is not an argument dressed in polite clothes.

An argument, you see, has two sides—yours and the other guy's—and it always ends winner take all.

A negotiation, meanwhile, has three—yours, theirs, and common ground— and the only limit on the number of winners is the number of participants.

To change an argument into a negotiation instantly, all you've got to change is the limits you place on winning. Simply by allowing more than one person to win, you cannot fail to come out with more than you had going in.

"They told us there had to be a temporary pay cut, so me and the wife tried to figure out what we needed rock-bottom to get by for a few months," reports

Todd Mahlenberk, 36, a Torrington, Connecticut foundry manager. "Their offer wasn't enough. My first inclination was to walk, but I held on. I told them I wanted to stay. I knew jobs were scarce, but I had to take care of my family. I had to have more than they were offering. They said they wanted to keep me but money was tight. They offered to put me on nights until things turned around. That's keeping my check almost the same as regular. Under the circumstances, with three daughters in parochial school and tuition bills coming in monthly, well, I don't think I gave more than I got."

Todd walked into the situation with a mental demand—my way or the highway!

As the conversation developed, an alternative appeared. It was far from perfect . . . but just as far from awful. It was a trade off, middle ground, and it served Todd's family interests. It may not have given him all that he wanted but it delivered most of what he needed.

When the conversation was over both he and his boss could honestly say that they were better off agreeing than not.

The Secret Weapon Every Successful Negotiator Must Possess

For roughly 25 years, I've researched the topic of negotiations—hundreds of books and lectures by political, business, and labor leaders; thousands of articles by professors, lawyers, and other experts in the field; even personal interviews with hands-on practitioners.

I was looking for the secret every negotiator must possess to succeed. I was out to find the universal principle—that one that worked everywhere and all the time—the one that consistently brings about meetings of minds.

And what I found was this. Every negotiation that ends in success begins with three questions. Negotiations in which at least one side raises and answers these three questions invariably produce the best possible compromises. Absent these, there is bound to be dissatisfaction between the parties.

It is these three questions that I want you to have straight away since these are the basis for the techniques I will be giving you as we move forward through this chapter.

Three Questions Guaranteed to Get You What You Want Every Time

The following questions are based first on knowing your needs, second on understanding theirs, and third on identifying the opportunity in between.

- What do I want?
- What does the other side want?
- Where is the common ground between us?

How to Determine What You Want

Secret 1: Put Your Own Interests First. "I used to get the short end of the stick coming to agreement with others because, being a trained sales person, the first thing they teach you is to look at the world through the customer's eyes," reports Cassandra Herman, 30, a Tulsa manufacturers' representative. "I got much better negotiating results, and so did they, when I started putting my own interests first."

By putting her interests first, it sounds like Cassandra is being selfish, doesn't it? Well, she's not. She's not basing her actions solely on what she wants, she's just following the advice of history—know thyself.

By determining in advance what she really wants out of the negotiation—not what she hopes or wishes or dreams about but, in concrete terms, what she is prepared to agree to—she establishes a solid foundation for further discussion.

This gives Cassandra several advantages: First, there's the comfort factor. Knowing exactly what she wants immediately scotches the possibility of confusion and self-doubt. She knows in advance what she will agree to and what she will not. This makes her feel more comfortable and relaxed, less likely to feel threatened and combative—even if the face of strong opposition.

Second, there's the control factor. She knows that by establishing her bottom line before negotiations begin rather than after, she can't be debated, detoured, or derailed by side issues. An amount of money, pledge of respect, a clause in a contract, a job offer—whatever she is after, she occupies a more powerful position by defining it than by not.

And third, there's the no-hassle factor. By keeping the focus on issues instead of the buildup of emotions that raises barriers to agreement, she doesn't get trapped in the dead end of who is right, or why me, or how do I feel about this? Instead, she asks the one question that empowers her to negotiate effectively—What do I want?

Secret 2: To Decide What You Want, Examine Your Options. If you have trouble deciding what you want in a particular situation, it is probably because you have too many general ideas competing for attention and not enough specific ones upon which to focus.

The way to beat it is this: Simply write down some possibilities of what you want.

Make them as specific as you can—not "earn more money" but rather, "make a six-figure income before I am 45."

Alongside each of these, note an alternative. List it even if the alternative seems outrageous and off the mark—"Earn $XX,000 next year."

Obviously, some of what you write down will not represent things you can act on, but they nevertheless serve a purpose.

What listing these options does for you is this: It jumpstarts your thinking, gets your mind working, prompts other approaches and ways of looking at things.

Eventually, you will run out of options and alternatives, and your list will narrow down to just a few specific points. These, you can be sure, are things of greatest importance to you under the circumstances.

All that remains is for you to decide what of these deserve priority. With sufficient practice, this process of noting possibilities and alternatives will become a mental rather than a written technique, an automatic part of your personality.

Unlike most of the options we can exercise, the ones associated with what we want don't cost anything to access . . . and plenty if you fail to.

Secret 3: Be Specific About Your Wants. "Once upon a time when the world was a little younger, I made disagreement rougher than it had to be, a battle of egos," reports Jeeter Byrd, seventy, a retired Washington, D.C. government worker. "Now I tell myself, well, this or that is exactly what I want. It looks like this, it weighs probably about this much, it's painted that color—you get my drift? The more I focus on the details of what I want, the less this becomes an ego issue for me. The other person might want something else, I know that. And that's okay too. That still doesn't give us the battle of the egos, it just gives us different points of view looking to somehow get together."

By focusing on specific details Jeeter takes the emotional conflict out of reaching agreement with other people.

When it comes to determining what you want, being specific saves time and eliminates the possibility of misunderstanding. Even if you are the only person dotting the "i's" and crossing the "t's," it's effects are sure to be felt.

The more specific you are about your wants, the less room you leave for emotional tensions to affect coming to terms.

Secret 4: Accept the Strengths and Weaknesses That Make You You. Deciding what you want in a negotiating situation is a whole lot less uncertain when you can speak from the honest conviction of your beliefs, values, and commitments.

There's just one source of these—yourself. Who you are, your strengths and your weaknesses. What you stand for. What's really important.

"It's a day-to-day thing, keeping in touch with myself," reports Atlanta bookseller Leigh Edin, 31. "Five years ago the most important thing in my life was to be a mother. Today, I still want to be a mother but the other biggest thing in my life right now is getting my own business up and running. Things don't change but the emphasis you put on them does. You've got to stay in touch with those changes or, the first thing you know, you are living in yesterday instead of today."

When I talk about knowing what you want, I mean it in the sense Leigh alludes to—knowing what you want *now,* not yesterday and not tomorrow but at this very moment.

Here are a couple of easy ways to start the process. Get out a piece of paper and rule it into three columns. Headline the first column "What," the second column, "Who," and the third column, "Targets."

In the first column, list the 10 most important things in your life.

Under the second headline, note down the ten most important people in your life. On the right, list your ten most important goals in life. When you've completed this exercise, I'd like to give you just one more.

Please rule a second sheet of paper into two columns. Label the left one "+" and the right one "−." Under the plus sign, list your five best personal strengths. Under the minus, list your five greatest weaknesses.

Once you have completed these exercises, you'll have a fair picture of who you are—your values, commitments, strengths, weaknesses, goals.

The rest is a piece of cake: next time you find it hard to decide what you want, think about the choices in terms of your profile—the real you.

Abracadabra!

You'll be amazed at how easily you come to a fitting conclusion about what you want.

Remember, the fastest and best way to figure out what you truly want is to figure out who you truly are.

How to Determine What Other People Want

Once you know what you want, the next thing to learn is what the others hope to get out of the negotiation.

Sometimes their expectations are unreasonable. And sometimes, people don't themselves honestly know what they want. Either way, you've got to get their position out on the table so you can deal with it. The best way, of course, is to ask.

"Most people are so flabbergasted when I ask them what they want, it takes them a minute or so to catch on that I really do want to know," reports

Chattanooga credit agency worker Lisle Krigel, 30. "A family owes a nursing home some money, says they are going to file a counter-claim for wrongful death if we go for a judgment against them. I ask them what they want. They're speechless. Then I say I can't promise to make it all happen but if I know their thinking, well, who knows? Maybe some of it can be worked out."

Lisle's message is as old as the Bible: It is a lesson very professional negotiator knows and never forgets. "Ask and ye shall receive."

Secret 5: Make the First Questions Broad. The broader your first couple of questions, the more information you are likely to get.

Sure, at first you'll get back answers that are as general as your questions . . . but that's okay: you can get to specifics as the conversation develops.

"Job training candidates come to me looking for helping getting into a new field," reports private education counselor Don Attwod, 36, who consults in the Silicon Valley. "The first thing I ask is what they're looking for out of life, where they see themselves 10 years from now. As we talk, I get a better idea of who they are and the way they see things. That gives me leads to more specific questions."

- What would you like out of this conversation? . . .
- Please tell me what you have in mind? . . .
- Can you tell me more about X? . . .
- How do you feel about X? . . .

There's no limit to the general questions you can invent to encourage people to start talking about what they want.

Secret 6: At First, Open-Ended Questions Are Best. In the early stages of negotiation, when you are exploring what others want, try to avoid queries that choke-off expanded talk, questions that can be answered either yes, no, or with a fact.

Instead, begin with open-ended questions, ones that require the other person to explain and talk more than a minimum. Encouraging them to go past what is absolutely necessary, combined with careful listening, gives you a better handle on the things that are important to them.

"I thought the first few minutes of our planning meeting was a disaster—interruptions, raised voices, ugh!," reports sanitary engineer, Oliver Pellington, 36, out of Charlottesville, Virginia. "The first thing I wanted to say was, hey, look, we're not getting anywhere, do you want to call this off? I thought it would be better to put a little nicer spin on things so I said seeing as how we couldn't get off the dime, what direction do you think we ought to take on this? That got us on a better track."

From the sound of things, I'd say that if Oliver followed his first impulse, asked them if they wanted to quit, there'd be as many yes and no answers. That would leave him in the dark about their wants, and leave them still fighting.

Instead, his open-ended question covered the same ground and it invited them to talk about how they saw things, what they wanted to do.

Secret 7: Consent to Advice.   Often, the best time to seek advice is when you need it least, and by this I mean at any point in the negotiations after you have determined what you want.

Asking for advice can be a subtle way of asking people to tell you what they want most. Rarely will you run into an individual whose advice is truly impartial. Nine times out of ten it's a reflection of what they'd like for themselves, what they want.

Asking them to share it with you shows a lot of respect. Whether you take it or leave it is another question.

"I bought these vitamins, and the gelatin gave me a rash. I brought them back to the health food store. The lady there started yelling—"No cash refund!," reports Shari Zein, 19, a New Hampshire college student. "All I wanted was a credit for the pills that were left. I asked her advice, how she'd like to handle it. She was so relieved I wasn't going to make a fuss I ended up with a free package of the hypo-allergenic kind."

There is ample evidence to think that free advice is worth precisely its cost. However, what is true of life is not quite as true of the hide-and-seek of negotiations. Here, even the worst counsel can be a valuable insight.

Secret 8: Playback Your Understanding of the Other Person's Desires.   It is never enough merely to listen to someone. You must listen in ways that tell them you are listening. One of these ways is playback. The idea is simple. They say something. You listen. Then playback—using your own words, tell them your understanding of what they want.

It goes like this.

He says, "I want to retire at age 55."

She says, "Let's see if I understand what you are saying. You'd like us to have your finances in such good shape by the time you reach 55 you never have to work again, right?"

He says, "Not quite. I'd like to leave the field I am in and start a little bed-and-breakfast up near Tahoe."

Playback confirms and clarifies your understanding at the same time it tells them they are being heard.

The process encourages them to share and develop their ideas. This works in your favor because the more you know, the easier it will be to establish a meeting of the minds.

Secret 9: When All Else Fails, Be Direct.   Let's face it: there are people who will do everything *but* name what they want.

"Couple times a day single women come up to the pharmacy counter and sort of don't want to talk about what they need," reports Pierre, North Dakota dispensary worker Karl Hess, 26. "I can't be a mind reader here and shilly-shally around—there are other customers. Would you like to speak with a woman pharmacist?, I ask."

When people are embarrassed to ask for what they want, or fearful they will be rejected, don't hesitate to use direct questions. These are your only hope of determining their stake in the outcome.

When all else fails, say as kindly as you can, words to the effect of:

"I've told you what I need. I'd like to work things out. But I can't if I don't know what you want. Please tell me."

Secret 10: Assume Nothing.   Words mean different things to different sorts of people . . . even to the same sorts of people at different moments . . . and even to the same sorts of people in different places.

"It was quite a surprise to learn that my eight means somebody else's eighty-thirty," reports Samantha Couerdelene, 24, who works in the banking business in New Orleans. "I invited people for drinks at seven-thirty and dinner at eight, but the couple from Buenos Aires didn't arrive until half past. They were surprised we had begun without them. I took the lateness as an insult. A friend told me later that, in Argentina, half an hour late is expected."

The trouble arises when we assume that everybody understands what we say in the way we want to be understood.

English comedian Benny Hill used to write **ASS - U - ME,** on the chalk board.

"When you assume," he'd say, "you make an *ass* out of *you* and *me*.

Don't assume what they mean is what you might mean if you spoke their words. Forget your assumptions. Check it out. Play it back.

"Do you mean that what you want is X?"

Secret 11: Keep Hopes and Fears Out of Listening.   When you are trying to find out what people want, it's important to make direct listening contact with what they are saying—not what you want them to say or are afraid they will say.

That means you must not filter their words through your hopes, fears, and anxieties.

Three Ways to Listen Better

- *It is counterproductive to listen for words that tweak your worst fears.* What you fear the most from the other person is very unlikely to happen.

- *Stop looking for hints that suggest you are less powerful than the other person.* You have more power than you are willing to allow. However, to experience its fullness, you must exercise it.

- *You mustn't lock-on phrases that lead you to hope everybody wants the same thing.* They never do.

Secret 12: Be a Stranger to Your Friends.   Because we tend to be too wary of strangers, we sometimes come across as skeptical. That gets in the way of coming to agreement.

LISTENING: AN ART

One of the biggest problems in many negotiations is the inability of one side, or both sides, to listen—*really listen*—to what the other party is saying. Much like one's personal life, the inability to listen carefully can lead to disastrous results.

You should always try to hear someone out completely. Interrupting is a surefire way to show you're more concerned about getting a word in edgewise than in hearing them out. Be sure to listen to the other person in total; focus on context. Don't lose the forest for want of a tree. See the big picture.

Also, try some techniques that help draw out the other person. There's no need to respond to everything they say. Sometimes the best technique is to answer the other person contemplatively by saying "Umm" and nodding your head, or saying "I see . . ." but not committing yourself to a definitive response one way or the other. Psychologists use this response as a trick to draw out more information from the other person. By paying more attention to what the other side is saying, and giving them the opportunity to provide more information, you are showing you value what the other side is saying and are gathering precious data that can help you craft your strategy.

On the other hand, we are often oh-so-casual about accepting what friends say; we usually don't bother to check it out. That gets in the way of a share-and-share-alike outcome.

"I sort of took it for granted my department head knew what I wanted. Jeez, we knew each other a long time, we even play poker a couple of nights a month. He kept telling me I'd get what I want at my annual review," reports Duane Leary, 27, who works in manufacturing in Winnetka, Illinois. "What I wanted was line responsibility. What I got was to stay in the same old staff job with a fairly nice raise. I know it sounds crabby to poo-poo a salary bump like that but, well, I thought he understood."

Here's a trade secret of professional negotiators that cannot fail to payoff:

Next time you find yourself trying to determine what people want—for themselves or for you!—treat friends like strangers and strangers like friends.

Secret 13: Empathize, Empathize, Empathize! Got a coin handy? A quarter? Better yet, a silver dollar? I want you to close one eye. Then, hold the coin very close to the open one. What do you see? The coin, of course, Now open both eyes . and hold the coin out at arm's length.

Tell me what you see.

Sure, you are still looking at the coin but now your view also includes your hand, the wall and floor in the distance, and so on.

My point is this: What you see depends on the breadth of your perspective. The same thing holds for any situation in which you are trying to discover what other people want.

Persist in seeing things from your own narrow point of view and you'll never get a complete picture of how your desires affect the other parties, cause them to do and say the things they do.

On the other hand, take a look at your ideas from their perspective, and you open a direct route to the part of them that understands and can connect with your thinking.

"We've had a very good little hair-care business with a special line for African Americans. When the time came to get out, I was surprised and disappointed, too. My son-in-law, Anfernee, who had worked with me for 12 years, didn't want any part of it. Said he did it for the family's sake but never liked it," reports Chicago entrepreneur Mason Wattley, 63. "If I'd've bothered to go over things from his point of view, I might've made changes along the way, gradual, and kept the company in the family—for my grandchildren."

Mason's family interests are admirable in any circumstance but insofar as his son-in-law, they weren't sufficiently compelling to keep him in the business.

The business didn't excite him in the way he wanted to be excited, didn't offer him a way to get what he really wanted out of life.

Seeing people as they see themselves, viewing life from their vantage point, forces you to align your thoughts in terms of their views.

There's a word for the ability to see things their way without necessarily agreeing with them. The word is empathy.

How to Develop Empathy

To be empathetic is to be aware of what makes the other fellow the other fellow.

It's not difficult to do.

Just ask yourself some questions, among them:

What drives their engine?

- Are they more concerned with show than with substance? Do they look up to anybody special?
- Do they enjoy life or do they seem to be having a hard time?
- What do they like and what do they hate?

How does what they are affect what I want?

- Will they see potential pressure points in your thinking, and what can you do to work around them?

By mentally raising these questions, you heighten the empathy in each of your encounters. This automatically aligns your thinking more with theirs—no matter who they are, no matter where you encounter them.

Secret 14: Read Body Language.   Here's my 10-second theory about the way impressions are formed.

Everything you need to know about a person you pick up in the first ten seconds of contact.

All the rest—hours, days, months, even years!—is a matter of confirming your gut-level impressions.

What I am saying here is that, in no time flat, nonverbal signals tell you all you ever have to know.

They either confirm or condemn the words people speak. Read properly, nonverbals are the litmus test of truth.

Gestures, postures, and actions tell you if a party to the negotiations is credible, aggressive, confident, easy to be with. Even the way they walk into a room can speak volumes.

"So the thing I hate about working with women is how much time it takes them to get down to business," reports N. C. Kiefer, 40, who is in the entertainment field, in Tampa. "She comes in . . . she takes off her coat . . . she fluffs her hair . . . she puts down her handbag, her attache case, and her computer . . . she arranges things at her place at the table . . . she fidgets with the waist of her skirt . . . she looks for a pen in her handbag . . . she removes a calculator from her briefcase . . . she checks her watch and asks if she can make a call—all this before she even sits down. I'll tell you, I'm going to be very skeptical about anything she says that includes the words 'businesslike' or 'efficiency.'"

Psycholinguists say that we extract about three times more meaning out of nonverbal signals than we do out of verbal ones. No wonder N. C. nets out where he does.

People pass important information via body language, especially in negotiations.

Tone of voice is an almost perfect barometer of their personal confidence level. The higher their tone, the less self-assured they are about their wants.

The faster their words pour out, the less comfortable they are about yours. *The attitude, posture, and movement of the body is an instant rating system: it tells you in a flash how they feel about what you are saying.*

The more they fidget, the more you can be sure that something about your thinking provokes emotional tension.

The more their feet turn away from you, the more certain you can be they'd rather not be in a give-and-take with you.

In general, you are most likely to find common ground with people who appear comfortable in their posture whether seated or standing, who ever-so-slightly lean towards you when you speak, and who don't juggle their fingers a lot.

Because, to the careful observer, eyes cannot lie, in them you can often read a person's truest feelings.

The secret is to go beyond the conscious gestures made with the eye. Its attempts, for instance, to alarm, bedevil, bemuse, comfort, and seduce. Instead, focus on the eye's *unconscious* eye movements . . . the ones that come up when a person isn't trying. Notice the pupils, if you can. When they seem to grow wider, something you said either surprised or pleased.

Observe the blink rate. If they blink much faster than six times a minute when they are speaking, the things they say they want may not be the things they *really* want. To play it safe, check out your specific understanding every step of the way.

If, on the other hand, they blink rapidly while you are speaking, it signals their immediate discomfort with the last thing you said. Unless you get the discomfort factor resolved—finesse it or overcome it—your chances of reaching agreement are compromised.

How to Find Common Ground

Earlier in this chapter, I told you there were three basic questions that determine the success of all negotiations.

The first concerned how to determine what you really want before negotiations begin.

The second was devoted to determining the desires of others.

Knowing clearly what's wanted on both sides sets the stage for the third and final question, Where's the common ground—the point of comfort at which, precisely and invariably, equals give and take?

FOCUS ON THE PROBLEM

One surefire way to end any negotiations is to let personal quibbles get involved. "I can't talk with her if she continues with that attitude of hers!" "He is an impossible person, he'll never listen to reason!" Words like these are bound to make anyone emotionally involved and will likely trigger an end to even the most rational discussion.

When negotiating make special pains to avoid these types of ad hominem attacks. You may think it. You may be 100 percent correct. But keep it there. Do not express it out loud. It only leads to needless mud-slinging. Your best plan of action is to focus on the issues at hand and keep personalities out of it altogether.

You may be dealing with literally the most impossible human being in the business world across the table, but you will win no points for saying this out loud. Keep the discussion professional and on the subject at hand. You are not going to change their personality, and they are not going to change yours. You may correct people when they are truly out of line, but remember, the point of negotiations is to build bridges where agreement can be reached, not to hurl slings and arrows at each other for sport. That leads to nowhere in the business world.

Common ground comes in every form you can imagine and several that might surprise. In a moment I will give you a number of ways to identify it in its various forms.

But first, a point needs to be made. They say the foundation of negotiating success is preparation. That the realization of it is courage. The limit on it is imagination. But what they don't say is what drives it. I say the engine is attitude. I'm talking about the attitudes of good will and spiritual generosity we bring to the table:

The goodwill that enables us to see things not as better or worse but as choices, to respect difference without feeling the need to agree with it, to be able to disagree without disengaging; the spiritual generosity that commits us to expect others will do the very best they can under the circumstances.

"If there was goodwill on either side they wouldn't need me," reports Russell Kirk, 40, who does conflict resolution for the American Arbitration Association on Michigan's upper peninsula. "Let's face it: good attitudes make good deals."

According to basketball coach Pat Riley, "Attitude is altitude." The same holds true of negotiating. Good attitudes make the best deals.

Secret 15: Put Their Case First. When you put forward your own needs first, only you are interested in what is being said. On the other hand, when you put their needs first, both sides are immediately drawn together on common ground: a shared interest in their desires.

Imagine, simply by speaking to their case first, you give them a personal reason to listen to, respect, and remember you.

So it stands to reason that when you begin talking about satisfying wants, you are best off identifying and speaking to theirs before you address your own.

"Now look, I know these folks before me aren't all sprouting wings and halos, but that's no reason to make things rougher than they have to be," reports Denver parking violations bureau officer David Laryton, 37. "I always talk about what they want first to reassure them that I am going to listen to what they have to say and take their story into account. That usually gets the tension down a smidgen."

Speaking to the needs of others before you talk about your own is a simple and powerful approach. It costs nothing, takes no time at all, and makes positive results more likely.

Secret 16: Build Two Bridges. Once you've got their wants out on the table, the next step is to relate them to yours.

Imagine, if you will, a picture of the negotiating situation as two banks of a river. Between them lies an island.

Your task is to build two bridges, one between your side and the island, and a second between the island and their side.

"They wanted me to transfer to Dallas but with a computer and a modem, I knew I could handle 90 percent of the load from Des Moines, with a couple of short trips a month," reports Barbara Liskin, 31, a package designer. "When I met with my boss I began by talking about the objections he had. Then I showed him how I could establish a presence in the Dallas market while operating out of the Iowa office, and save money while I was doing it. We set up a test for six months. That was a year-and-a-half ago."

Barbara first spoke to her boss's concerns about her ability to work out of the Des Moines office. Then she identified common ground—the need for more business out of the Dallas market. Finally, she went into how she could be as effective from Iowa and save money to boot.

Use the bridge building technique to span the gap between your interest, their interest, and common ground. It's quick. It's sensible. And nine times out of ten, it is going to work.

Secret 17: Offer a Choice.   When you talk somebody into something with a take-it-or-leave proposition, chances are any agreement you reach will not last.

That is because when people are forced to assent they end up feeling they never had a strong a say in outcome.

The way to get around it is simple:

Give people two choices, either one of which suits your interests.

By freely selecting an option, they stake a claim to the results and are more likely to see things through.

"I always give my children a choice when it comes to yard chores," reports Howard Sochurek, 38, a Wilmington, Delaware administrator. "They can rake the lawn on Friday afternoon and have the weekend free, or they can get it done by Sunday evening. Either way is fine by me."

Even if the choice you offer is not precisely what others want, the opportunity to choose—or suggest yet another alternative—commits them to active participation in the outcome, hence to its success.

Secret 18: Give to Get.   Offering something without being asked for it sets up a situation that leads others to feel obliged to do as much for you—even if it is only to listen.

"We offer everybody who comes into the gallery a cup of tea or coffee or bottled water," reports Berkeley, California oriental rug dealer John Whelan, 36.

"If the person eventually shows real interest in a particular piece, I might concede a point of negotiation unilaterally—for instance, right up front I might offer to pay for an independent appraisal, or offer free shipping."

By giving people something they do not expect, you make them feel special. This leads them to be more reasonable and encourages their active participation.

Secret 19: Defuse Conflict.   There are two ways to look at disagreement.

You can see it as the beginning of the end, in which case all is lost. Or you can see it as the end of the beginning, in which case you are almost certain to bring negotiations to a successful conclusion by overcoming the objection.

The best way to defuse conflict and move toward success is simply to air it openly. After all, you can't resolve differences you can't talk about.

"The morning before the sale of my house was supposed to close, my lawyer got a call from the buyer saying the deal looked like it was off," reports Ida Foukarini, 34, a Seattle department store assistant manager. "I called them and said that whatever might be in the way of a closing I would do my best to clear up. It turns out they wanted one of the skylights replaced. I told them I would have my lawyer put it into the contract immediately."

Unacknowledged differences rarely go away by themselves. Worse, they drive people apart. Working things out brings people together. The process begins when you air things openly.

Secret 20: Find Something to Admire.   The tougher it becomes to find common ground, the more important it is to find something about the other side's position to admire.

Your interest in their best qualities encourages them to be cooperative.

"To tell you the truth I hate dealing with the know-it-alls fresh out of business school," reports Digby Kates, 47, who is comptroller of a Fortune 500 company headquartered in Oklahoma. "Short-term thinking, immediate payoffs—they drive me nuts. But in the end, I try to find something to admire—maybe they're newly married and want to make a quick reputation so they can provide for their families. It's not much but without it things might break apart."

When the going gets toughest, when you least feel like doing so, find something to admire about the other fellow. It may prove the key to bringing your negotiation to a successful conclusion.

Secret 21: Don't Make Quitting an Option.   When you've reached the end of your string, don't offer others the option of quitting.

Instead, ask them to identify the benefits of continuing.

"Quitting in the middle may look like the easy way out but it is really the road to nowhere," reports Rhode Island marriage counselor Crystal Ellis, 44. "I try to turn the conversation around by comparing the benefits of going on versus the certain disaster of throwing it all over. If you go on, I say, the worst that will happen is that you will get some of the changes you want. But if you quit, things will never be any better and you will have wasted a lot of time and money."

Another way to get people back into the game is to review the progress that's been made so far.

"It was late, they were frazzled, and things were getting ugly," reports lawyer Jack Kaptur, 37, house attorney for a shopping center developer on New York's Long Island. "Look, I said, we've gotten past the biggest hurdle by selecting the site. All that's left is to work out the details and we can all go home knowing we've got an agreement both our companies will be proud of."

It is almost always better to continue than to quit.

When you feel the urge to take your bat and ball and go home, do not make quitting an option. Instead, treat the very idea of the impasse as an issue of the negotiation.

Indicate your interest in continuing. Ask them for their views.

In the end, you may have to give a little but that is far better than complete failure.

Secret 22: Stake Their Claim Every Step of the Way.   When the going gets tough, staying power is tested.

According to one arbitration organization's guidelines, the biggest reason people quit is that they lose sight of the benefits that will come to them through agreement.

To keep them involved and interested every step of the way, make sure they know that's in it for them—either personally or for the organization they represent.

"The danger in getting a youthful offender to agree to a visitation schedule is they begin to think it is jail without the bars. Some of them get the idea it might be better to be inside," reports Chicago probation officer Tammy Tatreau, 29. "When it looks like they are going to walk I tell them that the court allows some flexibility and that I will do my best to be sure some of what they want happens, but first I've got to have their input."

Making certain others are aware of their stake in negotiations increases your chances of coming out with satisfying results for all concerned.

Before we leave the subject of negotiation, let me give you a quick recap of the major points we've been working with in this chapter.

1. When you develop negotiating skills, two benefits are yours for a lifetime
   - You give your career the growing influence and visibility higher-management recognizes.
   - Your personal agreements will stick and your relationships will grow stronger.

2. Successful negotiators always ask three questions
   - What do I want?
   - What do they want?
   - Where is the common ground between us?

3. Four techniques to determine what you want
   - Put your own interests first.
   - Examine your options.
   - Be specific.
   - Accept the strengths and weaknesses that make you you.

4. Ten techniques to determine what other people want.
   - Make the first questions broad.
   - Ask open-ended questions.
   - Consent to advice.
   - Playback what you hear.
   - When all else fails, be direct.
   - Assume nothing.
   - Keep your hopes and fears out of listening.
   - Be a stranger to your friends.
   - Empathize, empathize, empathize.
   - Read body language.

5. Eight techniques to find common ground
   - Put their case first.
   - Build two bridges.

- Offer a choice.
- Give to get.
- Defuse conflict.
- Find something to admire.
- Don't make quitting an option.
- Stake their claim every step of the way.

Summary Points

- Negotiators ask three principal questions: What do I want? What does the other side want? Where is there common ground?
- To determine what you want:
  - Put your interests first.
  - Examine your options.
  - Be specific.
  - Accept strengths and weaknesses in yourself.
- To determine what others want:
  - Make the first questions broad.
  - Ask open-ended questions.
  - Consent to advice.
  - Playback what you hear.
  - When all else fails, be direct.
  - Assume nothing.
  - Keep your hopes and fears out of listening.
  - Be a stranger to your friends.
  - Empathize!
  - Read body language.
- To find common ground:
  - Put their case first.
  - Build two bridges.
  - Offer a choice.
  - Give to get.

- Defuse conflict.
- Find something to admire.
- Don't make quitting an option.
- Stake their claim every step of the way.

CHAPTER 19

CLOSING THE DEAL: COMING TO CLOSURE

You can almost see the finish line. You've been negotiating for weeks, maybe even months. Haggling over the smallest details and eventually ironing out the differences. After awhile you've almost gotten numb to the give-and-take. But there comes a time when you have to reach closure. No negotiations can be considered successful unless they're brought to an end—at some point. Don't get caught snatching failure from the jaws of success!

If timing is critical during the actual course of negotiations, it's just as critical to get the timing right for when to bring it to an end. Sometimes, you have to re-shuffle the deck to get negotiations back on track and successfully completed. Sometimes, time can be used for leverage, or it may reach the point where someone has to call and end to the whole process without losing face. No two negotiations are the same.

George Fuller's *Negotiator's Handbook,* excerpted below, details just what you should do in a variety of situations to help bring negotiations to successful conclusions—and as much to your advantage as possible. The chapter details how to project to the other side when your limits have been reached, how to cut through the red tape, and how to use time as a means of leverage to your advantage.

TECHNIQUES FOR CLOSING NEGOTIATIONS

When negotiations near the stage of wrapping the deal up, there are several elements to consider that can assist in closing negotiations. For one thing, you have to be realistic and know when to quit pushing for better terms. Alternatively, it's smart to look for ways in which you can further your objectives in the future. This can sometimes be done by getting the other side to agree to conditions that will help you accomplish this.

Timing is another factor that's very important in bringing the bargaining to a conclusion. Arguably, there may be no such thing as the right moment to make a closing pitch, but certain times are better than others. Unfortunately, in some instances, getting a deal concluded means perfecting your ability to slice through reams of red tape. Above all else, getting to the end of the road may mean that you have to assert yourself in various ways. This chapter explores a variety of tactics that can help you bring negotiations to a satisfactory close.

Knowing When to Quit While You're Ahead

You may have the good fortune to engage in negotiations where you have a distinct advantage over your adversary. This may be due to a real or perceived position of strength, or from something as basic as a less than skilled negotiating opponent. Whatever the cause, it's generally wise not to exploit this advantage beyond its reasonable limits. Pushing an opponent too far may (1) startle them into suddenly walking away, (2) force them into a bad deal, or (3) leave you holding the bag down the road when they experience difficulty performing an agreement they shouldn't have accepted in the first place.

When people are in a position of strength, there's a tendency to try and squeeze the last dime out of a deal. Such an attitude tends to overlook the long-term consequences. This is especially true where the agreement will result in the other party performing their part of the deal over a protracted period of time.

Every once in awhile, those who for one reason or another have a weak negotiating position, will accept less than palatable terms on the assumption that a bad deal is better than no deal. This can result in quality defects, delinquent deliveries, and most any other unpleasant event imaginable. The bottom line is that the lowest price you can get isn't necessarily the best price over the long haul. Consequently, although your primary focus should always be on protecting your own interests, it's necessary to recognize that not forcing unreasonable terms on your opponent is part of that process.

Negotiating Terms to Get Later What You Can't Get Now

Negotiations often get stalemated by impasses linked to a failure to reach agreement on an item that is of extreme significance to one of the parties, and equally objectionable to the opposition. One technique for overcoming this obstacle is to search for some way to make the undesirable item more acceptable to the other side. However, frequently even this approach is doomed to failure, especially if it's a deal breaking provision from the viewpoint of the objecting party.

When this happens, it's worthwhile to regroup and assess precisely what it is you want to accomplish. It may well be that rather than scuttle the deal, your long-term goals are better service by looking for ways to get what you want later rather than sooner. This can sometimes be done by negotiating terms that will achieve your aims at some future date. There are all sorts of provisions you can negotiate that will serve your long-term interests when you're unable to reach agreement on what you want at the present time. Let's look at a few typical examples:

1. "A" wants certain performance specifications written into the contract, but "B" won't accept them. "A" in an attempt to close the deal suggests putting an incentive provision in the contract that will reward "B" for meeting "A's" performance specs. The use of various performance incentives can be a hand substitute for the inability to negotiate more stringent performance provisions into a contract.

2. "C" wants a higher unit price than "D" is willing to pay. Rather than negate the deal, they agree to a price escalation factor that will increase the price if agreed-upon inflation indicators exceed certain limits.

3. "L" is reluctant to accept an agreement based on the quantities that "M" wants to buy. They resolve the dispute by putting an option provision in the contract.

4. "X" wants to buy two buildings from "Y," who is willing to sell only one. They agree instead to include a provision giving "X" a right of first refusal if "Y" decides to sell the other building at a later date.

The range of possibilities for negotiating provisions that can overcome an immediate deadlock is endless. It may not always give you everything you want, but often half-a-loaf is better than none, particularly when the alternative is no deal at all. Quite often, the major impediment is nothing more than a failure to look beyond the focus of the current agreement. So, anytime you find yourself essentially stuck over an inability to get the terms you want, look for ways to accomplish this by some other means.

Why Negotiators Sometimes Go Beyond Their Limits

Despite the use of all of your negotiation skills, there may come a time when you have made every concession you can, without reaching agreement with the other party. In short, you have made an offer which corresponds with the minimum acceptable position you prepared during your pre-negotiation planning. This has, of course, been amended during bargaining sessions to take into account any unexpected and/or unknown factors that were brought to your attention which would justify changing your position. All of this has been to no avail, and you have apparently reached the end of the road in terms of what you're willing to offer to reach agreement.

Yet, despite the fact that it flies in the face of the facts and figures you have worked so diligently to prepare, you don't want to give up the deal. There's something inside you that says, "Even if I don't get the minimum deal I wanted, I would rather have less of a deal than no deal at all."

Should you avoid logic, and give the other party what they want—or at least make another offer which is beyond what you had planned? The simple answer is "No," however, very little is very simple when emotions come into play. On a personal basis, people day in and day out deviate from their predetermined goals at the last minute to get something they want. Perhaps you, or a family member, has at one time or another set out to purchase an automobile, solemnly swearing not to spend more than a certain amount of money. Nevertheless, not too long thereafter, a car costing considerably more is lovingly maneuvered into your driveway.

Of course, business deals are somewhat different—and generally have a lot more riding on them—than a love affair with a new automobile. Yet, here too, emotions can enter into the process. Likewise, deals can be made for sums that far exceed their value when viewed from a detached standpoint. For example, it's not uncommon to read in the business press about a company paying substantially more to buy another business than financial analysts view the acquisition to be worth. On a different level, many a real estate developer has spent more for land or buildings than is deemed appropriate by the experts.

Sometimes these gambles pay off, and other times they don't. When they do, the one-time foolish buyers suddenly become geniuses. It is luck, intuition, or a little of both? Obviously, critics will deem it to be luck, while the fortunate buyer will modestly call it business acumen. What's important is that people can and do negotiate deals that on paper look lousy, but sometimes turn out to be astute buys.

Does that mean you should always throw caution to the wind and offer whatever is necessary to get the deal you want? Of course not, but there are occasions when you may consider making an offer that on paper appears to be a tad unreasonable. For instance, a plant site may have attractions for a company that outweigh the relatively high price being asked for the land. Or perhaps it's worth paying a premium for a competing business for no better reason than to eliminate a bothersome competitor.

So, all in all, there may be a time or two when you opt to offer more to get an agreement than might appear to be justified. It's certainly not wise to make a habit of it, but if the circumstances are such, there may be occasions when you can't be faulted for going ahead anyway.

How Solving Someone's Problem Can Save the Day

Sometimes when a negotiation hang-up occurs, there's no apparent reason for it. You may have offered very favorable terms, but find yourself unable to bring the bargaining to a conclusion. This dilemma is sometimes the result of a reluctance of the other party to close the deal for reasons that aren't apparent on the surface. In fact, they may have nothing at all to do with the terms and conditions of the proposed agreement.

When you're confronted with such a quandary—and the possibilities are endless—it's impossible to solve the problem until you know what it is. On occasion, the other negotiator may be willing to level with you. This is especially true if you have established good rapport during the bargaining sessions.

At other times, you may be left to fend for yourself in trying to figure out what the problem is. About all you can do is look for any clues that may have surfaced during the negotiation meetings. Of course, there's nothing to prevent you from asking what the problem is, and hopefully your counterpart will level with you. If that happens then it isn't always that difficult to come up with some creative way of resolving the difficulty. A few examples of such problems and how they can be resolved include:

- A difficult boss who is making it hard for the negotiator to close the deal. (Get your boss to carry the ball to his counterpart.)
- A business owner reluctant to sell because of a long-term attachment to the business. (Keep her on to manage the business.)
- A supplier worried about cash flow. (Include a provision for progress payments in the contract.)
- A buyer concerned about financing. (Arrange to help out with the financing.)

The bottom line in closing any deal is the ability to pinpoint any problems your adversary may have and then provide the solution. Admittedly, it's not always easy to do, but it certainly is worth the effort to bring a deal to a close.

The Importance of Timing in Reaching Agreement

An awareness of the importance of timing is essential throughout the negotiation process. All the way from knowing when the timing isn't right to begin negotiations to the most opportune moment to make your closing pitch, proper timing can't be ignored. For instance, there are numerous circumstances where it's wise to postpone opening negotiations such as:

- With suppliers who have large backlogs. (If they don't need the business, they may be hard to deal with.)

- When the local real estate market is overheated.

- When you're in the wrong end of a supply and demand cycle. (For instance, a commodity you buy has escalated in price due to temporary market conditions.)

Actually, the number of factors that can influence the proper timing to initiate a business transaction are endless. On the other hand, you can't always put off negotiations until conditions are conducive to getting a bargain. The best you can do in this regard is to be aware of any timing influences that can impact upon negotiations and plan accordingly. Of course, the flip side of the coin is to attempt to schedule negotiations when conditions are most favorable for you, such as when your counterpart has compelling reasons to be cooperative.

Apart from considerations in initiating negotiations, proper timing is equally important in bringing the bargaining to an end. It helps in this regard if you plan for it as negotiations proceed. One good approach is to hold in reserve the resolution of a particular issue which is of obvious importance to your counterpart. Even though you know you can reach agreement on the matter during negotiations, keep your suggestions to yourself. Then, when negotiations wind down toward the nitty-gritty, this item will remain as the major unresolved matter.

At an opportune moment, when everything else is settled and it appears that the open item will be the stumbling block that kills the deal, make your closing pitch. Say something such as, "Carl, here's how we can get the deal done." Then, go on to offer your resolution of the issue. Generally, your suggestion for resolving the matter will provide the momentum for wrapping things up. More often than not, the sheer relief of your counterpart in settling an issue that was thought to be a deal breaker will propel the other side toward agreement.

Beyond anything else proper timing requires a keen sense of just where the negotiations stand. This isn't always as easy to discern as it would appear to be, especially if you're dealing with an experienced negotiator who knows how to play a negotiation table version of poker. Yet, even here it pays to look for subtle signals that indicate the other side may be susceptible to a pitch to close the deal.

Use Time as Leverage

As the saying goes, "time is money," and nowhere more so than when your opponent has a self-imposed deadline to complete negotiations by a certain date.

There's no quicker way to close negotiations—other than giving the store away—as watching the time roll toward what you know is a deadline staring your counterpart in the face.

Once you know for a fact, or can pretty well assume, that your opponent is under deadline pressure, you have an obvious advantage as negotiations near the wire. However, before you go about playing this ploy for all it's worth, a few precautions are in order. First of all, how useful the deadline is to you, depends upon what sort of alternatives the other side has if negotiations can't be completed. Furthermore, it's smart to be cautious about not forcing the issue too far, since your opponent isn't likely to accept unreasonable terms under any circumstances.

Finally, absent knowledge that confirms the fact, the alleged deadline may be merely a tactic being used by the other side to speed things up. Why would someone do this? Perhaps they don't want you probing too deeply into the details of their offer, and are using a deadline as an excuse to keep you from doing so. A clue to look for in this regard is if the other negotiator lets you know right from the beginning that there are time constraints imposed for completing negotiations.

In terms of getting the best results when your opponent has a deadline to meet, the following guidelines are helpful:

1. Avoid mentioning your knowledge of the other side's deadline pressures. Telegraphing your awareness of the fact alerts them to the possibility that you will use this knowledge to push for last minute concessions.

2. If your opponent lets you know there is a deadline to be met, don't signal that you attach any particular significance to it.

3. Actively negotiate right down to the wire so as not to raise suspicions that you're deliberately dragging things out.

4. Let your opponent make the last offer which should come shortly before the deadline arrives.

5. Take some time to give the offer due consideration. Even though you know you won't accept it, you don't want your adversary to know that.

6. Reject the offer and make a counter-offer that's more beneficial to you. If it's accepted, you have a deal.

7. If your adversary refuses your counter-offer, just keep on talking. Let them make the next move, since they are the ones with deadline pressures. They will either finally concede, make another counteroffer, or break-off the negotiations. At what point a deal is reached will depend upon your best judgment as to when to call it quits.

8. Always keep in mind that the other side may have a built-in time lag as to when the actual deadline is. Therefore, even after the supposed deadline has passed, they may continue to negotiate.

9. Don't overdue it in trying to squeeze last minute concessions when the other party has a deadline to meet. After all, if you kill the goose, it won't be around to lay other golden eggs in the future.

How to Slice Through Red Tape Bottlenecks

Negotiating a satisfactory agreement is troublesome enough in itself, but your headaches don't always end there. In trying to get a deal wrapped up, you can encounter obstacles on both sides of the fence. When the bottleneck rests with the other party, you have to get through to someone who can make a decision on the agreement as previously discussed.

Even more irksome than circumventing roadblocks erected in the opposition camp, is having to work your way around stumbling blocks on your side of the aisle. These can take a variety of forms ranging from indecision within the approval loop, to outright resistance by people who oppose the agreement. First, let's look at how to address the problem of getting around those individuals within your organization who openly oppose approval of an agreement you have negotiated.

In a perfect world, corporate infighting and internal politics would be passé. However, even the most optimistic crystal ball gazer would hesitate to include that prediction in any forecast for the future. As a consequence, it's inevitable that internal conflicts will arise over negotiated agreements. These differences of opinion can range from petty politics generated by power struggles and bickering, to sincere disagreement over the viability of the subject matter of the negotiation.

Most of the time, the battles are fought before the go-ahead decision is made that results in the negotiation taking place. However, some wounds heal faster than others, and on occasion, those opposed to a project will carry their fight right down to the point where a negotiated agreement goes through the approval cycle. As a result, you may find yourself fighting a rearguard action as you seek internal approval. When this happens, it shouldn't be taken lightly, since if the opposition succeeds in shooting enough holes in the deal, you will find yourself right back at the bargaining table. Therefore, let's look at some measures you can take to overcome this difficulty. They include:

1. Pinpointing potential supporters and detractors in the approval loop.

2. Building a power base of supporters before you formally present the agreement for approval.

3. Trying to co-opt the opposition by gaining their support. If possible show them how their ideas and/or objectives have either been included in the negotiated agreement, or will be furthered by its approval.

4. Assessing potential objections to the agreement. When you seek approval, raise these objections yourself, and then proceed to show why they are not valid. Doing this is akin to blowing up the enemies' ammunition dump.

5. Making a solid presentation. You obviously worked long and hard to negotiate the deal, so labor just as hard to get it approved.

6. If it appears that you are being cut out of the approval process, take whatever measures are necessary to get through to the decision maker. After all, you negotiated the deal, and are therefore the proper person to explain and defend it. When someone wants to shoot down an agreement, it's a lot easier to do so if the negotiator isn't present at the meeting to defend it.

Aside from any organized resistance to a negotiated agreement, you may also have to overcome a wide variety of run-of-the-mill hurdles that are common to any organizational environment. These include indecisive people (work around them) restrictive policies, (interpret them in your favor) and a myriad of details (handle them after the fact). It isn't a rewarding experience to have to overcome a bevy of bottlenecks to get a negotiated agreement approved. However, it's part of the process, and shouldn't be ignored, since bottlenecks in your own camp can unravel a deal a lot faster than the time it took to get it negotiated.

Letting the Other Party Know Your Limit Is Reached

Sooner or later, it's necessary to bring matters to a head, and either close the deal, or recognize that an agreement just isn't in the cards. Sometimes, negotiations drag on endlessly simply because neither party is willing to take the initiative to conclude matters. Part of the problem lies in the natural reluctance of either party to be the one that makes the last offer. There's an inevitable feeling that it won't be accepted, and/or the other side will come back with yet another less desirable offer.

Overcoming this hurdle requires the fortitude to exercise a bit of brinkmanship. However, once you have exhausted every possible means of reaching agreement, you have to not only make a decision that your limit has been reached, but also convey this to your counterpart. So, sooner or later, when you make your last concession or offer, it's necessary to emphasize the fact that you are at your limit.

Don't be hesitant about calling it quits. More often than not, the other side will play out the string as far as it will go—which includes rejecting your final offer. They, quite understandably, won't accept it as the best they can get until you prove it is. Therefore, there will come a time when you simply have to get up and walk away.

Experienced negotiators know this, and don't have any hesitancy to do so at the proper moment. Complex negotiations can have the parties breaking off negotiations, and subsequently resuming talks several times over a period of weeks and months. The key is the ability to walk away after giving the other side the impression that you have had enough, while at the same time leaving leeway for them to initiate further contact.

On the one hand, conveying finality is necessary to convince the other side that you are at your limit. The flip side of the coin is that this be done in such a way that your counterpart won't be discouraged from contacting you later and accepting your last offer. Furthermore, you never know when an unexpected, but satisfactory, alternative may be proposed if and when the other side does contact you. Does all of this sound like it requires a little bit of acting ability? As they say, it isn't necessary, but it sure helps.

Using Ultimatums as a Last Resort

As just mentioned, when you have reached your negotiation limit, you want to let your adversary know that fact in no uncertain terms. Yet, as a rule, you want to leave the door slightly ajar—at least to the extent that the other side may be willing to call and accept your last offer. Aside from that, you never know what future negotiation opportunities may arise with the same people.

Consequently, no matter how frustrating an apparent failure to reach agreement may be, it doesn't pay to end everything with an emotional outburst. You certainly can use some form of ultimatum such as a deadline to force the hand of your counterpart, but going beyond that isn't good business sense. Ultimatums are to a large extent overplayed, since no one takes kindly to being threatened. Therefore, no matter how bitter you may feel, take your frustrations out on a golf ball or some similar form of tension reliever.

NOTE: In certain limited situations, a dead deal can be resurrected time and time again. Examples include repeated attempts to buy a business, or purchase a piece of real estate. Although such cases aren't the norm, when there is no particular urgency to reach agreement you can keep trying. It's not only that persistence may pay off, but also the fact that conditions change as time passes. The economy, personal and/or business circumstances, and individual motivations, are all subject to fluctuation. In fact, something as simple as establishing a good relationship with the other party over a period of time may bring success. As a result, if you ever confront such a situation, don't just give up, and most important, don't issue any ultimatums, since you have nothing to gain and everything to lose by doing so.

Summary Points

- Know when to quit. You *can* overdo it.
- Helping solve the other side's problems at the end can help bring about a successful conclusion.
- Don't mention the other side's deadline pressure. You're telegraphing intelligence you're better off not sharing.
- Take time to consider offers you know immediately you won't accept.
- Let your opponent make the last offer.
- At some point, you will need to communicate that your limit is reached.
- No one likes threats. Don't use ultimatums.

INDEX

INDEX

A

B

C

D

E

M

N